Shakespeare and Indian Cinemas

This book is the first to explore the rich archive of Shakespeare in Indian cinemas, including less-familiar, Indian-language cinemas, to contribute to the assessment of the expanding repertoire of Shakespeare films worldwide. Essays cover mainstream and regional Indian cinemas, such as the better-known Tamil and Kannada, as well as the less-familiar regions of the North-Eastern states. The volume visits diverse filmic genres, from the earliest silent cinema to diasporic films made for global audiences, television films, independent films and documentaries, thus expanding the very notion of 'Indian cinema' while also looking at the different modalities of deploying Shakespeare that are specific to these genres. Shakespeareans and film scholars provide an alternative history of the development of Indian cinema through its negotiations with Shakespeare, focussing on the intertextualities between Shakespearean theatre, regional cinema, performative traditions and literary histories in India. The purpose is not to catalogue examples of Shakespearean influence but to analyse the interplay of the aesthetic, historical, sociopolitical and theoretical contexts in which Indian-language films have turned to Shakespeare and to what purpose they have done so. The discussion extends from the content of the plays to the modes of their cinematic and intermedial translations. It thus tracks the intra-Indian flows and cross-currents between the various film industries and intervenes in the politics of multiculturalism and inter-/intraculturalism built up around Shakespearean appropriations. Contributing to current studies in global Shakespeare, this book marks a discursive shift in the way Shakespeare on screen is predominantly theorised as well as how Indian cinema, particularly 'Shakespeare in Indian cinema', is understood.

Poonam Trivedi was Associate Professor in English at Indraprastha College, University of Delhi, India, and is currently the vice-chair of the Asian Shakespeare Association.

Paromita Chakravarti is Professor in the Department of English at Jadavpur University, Calcutta, India.

Routledge Studies in Shakespeare

25 Shakespeare's *Hamlet* in an Era of Textual Exhaustion
   Edited By Sonya Freeman Loftis, Allison Kellar, and Lisa Ulevich

26 Shakespeare's Suicides
   Dead Bodies That Matter
   By Marlena Tronicke

27 The Fictional Lives of Shakespeare
   Kevin Gilvary

28 Jonson, Shakespeare, and Aristotle on Comedy
   Jonathan Goossen

29 Shakespeare and the Cultivation of Difference
   Race and Conduct in the Early Modern World
   Patricia Akhimie

30 Casual Shakespeare
   Three Centuries of Verbal Echoes
   Regula Hohl Trillini

31 Shakespearean Temporalities
   History on the Early Modern Stage
   Lukas Lammers

32 Rethinking Shakespeare Source Study
   Audiences, Authors, and Digital Technologies
   Edited by Dennis Austin Britton & Melissa Walter

33 Shakespeare and Indian Cinemas
   'Local Habitations'
   Edited by Poonam Trivedi and Paromita Chakravarti

For a full list of titles published in the series, please visit www.routledge.com

Shakespeare and Indian Cinemas
'Local Habitations'

Edited by Poonam Trivedi and
Paromita Chakravarti

NEW YORK AND LONDON

First published 2019
by Routledge
711 Third Avenue, New York, NY 10017

and by Routledge
2 Park Square, Milton Park, Abingdon, Oxon OX14 4RN

Routledge is an imprint of the Taylor & Francis Group, an informa business

© 2019 Taylor & Francis

The right of the editors to be identified as the authors of the editorial material, and of the authors for their individual chapters, has been asserted in accordance with sections 77 and 78 of the Copyright, Designs and Patents Act 1988.

All rights reserved. No part of this book may be reprinted or reproduced or utilised in any form or by any electronic, mechanical, or other means, now known or hereafter invented, including photocopying and recording, or in any information storage or retrieval system, without permission in writing from the publishers.

Trademark notice: Product or corporate names may be trademarks or registered trademarks, and are used only for identification and explanation without intent to infringe.

Library of Congress Cataloging-in-Publication Data
CIP data has been applied for.

ISBN: 978-1-138-94692-7 (hbk)
ISBN: 978-1-315-67040-9 (ebk)

Typeset in Sabon
by codeMantra

Contents

List of Figures ix
List of Contributors xi

Introduction: Shakespeare and Indian Cinemas: 'local habitations' 1
POONAM TRIVEDI AND PAROMITA CHAKRAVARTI

PART I
Indigenising the Tragic 21

1 Woman as Avenger: 'Indianising' the Shakespearean Tragic in the Films of Vishal Bhardwaj 23
   POONAM TRIVEDI

2 *Eklavya*: Shakespeare Meets the *Mahabharata* 45
   ROBERT S. WHITE

3 Reworking Shakespeare in Telugu Cinema: *King Lear* to *Gunasundari Katha* 62
   NISHI PULUGURTHA

4 Shakespeare in Malayalam Cinema: Cultural and Mythic Interface, Narrative Negotiations 75
   C.S. VENKITESWARAN

5 'Where art thou Muse that thou forget'st so long,/To speak of that which gives thee all thy might?': *Qayamat Se Qayamat Tak* (1988) – A Neglected Shakespeare Film 93
   KOEL CHATTERJEE

vi *Contents*

PART II
Critical Innovations: Historiography of Silence and Poetics of Rasa 111

  6 The Indian 'Silent' Shakespeare: Recouping an Archive 113
     AMRIT GANGAR

  7 Shakespeare, Cinema and Indian Poetics 127
     ANIL ZANKAR

PART III
Between the Global and the Local 141

  8 *Such a Long Journey*: Rohinton Mistry's Parsi *King Lear* From Fiction to Film 143
     PRETI TANEJA

  9 Cinematic *Lears* and Bengaliness: Locus, Identity, Language 161
     PAROMITA CHAKRAVARTI

  10 Shakespeare and Indian Independent Cinema: *8×10 Tasveer* and *10ml Love* 180
     VARSHA PANJWANI

  11 'Singing Is Such Sweet Sorrow': *Ambikapathy*, Hollywood Shakespeare and Tamil Cinema's Hybrid Heritage 200
     THEA BUCKLEY

PART IV
Reimagining Gender, Region and Nation 219

  12 Gendered Play and Regional Dialogue in *Nanjundi Kalyana* 221
     MARK THORNTON BURNETT

  13 Not the Play but the Playing: Citation of Performing Shakespeare as a Trope in Tamil Cinema 238
     A. MANGAI

14 Indianising *The Comedy of Errors*: *Bhranti Bilash* and
   Its Aftermaths   251
   AMRITA SEN

15 Regional Reflections: Shakespeare in Assamese Cinema   268
   PARTHAJIT BARUAH

PART V
Interviews   283

   Interview with Pankaj Butalia by Paromita Chakravarti
   and Poonam Trivedi, 20 September 2015   285

   Interview with Roysten Abel
   by Poonam Trivedi, 26 February 2016   292

   Interview with Aparna Sen
   by Paromita Chakravarti, 3 January 2016   304

PART VI   317

   Shakespeare Films in Indian Cinemas:
   An Annotated Filmography   319

   Filmography Chronological   328

   Index   333

List of Figures

1.1	Nimmi/Lady Macbeth wins love at gunpoint in *Maqbool*	30
1.2	Indu/Emila's flash of avenging fury in *Omkara*	34
1.3	Ghazala/Gertrude with Haider/Hamlet admiring her before her wedding with Khurram/Claudius	39
2.1	Flashback to Eklavya and Prince Harsh as a child	53
2.2	Prince Harsh, his sister and lover flying a kite	57
3.1	Poster of *Gunasundari Katha*	66
3.2	Gunasundari praying to Lord Shiva and Goddess Parvati	69
4.1	Rudran/Hamlet as a *kelipatra* (yogi)	87
5.1	Poster for *QSQT* that was manually distributed by Amir Khan in Mumbai	99
5.2	*QSQT* was one of the first few films that boasted on-screen kisses	103
8.1	When Tehmul dies, Gustad lays him down on the bed with Roshan's white-skinned bridal doll	156
9.1	*36 Chowringhee Lane*: Miss Stoneham reciting *Lear* to a dog	165
9.2	*The Last Lear*: Harry and Sidharth watch CCTV images of Calcutta like 'god's spies'	166
9.3	*Life Goes On*: Diya rehearses Cordelia's role in *King Lear*	168
10.1	Jai/Hamlet finds his mother embracing his uncle	183
10.2	Mechanicals carving out time for rehearsal between chopping vegetables	192
11.1	Amaravathi and Ambikapathy singing a love duet	203
11.2	The balcony scene	208
12.1	Devi/Katharina, reformed, greets her parents	234
13.1	Sivaji Ganesan as Hamlet – a new lease of life on stage in *Rajapart Rangadurai*	242
13.2	Sivaji and Savitri as Othello and Desdemona in the college play in *Ratha Thilagam*	244
14.1	*Bhranti Bilash*: Chiranjeet and Chiranjeev finally meet, as do the two Kinkars	256

14.2	*Angoor*: Ashok, Sudha and Tanu play cards	263
14.3	*Double Di Trouble*: Switched father and son	264
15.1	Mun with his autorickshaw named 'Othello'	276
15.2	Bankim, the failed Communist, spends his time making busts of revolutionaries in *We Have Our Othellos Too*	279
15.3	Arjun, Tina, Bankim, Pabitri and Mun in the '*Othello* within Othello' scene	280

List of Contributors

Parthajit Baruah is a film scholar and an award-winning documentary film-maker. He received the Prag Channel Film Critic Award for his book *Chalachitror Taranga* (2010). His latest book, *Face To Face: The Cinema of Adoor Gopalakrishnan*, has been widely acclaimed. He is the recipient of a research fellowship at the National Film Archive of India, Pune. He was a preview committee member at the 1st Guwahati International Film Festival – 2017. He presented his paper on Shakespeare and Assamese cinema at an international seminar in London in 2016. His documentaries, including *The Dhemaji Tragedy*, have won multiple awards at national and international film festivals.

Thea Buckley is Visiting Lecturer at the Shakespeare Institute, University of Birmingham and University of Staffordshire. She has worked for the Royal Shakespeare Company, Shakespeare Birthplace Trust and British Library, and with the British Film Institute while co-chairing 'Indian Shakespeares on Screen' in 2016. Having grown up in Kerala, her recent doctoral thesis focussed on performing *Macbeth* in Malayalam, and she has published on Shakespeare on stage and screen across the subcontinent in *A Year of Shakespeare*, *Cahiers Elisabethains*, *Multicultural Shakespeare*, the *Shakespeare Institute Review* and the *Birmingham Journal of Language and Literature*.

Mark Thornton Burnett is Professor of Renaissance Studies at Queen's University, Belfast. He is the author of *Masters and Servants in English Renaissance Drama and Culture: Authority and Obedience* (Basingstoke: Macmillan, 1997), *Constructing 'Monsters' in Shakespearean Drama and Early Modern Culture* (Basingstoke: Palgrave, 2002), *Filming Shakespeare in the Global Marketplace* (Basingstoke: Palgrave, 2007; 2nd ed. 2012) and *Shakespeare and World Cinema* (Cambridge: Cambridge University Press, 2013).

Paromita Chakravarti completed her doctoral studies on discourses of madness on the Renaissance stage at the University of Oxford. She is Professor of English at Jadavpur University, Kolkata, and teaches Renaissance drama, women's writing and queer and film studies. She has been the Director of the School of Women's Studies, Jadavpur University, and has co-edited a volume of essays, *Women Contesting Culture* (Stree, 2012). She has published widely on Shakespeare in film in journals and edited volumes, and has recently co-edited the special volume of *Essays and Studies* (vol. 30, 2016), the Jadavpur University journal, on 'Materiality and Cultural Life in early Modern Europe'.

Koel Chatterjee completed her PhD on the evolution of Bollywood Shakespeares at Royal Holloway, University of London. Her research focus is the adaptation of Shakespeare in the Hindi film industry after postcolonialism in India. She has presented papers on Bollywood Shakespeare adaptations at conferences and is a freelance writer for *Shakespeare Magazine*. She was the originator and co-organiser of the Shakespeare and Indian Cinema events in 2014–2016, organised under the aegis of the English Department at Royal Holloway. She is currently working on a book on the history of Bollywood Shakespeares which combines original first-person interviews with archival material uncovered during her doctoral research.

Amrit Gangar is a Mumbai-based writer, historian, curator and film theoretician. He has a number of publications to his credit, both in English and in Gujarati. He has curated numerous programmes, including Shakespeare and Cinema, in addition to presenting Indian 'silent' film programmes. For the past decade or so, he has been engaged with theorisation of his new concept of the Cinema of Prayoga. He has been on film festival juries in India and abroad. His book *Music That Still Rings at Dawn, Every Dawn: Walter Kaufmann in India, 1934–1946*, published by the Goethe Institut Mumbai in 2013, has been widely acclaimed.

A. Mangai is the pseudonym of V. Padma, who taught English in Stella Maris College, Chennai. She has been actively engaged in Tamil theatre as an actor, director and playwright for almost three decades. She hopes that her academic, activist and artistic selves can find a vibrant intersection. Her fields of interest are theatre, gender and translation studies. She writes both in Tamil and in English. She has twice been a recipient of the Fulbright Fellowship. She was given the Rockefeller-Bellagio Residency for four weeks to work on her monograph on gender and theatre in India in 2009, published as *Acting Up* (2015).

Varsha Panjwani teaches at Boston University (London) and New York University (London), and is an honorary Research Associate at the University of York. Her research focusses on the way in which Shakespeare is deployed in the service of diversity in theatre and films. As well as publishing in international journals, such as *Shakespeare*

Survey, and *Shakespeare Studies*, and in prestigious collections, such as *Shakespeare, Race and Performance*, she has co-edited the special issue of *Multicultural Shakespeare* (2017). In addition to her individual research, she was one of the principal investigators of the multi-grant-winning project 'Indian Shakespeares on Screen' (2016).

Nishi Pulugurtha is Head and Associate Professor, Department of English, Brahmananda Keshab Chandra College, Kolkata. Having earned her PhD on Coleridge's poetry she has completed two University Grants Commission Minor Research projects – on poetry written in English in Bengal in the nineteenth century and on diaspora poetry – and is now working on a project on Telugu films and the diaspora. She has been awarded an associateship at the Indian Institute of Advanced Study, Shimla, India. Her areas of interest are British Romantic literature, Indian writing in English, diaspora and film. She also writes on travel and Alzheimer's disease.

Amrita Sen is Associate Professor of English and Humanities at Heritage Institute of Technology and The Heritage College (University of Calcutta). She taught at Oklahoma City University for several years, first as Assistant and then as Associate Professor of English before moving back to India. She has published essays and reviews in edited collections as well as in journals like *Genre*, *South Asian Review* and *Shakespeare Quarterly*. She is the co-editor of the *Journal for Early Modern Cultural Studies* special issue on 'Alternative Histories of the East India Company' and is currently co-editing a book on early modern civic pageantry.

Preti Taneja's debut novel *We That Are Young* (2017) translates *King Lear* to contemporary India. Hailed as 'a masterpiece' by *The Spectator*, it was a Book of the Year pick in *The Hindu*, *The Guardian* and *The Sunday Times*, among others. She is a Leverhulme Early Career Research Fellow at Warwick University, working on Shakespeare by practitioners in current conflict and post-conflict zones. Her fieldwork includes projects with Syrian refugees, in Kashmir and the Balkans. She holds an honorary fellowship at Jesus College, Cambridge University, and is an Arts and Humanities Research Council/British Broadcasting Corporation New Generation Thinker, broadcasting on culture, world literature and human rights. www.preti-taneja.co.uk.

Poonam Trivedi was Associate Professor in English at Indraprastha College, University of Delhi. She received her doctorate from the Shakespeare Institute, University of Birmingham, UK, and has co-edited *Shakespeare's Asian Journeys* (2017), *Re-playing Shakespeare in Asia* (2010) and *India's Shakespeare: Translation, Interpretation and Performance* (2006). She has authored a CD-ROM, 'King Lear in India' (2006), and published articles in national and international journals on Shakespeare in India, performance and film versions, women in Shakespeare and Indian theatre. She was the secretary of the Shakespeare Society of India from 1993 to 1999 and is currently the vice-chair of the Asian Shakespeare Association.

C.S. Venkiteswaran is a film critic, curator, columnist, documentary film-maker and writer living in Kerala. He writes on film and media, in English and Malayalam, in various magazines and journals, and won the National Film Award for Best Film Critic in 2009. His books include *Samanthara Yathrakal – K R Mohanante Cinema*, *Malayala Cinema Padnangal*, *Udalinte Tharasancharangal*, *Cinema Talkies* and *Television Padanangal*. He has also edited *A Door to Adoor* with Lalit Mohan Joshi. His documentary film, co-directed with M.R. Rajan, *Pakarnattam – Ammannur the Actor* won the National Award for Best Arts/Cultural Film in 1995. He has curated film packages for several international film festivals in India and was the artistic director of SiGNS Film Festival.

Robert S. White is the Winthrop Professor of English at the University of Western Australia and a Chief Investigator for the Australian Research Council Centre of Excellence for the History of Emotions 1100–1800. He has published extensively on Shakespeare and Keats, and White's latest books are *Shakespeare and Emotions* (2015), *Avant-Garde Hamlet* (2015), *Shakespeare and the Cinema of Love* (2016), *Ambivalent Macbeth* (2018) and *The New Fortune Theatre: That Vast Open Stage* (2018). He is now working on another book on Keats and an Arden volume on *A Midsummer Night's Dream*, both due to be published in 2019.

Anil Zankar is a film-maker and Visiting Faculty at the Indian Institute of Science Research and Education (IISER), Pune, teaching Direction, Screenplay-Writing and Film Appreciation. He has won two national awards: Feature Film Script, 1982, and Best Book on Cinema1, 1997. He has produced twenty-one short films and was the conceptualiser for the Mass Media Studies Course, Central Board of Secondary Education. He has been on the Jury, Indian Panorama (International Film Festival of India 2010, 2013) and in international film seminars in Poland (2006) and Japan (2014). His publications include *Mughal-e-Azam* (2013), chapters in *Routledge Handbook of Indian Cinemas* (2013) and *Encyclopaedia of Hindi Cinema* (Britannica, 2001). Forthcoming are a documentary on Dr M.S. Swaminathan and a book on the city of Mumbai.

Introduction
Shakespeare and Indian Cinemas: 'local habitations'

Poonam Trivedi and Paromita Chakravarti

If there is one thing which has clearly placed Shakespeare in the international sphere it is the worldwide exponential growth of films based on his works in the past few decades. Not just Anglo-America but also diverse cultures across the globe are turning to Shakespeare and film to express themselves. Shakespeare, the most widely read, translated and performed single author in history, is now the most filmed too. And it is not just celluloid: a range of digital screens and media have also adopted Shakespeare. Shakespeare and the moving image seem to increasingly feed into each other. While some of this cinematic resurgence is the result of the evolving dynamics of the film industry, the growth of multiplexes, the corporatisation of finance and the development of technology, it is the establishment of film studies and Shakespeare film studies, especially, as disciplines which has conferred canonical status to these necessarily commercial ventures. However, though Shakespeare on film and media is one of the fastest growing and challenging subfields in Shakespeare studies, interest in the range of the international Shakespeare film has been slow to take off. Entrenched conservatism towards what constitutes the 'authentic' Shakespeare has relegated a vast number of innovative and transgressive 'foreign' reappraisals of Shakespeare on film to the margins of this new discipline.

Shakespeare Film in Indian Cinemas

Among the several cinemas of the world, the Indian Shakespeare film was, until very recently, virtually invisible except to a few aficionados. It was virtually unknown in Shakespeare film history and criticism: the standard filmography of a hundred years appended in Kenneth Rothwell's *A History of Shakespeare on Screen* (1999) lists only five films from what has been for many years the largest film industry in the world, one which began in 1913 and now produces almost 2,000 films a year; the Central Board of Film Certification lists 1,986 feature films in 2016–2017 in 43 languages.[1] International interest in Indian cinema until recently had been confined to the art films of Satyajit Ray. While the Shakespeare films of Vishal Bhardwaj over the last ten years have garnered international attention, Indian cinemas, and the Indian Shakespeare film on the whole, have virtually remained areas of darkness in critical discourse. And though there is a current boom in writings about Bollywood and Indian cinema in general, catalysed by film studies and South Asia departments, there is as yet no extended study of the Indian Shakespeare film.

The chief aim of this volume is therefore to recoup and foreground for scholarly and critical attention this rich archive. The filmography appended to the volume lists, for the first time (and to our immense satisfaction), a total of 115 titles of feature films, establishing a canon of the Indian Shakespeare film, extending from the earliest movie in 1923 to 2016, many movies having been unearthed in the process of this research. It shows that eighteen plays have been adapted in Indian cinemas in thirteen different languages: *Romeo and Juliet*, predictably, has the largest number of adaptations – seventeen – with the *Taming of the Shrew* coming a close second with sixteen films, and *Hamlet* coming third with twelve versions. Twenty-five films which incorporate scenes, characters, citations or close resonances from Shakespeare are listed separately to underline the multifarious presence of Shakespeare in Indian films. While the filmography cannot claim comprehensiveness, given the sheer size of the output, it does map the territory substantially. It also demonstrates that Indian cinemas contain the largest corpus of Shakespeare films in the world, a fact that is corroborated by Andrew Dickson's findings in his recent journey tracking Shakespearean legacies across the world, in which he asserts that there are 'more versions of Shakespeare in Indian cinema than anywhere else on the globe.'[2] The filmography also reveals the many complex and creative dimensions of the encounter between Shakespeare and the several Indian cinemas over almost a century, the exploration of which is the task of the book.

Though the first Shakespeare film (1899, *King John*, dir. Beerbohm Tree, a short extract, silent) appeared soon after the advent of cinema, and the first sound full-length feature appeared in 1929 (*The Taming of the Shrew*, dir. Sam Taylor), the Shakespeare film per se emerged slowly and intermittently. Shakespeare was not considered fit material for the box office in Hollywood until the 1950s, while in England, cinema was not considered a fit artistic medium capable of embodying the bard's works. Consequently, 'only a handful' of films were produced in the early years, and as observed by Russell Jackson, 'relative to the total output of the various producers, there have not been many Shakespeare films in the English-speaking cinema.'[3] European and world cinemas, however, were freer to appropriate Shakespeare, and Indian cinemas too were quick to exploit this rich resource. Based on current information, up to the 1950s, twenty-four films on Shakespeare's plays were made in India, which included, interestingly, seven silent films (of considerable length), the world's first full-length talkie of *Hamlet* (*Khoon ka Khoon*, 1935, dir. Sohrab Modi, Urdu/Hindi) and, incidentally, later, the first full-length *The Comedy of Errors* too (*Bhranti Bilash*, 1963, dir. Manu Sen, Bengali), again facts which have been entirely ignored in the Western academy. While cinematic experimentation with Shakespeare continued, it is since the 2000s that Indian cinema has shown a Shakespeare efflorescence, partly inspired by the Shakespeare film renaissance in the West. Throughout this long history, films in the major Indian languages have adapted and embedded Shakespeare's plots, characters, scenes and dialogues in a variety of genres and modes for local audiences. Beginning with historicals, melodramas, romantic comedies, family socials, stunt-action dramas, political satire and even mythologicals or art films, extending to docudramas and diasporic, independent and television films, Shakespeare is to be found everywhere, 'translated', like Bottom, in mind-boggling Indianised shades and shapes. While a few approximate to the original text, most of the films show differing degrees of transculturation, transformation and citation. In keeping with the unique template of popular Indian cinema, Shakespeare films incorporate songs and sometimes dance numbers too. Many were very successful at the box office, popularising Shakespeare, often without the audience being aware of it, much like the early Indian theatre adaptations.

National, Regional and Local Cinema

Internationally, and nationally, Indian cinema, and even Indian culture to some extent, is commonly considered synonymous with 'Bollywood', the prolific Hindi film industry based in Mumbai. Current academic discourse too has almost exclusively directed its attention at Bollywood, which is held to be the norm. The term, originally a journalistic coinage, has acquired wide currency, despite its disturbing cloning implication (linguistically echoing Hollywood), as a shorthand and is now even being used, at times, to refer to all of Indian cinema. In the globalised world of the media, the term has also come to represent a 'brand': a particular Indian *filmi* style, a mixture of realism and fantasy, melodrama and lush musicality and an internationalised fashion and the glamour associated with it.[4] The term, however, has led to the erasure and scholarly neglect of the thirteen full-fledged regional language cinemas in India. Since Hindi is the largest spoken language (53.60% first-language speakers, 2001 census) and a designated national language (along with English), its cinematic dominance is numerically accountable. But, though the regional film industries also cater primarily to their own language constituencies, each has a distinct cultural identity and historical trajectory, and independent modes of financing and production. Further, these cinemas have been in keen competition with each other: Bengali cinema, being closest to the centre of power in the colonial period, began early and developed its distinct profile, influenced by literature; Marathi cinema, which was the first to initiate production in 1913, suffered from the proximity of Hindi cinema in Mumbai. Malayalam has generated more art films inspired by world cinema than any other regional cinema, and since 1979, Tamil and Telugu have been producing more films every other year than the Hindi film industry.[5] Some of these cinemas are especially vibrant today, bigger and more trendsetting than Hindi cinema: e.g. Telugu cinema has had an unprecedented box-office success with the global release of *Baahubali* (2015) and its sequel *Baahubali 2: The Conclusion* (2017), which is estimated to have grossed $270 million (Rs. 1,706.5 crores) worldwide.[6]

This book aims equally to foreground the regional movies in India which have been overshadowed by Hindi films' discursive dominance. All these cinemas (except Gujarati and Oriya)[7] have embraced Shakespeare too, but because they usually lie outside the circuit of international film festivals and distribution networks, the regional Indian Shakespeare film has been even more invisible in scholarly discussion. Redressing this imbalance, this volume seeks to focus on these regional cinemas and bring their particular histories of literary and theatrical engagement with Shakespeare into the larger and a more interactive picture. The volume appropriately has two chapters on Tamil cinema, which has been the second most pioneering and productive film industry in India, topping production in 2013.[8] There are essays on Telugu, Kannada, Malayalam, Bengali and Assamese cinemas too. Smaller film industries like Punjabi and Mizo are also discussed, along with the diasporic film in English, preoccupied with regional locations and identities. The chapters not only detail the larger contexts of the development of regional cinema but also pay particular attention to the specific modes or 'local habitations' through which Shakespeare has been absorbed in the diverse cultures of India.

The regional films, however, exist in a dialectical tension with the national or pan-Indian cinema. At the industrial level, there has always been a robust symbiotic relationship between Bollywood and regional cinemas, manifested in the regular movement of technicians and cine professionals between the various film industries. A competitive interdependence can particularly be seen in the increasing number of 'remakes' (a standard Bollywood practice) of films from one Indian language to another, from Hindi into regional languages and, more regularly, vice versa. Even the niche Shakespeare films reflect these developing tendencies of Indian cinemas. For instance, the history of *Romeo and Juliet* films reveals this clearly: a 1978 Telugu version was remade in Hindi within a couple of years with the same actor, and a recent Marathi version, *Sairat* 2016, has done so well that remakes are being planned in Hindi, Kannada, Telugu, Punjabi, Malayalam and Tamil. The early Telugu 1949 *Gunasundari Katha*, an adaptation of *Lear*, was so successful that it was remade in Tamil in 1955. *Marmayogi*, a 1951 Tamil version of *Macbeth*, was immediately reshot in Hindi; the 1997 Kannada *Ulta Palta* version of *Comedy of Errors* was remade into Telugu within a year.

Technology and the Local

Today, films are being dubbed into different Indian languages for wider circulation and even being shot simultaneously in multiple languages: e.g. *Veeram* 2016 (*Macbeth*), the latest Shakespeare film from Kerala, was shot in Malayalam, Hindi and English. Modern technology is overcoming the linguistic regional compartmentalisation in the industry and thus aiding film circulation and commerce. Pan-Indian distribution and marketing of regional films is challenging Hindi cinema and claiming a larger share of the national market. Multilingual film-making is also targeting the different linguistic groups among the diasporic Indians abroad. Indians are said to constitute the largest number of filmgoers put together anywhere in the world. Cinematic technologies are thus questioning the broad metonymic identification of Indian cinema with the nation by increasingly blurring the boundaries of the politicised linguistic identities and making the categories of the local, regional and national subtler and more challenging. What needs underlining is that while at one level, the regional is extrapolating to the national, even in the global, at another, it is the flavour of the local that continues to create the stories and bring in the audiences. And, again, this is found in the Indian Shakespeare films, in which the regional/local has been a major source of their success, whether it is the use of the *janapada* folk music in the Telugu *Gunasundari Katha* (*Lear*) or the myth of *kelipatra* from north Kerala in *Karmayogi* (*Hamlet*). The local tension between theatre and film cultures in pre-independence Tamil Nadu, for instance, is encapsulated in the Hamlet cameo in *Rajapart Rangadurai*, while the recent political instability in Assam is boldly tackled in *Othello* (*We Too Have Our Othellos*). Bhardwaj's Shakespeare trilogy, despite its global Bollywood reach, is rooted in the specific contexts, language and mannerisms of the Mumbai underworld (*Maqbool*), the badlands of middle India (*Omkara*) or the insurgency torn Kashmir (*Haider*). Even English-language diasporic Shakespeare films like *Life Goes On* or *Second Generation*, based on *Lear*, turn on the nuances of immigrant Bengali lives. Though cinema is primarily a visual medium, it is language, the spoken word, which has played the key role in localising the regional film industries.

Translation, Performance and Parsi Theatre: Local and National

Shakespeare translated into the major Indian languages starts appearing in performance (*The Taming of the Shrew*, Gujarati, 1852) and in print (*Merchant of Venice*, Bengali, 1853) from the mid-nineteenth century. Though a consolidated and up-to-date checklist of all Shakespeare translations in the recognised twenty-two official languages of India is yet to be produced, at a conservative estimate, it will number several hundreds. This meant that there was a substantial ready corpus of translated Shakespeare for Indian film-makers to appropriate. What it also meant was that while the English-educated elite were reading Shakespeare in the original – he was quickly incorporated into school and college syllabi – a popular, adapted Shakespeare was circulated in translations through performances, particularly those of the Parsi theatre, the first modern theatre in India, from 1860s onwards. Parsi theatre has been recognised as a precursor of the film industry: its plays were in Urdu/Hindi, and it evolved a hybrid style of performance, spectacular, melodramatic and histrionic, of multiple plots with song and dance – elements which were in part drawn from a tradition of Shakespearean adaptations, one of the sources of this theatre. These features continue to characterise Indian cinema. With the coming of the talkies, this mass medium proved more lucrative, and there was a wholesale migration of actors, directors, playwrights, musicians, singers and technicians from Parsi theatre companies to film studios. In fact, the rise of cinema signalled the demise of the Parsi theatre. Many of the early silent films and talkies were filmed versions of the Parsi stage plays. The first Indian talkie, *AlamAra* 1931, was based on a Parsi stage play, and so was the first synchronised sound *Hamlet*, 1935, by Sohrab Modi. Parsi theatre companies toured the subcontinent, establishing an all-India presence: their impact in creating a taste for and a model of popular entertainment was far reaching. Indian-language Shakespeares not only found expression in regional film industries: Parsi theatre's Shakespeare appropriations also helped to create a national template of Bollywood cinema. Thus Shakespeare plays an important role in the shaping of and negotiations between national, regional and local Indian cinemas. And if today Bollywood has acquired a global recognition, the Shakespeare trilogy by Vishal Bhardwaj has had a salient role in it.

Reading the Indian Shakespeare Film

The critical estimation of Shakespeare on film has posed a challenge from the beginning. Initially, Shakespeare studies frowned on the new medium, considering it a 'menace,'[9] its mass appeal necessitating concessions and dilution. Serious evaluation did not begin until the 1970s, and early criticism laboured under the burden of the book to judge the fidelity of the visual to the word. It is only from the 1990s, with the consolidation of cultural and film studies, that the Shakespeare film has been seen in its own right, as a cultural product determined equally by the economic, industrial, social and political imperatives as by textual and artistic ones. In India too, early cinema was decried as a corrupting force by intellectuals. Foremost Hindi writer Premchand (1880–1936), who took up a contract as a scriptwriter in Bombay, was alienated by the commercialism of the industry and returned within a year: 'The cinema is not the right place for a literary person ... what can an industry have to do with taste and its correction? All it knows is how to exploit', he wrote.[10] Indian cinema as a whole has not had a favourable reception in the West until recently, even though it has had a wide viewership in South-East Asia, Far East, large parts of Africa and the Middle East. Its episodic narrative style, with its structures and semiotics largely dependent on emotionalism, melodrama and music for their effects, is seen as opposed to the needs of realism. Indian critics too, beset by postcolonial anxieties, have labelled the Indian mode of film-making as 'a counter naturalism emerging out of a pre-industrial, mythic mode of discourse' (Dasgupta),[11] producing escapist fantasies (Rangoonwalla) and vicariously feeding desires and needs emerging out of the tensions of modernity and tradition (Valicha, Nandy). Leftist ideological analyses (Madhava Prasad), which see Indian cinema as an expression of the struggle with the evolving nation state and subjectivity, do counter such reductive views but cannot account adequately for the pleasures and popularity of Indian movies. And though there are now increasing attempts to theorise these films in their own terms (Vasudevan, Dwyer, Misra), critiquing narrow definitions of realism and positing a 'psychological realism' (Kakar) instead, the multiple meanings, both textual and contextual, of Indian cinema continue to pose a challenge.

As in the West, the Indian Shakespeare film too has traversed a vast range of forms since the first moving picture, and it would be hazardous to try to define a clear category of 'the Shakespeare film', which has evolved through almost a hundred years from the earliest silent (*Champraj Hado* 1923, *Cymbeline*) and then talkie versions (*Khoon ka Khoon* 1935, *Hamlet*) of the histrionic play to assimilative Indianisations of the full play (*Angoor* 1982, *Comedy of Errors*) to spectacular but astute Bollywoodisation (*Haider* 2015, *Hamlet*) to the beauty of a polished art extravaganza (*Veeram* 2016, *Macbeth*). Critical attention to the Indian Shakespeare film in the Western academy has been catalysed chiefly by the appreciative reception of Bhardwaj's trilogy (2006–2016) but is almost exclusively centred on Bollywood. Interest in the conventions and traditions of Hindi cinema has been stimulated, but much of the writing measures the films against set frameworks – of Bollywoodisation and globalisation for instance – and often schematically so. This would go some distance to unpack the intricacies of such an indigenous product as the Indian film if much of it were not from the periphery as it were, guided by Western norms without taking into account the divergent tastes and practices that determine Indian cinema. This criticism tends to reify the categories of 'Bollywood' or 'globalised Indian films' by paying inadequate attention to the dynamic and evolving nature of these cinemas.[12] As noted before, not only is Shakespeare 'a knotted ... entity', posing a challenge in unpacking all his 450 years of encrustations, but equally so is Indian cinema in its multitudinous manifestations, layering and associations, both in India and abroad.[13] Addressing this challenge, Craig Dionne and Parmita Kapadia (*Bollywood Shakespeares*, 2014, the only book on the subject as yet) propose seeing Shakespeare in Indian cinema as 'cross-hatched ... 'two worlds necessarily separated but oddly aligned in their aims' which need to be read through a 'dissensus', i.e. by cracking open regimes of naturalised perception from the inside.[14] Yet, since the book confines itself to Bollywood, it does not have interactive and pan-Indian perspectives on Indian cinema as a whole. Mark Thornton Burnett, the leading critic to look at Shakespeare and world cinema (including Indian films) paying equal attention to both, clears more critical space. He calls for 'an approach that takes us away from the separate bracketing of "foreign Shakespeare" and towards a new sensibility' and for 'a praxis of interpretation which would allow us to challenge the channels through which we have access to Shakespearean production'. He further argues for 'an alteration in the canon of Shakespeare on film' because Shakespeare's international screen presences 'cannot be seen as "the other", for the simple reason that they are us.'[15]

Theorising Appropriation in Media and Film

However, the widespread appropriation of Shakespeare in diverse media has provoked a backlash reaction too. Of note are the polarised views of Richard Burt, important because of their special attention to Indian screen Shakespeares. In a move to prise Shakespeare film criticism out of the postcolonial and globalisation groove and position it within the transnational frames of film and media analysis, Burt holds that 'Cinematic Shakespeare functions as a type of currency without particular meaning, location [or] traceable source of value' and that in the 'post diasporic placelessness' of today's world, Shakespeare's post-canonical status means that he is 'no longer connected to gold standard.'[16] Focussing only on citational fragments of Shakespeare in Hindi film, Burt finds, not surprisingly, that Indian cinemas present us with a 'diminished, fragmentary, even forgettable Shakespeare.'[17] While Burt is surprised at the extent of Shakespeare in Hindi cinema, 'Shakespeare has become almost inescapable in Bollywood film,'[18] Burt's postmodern perspective, in which the 'local' is only 'an effect of a cinematic framing', leads him to conclude that Shakespeare in Indian cinema 'serves not to localize or indigenise ... but to use Shakespeare's obsolescence [result of mediatised commodification] as a means of entering into world cinema.'[19]

While Indian film-makers indeed aspire to international breakthroughs (meaning Western since Indian cinemas continue to enjoy considerable viewership in other parts of the world), it is the mammoth local market that gives their films a financial viability and which film-makers have to astutely balance with the international. And while the technology of film is indubitably transnational, it is the nature of its deployment to express the local that is of intellectual interest. Failure to attend to these local axes of film production leads to views like Burt's which gloss over centuries of Indian interaction with Shakespeare, second only to Germany (which, however, lacks the large number of Shakespeare films found in India).

Modification of this view may be found in a few critics willing to question the Western normative: Lucia Kramer's analysis of Bollywood's particular practices of adaptation as an 'industrial' category is a timely acknowledgement of what she calls 'crucial differences from the hegemonic Hollywood model'. She notes how the avoidance of literary adaptation in favour of 'remakes' in Bollywood, in which 'presentation' becomes more important than 'originality of story', 'encourages a comparative mode of reception, downplaying the western discourse of fidelity to the original'. Adaptation is instinctive in the Indian creative sphere; stories from mythology and the epics are constantly being reworked and presented as fresh creative acts. Borrowing is not frowned upon because, as elaborated elsewhere, and as quoted by Kramer in support, in the Indian literary tradition 'translation, adaptation, rewriting and transformation have been sanctioned practices of literary creation' and 'legitimate modes of alterity.'[20] Kramer concludes, 'investigating adaptation in Bollywood holds various corrective implications for Euro-American adaptation scholars who take the Hollywood model as the unmarked case.'[21]

Another salutary recognition taking cognisance of the 'inside' as it were comes from Bill Ashcroft's theorisation about the type of postcolonial resistance which results in transformation rather than opposition, a transformation which is different from acculturation, which is not joining or mingling with the dominant but changing it, which priorities the agency of the subjected and produces alternative modernities. He makes a strong case for reading Bollywood as 'a very dynamic example of the transformational and transcultural process by which globalisation proceeds ... a form that has so exceeded its Western origins that it offers a stunning example of the possibilities of transformation', citing the example of the idiosyncratic narrative and visual style which Bollywood has forged and which needs to be seen as not 'peculiar' but particular.[22]

Shakespeare came to India with colonialism for the entertainment of the expatriates, and though he was requisitioned in the teaching apparatus of the empire, it was through performance, through amateur productions in schools and colleges, and in translation on the public stages that he was popularised. However, it is in cinema, also a Western import, that Shakespeare in India has been truly 'homed', not just translated and adapted but adopted and assimilated as one of our own. Here the liberty to transform and transmute his space and place for our own purposes is seen most clearly in his stories, scenes, characters, citations, traces and echoes in a multitude of Indian films. In fact, it is virtually impossible to track all Shakespearean usage for new titles keep emerging all the time in the several language cinemas. The subtitle of this volume, 'Local Habitations', signals this guiding principle which animated it and around which all the contributions are centred.

***

The fifteen essays of the book are divided into four parts which thematically span the major aspects of the treatment of Shakespeare in Indian cinemas. The fifth part comprises interviews with three film-makers who have risked unusual cinematic engagements with Shakespeare. This is followed by a filmography, assembled for the first time, which lists the Indian Shakespeare films according to (a) plays and (b) chronologically, and which will provide a vital resource for further studies in this area. It will also help to position the Indian Shakespeare film within the expanding repertoire of Shakespeare cinema worldwide. The parts of the book are as follows.

Indigenising the Tragic

Shakespeare's tragedies represent the acme of his achievement, and the opening part of the volume features a group of five essays which examine how Indian films, whether Bollywood, art-house Hindi cinema or regional movies, adapt the tragedies into their own artistic idioms and conventions, given the absence of the tragic genre in indigenous aesthetics.

Poonam Trivedi's 'Woman as Avenger: "Indianising" the Shakespearean Tragic in the Films of Vishal Bhardwaj' shows how Bhardwaj transforms the Shakespearean tragic form through his reframing of the female protagonists as active instruments of redemptive justice. While women in Shakespeare's tragedies appear as either victims or instigators of violence, in *Maqbool*, *Omkara* and *Haider*, they take a leading role, often displacing the male heroes, and emerge as authors of the tragic resolution which is significantly different from the original denouement of the plays. Lady Macbeth/Nimmi's child in *Maqbool* representing the hope for a less violent future, Emilia/Indu's expiatory killing of her husband Iago/Langda in *Omkara* and Gertrude/Ghazala's suicide disrupting the male cycle of retribution infuse Shakespeare's tragedies with a sense of justice and closure, distinct from the ideas of waste, pity and fear generated by the death of male heroes. Thus, it is argued, the re-organisation of gender leads to a reformulation of genre in Bhardwaj's films, making for a unique kind of 'Indianisation' of the tragic within Bollywood conventions.

Robert S. White's '*Eklavya*: Shakespeare Meets the *Mahabharata*' reads Vidhu Vinod Chopra's 2007 film *Eklavya: The Royal Guard* as a tapestry of influences from the Shakespearean tragedies *Macbeth*, *Lear* and primarily *Hamlet*, as well as the sonnets, woven together with Indian epic and myth. The story of Eklavya from the *Mahabharata* and the repeated references to *dharma* complicate and disrupt the tragic frame of *Hamlet* and its politics of male revenge. Like Trivedi, White also indicates how it is women's moral agency (Rajjo/Ophelia's forgiveness of Harsh/Hamlet for causing her father's accidental death) that breaks the cycle of retributive violence. This helps *Eklavya* to go beyond tragic calamity and garner a peace which White likens both to the *santa rasa* or the mood of equanimity described in Indian poetics (*Natyashastra*) and the spirit of reconciliation in Shakespeare's late romances.

Nishi Pulugurtha's essay 'Reworking Shakespeare in Telugu Cinema: *King Lear* to *Gunasundari Katha*' studies how the frame of Shakespeare's harrowing tragedy in K.V. Reddy's 1949 Telugu film, the first redaction of *Lear* in Indian cinema, is appropriated to create a typical example of the indigenous mythological and folkloric blockbuster. The love test, banishment and victimisation of Cordelia (she is married to a blind and lame beggar) are used to project filial and wifely devotion through the popular musical form of the *janapadam*, and the bleak and godless universe of *Lear* is transformed into a devotional and fabulous one in which the gods descend to punish the sisters and reward the loyalty of Gunasundari/Cordelia. Lear survives, and the bind beggar transmutes into a handsome prince for a comic rather than tragic resolution.

'Shakespeare in Malayalam Cinema: Cultural and Mythic Interface, Narrative Negotiations' by C.S. Venkiteswaran examines four Malayali films, Jayaraj's trilogy – *Kaliyattam* (1997), *Kannaki* (2001) and *Veeram* (2016) based on *Othello*, *Antony and Cleopatra* and *Macbeth*, respectively – and V.K. Prakash's *Karmayogi* (2012), an adaptation of

Hamlet, to demonstrate how the mythical, storytelling and performative traditions of Kerala create a specific local tragic idiom. Jayaraj's films set Shakespearean plots in rural communities, some in a distant past, engaged in traditional performances like *theyyam,* cockfighting or *kalari,* which generate intense rivalry and hatred, leading to terrible consequences. Shakespeare's lonely tragedies of individual waste are fitted into mythic stories of ritualistic transgression and punishment. Prakash's *Karmayogi* ends not with the death of the hero, Hamlet/Rudra, but with his renunciation of the world to embark on a spiritual journey, a closure that Venkiteswaran reads as marking an Indian unease with the 'moral void' of the Shakespearean tragic ending.

Pointing to this same disinclination in Bollywood's avoidance of tragedy (particularly in musical love stories), Koel Chatterjee's '*Qayamat Se Qayamat Tak:* A Neglected Shakespeare Film' argues for the singularity of director Mansoor Khan's popular Bollywood adaptation of *Romeo and Juliet,* which retained Shakespeare's tragic ending against commercial logic. Although a happy ending version of the film had been scripted and shot, Khan felt that the story demanded a tragic closure and decided to reshoot the final scenes. Borrowing images, motifs and dialogue from the original play, and particularly its popular reincarnations, like the 1961 American musical *West Side Story* and the 1981 Hindi film based on a Telugu original *Ek Duuje Ke Liye,* Khan created a tragic template for *Romeo and Juliet* adaptations within Bollywood which has influenced more recent versions. like *Ishaqzaade* (2012), *Issaq* (2013) and *Ram-leela* (2013).

Critical Innovations: Historiography of Silence and Poetics of *Rasa*

The second part comprises two essays which introduce critical and methodological challenges to the historiography and aesthetics of Indian film studies. While Amrit Gangar's essay, 'Silent Shakespeare: Recouping an Archive', attempts to reconstruct a history of the little-known and now lost films of the silent genre based on Shakespeare, Anil Zankar's essay, 'Shakespeare, Cinema and Indian Poetics', explores the modalities of deploying the *rasa* theory of Sanskrit poetics as an interpretative tool for analysing all films. Relying on tertiary material, posters, reviews and discussions, Gangar resurrects his absent subjects – seven silent Indian Shakespeare films, the prints of which are lost – raising critical questions about archiving, retrieving and reconstructing their histories, particularly in the context of missing materials. His intensive research has unearthed a wealth of details about these films but, most importantly, has discovered a hitherto unknown silent film, *Champraj Hado,* adapted from *Cymbeline,* which pushes the date for the first Indian Shakespeare film further back to 1923. The essay evokes the excitement of the new movie technology which inspired film-makers to go beyond the early mythologicals and take up challenging subjects like Shakespearean plays and traces the evolution of these films from translations, adaptations and popular stage versions, especially those from the Parsi theatre.

Anil Zankar's essay, 'Shakespeare, Cinema and Indian Poetics', explicates the Sanskrit *rasa* theory and its applicability to film criticism in general and to the *mise en scène* in particular. It demonstrates how reading oriental adaptations of Shakespeare on screen through the lens of *rasa* reveals different facets about them through a comparative analysis of Kurosawa's *Throne of Blood* and Bhardwaj's *Maqbool*, *Omkara* and *Haider*. The essay thus suggests an alternative and comparative mode of understanding the aesthetics of Shakespearean film adaptations.

Between the Global and the Local

The third part examines how the engagement with Shakespeare provides a site of intercultural dialogue and intertextuality between Anglophone cinematic genres (produced and distributed internationally or nationally) on the one hand and the exploration of Indian regional identities and idioms on the other. Ranging from classic Hollywood to low-budget 'Indie' movies, from internationally produced and distributed 'festival' films to diasporic cinema and television series, the four essays study how English-language Shakespeare films help to articulate diverse local ethnicities and traditions in India.

Preti Taneja's 'Such a Long Journey: Rohinton Mistry's Parsi *King Lear* from Fiction to Film' reads both Rohinton Mistry's 1991 English novel *Such a Long Journey* and Sturla Gunnarson's 2002 Indo-Canadian English film based on it as diasporic Anglophone productions (Mistry and the screenwriter, Taraporewala, are both diasporic India-born Parsis), although they are set squarely in the lives of the Parsi community of 1970s Bombay. The novel deploys *King Lear* to express the relationship between tradition and modernity, East and West in postcolonial Parsi lives and their nostalgic looking back at the British Raj, metonymically represented by Shakespeare. However, the film, made for a global market, limits the *Lear* references in the novel to create perhaps a more 'pure' and exoticised notion of 'Indianness' uncontaminated by 'Western' influences. Both the presence and absence of Shakespeare's mediation in narrating the Parsi identity in the novel and the film throw up important questions regarding the dialogue between the global and the local, the diasporic and the 'native'.

In conversation with Taneja's essay on *King Lear* and Parsi identity is Paromita Chakravarti's 'Cinematic *Lears* and Bengaliness: Locus, Identity, Language', which examines how Shakespeare's play affords a productive location from which to explore questions of Bengali identity in four English films aimed at an international audience – Aparna Sen's *36 Chowringhee Lane* (1981); Jon Sen's two-part *Second Generation* (2003), made for Channel 4 television; Rituparno Ghosh's *The Last Lear* (2006); and Sangeeta Datta's *Life Goes On* (2009). The essay examines how these films deploy *Lear* to delineate a 'Bengaliness' poised between the West and the East, tradition and modernity, colonial and postcolonial legacies. While *Lear* in these films provides an image of lost worlds, broken families and rejected patrimonies, it also supplies possibilities of reconciliation and recovery through an acceptance of change, otherness and hybridities. Whereas in *36 Chowringhee Lane* and *The Last Lear*, both set in Calcutta, Shakespeare is more of a cultural relic upholding an elitist Bengali modernity evolved through colonial education, in the two diasporic films there is a gesture towards a different negotiation with Shakespeare and the forging of a new and more inclusive Bengali identity.

Varsha Panjwani's essay, 'Shakespeare and Indian Independent Cinema: *8 × 10 Tasveer and 10 ml Love*', explores *8 × 10 Tasveer*, Nagesh Kukunoor's 2009 reworking of *Hamlet* as a murder mystery, and *10 ml Love*, Sharat Katariya's 2012 take on *A Midsummer Night's Dream*. These films represent a new genre of independent (indie) non-Bollywood and non-parallel/-art, low-budget films made in 'Hinglish', a combination of Hindi and English which is spoken by a large section of educated, urban Indian youth. Panjwani demonstrates how in this genre Shakespearean plots enable the expression of a new middle-class, transnational, cosmopolitan identity in a globalised, urban India. She speculates that the directors' choice of both these Shakespeare plays, concerned with self-reflexivity, reflects their own concerns, as do the metatheatrical references to the material conditions of playing, which resonate with these edgy, low-budget movies filled with ironic asides to the difficulties of resource-strapped film-making. She argues that these movies represent the rise of new markets and audiences in English-speaking, neo-liberal India.

'"Singing Is Such Sweet Sorrow": *Ambikapathy*, Hollywood Shakespeare, and Tamil Cinema's Hybrid Heritage' by Thea Buckley places the intercultural dialogue between English-language, Western Shakespeare films and regional Indian identities not in a globalised world but in an earlier, imperial history of the emergence of Indian cinemas in the late 1930s. The essay shows that, in the context of growing audience demand for local stories, the visiting American film director Ellis R. Dungan made *Ambikapathy* in 1937, inspired by George Cukor's 1936 Hollywood *Romeo and Juliet*, but set it in the world of classical Tamil myth – the love story of the legendary Chola princess Amaravathi and Ambikapathy, son of the twelfth-century Tamil poet Kambar. Dungan's film represented one of the earliest successful, subversive and creative dialogues between Western romance and regional myth and music which ran to full houses for months. Buckley points out how much of the appeal of the film actually lay in its crucial borrowings, of poetry, the balcony scene and the on-screen kiss, from Shakespeare and the Hollywood original. The triumph of this Shakespearean hybrid led to a 1957 remake and established cinema as a new vehicle for Tamil culture.

Reimagining Gender, Region and Nation

While the previous part explored the continuities between the global and the local, the essays in this fourth part focus on the relationship between the region and the nation as it is mediated through the lens of changing gender relations. Shakespeare's portrayal of women in his plays offers templates of modernity (as attested by the essays of Bankim Chandra and Tagore, discussed in Amrita Sen's essay) through which a complex politics of local and national identities are articulated in regional Indian Shakespearean cinemas.

Mark Thornton Burnett's 'Gendered Play and Regional Dialogue in *Nanjundi Kalyana*' analyses the adaptation of *Taming of the Shrew* in S. Rajashekar's 1989 Kannada film as an assertion of Kannada culture and pride. Shakespeare's plot provides a narrative of the domestication of a Westernised, English-speaking, shrewish Devi/Katharina figure into a demure Kannadiga woman, respectful of *dharma* and appropriate familial and conjugal values. This story of transformation recapitulates some of the nationalist arguments against the anglicised and educated 'New Woman' of colonial India. The essay highlights how the identity of regional cinema pitted against Bollywood is articulated in the film through subtle variations on the tropes of mainstream Hindi cinema. It demonstrates how Shakespeare is deployed to support the vitality and uniqueness of a regional culture and film industry in its relationship with the nation.

Concentrating not on full-length films but on citations, A. Mangai's essay 'Not the Play but the Playing: Citation of Performing Shakespeare as a Trope in Tamil Cinema' explores the overlaps between the Shakespearean presence in Tamil drama and cinema, discussing films in which inset scenes of the theatrical performance of Shakespearean plays provide key moments articulating motifs of modernity and transition in Tamil cultural history. In P. Mathavan's 1973 *Rajapart Rangadurai*, the cinematic citation of a stage performance of *Hamlet* marks the coming of a modern acting style in Tamil theatre history. In the 1963 film *Ratha Thilagam*, directed by Dada Mirasi, the protagonists fall in love during a college production of *Othello*, the ethos and plot of which then inform the narrative. Set against the 1962 India-China war, the personal themes of suspicion and loyalty in the play are transported to the political realm in the film. Portrayed as an assertive, modern woman the Desdemona figure sacrifices individual interests for service to the nation, and though initially misunderstood by Othello, she is forgiven in death. The film demonstrates how Shakespeare becomes a site through which local Tamil cinema finds modes of accessing a paradigm of national modernity. Significantly, *Ratha Thilagam* echoes themes of an earlier Bengali film, *Saptapadi* (1961), set against the Second World War, which also uses the trope of a college performance of *Othello* as a framing device. By unearthing connections between the Tamil and Bengali films, Mangai's essay initiates a line of potential research into the complex web of intertextualities across various regional language cinemas based on Shakespearean plays.

Intertextualities across various regional as well as Bollywood adaptations of *The Comedy of Errors* are the subject of Amrita Sen's essay 'Indianizing *The Comedy of Errors*: *Bhranti Bilash* and Its Aftermaths', which examines the curious fit between the comic conventions in Shakespeare's play and the stock devices of popular Indian cinema. Though separated twins and mistaken identities are common in Indian cinemas, the deployment of two sets of twins is Shakespearean and leads to more versions in Indian cinemas (seven) of *The Comedy of Errors* than in other cinemas and, moreover, all commercial hits. Focussing on the 1963 Bengali adaptation, *Bhranti Bilash*, based on Vidyasagar's prose translation, Sen's essay examines two Bollywood, one Kannada, and a recent Punjabi version, underlining the use of local performative traditions in interpreting the play. The depiction of the Luciana figure as an assertive and modern woman who is romantically linked with the unmarried twin in the Bengali film influences other Hindi and regional language adaptations, and helps to tone down the sexually transgressive scenes in Shakespeare's play and transform the raucous farce into romantic comedy, even domestic melodrama. Thus the Indian *Comedy of Errors* films draw upon each other as much as they do on Shakespeare and Bollywood, setting up a subgroup within the mistaken identities film genre.

Parthajit Baruah's 'Regional Reflections: Shakespeare in Assamese Cinema' argues that the Western influence and assimilation of Shakespeare, and of the cinematic medium into Assamese culture have been deployed for articulating a peculiarly regional selfhood in its contestations with nationally imposed identities. Locating Hemanta Kumar Das's award-winning Assamese film *Othello* (*We Too Have Our Othellos*) (2014) in a local tradition of political film-making, Baruah contends that notions of otherness and marginalisation from Shakespeare's play inspire a bold critique of the movements for self-determination that have been raging in the state for several decades. The film shows how it is not the various Othellos, socially disaffected male figures who try to cope with their political and social failures, but the

Desdemona figure, transformed into a bold, non-conforming 'fallen' woman, who manages to carve out a unique, nurturing space for herself and, by association, others. It suggests that a radical politics of identity can perhaps be better articulated within the ambit of the personal spheres of women's lives rather than in the male realm of people's rebellion.

Interviews

Much of the scholarship on Shakespeare on screen is dominated by literary critics and scholars whose analyses focus, sometimes lopsidedly, on the content of the films and their relationship to the 'original' plays rather than on the specificities of the cinematic medium, the vision of directors and the material contingencies of film-making. In an attempt to redress this bias, a part on interviews with three film-makers is incorporated. This includes a conversation of the editors with Pankaj Butalia, director of the documentary *When Hamlet Went to Mizoram* (1990), a particularly valuable film since its print had been lost and has only recently been restored for limited circulation. It represents the under-researched genre of the Shakespeare-themed documentary as well as the little-known subject of Shakespearean influence on North-Eastern culture in India. The second interview is with Roysten Abel, director of the play *Othello: A Play in Black and White* (1999), one of the first Indian contemporisations of Shakespeare's play, which won the Fringe First award at Edinburgh, and the art film based on it, *In Othello* (2003). Like Butalia's documentary, Abel's experimental movie is difficult to access, and there is little scholarly work on it. The film-maker's retrospective analysis of the film therefore forms a critical resource for scholars of Shakespeare in Indian cinemas. The final interview is with Aparna Sen, actor-director, who speaks extensively on Shakespeare's influence on her as a film-maker, manifested both in her 1981 film *36 Chowringhee Lane* and in her recent Bengali version of *Romeo and Juliet*, *Arshinagar* (Mirror City, 2015).

Looking at Indian cinemas through the prism of Shakespeare is thus to view aslant the evolution of the Indian film industry and provide an alternate synoptic perspective on its growth, movements and current concerns. The Indian Shakespeare film marks all the stages of its development. The research and analyses of the essays of this collection not only unearth and bring to fore many forgotten chapters and details of this history, but they also unsettle and refract many givens: qualifying the dominance of Bollywood by foregrounding its intertextualities with the several regional cinemas and challenging the accepted, largely Anglocentric, modes of reading the Indian film. Instead the collection focusses on indigenous traditions, practices and aesthetics, looking at the epics, *rasa* theory and the Indian ambivalence towards the tragic to open up the specificities of the Indian cinematic engagements with the Bard. Hence it shifts attention from content and convention, and directs it towards genres, histories – literary, theatrical and musical – and the material conditions of film-making, including the international, to parse out how they are intermedially translated into Shakespeare films. And how the intermeshing of Hollywood, Bollywood and regional, i.e. the politics of the imperial, national, global and local, impacted the configurations of the diverse Indian Shakespeare films.

Tracking this considerable circulation of Shakespeare in Indian cinemas (115 titles and growing!) is also to uphold the transcultural appropriative as a legitimate mode of interpretation. A re-textualisation takes place here, juxtaposing and repositioning in new contexts, even in citations and afterlives, which extends and provokes meanings, enabling us to see anew the plays and Shakespearean potentialities. It shows that Shakespeare forms a benchmark in our cultural imaginaries: the changing attitudes towards him and the evolving iterations of his words and works position both the distance from our past and the signages for the future.

Notes

1 See Film Federation of India website, www.filmfed.org/IFF2017.html. Not all the certified films may have been finally produced, and in seventeen languages, there was only one film in the year. Last accessed December 2017.
2 Andrew Dickson, *Worlds Elsewhere: Journeys Around Shakespeare's Globe* (London: Vintage, 2015), 181.
3 Russell Jackson, *Shakespeare and the English-speaking Cinema* (Oxford: Oxford University Press, 2014), 10.
4 On the use of the term 'Bollywood', see M. Madhava Prasad, 'This Thing Called Bollywood', *Seminar* 525 (May 2003), Ashish Rajadhyaksha, 'The Bollywoodization of the Indian Cinema: Cultural Nationalism in a Global Arena', in *City Flicks: Indian Cinema and the Urban Experience*, ed. Preban Kaarsholm (Calcutta: Seagull, 2004) and the latest M.K. Raghavendra, *Bollywood*, Oxford India Short Introductions (New Delhi: Oxford University Press, 2016).
5 See tables in *Encyclopaedia of Indian Cinema*, ed. Ashish Rajadhyaksha and Paul Willemen, new revised ed. (New Delhi: Oxford University Press, 2002), 31 and 32.
6 Figures for *Baahubali 2* represent the expanding possibilities for Indian cinema. Its first day collection worldwide was $34 million, and it was released in 9,000 theatres. It was made in Tamil and Telugu, and dubbed into Hindi, Malayalam, German, French, Japanese and English. From *International Business Times*, September 2017.
7 Marathi has two films, *Natsamrat* (2016) and *Sairat* (2016).
8 N. Kalyan Raman, 'Dream-World: Reflections on Cinema and Society in Tamil Country', in *Beyond Bollywood: The Cinemas of South India*, ed. M.K. Raghavendra (Noida: Harper Collins India, 2017), 3.

9 Lawrence Kitchen, 'Shakespeare on Screen', *Shakespeare Survey* 18 (1965): 74.
10 Amrit Rai, *Premchand: A Life*, tr. from the Hindi by Harish Trivedi (New Delhi: People's Publishing House, 1982), 321.
11 Chidananda Dasgupta, *The Painted Face: Studies in India's Popular Cinemas* (New Delhi: Roli Books, 1991), 59. See also Firoze Rangoonwala, *75 Years of Indian Cinema* (New Delhi: Indian Book Company, 1975); Kishore Valicha, *The Moving Image* (Bombay: Orient Longman, 1988); Ashish Nandy, ed. *The Secret Politics of Our Desires: Innocence, Culpability and Indian Popular Cinema* (New Delhi: Oxford University Press, 1998); M. Madhav Prasad, *Ideology of the Hindi Film: A Historical Construction* (New Delhi: Oxford University Press, 1998); Ravi Vasudevan, ed. *Making Meaning in Indian Cinema* (New Delhi: Oxford University Press, 2000); Rachel Dwyer and Christopher Pinney, eds. *Pleasure and the Nation: The History, Politics and Consumption of Public Culture in India* (New Delhi: Oxford University Press, 2001); Vijay Misra, *Bollywood Cinema: Temples of Desire* (New York: Routledge, 2002); and Sudhir Kakar, *Intimate Relations: Exploring Indian Sexuality* (New Delhi: Penguin, 1990).
12 See articles by Rosa M. Garcia-Periago, 'The Ambiguities of Bollywood Conventions and the Reading of Transnationalism in Vishal Bhardwaj's *Maqbool*' and Brinda Charry and Gitanjali Shahani, 'The Global as Local/Othello as Omkara', in *Bollywood Shakespeares*, ed. Craig Dionne and Parmita Kapadia (New York: Palgrave, 2014); Susanne Gruss, 'Shakespeare in Bollywood? Vishal Bhardwaj's *Omkara*', in *Semiotic Encounters: Text, Image and Trans-Nation*, ed. Sarah Sackel, Walter Gobel and NohaHamdy (Amsterdam: Rodopi, 2009); and Florence Cabaret, 'Indianizing *Othello*: Vishal Bhardwaj's *Omkara*', in *Shakespeare on Screen: Othello*, ed. Sarah Hatchuel and Nathalie Vienne-Guerrin (Cambridge: Cambridge University Press, 2015).
13 See Poonam Trivedi, 'Afterword', in *Bollywood Shakespeares*.
14 Craig Dionne and Parmita Kapadia, 'Introduction', in *Bollywood Shakespeare*, 3 and 6.
15 Mark Thornton Burnett, *Shakespeare and World Cinema* (Cambridge: Cambridge University Press, 2013), 3.
16 Richard Burt, 'Shakespeare and Asia in Postdiasporic Cinemas: Spin-Offs and Citations of the Plays from Bollywood to Hollywood', in *Shakespeare the Movie II: Popularising the Plays on Film, TV, Video and DVD*, ed. Richard Burt and Lynda E. Boose (New York: Routledge, 2004), 268–69.
17 Richard Burt, 'All That Remains of Shakespeare in Indian Film', in *Shakespeare in Asia: Contemporary Performance*, ed. Dennis Kennedy and Yong Li Lan (Cambridge: Cambridge University Press, 2010), 76–77.
18 Burt, 'Shakespeare and Asia in Postdiasporic Cinemas', 271.
19 Burt, 'All That Remains of Shakespeare in Indian Film', 75 and 73.
20 For a longer discussion, see Poonam Trivedi, 'Reading Other Shakespeares', in *Remaking Shakespeare: Performance across Media, Genres and Cultures*, ed. Pascale Aebischer, Edward J. Esche and Nigel Wheale (London: Palgrave, 2003), 60.
21 Lucia Kramer, 'Adaptation in Bollywood', in *The Oxford Handbook of Adaptation Studies*, ed. Thomas Leitch (Oxford: Oxford University Press, 2017), 251, 261 and 262.
22 Bill Ashcroft, 'Bollywood, Postcolonial Transformation and Modernity', in *Travels of Bollywood Cinema: From Bombay to LA*, ed. Anjali Gera Roy and Chua Beng Huat (New Delhi: Oxford University Press, 2012), 3.

Part I
Indigenising the Tragic

1 Woman as Avenger

'Indianising' the Shakespearean Tragic in the Films of Vishal Bhardwaj

Poonam Trivedi

Vishal Bhardwaj has been called Hindi cinema's 'Renaissance man,'[1] a tribute based not only on his three Shakespeare films, more than any other Indian film-maker, but also on the critical attention they have garnered, cross-culturally and internationally. These films have instigated a new approbation, a shift of attitudes akin to a rebirthing of the Indian film industry in a new, crossover light. Until the past few decades, Indian cinema spoke mainly to the local, though millions, of the subcontinent. The growing diaspora created a space for it in many other parts of the world. But Vishal Bhardwaj's Shakespeare films have in no small measure changed this; they have become the 'global' face of Indian/Hindi cinema. Since renowned Shakespeare thespian Sir Ian McKellen offered to start learning Hindi in a conversation with Bhardwaj during the festival of his Shakespeare films at the British Film Institute in April 2016, we can be confident that Indian cinema has crossed into another threshold.[2]

Bhardwaj's reputation is also based on the fact that he has started his reckoning with the core of the Shakespearean canon, the major tragedies. While there has been considerable comment on his films, what has been little noticed is how he has modified the configuration of the genre, mainly through changes in the endings and the role of women, in the process putting an unmistakable Indian stamp on it. If there is a common thread running through Vishal Bhardwaj's film versions of Shakespeare's tragedies, *Macbeth*, *Othello* and *Hamlet*, that is, *Maqbool* (2004), *Omkara* (2006) and *Haider* (2014), it is that all three foreground their relocation in specific cultures of violence: urban, rural and of the state. Violence and the tragic have a symbiotic relationship in Shakespeare; the background of war and power struggles infects the heroes, who embark on a fatal course of action from which there is no return. Macbeth is introduced as 'Bellona's bridegroom' (1.3.54), identified with a sword 'smoking with bloody execution' (1.3.18); Othello is called a 'savage' (4.1.52) whose attraction is 'the dangers I had passed' (1.3.166); and Hamlet debates whether to take up arms in a state which is 'rotten' (1.4.67).[3] Entire societies seem to reel under the onslaught of violence, both physical and emotional. Women are not spared either, but their roles in Shakespeare tragedies, apart from Juliet and Cleopatra, are limited to being either instigators or victims, or both, but not protagonists of the violence. Contemporising of Shakespearean drama often challenges these given positions, creating new localisations of the narrative which shift the dynamics of character and action. Vishal Bhardwaj's relocations of the tragedies in contemporary India enhance their equation with violence to make pointed political statements. His retellings critique 'systemic violence,'[4] i.e. spheres of organised violence – the criminal underworld of Mumbai in *Maqbool*, rural gangsterism in *Omkara* and the army excesses versus insurgency in Kashmir in *Haider* – all critical flash points of independent India. They show characters, male and female, trapped within the excesses of violence that they themselves generate. His other films too, like *Kaminey* (2009), an underworld thriller, and *Matru Ki Bijili Ka Mandola*, a satiric dig at land scams, scour the economic violence of corruption. Bhardwaj seems committed to exposing the cancer of violence in modern Indian society. While *Haider* is obviously the most political of the three films, the other two, contrary to what some critics believe, are equally concerned with contentious issues, asking serious questions of the state.

This exposé is mainly effected through the changes he makes in the role of the women, unpicking the accepted equation between women and violence in the tragedies and shifting the onus of establishing the final justice and executing vengeance upon the females in the play, almost akin to the manner in which women playfully sort out the situation in Shakespearean comedies. Bhardwaj's films, while remaining true to an essence of the plays, interpolate, extend and excise to subtly 'fill out' suggestions and echoes, re-textualising submerged meanings and re-placing events in their contemporisation of the plays. Anthony Howard, in his review of *Haider*, put his thumb squarely on it: 'One of Bhardwaj's greatest strengths is his readiness to rebalance Shakespeare, giving new speeches to the silent and bolstering relationships.'[5] A salient feature of this mode of adaptation, which has not been picked up in critical discourse, is the change Bhardwaj effects in the agency of the female figures. His versions of the tragic women, though infected by the violence around them, are more proactive, more instrumental in the expanded roles they are given. Individuals in their own right, they are not simply the 'other' of the masculine self. They intervene, interrogate and instigate resolutions that mere men cannot. In addition to their original role and function in Shakespeare, they promote and deflect the challenges faced by the male protagonists, courting violence and helping resolve it. Nimmi (Lady Macbeth) in *Maqbool*, who is Duncan's mistress in the film, forces Maqbool (Macbeth) at the point of a gun to accept her love for him, a relationship which proves to be both his undoing and his redemption. Dolly (Desdemona) in *Omkara* pursues Omi far more aggressively than the 'fair' Desdemona would ever dream of doing, and Emilia, not content in a supportive role, morphs into a slasher for justice. Gertrude, Shakespeare's most misunderstood woman, in *Haider* as Ghazala, takes over the role of the bloody avenger from Hamlet, blowing herself up in the process. Innocent Arshia (Ophelia), too, handles not flowers but a pistol.

Clearly, Vishal Bhardwaj's reconfiguration of Shakespeare's tragedies hinges upon the transgressive dimensions of the women's extended roles. In fact, it is possible to read his tragic trilogy as 'women's films'; Bhardwaj has said over the course of his interviews that he believes women to be stronger than men and that he finds it much easier to work with female actors – they 'leave it to you and are not a problem' – and wished that he could make female-oriented films (*The Times of India* 12 December 2012). This essay will investigate these dynamic changes of a re-gendering of the course of justice and their implications in the reading of not just the women but also the dimensions of Shakespearean tragedy on film. It will contextualise these changes by looking at the place, influence and assimilation of Shakespearean tragedy in Indian literary and performative cultures; the filming of Shakespeare tragedies in Hindi cinema; and the genres and conventions the particular films intersect with. It will argue that Bhardwaj's particular slant in his adaptations, not just in the mise en scène but also in the cultural and philosophic dimensions, is determined by his deep roots in Indian society and culture. It will demonstrate how his versions of the women emerge out of many complex symbolisms and tropes concerning women in Indian culture, which form the breeding ground for his imaginative recreations.

Shakespearean Tragedy in Indian Cinema

Indians have not been entirely comfortable with the tragic genre. Though it has been commonly accepted, it is observed more often in violation. Tragedy as a genre was introduced to Indian literary culture through Greek and Shakespearean drama in colonial times. Sanskrit poetics did not conceive of tragedy – depiction of death on stage was proscribed in the Natya Shastra. Hindu philosophy, positing rebirth, did not hold death as a finality but as a stepping stone into a future existence. Hence the aim of creative expression was to show the ultimate harmonisation of the earthly and metaphysical realms. Even though tragedy was opposed to traditional beliefs, it intrigued Indian intellectuals, stimulated debate, wielded influence and was accepted and assimilated in various ways.[6] And as with all Western genres, it was often modified to suit popular taste. For instance, a very popular early stage version of *Romeo and Juliet*, in Kannada, had the god Vishnu descend from the heavens at the end, to revive, bless and marry the lovers. Indian film genres too have adapted and remoulded their borrowings comprehensively. Popular

Indian cinema, as we know, has charted an altogether different track to the accepted modes of film-making, creating what has been termed a 'different universe.'[7] Shakespeare's tragedies were prominent in Indian cinema right from the beginning. *Hamlet, Khoon-e-Nahak* (Unjust Assassination, 1928) and *Macbeth, Khooni Taj* (Bloody Crown, 1930) are to be found among the early silent films. One of the earliest talkies, Sohrab Modi's *Khoon Ka Khoon* (Filial Murder, 1935), has the distinction of being the first full-length Indian Shakespeare film as well as, according to Kenneth S. Rothwell's filmography, the very first known talkie of the play globally![8] The pioneering Indian film-makers, busy with mythologicals and historicals, did not shy away from Shakespeare or tragedy. Almost all the Indian-language cinemas continued to experiment with Shakespeare's plays, taking up the challenge to embed them in their own cultural milieus, Tamil and Hindi producing the most versions. And by the time we come up to the twenty-first century, it is Vishal Bhardwaj's acclaimed Shakespeare tragic trilogy which has in no small way contributed to the internationalisation of Indian cinema. Interest in Bollywood had been burgeoning, but the trilogy has added a crucial critical esteem.

Vishal Bhardwaj's Shakespeare films achieve their impact through opposites: simultaneously global yet very local, they are reasonably close to the original texts but introduce critical changes. They are produced as full-scale commercial films but are characterised by an auteuristic vision. In their intensive engagement with the central icon of English literature they seem to be addressing the growing anglophone younger generation; yet the story, sounds and mise en scène of the films remain authentically indigenous and regional. And though there is the tragic, inevitable but unmerited death of the protagonists at the end, the films are all topical, with decided political overtones. In all the three films, the heroes are underplayed in favour of the women who rise up to become the avenging protagonists. What is most striking is that while the women are given a transgressive individuality, it is the changed gendered equation with violence which instruments the resolution of redemptive justice. Bhardwaj himself does not belong to the anglophone generation: he says that he had no schooling in Shakespeare but came to him as an adult. He has also repeatedly said that it is the stories that interest him most in Shakespeare. Hence, he has no hesitation in acculturating the stories into Indian situations, and he is not hampered by the residual colonial awe which still afflicts many Indians. It therefore becomes imperative to unpack his versioning of the Shakespearean tragic in which women are more deeply implicated in the violence when they finally turn towards a resolution, sacrificing their lives nevertheless. What is the gain of this gendering of justice? How and what do the women reframe and affirm through violence? Are these changes of characterisation to be considered monstrous or heroic? What social, psychic or ethical compulsions do they satisfy? And do they achieve a curative or regenerative impact? These are some of the questions that Bhardwaj's films provoke.

The Avenging Woman in Film and Culture

The figure of the violent avenging woman in Indian films is not exceptional. She has appeared in different forms from the early decades of Indian cinema. As a matter of fact, the considerable presence of this figure has created a subgenre in Indian cinema: the 'avenging woman' film, which intersects with other subgenres, like the 'vigilante woman' film, the 'rape and revenge' film and the early 'female action' film. These films have provoked considerable discussion, especially among feminist critics, who confront the contradictory readings which surround such 'women's' films. They were dismissed earlier as 'hackneyed' responses to the wave of violence and breakdown of the state (especially during the Emergency), seen as a 'welcome break' from the dominant stereotypes of the submissive women or seen as male fantasies recycling the old victimisation and masquerading as the female power trope. The proliferation of the genre, especially since the 1980s, has led to competing analyses testifying to the complexities and contradictions inherent in it. Issues of 'scopophilia and spectatorship', 'censorship and state' also form, as Lalitha Gopalan, in one of the earliest essays on the topic, put it, 'intertextual relays between them.'[9] This critical trajectory, incidentally, resembles the turns and counter-turns familiar from the feminist estimation of Shakespeare's tragic women, who were earlier undermined in binary readings of victim versus monsters, seen only as the 'Other' of the masculine Self or as fictions covering up oppressive reality.[10] Just as later, third-wave, feminism has attempted to recoup an agonistic reading of Shakespeare's women, so have Indian film critics had to rethink their positions on Indian women's film (*Bandit Queen*, dir. Shekhar Kapoor, 1994, sparked a huge debate). If Shakespeare's avenging women have yet to receive full critical estimation, the Indian counterpart too needs a consensus of views.

Further, Indian cinematic representation is fed, one needs to remember, by multiple streams of signification, not the least from the evergreen Indian epics, folklore and history. The figure of the avenging *virangana* or the warrior woman in different forms is to be found everywhere. Draupadi, the common wife of the five Pandava brothers in the *Mahabharata*, is usually seen as the vengeful one, burning with anger at her disrobing by the Kauravas. Though she does not don male disguise or take up arms herself, she constantly argues in favour of battle and instigates her Pandava husbands to take revenge. Kannaki, the heroine of the Tamil epic *Silappatikaram*, tears out her breast and throws it to burn down the city of Madurai as retaliation for the unjust killing of her husband. The legendary Rani of Jhansi (1828–1858) is the historical example of a warrior queen who fought on the battlefield against annexation by the British in 1857. Many other historical female figures of local/regional renown, like Rani Kittur Chennamma (1778–1829) of Karnataka, freedom fighters like Hazrat Mahal and Uda Devi of Lucknow (1857), who laid down their lives in violent resistance and protest, are part of the pantheon of Indian female heroes. Above all, there is the mythological figure of the goddess Kali, a symbol of primeval energy (Shakti) and moral vengeance, representing both life and death, both a giver and a destroyer of life, a mother and a demon. The existence of all these icons freely available to be summoned informs the images and tropes of Bhardwaj's creativity and the adaptive changes he makes in filming Shakespeare's tragedies. As Elaine Showalter has argued in her pioneering essay on Ophelia, the most nuanced way of entering the life of characters is not always through the play as such but through their afterlives, the appropriations and adaptations. Contextualising Bhardwaj's reconfiguration of the tragic women, we find that they mesh with several of these archetypes but also move beyond them, shaping new personages and alliances between the Indian mythic and the contemporary: they are neither rape-revenge victims redressing some personal dishonour, the pure stunt heroine with fantastical powers of the action film nor even fully the vigilante women restoring social order or full bloodied warrior women. Structured by the Shakespearean narrative, they extend and intervene in the Bollywoodian economy of the evolving representation of the new woman of the millennium, who moves beyond the normative domestic into agonistic drives of desire and power. The old stereotypes of the moll/vamp, the submissive beloved, the talkative companion and the melodramatic mother are all challenged, infused with an agency and infected with the hubris of the avenger to new and startling effects. Their visualisations too are distinguished by an atypical de-aestheticisation (of the new wave films) which deglamourises and destabilises the given identities and equations of gender and power. It is the motives behind their transformations that interest us.

Maqbool/Macbeth ... 'our love was pure, wasn't it?'

In literary criticism, Lady Macbeth is a female who is usually demonised as a villain, an evil genius leading her husband into a river of blood. Shakespeare provides an ameliorating dimension by letting us glimpse a backlash nemesis for her actions: she loses her husband's love, is haunted by the smell of blood, the shedding of which she has herself instigated, and finally, ends her torment by taking her own life. Feminist criticism, while not able to exactly 'save' her, has succeeded in humanising her. Today, she is seen as 'repentant, heroic, even innocent – and above all, a maternal – Lady Macbeth.'[11]

Bhardwaj's version keeps the main features of Lady Macbeth's characterisation, her ambition, her use of sexuality to goad Macbeth into taking the final step and her downfall, but makes a singular radical change – she, Lady Macbeth/Nimmi, is not the wife but Duncan/Abbuji's discontented mistress, making Maqbool's murder of Abbuji doubly treacherous, guilty of both patricide and adultery. In an interview, Bhardwaj said that he was not convinced that power was enough motivation for Maqbool to kill his father figure; he needed some other reason too. This change has been referred to as 'one of the film's most creative developments' and as an example of a 'cross-fertilizing Shakespearean appropriation' with an antecedent in *Pulp Fiction*, where too Vincent succumbs to sleeping with boss's wife.[12] As Bhardwaj has put it in the Preface to the printed screenplay of the film, 'This changed the dynamics of the relationships completely. Suddenly the sexual conflict became the core of the screenplay. For Macbeth, the Lady Macbeth became the throne herself.'[13]

Bhardwaj makes Nimmi the aggressor in love, and she unabashedly pursues her sexual attraction for Maqbool. She exploits every opportunity to get close to him: faking a vow to walk to the dargah, deliberately injuring her foot to force him to touch her and remind him of her love. The Sufi song being sung at the dargah, *'tu mere ru ba ru hai / aakho ki ibadat hai'* (you are face to face with me/my eyes worship you), like many such devotional songs, has a dual meaning, both sacred and profane, signalling what is going on in her mind too. The Don, Abbuji, is old and obese, and she confesses she is repulsed by his corporeality. Further, Nimmi feels betrayed by Abbuji, who promised to get her into films but is keeping her for himself. But when he begins courting a new Bollywood starlet, she knows her time is limited. She is also quick to perceive that Abbuji's daughter, Sameera, and Guddu/Fleance, Banquo/Kaka's son, are romancing and that it will only be a matter of time before they inherit the Don's position, displacing his right-hand man, Maqbool. Hence the urgency for usurpation by murder. She plays upon Maqbool's insecurities, openly suggesting doing away with the Don. And as if the motivations of Shakespearean characters were not complex enough, Bhardwaj adds further twists to them. Lust, love and ambition, but all inextricably mixed, drive both Nimmi and Maqbool. It is made very clear that were it not for Nimmi's seductive shrewdness, Maqbool would have remained Abbuji's right-hand man. It is the controlled and subtilised performance by Tabu, not in the least like the coquetry and tantrums of typical Bollywood heroines but convincingly understated, that tends to let the viewer get taken in by the 'romance'. Nimmi is shrewd in her pursuit of Mian Maqbool. As Antony Gunratane has observed, she is the 'dangerous' mistress (Figure 1.1).[14]

Ironically, it is a Bollywoodish love scene and song in which she forces him at the point of a gun to accept her love, which establishes

Figure 1.1 Nimmi/Lady Macbeth wins love at gunpoint in *Maqbool*.

her masculinist aggression, her burgeoning sexuality and her need for a protector. This is during the preparations for Sameera's engagement which Nimmi has gone to oversee. The two go out when, suddenly, she pulls a gun on him and forces him to repeat '*meri jaan*', my life/love, again and again, until he succumbs to her wiles and before she returns the gun to him. Maqbool immediately hits out and abuses her, calling her a whore. 'Why don't you return to Lucknow?' he snaps at her. 'If you were coming me with me, I'm even prepared to go to heaven', she retorts. They embrace, the camera moves back and pans to show them standing on a precarious promontory, high above the calm sea spread out below them. They have scaled the rocky terrain of love and, poised at the summit, seem one with the beauty of nature. The scene is replete with telling symbols: the phallicity of the gun (all of Bhardwaj's heroines play around with guns!), the passionate blood red of her outfit, the violence she does to him, the physical knocks he gives her, the laughter and tears, his wiping them with the muzzle of the gun, making him go back to search for her lost earing in the dark, leading to the consummation, all these betoken an enhanced masculinist agency for Nimmi. The plaintive notes of the song which plays in the background, '*rone do ... jee bhar ke* (let me weep my heart out ...)', which seem to undercut the Bollywoodish foreplay, simultaneously voice Nimmi's fears, 'live for the day', the song implies, 'love will diminish, all have their woes'. Ruby Cohen in 1976 remarked that 'Perhaps today's Lady Macbeth needs Women's Liberation'[15]; in *Maqbool*, this need has become redundant.

In the several generic shifts that the film effects, the gangster's moll is reconfigured; Nimmi is no voluptuous sex toy or hard-headed cynic but a poignant portrait of a search for love and self-validation. If Nimmi is responsible for pushing Mian Maqbool into a river of blood from which there is no wading back, she also becomes, inadvertently, liable for her own and his final collapse. She is haunted by the blood which was sprayed on her and the walls at Abbuji's shooting and which she hysterically tries to wash off. Maqbool, after Kaka/Banquo's murder, finds it increasingly difficult to hold the gang together; fissures in the loyalties creep in, rivals take advantage, but Maqbool is preoccupied, nursing the pregnant but distracted Nimmi. As one aide quips, 'that whore will be the death of all of us'. Unlike, Macbeth who becomes hardened, who has no time to mourn his wife's death – it is ill-timed for him – Maqbool risks his all for Nimmi. When his world is collapsing around him, he lifts her from the hospital bed to flee the country along with her, but it is too late. She dies in his arms, too weak after severe blood loss in childbirth but asserting until the last breath the purity and legitimacy of their love.

If it is the violence of her desire that brings down Nimmi, and later Maqbool, it is her child, the product of the same feelings that redeems her, and finally, Maqbool. Though Lady Macbeths today are increasingly seen as maternal, tormented by the lack of a child, no actual living babe of the Macbeths has made an appearance in any production or adaptation on stage or screen. Justin Kurzel's *Macbeth* (2015) with Michael Fassbender opens with the funeral of an infant assumed to be the Macbeths'. The 2016 Globe Theatre production of *Macbeth* directed by Iqbal Khan interpolated a young boy as a constant but spectral presence on stage suggestive of a subliminal influence. As Blair Orfall has noted, 'the appearance of a child' is the strongest influence on Bhardwaj of *Throne of Blood*, 'a deviation not seen in other Macbeth adaptations.'[16] Asaji announces her pregnancy very opportunely to manipulate Washisu. However, the child does not survive, and suspicions arise if Asaji's assertion was true.[17] Though the paternity of Nimmi's child remains uncertain, it takes on the form and function of the most famous image in the play, of 'Pity', which 'like a naked new born babe' drives the 'horrid deed[s]' (1.7.21, 24) in Maqbool's own eyes, creating a moment of *anagorisis*, making the very sight of the babe, being lovingly cradled by Sameera and Guddu, overwhelm him. As he watches through the glass door, his eyes brim over, he drops his gun and walks out of the hospital. Nimmi's child is central to the resolution posed by the film; it becomes the instrument of the tragic catharsis. Maqbool gives up his life of bloodshed, abdicates violence, is killed soon thereafter, and appropriately, seems at peace. Nimmi's child brings about a reprieve: as Maqbool falls to the ground and his eyes shut, the camera swivels up to show a blue sky, and birdsong and spiritual music flooding in.

Thus Nimmi, who leads Maqbool into treachery and murder, through her babe, redeems him from them. Her aggressive sexuality and the procreative maternity both impact him, 'make' him in all senses. In the play Lady Macbeth remains sterile, while Nimmi is generative, both destroyer and creator, a quasi Kali figure of the opposites. In contrast, the Kurzel Macbeth comes to an opposing view; it 'intuits ... that Lady

Macbeth's grief (at the loss of her infant) is twisted into murderous ambition' (P. Bradshaw, *Guardian*, 1 October 2015). The surrender of arms and self by the protagonist is of course an un-Shakespearean action for the tragic protagonist who needs must die fighting, protesting until the end. Bhardwaj quietly modifies the generic ending, to suit his milieu, both philosophically and politically: making the gangster hero-villain, Maqbool, accept his fate and abjure the life of violence. All this stems from the procreant mistress and her babe – to be nurtured by Hindu Guddu and Muslim Samira – symbolic of an ideal communal amity for the future of the nation.

If the Weird Sisters are masculinised as cops, Duncan's sons are replaced by a daughter (Sameera) who has more agency and instrumentality than Malcolm and Donalbain, who flee the scene of action. Both Sameera and Nimmi have a hold and assert a power on Abbuji and later Maqbool. A female penumbra enfolds Maqbool, pushing him into directions not of his own choosing. The eloquent visual of the warm and loving acceptance of the infant inheritor, either Abbuji's or Maqbool's son, by Guddu (hinted severally that he will eschew the life of violence) and Sameera, is signalled as the way forward.[18] A strand of *Macbeth* criticism reads the ending as cyclical: with Donalbain's absence, the old treachery and revenge beginning again. The end of *Maqbool* points towards a more formal tragic cathartic ending, of a forward seeming calm after the purging of the violence.

Omkara/Othello: 'we may walk through fire, but are still not called loyal but treacherous'

In his second film, *Omkara*, based on *Othello* (2006), Vishal Bhardwaj makes more radical changes. Some are expansions of suggestiveness in the text, while others are interpolations required by the reworking; they all deepen and make explicit the women's equation with violence.

To begin with, Dolly/Desdemona is more than 'half the wooer' (1.3.175). When Omkara arrives at her house wounded and bloodied and she nurses him back to health, she falls hugely in love with him and is not ready to let him go. Though Desdemona, too, is charmed and seduced by the tales of the battles that Othello has fought, Dolly comes face to face with their injurious aspect, something which the visuality of the cinematic medium can only make more visceral. She is bloodied and besmirched by Omi's wounds as she supports him indoors, almost faint with the loss of blood. In an inversion of the accepted gender roles, she takes the initiative and presents a jewel – her engagement ring (connoting her sexuality) – to him in a tea cup during her engagement party. She pursues him aggressively, confessing her love in a letter and threatening suicide if he does not rescue her. Her transgressive wooing is symbolised by the askew letter 'D' which has become unfixed and hangs upside down on the signage at her wedding. We are forewarned about further inversions to come: the *barat* with the groom is waylaid, and Dolly elopes with Omkara. The phallicity of her enhanced role is underlined when she, teased by Omi, picks up a shotgun and chases him across the fields, pinning him down finally at the point of the gun forcing him to explain his words. Later, she persists until he agrees to reinstate Kesu/Casio on their wedding day. The violence of Dolly/Desdemona's end, her murder at her husband's hands, is precipitated by this same intensity of her feelings, when she looks entirely baffled, unable to grasp his intentions.

A more acute change occurs in the role of Indu/Emilia: she is made Omkara's sister, not a sibling but an affiliate sister, along with being Langda/Iago's wife. All three are thus tied in a familial relation and reciprocity which has been seen as a 'radical addition.'[19] The betrayal of these bonds serves to deepen the crime and the resultant violence. Indu is also endowed with a vivacity and agency unlike Emilia. She picks up Dolly's cummerbund, the precious heirloom gifted by Omi, at her own volition, without Langda's prompting. She is aware of its significance as a sexual talisman and uses it to entice her husband to bed her. A certain fulfilment is signalled here: earlier she has shown resentment about her husband's lack of attention towards her – he is either away on jobs or just lazes around. Indu is also a friend and confidant to Dolly, a role that younger sisters-in-law often fulfil. She suspects that something is amiss between Omi and Dolly when the latter is quiet and withdrawn. She speaks out to Omi defending Dolly but advises him against marriage if he is not sure about her. When she does finally find out the truth about how her own husband has been poisoning the mind of her brother Omi against Dolly and her own inadvertent role in it in taking away the cummerbund and in Dolly's death, this strong and sensible Indu is so enraged at the injustice of the events that she picks up a sickle and instantly slashes Langda's neck, killing him on the spot – with a household implement she is first glimpsed using to cut fodder for the cows. The camera closes up on her face, especially focusses on her eyes, looking straight out at the audience, and like Chandi, the ferocious aspect of the goddess Kali/Durga, with sword in hand, her eyes goggling, Indu transforms into the demon slayer. She becomes the instrument of justice and moral retribution, something which has been found lacking in Shakespeare's ending. Iagos are usually taken away, after Othello is prevented from attacking him, to be delivered to their just deserts, later, offstage/screen. Orson Welles' image of Iago trapped in a cage, hoisted above the ramparts of the fort being the only exception. Precedents for such avenging female metamorphosis are to be found in other Indian films too: *Damul* (1985), a critique of the oppression of bonded labour by activist director, Prakash Jha, shows how at the very end, when the meek wife sees her husband killed by the grasping landlord, she suddenly stands tall, picks up a sickle and, in a manner similar to Indu, beheads him. When all fails, women step in, a transformation sanctioned by mythology (Figure 1.2).

It is what happens to Indu afterwards, however, that has become a matter of debate. Indu is last shown peering down a well, splattered with blood, crying hoarsely. The last but one scene is of water splashed in the well, after which the camera moves back, pans the wider space of the courtyard of the house, ironically dressed up in festive lights for the wedding but now resonating with a harsh, anti-choral music – a house of death – where no one is seen. What happens to Indu/Emilia? The final screen image is ambiguous, and many speculations have been made: that she tips her husband's body into the well (Mark Thornton Burnett) or that she kills Langda to avenge family honour/*izzat* and is venting grief (Mike Heidenberg). Only one commentator (Lalitha Pandit Hogan) has been able to surmise that Indu throws herself into the well: hence Indu/Emilia's end needs further elaboration.[20] With her husband dead, and killed by her, she has nothing to live for; she would probably be arrested and sentenced for murder.

Jumping into a well was, and still continues to be, the most common mode of female suicide in India, especially in rural areas. Wells were the only sources of water in most areas; it was the woman's chore to fetch and carry water from the well to the house. Woman and wells are frequently twinned in many stories, folklore, songs and rituals.[21] This common, essential and celebrated feature of a village also afforded a last resort to many a desperate woman. Hindi films are replete with scenes with wells, and women trying to jump in, though more often than not they are saved in the nick of time by the hero, given the romantic, feel-good propensity of most Indian films. The last evocative shots of the film *Khamosh Pani* (Silent Water, dir. Sabiha Sumar, 2003), a post-partition

Figure 1.2 Indu/Emilia's flash of avenging fury in *Omkara*.

trauma tale, are of water ripples in the village well that cannot reveal to the world the desperate suicide of a Sikh converted Muslim woman whose radicalised son starts questioning her communal identity. This suicide is doubly tragic because as a young girl, during the partition, she had refused to jump into the same well and martyr herself when ordered to do so by her father to save her from the riotous mob which was neigh. (She runs away but is caught, abducted, raped and forced to convert and marry and live out a shadowy life.) The most well-known instance of the well as a desperate refuge in the face of violence was during the firing by the British army on unarmed political protestors at Jallianwala Bagh (13 April 1919), who had no other exit except to jump into the garden well. One hundred and twenty bodies were reported to have been recovered from it.[22]

Further, water and the immersion or *visarjan* of images of the goddess Durga/Kali are an essential part of the celebration; once the prayers are over, submerging the idols in water is the consecrated end ritual. Inexorable cultural logic deems that Indu, who has morphed into an avenging goddess fury, would naturally immerse herself in water once the deed was done.[23] In a Question and Answer session Bhardwaj revealed that they had a final shot of the sound and image of something falling into water but later decided to cut it, preferring to leave it to the audience's imagination to complete Indu's end.[24] As in Shakespeare, Indu/Emilia dies at the end, righting the wrongs but by taking her own life after her whole family has been devastated.

Among Bhardwaj's trilogy, the ending of *Omkara* is the most devastating and bleak and more than in Shakespeare. The disrupted wedding, the senseless killings, the garish lights and the harsh music as the camera pans at the end, the final shots suggest a village orphaned, like Golu, Indu/Langda's son, with no redeeming feature left, the net result of the gangsterism of the 'Wild West' of rural regional areas. As Kesu says at the end, 'is there anything left …' (*khatam hone ke liye kuch bacha hai …?*). Unlike the individualised tragic failure of *Othello*, *Omkara* is a severe indictment of the failure of the state through the expose of the nexus between the political class, police and local strongmen who all resort to brutality to serve their own ends, leaving festering violence that forces people to take up arms for herself/himself.

Haider/Hamlet: 'Revenge cannot make you free …'

It is in the third film, *Haider/Hamlet* 2014, that Vishal Bhardwaj's mode of relocation into an area of extended violence which substantially involves women comes fully into its own. As Bhardwaj himself has put it, '*Haider* is an extension of what I've attempted in *Maqbool* and *Omkara*' (*The Indian Express*, 5 October 2014). Set in Kashmir during the peak of the insurgency movement in 1995 and the consequent Indian army reprisals, it tells the story of the 'disappearance' of Old Hamlet, an idealistic doctor, named Hilal Meer; the anguished search and revenge for him by his son Haider; the duplicitous role of the brother Khurram; and the involvement of the wife and mother Ghazala – all these are deftly woven together with key themes, scenes and characters of Shakespeare's play, recast but absorbed and informing the whole. The film's primary purpose is to make an open political statement about the violations of human rights by the Indian army, but its success lies in embedding it in the life of a middle-class family which is unwittingly caught up in the internecine power struggle and violence of revenge. Unlike the earlier two films, *Maqbool* and *Omkara*, however, *Haider* does not depend solely on the Shakespearean narrative but interpolates its own strong storyline, thereby creating greater space to expand and fill out the allusions and suggestiveness of the Shakespearean text. This, as noted earlier, is Bhardwaj's usp: he unerringly bolsters and foregrounds submerged elements, giving Shakespearean characters their back stories, as it were, to help explain their actions in the present. In *Haider*, the major change is with Gertrude/Ghazala who is moved to the centre, and the story revolves largely around her, not Hamlet/Haider. Rachel Saltz was quick to note this: in 'Shakespearean Revenge in a Violent Kashmir' she remarked that 'Instead of Haider, the director Vishal Bhardwaj might have considered calling his fast-loose adaptation of "Hamlet" "Ghazala" after its Gertrude character' … [she] 'has such depths and mystery that she hijacks the movie' (*The New York Times*, October 2014).

Gertrude is perhaps the most misinterpreted woman in Shakespeare. For centuries, she has been maligned for infidelity, concupiscence and culpability in murder without any hard textual evidence. She has limited lines in the text, not enough to explain herself, which has allowed other characters' views, particularly the men, to colour her critical estimation. Feminist criticism too has not been able to substantially provide adequate redress;[25] hence Bhardwaj's expansion of her role is seminal: 'one of the most complicated characters of Shakespeare' he believes,[26] it does not exonerate but fleshes out her dilemmas, providing the links between her actions and her words. Like Gertrude, Ghazala is dissatisfied with her marriage; if Old Hamlet was too busy with the wars, her doctor husband is too absorbed in saving lives. He too is associated with blood; 'his body reeked of blood day and night', says Ghazala of the doctor. Unlike Gertrude, however, whose backstory is not available, the brother-in-law Khurram/Claudius becomes a trusted confidant, a position which is misused by him to get the elder brother arrested by the army. When she becomes a 'half-widow' Ghazala naturally leans on him, an action mistaken by the son for infidelity. She remarries only after the death of her husband, at the hands of the military, is confirmed. Her search is to 'become whole' (*ek baar poori ho jaun*) something which remains elusive, with her son reacting adversely to the marriage. Played with much subtly and control by Tabu, her story draws attention, sidelining to an extent, her son, Hamlet.

However, Ghazala does, unwittingly, become the instrument of violence, unlike Gertrude, when she informs Khurram that her husband has secreted home a wanted militant leader for minor surgery. Next morning, he is arrested for harbouring a militant, their house is blown up and the spiral of revenge, of brother against brother, is set off. Ghazala's story develops with an accelerating association with arms and violence. In a central flashback sequence, when she discovers a pistol in Haider's school bag and is terrified that he might cross the border and join the militants, the parents decide that the only solution was to send him away from Kashmir for his higher studies. Predictably, the young Haider refuses to leave his friends and home in Srinagar, whereupon Ghazala strides out into the field where the kids are playing cricket with a pistol poised at her temple, and threatens to blow her brains out, in an act of public blackmail, to force Haider to agree to leave Kashmir. In the equivalent of the closet scene, in the backdrop of their bombed-out house, realising that Haider is determined on revenge, Ghazala clasps his hand holding a pistol and, pointing it to her own forehead, begs him to kill her. Guns and Ghazala are twinned; they bestow a purposive agency and a phallicity on an almost hysterical mother. Not only does she precipitate violence of revenge and suffer the consequences of death and widowhood, but she has to resort to violence, or a threat of it, again to exert any control over her son. At the end, knowing that Haider has been co-opted by the militants and that he has sworn to kill Khurram, now her husband, but who was traitor to his brother, her first husband, Ghazala, in a repeat act to persuade her son, this time to surrender and give up revenge, dares to approach him, holed up in the graveyard surrounded by the army, speaks to him, and when he refuses to listen to her, this time, she does pull the trigger of her grenade-lined vest and blows herself up to stop the cycle of revenge as the final resolution.

Gertrude, the passive, pushover queen, manipulated by all, is reinvented in *Haider* as a suicide bomber in Ghazala to become a virtual embodiment of violence, paradoxically advocating surrender and peace. This is the key startling new twist in this re-versioning of *Hamlet*. How and why does Bhardwaj arrive at this? Several intertextualities can be traced: Sulayman Al Bassam's *Al Hamlet Summit* (2002), which has Ophelia turn into a Palestinian suicide bomber, is the most immediate.[27] But for Gertrude, this has to be a first. Female suicide bombers are, unfortunately, increasingly encountered in the contemporary world. From our own homegrown Dhanu, the assassin/martyr of Prime Minister Rajiv Gandhi (1991), to the Palestinian instances, the discourse around these figures is muddled and mixed: while their zeal for martyrdom as '*shahidas*' is valorised, media tends to personalise and domesticate them, undermining the politics which set them up. Hindi cinema took up their stories too in Mani Ratnam's *Dil Se* (1998) and Santosh Sivan's *The Terrorist* (1999), the heroines of both of which have been seen as allusions to Dhanu. And even though both films have been read as allegories of the challenge to the nation state, their scripts twin the bomber heroine with her sexuality: Megha in *Dil Se* dies embracing her lover as her bomb-laden vest explodes, while Malli in *The Terrorist* opts out of suicide when she learns that she is pregnant. Ghazala in *Haider* is both these women and more: from a typical Bollywood mother, making a last-ditch attempt to extricate her son from the morass of violence and revenge that he has fallen into, she is also, like Indu in *Omkara*, a Shakti figure who can suddenly stand tall and resolute. Gertrude's last actions in the original play also express her maternal concern for Hamlet: she notices Hamlet sweating during the duel and offers to wipe his face, and for the first time, asserts her will against Claudius to drink from the cup which, she does not know, is poisoned and meant for Hamlet. There is a submerged suggestion in the text that Gertrude dies protecting her son, and exposing Claudius, the deferred possibilities of which are harnessed by Bhardwaj.

Mother – nation – state equations too surface irresistibly in this case, especially as they deliver the messages of the moment, that 'revenge only begets revenge ... till we free ourselves from our revenge, until then no freedom will set us free'. Bhardwaj has said that 'Kashmir is the Hamlet of my film' with reference to *Haider* (*The Indian Express*, 5 October 2014), and a sacrifice of the mother nation is one way to placate the disturbed son – Kashmir. The trope of the female warrior and her sacrificial heroism too is well known in Indian myth and history, as noted earlier, but this territorialisation of the female body as nation received fresh impetus during the freedom movement and later in partition narratives. Bharata Mata (India as Mother), as a mother goddess, nurturer and protector, emerged as a popular rallying icon during the early twentieth century and the beginnings of the freedom struggle.[28] This feminisation of the nation was given further fillip with partition, viewed as the traumatic severing of a child from the womb. In Indian cinema criticism, the film *Mother India* (1957) directed by Mehboob Khan has frequently been held up as a prototype and allegory of the self-sacrificing mother/nation, who transforms into an avenging figure, killing her own son to save her village from ignominy. Seventy years post-independence, Ghazala, the mother, finds the roles reversed and must kill herself to save the territory and the son. As the reviewer from *The Hindu* put it, her 'story is so audacious that Mother India crosses the line of Control, not just metaphorically' (Sudhish Kamath, 3 October 2014). It is one of the assertions of feminist criticism that the female body has become a contested space, and familial, communal and national discourses all endeavour to construct and contain it in mutually contradictory ways. Finally, in a deeply indigenous layering, the convention of Urdu poetry in which the figure of the beloved is often a metaphor for the world, is also mobilised to this end. The recurrent and haunting stanzas of a well-known ghazal by Faiz Ahmed Faiz, *'gulon mein rang bhare, bag-e-bahaar aiye …/* let the breeze of spring colour the flowers', which become a code between the father and son and his ghost, are not just a plea to the absent beloved to come and enliven the garden but also voice the desire to rejuvenate (rehabilitate) the paradise of Kashmir *'Aa bhi jao ke gulshan ka karobar chale'*.

This politicised mother/son dialectic germinates in the personal. The mother-son relationship, a staple of much Indian cinema, is here radicalised. The oedipal motif has rarely been explored in Indian cinema; Bhardwaj in another first breaks the taboo in *Haider*. The thread of sexual attraction between mother and son, manifested in Hamlet's misogynist raving against his mother's hasty remarriage in the original text, runs through the film too. It is mirrored, literally and metaphorically, in two almost parallel scenes in which a young Haider, struck by the beauty of his mother, seen self-reflexively, dressing before the mirror, bends down to kiss her on the nape of her neck. And again, when she is preparing for her second wedding, resplendent in flaming red, now an older Haider confesses that he does not have the heart to share her with anyone, so 'drop-dead gorgeous' she is while he, in an erotic gesture, daubs perfume on her neck and then hastens to speck her cheek with black kohl to ward off any envious eyes (Fig. 1.3). This intense love-hate tension between the mother and the son peaks at the very end, informing their last dialogue, and is intertwined with the apocalyptic ending. Haider is

Figure 1.3 Ghazala/Gertrude with Haider/Hamlet admiring her before her wedding with Khurram/Claudius.

loath to agree with his mother to drop his weapons and surrender but cannot tear himself away from her. Finally, she seals her words with tender kisses, on his forehead, his eyes, and his lips, making him pause in his rejections, while she walks out and pulls the trigger on herself.

If Gertrude is reinvented, Ophelia is more clearly transfigured, but, in her essential core, she remains the same. Arshia, a childhood sweetheart, is merged with Horatio, the friend and confidant, to become a gutsy and feisty journalist. She is given all the agency that Ophelia never had: she is there for Haider as a right-hand mate, rescuing him out of tight spots, as at the beginning when he is held back at the border checkpost for his brash aggressiveness, then accompanying him in his search for his father, carrying secret messages of the militants for him, sharing his anguish and his love. Consequently, Haider/Hamlet suffers no sex revulsion; his anger at women's frailty is directed at a more tangible target: the Indian army and preventing its deflection on to Arshia. Like Nimmi, Dolly and Ghazala, Arshi too has her moments with a pistol, but in her case, it constitutes a turning point of her denouement. During a love scene she is shocked to find Haider handling a pistol; she snatches it from him and only after a lot of playful love talk hands it back. Like Ophelia in the play, she is persuaded by her father (Superintendent of Police in capital city Srinagar) to tell on Haider's possession of a pistol; in the film, she believes that she is protecting him from the terrorists, but her 'informing' triggers a series of events which will force Haider to flee. However, it is the pernicious corruption, political and patriarchal, the 'rotten' in the world of her father, and her brother, a multinational jobber, which kicks in, controls and finally crushes her. Unlike Ghazala, who though seemingly helpless, a 'half-widow' and in conflict with her son, always takes matters in her own hand; Arshee, though physically proactive and supportive, ends like Ophelia, a victim of circumstances. Devastated after her father's accidental shooting by Haider, she is seen abstractly singing Habba Khatoon's songs of separation, her mind as unravelled as the red wool of the father's muffler, strewn all around her, all the while fondling her father's pistol until it goes off.

Female intervention in *Haider* saves Hamlet from death, though the scene at the end of the film is more drenched in blood than is possible on stage. His mother's words echoing in his ears, Haider is unable to kill Khurram, leaving him in a pool of blood, both his legs blown off, to a fate worse than death. The convention/logic of the tragic end is severally modified: hero and villain survive to live not in abject surrender but in an acceptance and acknowledgement of the futility of the life of bloodshed, that true freedom lies beyond revenge, 'Readiness is all' (5.2.160). As Bhardwaj has stated, 'I strongly feel that Kashmir has been the biggest tragedy of modern Indian history and no film has been made to capture the real tragedy of what has been going on there for the last twenty-five years,'[29] ... 'our way of looking at Kashmir has either been cosmetic – only for shooting songs – or the rhetoric, where we show a man in a phiran, holding a Kalashnikov. *Haider* is the first film where we see Kashmir from the inside' (*The Indian Express*, 5 October 2014). Bhardwaj more than succeeds in his attempt: his analysis of the tragedy of Kashmir – of fratricidal enmities, of brother fighting brother, which will end only beyond revenge. In the context of the continuing militancy in Kashmir, it proposes an alternate, almost revolutionary resolution abjuring arms and violence as a condition for freedom, a message which is the need of the hour in a world fraught with terrorism. Shakespeare's most thought-provoking play gives out this answer for today. But in the process, Bhardwaj rejigs the dimensions of the genre of the tragic. His placing of women at the centre, establishing moral equity, seems to emerge from an infiltration of a female principle and perspective, modifying and gendering the logic of the tragic. If Hamlet's dilemma to bear arms seems sidelined (though Haider does debate whether Roohdaar/Ghost is true, and his 'mad speech' equates his existential angst with the trauma of Kashmir: '*hum hai ki nahi*'/Do we exist or not?), it is because the film allows the women to appropriate and challenge male power structures.

It has been noted severally that Bhardwaj's films break the Bollywood mould even while working within it. It can be added that his Shakespeare trilogy does the same to the genre of the Shakespearean tragedy. In the restructuring of the Shakespearean situations and relationships, and the fine-tuning of their psychologies, not only is a new narrative and critical perspective regarding women opened up, but also new questions are posed on the accepted interrelation between gender and genre, that is, the traditional trajectories of Shakespearean tragedy. As seen above, a feminisation of the tragic happens: an alternative space for female agency and heroism is created, and more critically, the resolutions of the conflicts, shaped by the women, abjure the dependence on arms, masculinity and violence that patriarchy has created. Maqbool does not die fighting, 'lay on …', Omi chooses not to kill Iago, leaving him to live and suffer the torments of the soul, and Haider, realising that revenge will not bring freedom, lets Khurram live. The reified tragic arc with its reassertion of justice, of the purgation through suffering and death and of the validation of the heroic male self, seems insufficient to resolve today's conflicts. Instead, women show the way, creating areas of nurturance, regeneration and conflict resolution, or summary justice, at the end, as the way forward. Vishal Bhardwaj's moral/spiritual and political arc resonates with aspects of Indian philosophy/mythology which reserves a stronger, more proactive potency for the female principle than the familiar Western Aristotelian division of male reason versus female nature. Indian goddesses are invested with powers that are not only in consonance with the male gods but also with paradoxically opposed attributes like the erotic and maternal, seductive and grotesque, life giver and destroyer.

The New York Times reviewer commented with reference to *Haider* that Vishal Bhardwaj's movies 'make Shakespearean tragedy seem a natural lens through which to view contemporary India' (2 October 2014). The formal structures of tragedy allow him the distance to critically engage with the urgent political and social issues of modern India while dovetailing them in compelling stories of families, men and women caught up in love and hatred, jealousies and treachery, ambition and power. As Bhardwaj himself has acknowledged, 'I like to fire the shots from Shakespeare's shoulders ... that gives me a lot of license' (*The New York Times*, 27 October 2014). His films bridge the micro and macro dimensions and mediate between the symbolism and the reality of the nation state with ease.

Notes

1. Amy Rodgers, 'Vishal Bhardwaj', *Shakespeare Bulletin* 34, no. 3 (2016): 500.
2. As reported in *The Times of India*, 28 January 2017.
3. All references to the text are from *The Norton Shakespeare*, ed. Stephen Greenblatt (New York: W.W. Norton and Company, 1997).
4. Alfredo Michel Modenessi, '"Is This the Noble Moor?" Reviewing *Othello* on Screen through "Indian" (and Indian) Eyes', *Borrowers and Lenders: The Journal of Shakespeare and Appropriation* VII, no. 2 (2012–2013), accessed February 2017, www.borrowers.uga.edu/7164/toc.
5. Antony Howard, 'Hamlet in Kashmir', *The BBA Shakespeare Blog*, 17 February 2015, accessed June 2015, http://blogs.warwick.ac.uk/bbashakespeare/entry/hamlet_in_kashmir/.
6. See Poonam Trivedi, 'Shakespearean Tragedy in India: Politics of Genre - or How Newness Entered Indian Literary Culture', in *The Oxford Handbook of Shakespearean Tragedy*, ed. Michael Neill and David Schalkwyk (Oxford: Oxford University Press, 2016) for a longer discussion.
7. Philip Lutgendorf, 'Is there an Indian way of Filming?', *International Journal of Hindu Studies* 10, no. 3 (2006): 227.
8. For further information on early Shakespeare films in Hindi cinema and for a longer discussion on *Maqbool* and *Omkara*, see my *Filmi Shakespeare*, revised version in *Narratives of Indian Cinema*, ed. Manju Jain (Delhi: Ratna Sagar, 2009).
9. Lalitha Gopalan, 'Avenging Women in Indian Cinema', *Screen* 38, no. 1 (March 1997): 44. See also Jyotika Virdi, 'Reverence, Rape and then Revenge: Popular Hindi Cinema's "Women's Film"', in *Killing Women: The Visual Culture of Gender and Violence*, ed. Susan Lord and Annette Burfoot (Waterloo: Wilfrid Laurier University Press, 2006) and Sangeeta Dutta, 'Globalisation and Representation of Women in Indian Cinema', *Social Scientist* 28, no. 3/4 (2000). See also Priyamvada Gopal, 'Of Victims and Vigilantes: The Bandit Queen Controversy 1997', in *Signposts: Gender Issues in Post-independent India*, ed. Rajeshwari Sundar Rajan (New Delhi: Kali for Women, 1999) for an overview of the contesting perspectives in feminist film criticism.
10. See Naomi Conn Liebler ed., *The Female Tragic Hero in Renaissance Drama* (New York: Palgrave Macmillan 2002); Marguerite A. Tassi, *Women and*

Revenge in Shakespeare: Gender, Genre and Ethics (Selinsgrove: Susquehanna University Press, 2011); and Melissa E. Sanchez, 'Impure Resistance: Heteroeroticism, Feminism and Shakespearean Tragedy', in *The Oxford Handbook of Shakespeare and Embodiment: Gender, Sexuality and Race*, ed. Valerie Traub (Oxford: Oxford University Press, 2016).

11 W.C. Carroll, 'Recuperating Lady Macbeth in Contemporary Adaptations', *Borrowers and Lenders: The Journal of Shakespeare and Appropriation* VIII, no. 2 (2013–2014), accessed February 2017, www.borrowers.uga.edu/7158/toc.

12 Mark Thornton Burnett, *Shakespeare and World Cinema* (Cambridge: Cambridge University Press, 2013), 58 and 62.

13 Vishal Bhardwaj with Abbas Tyrewala, *Maqbool: The Original Screenplay with English Translation* (Noida: Harper Collins, 2014), vi.

14 Antony Gunratane, *Shakespeare, Film Studies and the Visual Cultures of Modernity* (London: Palgrave Macmillan, 2008), 71.

15 Quoted in W.C. Carroll, 'Recuperating Lady Macbeth in Contemporary Adaptations'.

16 Blair Orfall, 'From Ethnographic Impulses to Apocalyptic Endings: *Maqbool* and *Throne of Blood* in Comparative Context', *Borrowers and Lenders* IV, no. 2 (2009) 'Asian Shakespeares on Screen: Two films in Perspective, sp. issue ed. Alexa Huang, accessed February 2017, www.borrowers.uga.edu/7158/toc.

17 A new-born male heir of the Macbeths is seen in a Kannada stage version, *Maranaanayakana Dristhanta*, by H.S. Shiva Prakash (1991), who is later killed by Duncan's son.

18 Disregarding the eloquent visuals of Guddu and Sameera cradling the babe lovingly, William C Ferleman sees the babe as Maqbool's 'blood thirsty heir' not promising any 'good'. In 'What if Lady Macbeth were Pregnant?: Amantiveness, Procreation and Future Dynasty in Maqbool', *Borrowers and Lenders*, IV, no. 2 (2009), accessed February 2017, www.borrowers.uga.edu/7158/toc.

19 Mark Thornton Burnett, *Shakespeare and World Cinema*, 80.

20 See Ibid., 81, Mike Heidenberg, 'No Country for Young Women: Empowering Emilia in Vishal Bhradwaj's *Omkara*', in *Bollywood Shakespeares*, ed. Craig Dionne and Parmita Kapadia (New York: Palgrave Macmillan, 2014), 98–101 and Lalita Pandit Hogan, 'The Sacred and Profane in *Omkara*', *Image and Narrative* 11, no. 2 (2010): 58.

21 See Heidi Pauwels, '"The Woman Waylaid at the Well" or *Paṇaghaṭa-līlā*: An Indian Folk Theme Appropriated in Myth and Movies', *Asian Ethnology* 69, no. 1 (2010): 1–33.

22 As stated on the memorial plaque at the site. See Brian Lapping, *End of Empire* (London: Paladin, 1985), 38 for a far larger estimate.

23 Diana E. Henderson makes an elaborate but wishful plea against Indu's suicide arguing that she has a 'community' of women to support her after the death of her husband. However, the household hinges only on an old grandmother and the reality for women in rural north India is rather grim, they are apt to be left destitute once the husband is no more. See 'Magic in the Chains: Othello, Omkara and the Materiality of Gender across Time and Media', in *The Oxford Handbook of Shakespeare and Embodiment: Gender, Sexuality and Race*, ed. Valerie Traub (Oxford: Oxford University Press, 2016), 681.

24 In response to questions by the author at the Question/Answer session via skype at the 'Bard in Bombay: Shakespeare in Indian Cinema' conference

at Simon Fraser University, Vancouver, November 2015. And in person at a similar session at the 'Indian Shakespeares on Screen' conference, London, April 2016.
25 Carolyn G. Heilbrun, *Hamlet's Mother and Other Women* (Columbia University Press, 1957) was the first feminist re-reading.
26 Vishal Bhardwaj with Basharat Peer, 'Preface', *Haider: The Original Screenplay with English Translation* (Noida: Harper Collins, 2014), vii.
27 Margaret Litvin, author of *Hamlet's Arab Journeys: Shakespeare's Prince and Nasser's Ghost* (Princeton: Princeton University Press, 2011) revealed in a presentation at the Shakespeare Globe, London, 22 April 2016, that Basharat Peer, the screenplay writer of *Haider* had read her book and had corresponded with her while working on the screenplay.
28 See Sugata Bose, *The Nation as Mother and Other Visions of Nationhood* (New Delhi: Penguin Random House, 2017).
29 Vishal Bhardwaj, 'Preface', *Haider: The Original Screenplay*, vi.

2 *Eklavya*
Shakespeare Meets the *Mahabharata*

Robert S. White

Eklavya: The Royal Guard (2007; DVD, Eros International), directed by the celebrated film-maker Vidhu Vinod Chopra, has been described as a version of *Hamlet*,[1] but the relationship between the two works and others by Shakespeare is more difficult to assess than it is in the sustained adaptations by Vishal Bhardwaj: *Maqbool* (*Macbeth*), *Omkara* (*Othello*) and *Haider* (*Hamlet*). A commercial failure (as Chopra expected, judging from his interviews), *Eklavya* attracted only lukewarm praise among Indian reviewers, who come close to dismissing it as pretentious. Baradwaj Rangan used the term 'self-indulgence' and described it as 'the most expensive art film ever made in our country', although saved by its presentation as myth and 'its glossy, beautifully-crafted surfaces.'[2] However, the movie has gained more positive, international, reception as an independent film and was nominated for an Oscar in the Best Foreign Film category. It is, of course, recognisably Indian in language, setting, dominant source and some central themes, such as 'untouchability', but it is not overtly a 'Bollywood' production in the popular understanding of that term. As many critics, including Mark Thornton Burnett, warn us, it is dangerous to generalise meaningfully about the Indian film industry as 'Bollywood' since the subcontinent is a behemoth, with as many regional varieties of moviemaking as languages interacting with each other.[3] However, some recognisable elements are noticeable: for example, *Eklavya* manifests the generic hybridity which is a hallmark of Hindi movies, shifting between murder mystery, romance, political thriller, musical (there is actually only one full-length song, but it is stunning in its effect) and so on. There is, however, a far more international dimension to *Eklavya*, including the ubiquitous referencing to Shakespeare.

The filming locations establish the setting as Rajasthan, specifically Bikaner, Jaipur and Udaipur, all filmed in sumptuous detail worthy of a quality travelogue. However, there is a political relevance to the fact that it is filmed in these places. Angma Dey Jhala notes that they are all 'princely locations' associated with wealthy, ruling families, and in the case of *Eklavya* there is a 'fascination for courtly aesthetics and royal drama.'[4] Specifically it is set in the fort of Devigarh, north of Udaipur, formerly a royal residence and now described in publicity material as 'fantastically restored into a luxurious, sophisticated and impossibly romantic retreat ... one of India's finest boutique hotels'. However, the fascination is tempered in Chopra's perspective with implied criticism of such opulence, conspicuous privilege and a taste of anachronism in the modern world. Not only is the king an unsympathetic murderer, but also the royal setting is especially significant in the film's subplot concerning the grievances of local farmers against greedy landowners, which becomes crucial later in the film. Prejudice based on caste, class and race; lack of democratic principles of equality and justice; and corruption are equated with the system of royalty, and the apparently admirable but misguided commitment to *dharma* pursued by 'the royal guard' is exposed in the end as a laudable but unhelpful relic from older tradition, just as, in one sense at least, the idea of revenge in *Hamlet* is ineffectual as a form of justice since by the end of Shakespeare's play, although it has effected justice in killing the villain, it also leaves the protagonist dead and his family destroyed. The film is also explicitly situated in the historical ambit of Indian myth since the central reference is to the *Mahabharata*.

However, seeking more ambitious, international credentials, Chopra, who took seven years to make *Eklavya*, uses style individually and with painstaking artistic craftsmanship, working in ways more comparable with Western *auteurism* than a branch of the contemporary Indian entertainment industry. There are flashbacks and flash-forwards, dream sequences verging on surrealism, carefully orchestrated alternations of sound through thunderous effects, haunting melodies and eerie silence, extreme slow motion and frantic action, and subjectively driven camera motions and angles, some of which will be mentioned later. These are signs of conscious art cinema, aimed at an educated elite and crafted to distance the film from mainstream, populist cinema conventions and large industrial systems of production.[5]

Intertextuality

In terms of Shakespearean allusion, a comparison may be the even more overtly cosmopolitan social comedy directed by the Indo-Canadian Deepa Mehta, *Bollywood Hollywood* (2002). In this film the grandmother in particular, slipping strategically in and out of Hindi and English, frequently (mis)quotes Shakespeare: 'Et tu Brute?', 'This is the winter of our discontent', 'All the world's a stage, and all men and women are mere players', 'But soft, what light through yonder window breaks. It is the east, and so is the sun [*sic*]', 'All the perfumes of Arabia will not sweeten this little hand'. Another character's dead father speaks to him like Hamlet's, though with more comic effect, from beyond the grave in a picture. There is a parody of the balcony scene from *Romeo and Juliet*. Behind this, and arguably behind most Indian films echoing Shakespeare, perhaps lies a cultural memory of Merchant Ivory's *Shakespeare Wallah* (1965), with its mixture of ambivalent tones, ranging from nostalgia and political significance in terms of the end of British colonisation, to the necessity for change in the face of an emerging independent nation. *Eklavya*'s intertextuality also invokes some of these associations but in a way that involves both contemporary reference and a longer historical perspective, weaving together sources which hold mythical and cultural status, including different works by Shakespeare. Both the *Mahabharata* and Shakespeare's sonnets are explicitly quoted from the beginning of the film, and echoes of *Hamlet* become increasingly insistent, supported by muted echoes of *Macbeth* and *King Lear*. 'The lineage of heroes, like the sources of a lordly river, is ever unknown' is written in the *Mahabharata*,[6] and something similar can be said of complex creative works with their interweaving of sources, some known and others unknown, conscious and unconscious, and their overlaying of received patterns. *Eklavya* is an example, and the quotation is especially pertinent to the film's central character since it occurs in a context which supplies the significance that even those of 'inferior birth' may become heroes.

Chopra himself has acknowledged in interviews that he came rather late to English as a language, not learning it until seventh grade at school, and in particular to Shakespeare, whose works he encountered not through the educational system but only later when he entered the Film Institute in Pune.[7] Chopra has become known as a versatile and individual film-maker who has made a mark in both 'Bollywood *masala*' films and a Western made in Hollywood, *Broken Horses* (2015), which was a remake of Chopra's earlier Hindi film *Parinda* or *The Bird* (1989), which had itself been hailed as an historic experiment in Hindi film and won several awards. Having discovered the bard he was quick to exploit the plays for his own filmic purposes, and in 1994 he directed *1942: A Love Story*, in which Shakespeare's *Romeo and Juliet* is copiously referenced and becomes a vehicle for exploring the relationship between Indian nationalism and the struggle for independence.[8] Shakespeare is not set up as an easy symbol for the superimposed English culture but instead as ambivalently poised on the side of neither the colonials nor the revolutionaries and framed by a typical Bollywood musical sequence aimed at local Indian audiences.[9] Chopra clearly sees Shakespeare as a complex and ambiguous symbolic force in Indian culture, neither fully accommodated nor fully alienated, neither obsolescent nor fully localised, but instead suggesting plural and hybrid forms, and associations entirely in tune with Indian cinema itself.

In *Eklavya* the cultural sources are even more intricately interfused, using myths and stories from the past, and although these are less systematically presented in ideological debates over political nationalism than in *1942*, the effect is again to suggest that the present is a complex amalgam of past conflicts. Accordingly, apart from the early sonnet quotation, the Shakespearean content is, in critical terminology borrowed from Derrida by Maurizio Calbi, 'spectral', allusively mediated and only sometimes explicit.[10] When recognised, the references stimulate, again in Calbi's phrase, 'uncanny temporal paradoxes' implicit in the act of overlaying a set of mythic pasts from East and West with the contemporary world.[11] Another way of conceptualising the relationship between the movie and the Shakespearean texts is to adopt Douglas Lanier's analysis of 'post-fidelity' adaptation as a form of 'rhizomatics' (borrowing the term himself from Deleuze and Guattari), the creation of new processes by grafting apparently very different root stocks. In his 'arboreal conception of adaptation', Lanier suggests,

> A rhizomatic structure ... has no single or central root and no vertical structure. Instead, like the underground root system of rhizomatic plant, it is a horizontal, decentred multiplicity of subterranean roots that cross each other, bifurcating and recombining, breaking off and restarting.[12]

It seems that we need metaphors – rivers and plants (and for Deleuze and Guattari, wasps) – to describe the process of creative adaptation. In 'Shakespeare's imbrication with cultural processes of adaptation'[13] the plays are not treated as privileged 'sources' but rather as 'collaborators' in a mutual act of recreation and creation, and in relation to local Indian sources.

The Mahabharata

The opening words in *Eklavya* are 'In the ancient times of the *Mahabharata*', thus establishing the primary source, the provenance of the story of the mythical archer Eklavya in this ancient Sanskrit epic. Knowledge of the *Mahabharata* may be every Hindu's birth right, but it reached Western readers through the work of orientalist scholars in the nineteenth century and has been popularised among Western audiences more recently through the multicultural dramatic adaptation directed by Peter Brook. His staged version toured the world in 1985 as a nine-hour performance and was later filmed in a 'mere' six-hour version in 1989. The vast, sprawling Indian epic represents in the form of myth the history of the world as comprehensively as does Aboriginal mythology from the Dreamtime in Australia or stories of gods and goddesses in the Greco-Roman world of Western Europe. The *Mahabharata* builds its interrelated stories as versions upon versions passed down through time, layers upon layers of structures, narratives begetting narratives with the fertility of births begetting births and tales within tales. Pamela

Lothspeich has shown how the epic has been constantly adapted into novels and movies which use the past to illustrate current problems, often relating to social injustice or reclaiming land (both of which are relevant in *Eklavya*) through the themes of caste untouchability, the exploitation of farmers by wealthy landowners, and the concept of *dharma* or personal duty as destiny. Without mentioning this film, Lothspeich sums up in terms which could be applied to it that

> The themes, problems, conflicts and personalities of the epic are timeless and can find expression in ever new forms, relevant to the present. And yet, if these works are any indication, the logic of *dharmic* morality in the epic seemingly does not hold sway in contemporary globalized India.[14]

In the *Mahabharata* we find the *ur*-story of Eklavya, a legendary archer who is deprived of his right-hand thumb because, as a prince from the house of Nishada, the lowest among the royal orders, he could not be allowed to rival the skill of the more high-born Arjuna. As the son of the king of the outcasts, he is an archetypal paradigm for untouchability, suffering because of his caste. However, despite his lost thumb he proves himself the supreme archer, though still reviled for his lowly social status and unkempt appearance: 'the Nishada of dark hue, of body besmeared with filth, dressed in black and bearing matted locks on head.'[15] These are the essential background facts adapted from the *Mahabharata* into the film, and they are succinctly summarised at its opening, audibly rather than visually (perhaps imaging Eklavya's blindness), in a voice-over narration. As Eklavya (the veteran actor Amitabh Bachchan) narrates to Princess Nandini the tale which explains his own name and role, the child voices a sense of injustice: 'No pain, no blood. No pain, no blood'. The speaker ends the story, 'But without flinching, Eklavya fulfilled his *dharma*. His sacred duty'. The child's voice protests, 'What kind of *dharma* is this? This *dharma* is wrong. I'd have refused. Eklavya was wrong [REPEATED, FADING]'. The phrase 'Eklavya was wrong' returns at the end of the film, when the royal guard admits his mistake in following a misguided formulation of his *dharma*. In a similar way, Hamlet's assumption of a duty to revenge will become an ambiguous part of the underlying critique of justice in the movie.

The prologue introduces themes such as the role of this 'untouchable tribal' in adhering to *dharma* as uncompromising duty, but we are left in suspense as to how these motifs and others will be developed. The present Eklavya, we gradually learn, has some differences from his ancient prototype. Although socially lowly, he is not an archer but a swordsman, and he is old and almost blind, though blessed with preternaturally acute hearing which allows him to throw a sword or shoot a gun with uncanny precision, even without the power of sight. His unswerving duty is to his occupation as the royal guard protecting the figure of the King, despite the latter's steadily emerging malevolence, perhaps an equivalent of the mythic Drona who exploits and downgrades his loyal guard because of his class. Later Eklavya uses his skills to effect poetic justice on wrongdoers, renewing the classic function of Eklavya as an agent of justice while also, as in *Hamlet*, raising broader ethical questions about *dharma*.

Shakespearean Resonances

To return to the film's opening, after the explanatory introduction, there comes a different beginning, a kind of parallel prologue, projected forward in time to the present day, via Shakespeare, as another voice intones the words of Sonnet 18 in English: 'Shall I compare thee to a summer's day?'[16] In a richly decorated boudoir the King (Boman Irani) recites to his queen (Sharmila Tagore), who is lying in bed with every sign of mortal illness ('every fair from fair sometime declines'), while in the background their daughter Princess Nandini (Raima Sen) on a rocking chair enigmatically smiles. The King asks his wife, 'Remember this sonnet? I read it to you when you first came to Devigarh. And you gifted me this flower. It has withered away now'. The Shakespearean elegy to time's destructiveness operates as both memorial recuperation of the past and to portend tragedy in the future. The King resumes reading, silencing with a reprimanding gaze the incongruous laughter of the princess: 'But thy eternal summer shall not fade/Nor lose possession ...'. The Queen keeps asking mysteriously for Eklavya, and the Princess repeats, 'Mother says call Eklavya'. Poonam Trivedi writes perceptively on how the recitation of Shakespeare's sonnet (repeated later in the film) has ongoing ironic reverberations: 'Love sonnet and tragedy are collapsed, courtship and death, love and betrayal are telescoped legitimizing each other', and she points out how Shakespeare's words are later used to undermine the low-born Eklavya.[17] We might add that this particular sonnet reveals other themes, such as the influence of the past on the present and the destructive effects of time on human lives. Also, contrary to expectations, the words are not privileged by being spoken by a sympathetic character, but instead they are increasingly aligned with power and murderous decadence. Shakespeare's words, however inspiring, far from being reverently presented, become as deeply ambivalent in the film as Hamlet's revenge.

We jump to a new scene. Eklavya, alone, is writing and sealing a letter to his son — a letter which will never be posted — finishing with the words, 'Yet gloom engulfs me. Putting this pen to paper is my only solace. Only through these letters can my heart speak'. Using Hamlet's phrase, he concludes, 'The rest is silence'. He is asking his son to return and help him run the fort, given his own ageing infirmity. However, the letter is never sent but instead bundled up as a kind of private diary which reveals more of Eklavya's lonely situation:

I am but a mere wall of this fort that exists only to protect the King. Each moment of my life is a brick in this wall. But this wall is now ravaged by age. The eagle eyes that once watched over this fort are going blind. But my ears miss nothing. What does it yearn for? Perhaps, your voice calling out to me. When an aging father's hands begin to tremble, it is his son's duty to give him a helping hand. Where are you my son?

In a camera movement which will be repeated time and again in the film, we move slowly around the figure, coming ever closer to see his haggard, almost sightless eyes, finally withdrawing and eventually coming to rest on an orange moon.

We move back to the Queen who persists in calling for Eklavya. The King rocks her in ever more agitation, and she dies under his grip. He certainly kills her, and the event is witnessed by Nandini, but as yet it is unclear to the viewer whether he is shaking her in a grief-stricken moment or whether he intentionally stifles or chokes her in his jealousy because she calls only for Eklavya as Othello smothers Desdemona. Later we learn from a graphic painting of the event by the intellectually challenged, child-like Princess Nandini, that it was indeed an act of deliberate strangling. The daughter riddles, 'Mother is dead. Now we don't need Eklavya'. The camera moves outside to the night scene where a large group of people wail in mourning beneath the moon.

All this happens in the first ten minutes of the film, establishing both the *Mahabharata* and Shakespeare as important points of reference in some way that has not yet been revealed or explained. For the whole time the camera moves stealthily around, always circling, as if it is a tactful spectator, a movement which is repeated over and again throughout the movie. In fact the camera virtually never stops moving throughout the film, one sign that Chopra as film-maker is ambitiously reaching for the effect of world cinema aesthetics; another being the use of constant, quietly melodic music sometimes including the human voice humming, chanting or wailing, without signs of the more intrusively celebratory musical and choreographed effects associated with Bollywood productions, until the very last scene. It is a restrained and lyrical but disturbing opening, full of portentous obscurity as to how events will develop from a set of complex but as-yet disconnected premises. It is a mark of the film that linkages are not offered until later as generic markers change, so that we do not have the full picture until towards the end. This makes critical analysis tricky – it is tempting to summarise using hindsight but misleading since this compromises the prevailing sense of mystery, *lacunae*, and gradual disclosures that make sense of the narrative in its own terms, as the past bears upon the present. Again, *Hamlet* comes to mind.

The film does not reproduce in any linear fashion the storyline of Shakespeare's *Hamlet*, and the characters have no easy one-to-one equivalents. Instead, there are similarities, analogies and echoes, in situations and also in roles, although these shift in a very fluid, allusive way. A significant purpose of the constantly changing correspondences is to control the levels of surprise in the shifting tale. Whereas, for example, in *Maqbool* the expectations derived from knowing the play *Macbeth* provide a foreknown, tragic inevitability which is important to the structure, in *Eklavya* it would actually spoil the plot to find a settled path or expectations based on *Hamlet*. We might be led to think a character like the King consistently is Claudius; however, later a switch of perspective places his own hypocritical brother in this role, revealing a different turn of the plot and nuance in the thematic design. The movie has as many twists and turns as a murder mystery (which, among other things, it is), and the clearest way to explain its relationship to Shakespeare's play is briefly to rehearse the unfolding plot and draw attention to some analogies.

The King's recitation of Shakespeare's sonnet gives the fort the anachronistic air of a relic left behind by time. This perspective opens up when the dead Queen's son, Prince Harshwardhan (Harsh, played by Saif Ali Khan), arrives in contrastingly modish fashion by helicopter and wearing shades, to be conveyed by chauffeur-driven car to the fort. Already, with the 'silence' quotation from Eklavya's letter in our minds, the film begins to offer analogies with *Hamlet*. As Shakespeare's young student prince returns to the castle at Elsinore from Wittenberg, so Prince Harsh comes back from the distant metropolis of London to a grief-laden Fort Devigarh, both prompted by the death of a parent, in this case a mother rather than father. We discover that Princess Nandini is his twin sister. This may be a change from the *Mahabharata* where there is a married couple named, respectively, Harsh and Nanda, perhaps a coincidence of names or perhaps showing again Chopra's strategy of subtly adapting his sources,[18] though this part of the plot seems not to be so directly indebted to the *Mahabharata* as the tale of Eklavya. Nandini's friend, who faithfully tended the Queen in her illness, is Rajeshwari or Rajjo (Vidya Balan), daughter of the royal chauffeur whose role equates to Polonius's. Rajjo loves Prince Harsh from afar, much to the concern of her own father: 'Lord, look after my daughter, she's innocent, she's naïve. Please don't break her heart'. Comparisons with Ophelia are unavoidable even down to Nandini's insanity, Rajjo's love for the prince and her father's closeness to the King, all of which will become significant. Other oblique parallels steadily emerge. Just as Hamlet is briefed by the Ghost of his father, so Harsh learns from a letter left by his mother that his own and his sister's true father was not her husband the current King, who has always been impotent (a detail reflecting his tenuous hold on the kingdom as much as his physical state), but Eklavya, who is now the family's loyal protector, the 'royal guard' of the title and the one whom the Queen had mysteriously called for on her deathbed. Now we have an inkling why she did so and why the King killed his wife. We realise

Figure 2.1 Flashback to Eklavya and Prince Harsh as a child.

also that the King is not Harsh's father but his stepfather – another implied comparison with *Hamlet*'s situation. The correspondences are not exact, but they resemble key issues in *Hamlet*, reconceptualised and glimpsed through a subtly distorting glass. In this case the ruler is an unsuspected and murderous stepfather to a young prince, and the true father is not him but in this case a man from a far lowlier social status, descended from Eklavya in the *Mahabharata*, whose mission is to protect the family and the fort. At one stage a flashback shows Eklavya playing with Prince Harsh as a child, splicing Eklavya's role with two from Shakespeare, the Ghost who is Hamlet's father, and also Yorick his childhood companion who died twenty-three years before, whom Hamlet recalls nostalgically as 'a fellow of infinite jest, of most excellent fancy. He hath borne me on his back a thousand times' (5.1.180–1) (Figure 2.1).

Dharma

The Queen's letter to her son concludes with a reference to the central philosophical concept in the movie:

> If your father learns that I've revealed this secret, he will believe I violated our vow, I failed my *dharma*. My sacred duty ... *Dharma* is born from reason. *Dharma* is born from intellect. It is what your heart, your mind feels is right. *Dharma* is what your soul accepts as true and sacred. I have fulfilled my *dharma*. Now son ... you must fulfill yours.

In *Hamlet* Polonius's line 'This above all: to thine own self be true ...' seems to gesture towards something of the nature of '*Dharma*', although Shakespeare's lines have a glibly sententious air when spoken by a garrulous, self-interested character. More pertinently, Hamlet comes to accept a duty of revenge for his father's murder as though it is his *dharma*. Here the *Mahabharata* becomes relevant, for in it *Dharma* is repeatedly referred to as 'the god of justice' and immensely powerful: 'If thou destroy Dharma, verily Dharma will destroy thee.'[19] As Vijay Mishra in *Bollywood Cinema: Temples of Desire* points out, *dharma* is 'a transcendental principle' and 'the ultimate Hindu Law', significant not only in religious belief but all spheres of life, its influence observable in Bombay cinema.[20] Its spirit thematically dominates the film since each character has a personal *dharma*, for good or ill, although its exact nature in each individual case may shift through circumstances. A comparable Western concept in the Renaissance, I believe, was Natural Law, the way living beings fulfil their own nature while following innate knowledge of right and wrong, and it is a principle that dictates apportionment of poetic justice at the end of plays.[21] However, a complexity in the movie is that belief in *dharma* is associated especially with the older generation of Eklavya including the Queen, and may be uncertain or problematic in modern circumstances, just as imperatives of natural law change with circumstances. Both the Queen and Eklavya are accused of breaking their *dharma*, though the ending exonerates both by suggesting that they followed a deeper destiny than they realised. There are variations: first, Eklavya does not realise that his duty should change once it is established that the King is corrupt, and second, without the Queen breaking her promise to conceal the secret of the twins' paternity, there would never have been closure based on poetic justice. Notwithstanding the Queen's wish to keep the secret, the King himself does find out from his brother Jyotiwardhan (Jyoti, acted by Jackie Shroff) that the twins are the children of Eklavya whom he regards as a low-class and 'worthless guard'. He had always known the twins were not his own children but had been persuaded that they were sired by a distant and respectable 'sage'. The King is humiliated by the revelation of the lowly paternity, prompting Jyoti to swear to kill Eklavya to save the honour of his brother the King. Meanwhile, Harsh's cousin, Uday (Jyoti's son), discovers through Nandini that the King strangled his aunt, and yet another allusive motif from *Hamlet* emerges – the cause for revenge of a nephew who hates his uncle and sees him as morally illegitimate. Through the family relationships there is also an implied alignment between Uday and Shakespeare's Laertes as pawns in the plots to assassinate the respective princes. It all sounds complicated, but by this stage the comparisons with *Hamlet* are enlightening.

Hamlet

A new, politically charged situation erupts, again with echoes from Shakespeare. The King has received a threat that he will die unless he gives back to farmers their land, which had been annexed since they had not repaid the debt on it. In fact, as we learn later, the farmers, far from being debtors, are victims of a conspiracy. In *Hamlet* the dispute over land is between the Danes and the Norwegians, the latter accusing old King Hamlet of defrauding them, leading to preparations for war in the kingdom as Fortinbras, the young nephew of the Norse King, approaches with an army. There is also civil unrest rumbling in Elsinore with hints that Prince Hamlet is the people's candidate as monarch. In both *Hamlet* and *Eklavya* the family and dynastic issues insistently interweave with the national and political. In the increasingly important issue of class difference, the King makes himself even more unsympathetic in our eyes when he treats abusively the two policemen who are making enquiries about the death threats on the King. They are both untouchables but aware of the modern law enshrined in the Indian Constitution, establishing non-discrimination as a fundamental right. Although to some extent comically presented with glances at Rosencrantz and Guildenstern and providing a parody of the famous line, 'to be or not to be', yet the policemen's grievances will become politically vital at the *dénouement*. As policemen employed to right wrongs, they may represent a more appropriate concept of *dharma* in modern India with all its injustices.

A different Shakespearean reference now moves into view from *King Lear*, as the rebellion of a starving farming population deprived of a living by the regime of a corrupt, ageing monarch, is revealed through the unlikely agent of the police commissioner (Sanjay Dutt) who turns into a would-be poet:

> KING: These damn farmers have gone mad! They have threatened to kill me.
> POLICE COMMISSIONER: I am not a bad writer myself, Your Highness, Why does the troubled King hide in his mighty mansion?
> Does he fear those poor naked farmers who harbour a secret passion?
> Should he not know that time and tide will wait for none?

The King responds, 'You dare mock me? Don't forget I'm King Jayawardhan. And you are a mere untouchable!', to which the policeman responds spiritedly, 'I wouldn't say that. In our democracy discrimination is a crime'. The exchange is a direct allusion to Lear's insight when he recognises the suffering of his people, 'poor naked wretches', although in the film the King needs to be told of his moral blindness by an equivalent to Shakespeare's wise Fool:

> Poor naked wretches, whereso'er you are,
> That bide the pelting of this pitiless night,
> How shall your houseless heads and unfed sides,
> Your looped and windowed raggedness, defend you
> From seasons such as these? O, I have ta'en

Too little care of this. Take physic, pomp,
Expose thyself to feel what wretches feel,
That thou mayst shake the superflux to them,
And show the heavens more just.
                    (*History of King Lear*, Scene 10, lines 25–33)

This political theme dominates the plot for a while, in the generic capaciousness – and sometimes capriciousness – of Bollywood aesthetics, and the Shakespearean allusion operates opportunistically, depending on a similarity of context rather than being part of a sustained narrative sequence.

Towards the Denouement

The extra role played by the senior policeman, adverting again to the *Mahabharata*, comes when he also reveals his reverence for Eklavya, and that he himself as a boy played a part in Eklavya's childhood feat, of which we had become aware through the voice-over narration beginning the film. Even though not only nearly blind but also blindfolded, Eklavya re-enacts the achievement, at the request of the policeman. In a stunningly filmed sequence, guided only by sound, he throws his sword to cut the cord of a bunch of bells hanging from the foot of a flying dove. As a boy, the policeman, also an untouchable, had been the one who caught the bells. We find out more of Eklavya's past. He explains that his father, also called Eklavya, had drowned (perhaps another recontextualised image of victimhood aligned with Ophelia's fate in *Hamlet* as well as derived from the *Mahabharata*), whereupon the boy's mother gave him his father's sword, called him Eklavya, and entrusted him with the sole *dharma* of protecting the King as a sacred duty. This duty now severely compromises Eklavya as the biological father of the King's children, and now a marked man as the King plans his murder. In a scene of filmic beauty and serenity, Harsh shares his grief for his dead mother with Rajjo and his sister, who sings one of their mother's lullabies, 'Moon-child' while they manoeuvre a kite in the wind (Figure 2.2).

The moment of rare harmony is heard from afar and shared by their real father Eklavya, whose acute hearing compensates for his lack of clear sight. Coming halfway through the film, the moment presages a gathering storm in the narrative, as it moves towards climactic violence and a change of genre to 'action movie'. Equally memorable in cinematic terms are the contrasting scenes that follow, as a herd of camels gallops dustily beside a racing train, photographed from ground level between the animals' legs. Spectacularly choreographed scenes such as these further establish Chopra's ambitious artistic intentions behind his direction.

Figure 2.2 Prince Harsh, his sister and lover flying a kite.

As the King is driven with the unsuspecting Eklavya in a car alongside the camel herd, he again obsessively quotes from Shakespeare's sonnet, but by now it is symptomatic of his neurotic possessiveness over the dead Queen and also his guilty paranoia. He ominously asks, 'Eklavya where would you like to be cremated?', followed by an equally threatening, 'you have served us too long' and a declaration that he will be cremated in the royal grounds. Eklavya's vow to protect the King is now put to a test, which in his own terms he fails. Presumed rebels attack them in a car, using as cover the flocking camels and a passing train. The chauffeur is shot and mortally wounded, Eklavya jumps out of the car into the thundering camel herd, and the King is also shot, apparently by the killer hired to assassinate Eklavya. Not knowing any of this, Eklavya is devastated by his apparent failure to protect the King, his feeling of guilt intensified by the memory of his mother saying that if he failed in this one *dharma*, then nine generations of their family would suffer in hell forever. He is also now mocked by the derisive accusations of Uday, who still plays Laertes's role in *Hamlet* and is the real murderer. Another role equivalent is Rajjo's father, whose situation and words place him anew in the same situation as Polonius. She had dreamed of marrying Prince Harsh but is willing to sacrifice her love for her father's sake. Unbeknownst to her, Harsh in fact inadvertently causes the death of her father, just as Hamlet had stabbed Polonius behind the arras. Harsh's words to Rajjo are full of sidelong allusions:

> Truth is I feel the same. But I remain silent. I can't express myself. Nandini can. She is the only sane person in this fort. You know this fort, it does terrible things to people. This citadel of customs, traditions, rites and rituals is driving me insane. Rajjo, I am no longer the Harsh of your dreams.

The speech holds glimpsed reminders of Hamlet: '... break, my heart, for I must hold my tongue' (1.2.159), and his decision to put on an 'antic disposition' (2.1.173). In context, the mild rejection has a similarly rejective function to Hamlet's 'Get thee to a nunnery speech', though Harsh's is delivered far more gently. There also hover echoes of *Hamlet*'s world-weary mood in 2.2, burdened by his surroundings in the castle: 'Denmark's a prison' (2.2.246), 'a dream itself is but a shadow' (2.2.262), 'in a fiction, but a dream of passion ...' (2.2.554) and 'How weary, stale, flat ...' (1.2.133). The description of Nandini as 'the only sane person in this fort' recalls Laertes's description of his sister's distracted words 'This nothing's more than matter' (4.5.174) and Ophelia's penetrating comments to the court in her madness. The speech also throws a critical light on doctrinaire *dharma* as a dubious relic of 'customs, traditions, rites and rituals', which overburden people with responsibilities derived from the past and interfere with spontaneous emotions in the present. Harsh turns away, leaving Rajjo bereft like Ophelia, though their emotional relationship is, by contrast, intact. Her father, in a posthumous sense at least, gets his stated wish granted, when a biological son of Eklavya (Harsh) agrees to marry his daughter, and his final act is to bless the marriage, allowing him to die happily, to his daughter's gratitude. She thanks Harsh for making her father smile on his deathbed, another apparent echo from *King Lear* when Gloucester's 'flawed heart ... burst smilingly' in the arms of his son (*History of King Lear*, Scene 24, lines 193–96), another example of the emotional context stimulating memory of a Shakespearean quotation.

From here on, against a backdrop of rumbling thunder of an approaching storm (again, *Lear* comes to mind), the genre shifts several times, though retaining a loose connection with Shakespearean sources. A contemporary, socio-political dimension enters with the indignant response of the disaffected farmers to the unjust accusation that they have killed the King: 'they hang our boys. They call us farmers but we don't have enough land for our own graves. First they take our land, now our sons ... It's a conspiracy. Enough, we can't take it any more'. The desperation of the downtrodden farmers may carry another allusion to *Hamlet*, in Claudius's description of the populace after the murder of Polonius: '... the people muddied,/Thick and unwholesome in their thoughts and whispers' (4.5.79–80). Eklavya himself is accused of being part of 'a brotherhood of bastards' because of his lowly birth and the fact that the farmers spared him. There is an ironic truth to this concept with the return of the untouchable policeman investigating the crime, as he seeks to save Eklavya whose life is in jeopardy. He has detected that the real killers of the King, and the ones who conspired to incriminate the farmers, are no less than Jyoti the King's brother and his son Uday – just as Claudius had manipulated Laertes in *Hamlet*. Eklavya discovers the plot and vows to revenge. He warns Harsh that he will be the next to be assassinated –'they will kill you for the crown'– but Harsh tells Eklavya to leave the fort and retire to his village. Eklavya responds rhetorically, 'Leave? With my King's death un-avenged?', and he refuses to abandon his *dharma*. Harsh, now King and aware from his mother's letter that Eklavya is his father, vows like Hamlet to undertake the *dharma* of revenge himself, again advising his father to leave the fort for his own protection. He writes, 'Father, return to your peaceful village. Enjoy the simple pleasures of farm life. I will bring you back to this fort only when I have driven out the maddening echoes of "*dharma*" and "duty" and replaced them with the cheerful laughter of your grandchildren. I want to see you smile. You have suffered too much', words stimulating more links with the sufferings of the blind Gloucester in *Lear*. But more generally, one of the running themes in the film, as in *Hamlet*, is the way the past not only determines but also burdens and distorts the present, by enjoining codes of duty, revenge and atonement on the living. However, Eklavya does not immediately leave as he is ordered, and instead kills Uday. In a cinematically daring scene, he hears the villain's breathing even in darkness, which allows him to aim the sword and throw it accurately.

Reflecting Bollywood cinema's tendency to introduce new surprises just as a resolution becomes more likely, things get even more complicated. In a sudden twist, Eklavya, having heard Jyoti's dying story, now accuses Harsh of in fact being the one who planned and ordered the killing of the King out of hatred. Now, still fixated on his understanding of *dharma* to avenge the King's death and proclaiming that '*dharma* is everything and must be followed', Eklavya tells Harsh that it is his duty to kill him, but his hands tremble at the prospect of killing his son. The prince denies he would kill for the crown but reveals that the evidence of Nandini's painting establishes the King had murdered his mother out of jealousy because she had been calling for Eklavya– a fact which Eklavya vehemently refuses to believe. Harsh himself is guilt-stricken for his indirect implication in the death of Rajjo's father, accidentally killed as Polonius is by Hamlet. In another creatively displaced Shakespearean allusion, this time to Lady Macbeth's sleepwalking words, Harsh confesses, 'My hands are stained with blood. The blood of Rajjo's father. I can never wash it away.'[22] By this stage the concept of *dharma* has been undermined by its apparent tendency to be compromised by complex circumstances and deliberate deception. Harsh tries to commit suicide but is stopped by Eklavya's unerring aim of his sword which knocks the gun out of Harsh's hand, even as we think he is aiming to kill Harsh: 'I didn't miss. That was my finest throw ever. Instead of cutting off my thumb, I struck the hand that was about to kill my son'.

Commenting on what initially looks like a funeral ceremony, the voice-over of Rajjo laments, 'Too many lives have been lost. Too much blood has been shed. Someone must stop this. Let it be me'. As the final scene of Bhardwaj's *Haider* (2014) shows, the only possible end to revenge killings based on uncompromising *dharma* is circuit-breaking forgiveness, and accordingly Rajjo forgives Harsh for playing a part in her father's death. It is reported that Harsh as the new King has restored land to the peasants, earning their undying gratitude in a radical act of democratic redistribution of wealth. Harsh now acknowledges Eklavya as his father, finally exonerating all the wrongdoings of the past. In a final twist, the policemen return with benevolently fabricated evidence that Jyoti and Uday committed suicide, thus exonerating Eklavya of their murder.

Conclusion

The film *Eklavya: The Royal Guard* incorporates many tones, even comedy (the policemen, who fill different roles at various points as do their counterparts in *Maqbool*), love, pathos and terror. With a perhaps inevitable link with ancient Indian aesthetic theory concerning emotions in art, codified in the exhaustive treatise, the *Nāṭyaśāstra*, it ends with the celebratory and resolved *rasa* of *shantam* [*sāntarasa*], described by one critic as 'the aesthetic mood of peace, or equanimity' most associated with the *Mahabharata,* denoting the closure of harmony and peace.[23] This is like the 'full close' of Shakespeare's tragedies, and recalls the spirit of his late romances in which families are reunited and 'Pardon's the word to all' (*Cymbeline*). With its intricately overlapping series of analogical and allusive relationships to the *Mahabharata* and various works by Shakespeare, especially *Hamlet*, and its invocation of different emotional states corresponding to different *rasas* according to ancient Indian aesthetic theory, the movie draws on a richly multidimensional river of sources. *Eklavya: The Royal Guard* is an ambitious work representing a form of cultural fusion of Bollywood, international film styles and aesthetics, and ancient Indian myth, overlapping past and present, in order to make from the old something vibrantly new and unique.[24]

Notes

1 See, for example, Baradwaj Rangan, *Dispatches from the Wall Corner: A Journey through Indian Cinema* (Chennai: Tranquebar Press, 2014).
2 Ibid., 352.
3 Mark Thornton Burnett, *Shakespeare and World Cinema* (Cambridge University Press, 2013), 55.
4 Angma Dey Jhala, 'From Zenana to Cinema: The Impact of Royal Aesthetics on Bollywood Film', in *Popular Culture in a Globalised India*, ed. K. Moti Gokulsing and Wimal Dissanayake (London: Routledge, 2009), 139–53, 140.
5 See Susan Hayward ed., *Cinema Studies: The Key Concepts*, 2nd ed. (London: Routledge, 2000), 16–18.
6 *The Mahabharata of Vyasa*, English Prose Translation by Kesari Mohan Ganguli (1883–1896), online scanned at sacred-txts.com, 2003 by Juliet Sutherland, Book I, Section CXXXIX, 290.

7 Chopra makes the point in various published interviews, for example, 'I have a Munnabhai in Me: Vidhu Vinod Chopra' in *The Hindu* 12 April 2015.
8 See Rosa Maria García Periago, 'Quitting India, Quitting Shakespeare? The Curious Case of *1942: A Love Story*', *Proceedings of the 34th International ADEAN Conference*, Almeira (2010), 1–6.
9 Richard Burt, 'All that Remains of Shakespeare in Indian Film', in *Shakespeare in Asia: Contemporary Performance*, ed. Dennis Kennedy and Yong Li Lan (Cambridge University Press, 2010), 73–108, 97–98.
10 Maurizio Calbi, *Spectral Shakespeares: Media Adaptations in the Twenty-First Century* (London: Palgrave Macmillan, 2013).
11 Ibid., 17.
12 Douglas Lanier, 'Shakespearean Rhizomatics', in *Adaptation, Ethics, Value*, ed. Alexa Huang and Elizabeth Rivlin (London: Palgrave Macmillan, 2014), 21–40, 28.
13 Ibid., 23.
14 Pamela Lothspeich, 'The *Mahabharata's* Imprint on Contemporary Literature and Film', in *Popular Culture in a Globalised India* (London: Routledge, 2009), 82–94, 92.
15 *The Mahabharata of Vyasa* (above), Book I, Section CXXXIV, 280.
16 The text is reproduced as it is spoken in the movie, but punctuation and other quotations are taken from Stanley Wells, Gary Taylor, et al. ed., *William Shakespeare: Complete Works*, 2nd ed. (Oxford: Clarendon Press, 2005).
17 Poonam Trivedi, 'Shakespeare in Bits and Bites in Indian Cinema', in *Cinematic Allusions to Shakespeare: International Appropriations*, ed. Alexa Alice Joubin (Basingstoke, UK: Palgrave Macmillan, forthcoming).
18 Book I, Section LXVI, 245.
19 Ganguli (trans.), *The Mahabharata of Vyasa*, Book I, Section XLI, 90.
20 Vijay Mishra, *Bollywood Cinema: Temples of Desire* (New York: Routledge, 2002), 14.
21 See R. S. White, *Natural Law in English Renaissance Literature* (Cambridge: Cambridge University Press, 1996).
22 Burnett in his Filmography in *Shakespeare and World Cinema* mentions only *Macbeth* as source for *Eklavya*, while Rangan in *Dispatches from the Wall Corner* cites both *Macbeth* and *Hamlet*.
23 Lothspeich, 'Mahabharata's Imprint on Literature and Film', 92.
24 The basic research for this essay (among other works) was supported by a grant from the Australian Research Council ('Shakespeare and Film Genres' DP 0877846).

3 Reworking Shakespeare in Telugu Cinema
King Lear to *Gunasundari Katha*

Nishi Pulugurtha

Gunasundari Katha (1949), a Telugu film which was a huge commercial success in its time, begins with Lord Shiva and his consort Parvati in their celestial abode as strains of a song waft up to heaven – it is a prayer, asking for divine intervention at a moment of crisis. On Parvati's questioning, Shiva draws attention to the sufferings of a young woman on earth. The film then unfolds in flashback as Shiva recounts the story of King Ugrasena of Dharanagaram, an egoistic king with three daughters. Few noticed the connection with Shakespeare's *King Lear*, but to fully appreciate its popularity the film needs to be read not only as an adaptation of Shakespeare but also in the context of Telugu cinema. Using a format that became the staple of the Telugu film industry, the mythological with folk music, the film reveals the multiple possibilities of reworking Shakespeare.

Early Telugu Cinema: The Mythological, Folk and Devotional Genres

The contemporary Telugu film industry, one of the largest in India, is based chiefly in Hyderabad, the capital of both the Telugu-speaking states of Andhra Pradesh and Telangana. Its popularity and big-budget productions rival Bollywood's. Its most recent box-office success is a 2015 film originally made in Telugu and Tamil, and dubbed into Hindi, Malayalam and French: *Baahubali: The Beginning* (The Powerful One). Directed by S. Rajamouli and described as the most expensive film to be made, it is credited with having the highest-grossing opening for any Indian film at the box office: 60 crore rupees.[1]

Andhra Pradesh is the first Indian state formed on the basis of linguistic organisation and came into existence in 1956. Three regions were integrated to form the state of Andhra Pradesh – Telangana (Telugu-speaking area of the erstwhile princely state of Hyderabad), Rayalaseema and the coastal districts of Andhra. Earlier in 1953, the new state of Andhra was created, with eleven Telugu-speaking districts of the Madras Presidency, and its capital was at Kurnool. Later on there was a demand to integrate other Telugu-speaking areas into this state, and in 1956, the states of Andhra Pradesh, Karnataka and Kerala were formed on the basis of language. In June 2014, it was bifurcated, and the new state of Telangana came into existence.[2]

The language-based creation of these states influenced film production in South India. Initially the Kannada, Malayalam, Tamil and Telugu film industries were all situated in Madras, the capital of the Madras Presidency, a commercial and political hub, and shared resources, themes and actors. The creation of new states led the actors to confine themselves to one region and language. Before that, most Telugu entrepreneurs since the early 1930s set up their studios in Madras. The first Telugu talkie, *Bhakta Prahlada* (1931), was directed by H.M. Reddy, a Telugu director who also directed the first Tamil talkie, *Kalidasa* (1931), in which the heroine spoke in Tamil and the hero spoke in Telugu. Both these early films demonstrated the traits of early Indian cinema in that they resembled stage plays, which is unsurprising given that they belonged to the repertoire of the popular Surabhi Theatres and depicted mythological and classical themes, respectively.[3]

In the era of the early Telugu talkies, the films produced were chiefly versions of company dramas based on popular plays and stories. Many of these were *padyanatakalu* or musicals, largely based on mythological stories and performed by theatre groups. These plays were in high sounding Telugu verse (*padyalu*), which was sung. Some of the popular mythological plays (written between 1890 and 1930) which travelled to cinema in whole or in part were *Pandava Udyoga Vijayalu* (The Victory of the Pandavas), *Satya Harischandra, Sati Savitri, Sri Krishna Tulabharam* (based on an episode in Lord Krishna's life) and *Prahlada*. These plays were famous for their songs and sung verses, the *padyalu*. The ability to deliver long monologues consisting of polysyllabic words and alliterative phrases was a much appreciated skill. The mythological films starring N.T. Rama Rao, the iconic Telugu actor who later became the Andhra Pradesh chief minister, demonstrate how these speeches were rendered. The audience of Telugu mythological cinema came to watch films with ears habituated to the monologues and *padyam* singing traditions. The early Telugu cinema, therefore, worked at reviving their memories of watching and hearing plays. The mythological genre, both on stage and later in film, was characterised by a conventional presentation of songs and dialogue, the gestures and poses of the characters were fixed and there was not much scope for improvisation.

Talkies came to India in 1931, and the first four decades of Indian film-making witnessed the production of innumerable mythological and devotional films. Although few Tamil mythologicals were produced, Telugu mythological films dubbed in other South Indian languages were popular among Tamil and other South Indian-language audiences. This is why this genre did not develop in other South Indian-language films.[4] The mythological films, called *pauranikam* in Telugu, drew upon stories from the epics the *Ramayana* and the *Mahabharata* as well as other Puranic literature. The devotional films (*bhakti chitralu* in Telugu) were mostly biographies of saints or pious devotees. The mythologicals depicted gods and goddesses, and showed the influence of the Sanskrit *Puranas* (narratives of gods). Oral in character, these oft-repeated stories are narratives in the folk format or the *janapadam*, sung by itinerant singers. The popularity of the Telugu mythologicals may also be attributed to their rootedness in a social narrative. Not only would these films be structured as a family melodrama, but comic elements and climactic fight scenes would also be assimilated, causing, what M. Madhava Prasad calls, the mixing of genres.[5] From the 1940s to the 1960s, Telugu cinema saw the production of a number of mythological and folkloric films. By 1983, when N.T. Rama Rao became the chief minister of erstwhile Andhra Pradesh, he had acted in 289 films, of which 42 were mythologicals, 55 were of the folklore genre and 11 were historical films.[6] Folk theatre and formats like the *janapadam*, and folk versions of the *Ramayana, Mahabharata* and *Puranas* became important resources for both theatre and films. Surabhi Theatres in undivided Andhra Pradesh used local traditions like the *Tholu Bommalata* (leather puppet dances, which were based on epics and folk tales and performed by itinerant entertainers) and *harikatha* (stories of the lord, in which the storyteller narrated and sang stories about gods and saints), and adapted them to the stage. The various theatre companies provided both Telugu and Tamil cinema with their repertoire and cast.

Telugu cinema also developed a genre of folklore films which can be regarded as localised mythologicals.[7] With *Balanagamma* (C. Pullaiah, 1942), an extremely commercially successful film about a woman who retains her virtue during her twelve-year abduction, the folklore or fantasy film attained great popularity in Telugu cinema. *Ratnamala* (P.S. Ramakrishna Rao, 1947), which portrays a young princess tricked into marrying a prince, with the gods descending to solve the problems, is another film in the same genre. It is in this context that *Gunasundari Katha* (1949), the film under discussion, was made and released. Fairy tales and folk pseudo-historical and mythological stories provided the subject matter of most Telugu films of this era, with the most successful of these being *Patala Bhairavi* (K.V. Reddi, 1951), which broke all box-office records.

Ashish Rajadhyaksha, in his study of Dadasaheb Phalke's early Indian mythologicals and 1920s silent cinema, notes that these films demonstrate a cinematic realism, 'not realism as plausibility but in its different guise, of realization: making it happen before your eyes.'[8] He quotes Phalke: 'Mountains, rivers, oceans, houses, human beings, animals, birds, everything on the screen is real. The miracle of the visual appearance of objects is sometimes caused by the play of light and shadow. This is the magic of the filmmaker.'[9] Early films used stylised acting, exaggerated body movements and frontal shots with characters looking into the camera and voicing dialogues. Supernatural events, a god's birth or a woman's heroic devotion to husband or father, comprised themes of early Indian films; these continued to be used well into the 1950s and are found in *Gunasundari Katha*, as demonstrated in the framing of songs, the use of mythology and folklore, and the deployment of the woman devoted to her husband. The popular devotional films in Telugu frequently presented the woman protagonist as a *pativrata*, blindly devoted to her husband. Gunasundari in *Gunasundari Katha* is shown reading stories of such women, thereby preparing the audience for her course of action.

The costumes of mythological characters, gods and goddesses in plays performed before cinema arrived in South India reveal the influence of the painter Ravi Varma.[10] At the turn of the twentieth century, Ravi Varma's paintings circulated in magazines and calendars, and influenced drama companies in Bombay and Madras. This influence was carried over to cinema,[11] as shown in *Gunasundari Katha*. The theatre's influence is also marked by the way characters enter and exit from the side of the frame after delivering their dialogue. The film's soliloquies recall the stage actor's direct address to the audience.

Like the Telugu films of that period, *Gunasundari Katha* (1949) drew heavily from the visual and histrionic codes of the theatre as well as the conventions of the mythological film; the orality, musicality and performativity of folk formats like the *janapadam*; and the power of social narratives in which Telugu mythologicals were also rooted (Figure 3.1).

Shakespeare and *Gunasundari Katha*

In *Gunasundari Katha* (1949) the Shakespearean text of *King Lear* has been incorporated into the mythological along with the folklore format, or the *janapadam*, in an interesting intercultural amalgam. In his work on Telugu literature and culture, Narayana Rao notes that the retellings of stories from the Indian epics and *Puranas* sought to bring them close to audiences by making them approximate to Telugu culture, and in this process the narratives would often be domesticated.[12] This essay contends that this mode of domestication is at work in the way Shakespeare's play *King Lear* has been retold in *Gunasundari Katha*.

The Telugu film-maker K.V. Reddy's decision to use the *janapadam* as a moral framework for the Lear story proved to be a masterstroke since the film became a huge success and helped to popularise this genre in Telugu cinema. Consisting predominantly of songs sung by itinerant singers, based on mythological and devotional stories, the *janapadam* is didactic in nature and devotional in content. This essay examines *Gunasundari Katha* as a cine narrative that uses an indigenous frame for a Shakespeare text. This intercultural adaptation works as an example of the ease with which Shakespeare can be assimilated into diverse cultural

Figure 3.1 Poster of *Gunasundari Katha*.

media. Shakespeare was taught[13] and excerpts from Shakespeare's plays were acted and recited in schools in colonial India. Translations, adaptations and enactments of the plays were prolific during the nineteenth century, mostly in Calcutta and Bombay, although translations were done in most Indian languages. The influence of Shakespeare on Telugu literature and drama was initially facilitated by Parsi drama groups that toured Andhra Pradesh in the nineteenth century. Vavilala Vasudeva Sastri (1851–1897) was the first translator of Shakespeare into Telugu. He translated *Julius Caesar* in 1876, cleverly indigenising the names of characters into Telugu while retaining the sounds of the original. Julius Caesar is rendered 'Juliusudu', Brutus 'Brutusudu'. In 1880, Gurazada Sriramamurti translated *The Merchant of Venice* as *Venusu Vanija Naatakamu* using both prose and verse, retaining the names of the dramatis personae and making modifications to suit the taste of a Telugu readership. Kandukuri Veeresalingam (1848–1919), the 'father of modern Telugu literature', translated Charles Lamb's *Tales from Shakespeare* in a lucid style, changing the names of characters, situations and incidents. C.S.R. Krishnamma translated *Macbeth* into Telugu prose in 1895 rendering Lady Macbeth as Macbeth Devi and Lady Macduff as Macduff Devi.[14]

Drama companies in the Madras Presidency were the chief source of popular entertainment in South India before the advent of cinema. Folk forms existed, but they lacked organisation and patronage. Following the success of touring Parsi theatre groups, local drama groups were set up chiefly in Madurai and Tanjore. These drama clubs attracted many Western-educated theatre aficionados. Most of the plays staged by these groups were based on the works of Kalidasa and Shakespeare.

With the coming of cinema it is the Tamil film industry which produced the maximum number of Shakespeare adaptations. A Tamil film *Shylock* (1940) was directed by Serukalathur Sarma who wrote and played the title role in the film. Interestingly the film retained the Shakespearean names for all the characters and even used the costumes used in the Elizabethan theatre. Other notable examples are *Katakam* (*Cymbeline*, 1947) directed by T.G. Raghavachari as well as adaptations of *The Taming of the Shrew* (*Arivali*, 1963 directed by A.T. Krishnaswami) and the *Romeo and Juliet*-inspired *Ambikapathy* (1937) directed by Ellis R. Dungan.[15] K. Ramnoth's directorial debut *Kanniyin Kathali* (A Maiden's Friend, 1949) is an adaptation of *Twelfth Night*, while his 1951 film *Marmayogi* has elements of *Hamlet* and Robin Hood.

Gunasundari Katha (1949) and *Yellamma* (1999), an adaptation of *Macbeth* set in feudal Telangana, are the main instances of Shakespeare adaptations in Telugu cinema to date. *Yellamma*, directed by Mohan Koda, is set in Karimnagar in Telangana in the turbulent backdrop of the 1857, 'Sepoy Mutiny'. Yellamma, after whom the film gets its title, is a holy woman, and her role is analogous to that of the witches in Shakespeare's play. Yellamma incidentally is also a goddess in the Hindu pantheon, worshipped by the *devadasis*, women who 'married' or dedicated themselves to the goddess and were dancers and singers in courts and temples. The film, however, did not get a public release, possibly indicating that a reworking of a Shakespeare play within a Telugu historical and political framework would not always work with the Telugu audience. However, fifty years earlier, *Gunasundari Katha* had worked well with audiences, perhaps because of the folk format it used. *Gunasundari* (1948) was also the name of a Gujarati film which does not have similarity to the film under discussion here.

Transculturation

Shakespeare adaptations in Indian languages provoke fresh readings of the plays. These recreations in film, stage and other sites engage in a postcolonial project that Salman Rushdie refers to as 'redescribing a world'. The adaption in a different and new cultural context extends the plays' scope and helps to create what Rushdie calls the 'necessary first step towards changing' a world through a new perspective.[16]

In *Repositioning Shakespeare: National Formations, Postcolonial Appropriations*(1999), Thomas Cartelli catalogues the different ways in which Shakespeare appropriation works: 'confrontational'– that 'which directly contests the ascribed meaning or prevailing function of a Shakespearean text in the interests of an opposing or alternative social or political agenda'; 'transpositional' – that 'which identifies and isolates a specific theme, plot or argument in its appropriative objective and brings it into its own, arguably analogous, interpretive field to underwrite or enrich a presumably related thesis or argument'; and 'dialogic'– a mode

> which involves the careful integration into a work of allusions, identifications, and quotations that complicate, "thicken," and qualify that work's primary narrative line to the extent that each partner to the transaction may be said to enter into the other's frame of reference.[17]

In the case of *Gunasundari Katha*, it is the second, the 'transpositional', that is at work bringing in a new world view.

Gunasundari Katha (Tale of the Virtuous Woman)

Folklores are oral traditions referring to myths, dramas and rituals which are the carriers of culture, social mores and customs. They present philosophical and metaphysical ideas in easily comprehensible formats– dramatisation, songs, simple gestures. These folk performances of the *janapadam* incorporate elements of the *Harikatha* and *Tholu Bommalata*, songs from the first and dramatisation from the second. One of the reasons why *King Lear* was chosen for the film adaptation could be the presence of folk elements in the Lear story which have an affinity with Indian forms. A common Indian folk story of a daughter who angers her father by telling him that she loves him as much as salt, neither

Figure 3.2 Gunasundari praying to Lord Shiva and Goddess Parvati.

more nor less, would have been available to the Indian audience, thus making the *Lear* plot appear familiar.

In 1949 Vauhini Productions, Madras, had already made six movies – *Vandemataram, Sumangali, Devatha, Bhakta Potana, Swarga Seema* and *Yogi Vemana*, the last of which was not commercially successful. It is then that film-maker K.V. Reddy decided to use a genre that was then new to the Vauhini stable – the *janapadam*, a folklore format that would eventually prove commercially viable, using the central theme of *King Lear*. The dialogues and the lyrics of *Gunasundari Katha* were written by Pingali and the screenplay by K.V. Reddy and Kamalakara Kameswara Rao. There is unfortunately not much discussion on the film, and material on the film is scarce. In fact, getting a copy of the film proved challenging (Figure 3.2).

Gunasundari Katha, like *King Lear*, is the story of a King Ugrasena with three daughters Rupasundari, Hemasundari and Gunasundari. His wife dies during the birth of the youngest daughter, and the doting king brings up his daughters lovingly. Refusing to remarry, he neglects state affairs, preferring to look after his daughters which he considers a more daunting task than administering the country. When asked to remarry for the sake of a male heir, the king refuses asserting that his daughters would be the future queens of his kingdom. Even during their childhood, the elder two are more interested in material things and dislike their younger sister. The youngest is of a quieter temperament and is loyal to her father. She also loves reading stories about dedicated wives – *Pativrata Kathalahari*, which narrates the lives of Sita, Sati and Savitri, among others. This interest prepares the audience for the answer that Gunasundari gives to her father's question about how much she loves him, something that the original play did not have. In Shakespeare's *Lear*, Cordelia's response comes as much as a shock to us as it does to her father. However, in *Gunasundari Katha*, Cordelia's character is built up in a way that her response seems justified.

Rupasundari and Hemasundari, the two older daughters, are married to their cousins, Haramati and Kalamati, respectively, in accordance with the Telugu social practice of consanguineous marriages. However, for his youngest daughter, the king takes great pains in searching for a suitable groom. Elaborate arrangements are made on the occasion of the king's sixtieth birthday celebrations, his *sashti poorthi*. He presents his three daughters to the court where they are praised for their devotion to their father upon which a courtier asks whether it is possible for daughters to love their father so much. Confident of his daughters' love and seeking to satisfy the court, the king asks how much they love him. This also marks a method through which they would be anointed as future rulers of the kingdom. The eldest, Rupasundari says, 'My father is my life. He is my god'. The Telugu word for father is *nana*, '*na*' in Telugu also means mine. 'I have never loved anyone more. I do not have words to express my love for my father' (my translation).What she says here is similar to Goneril's statement in *King Lear*.

> Sir, I love you more than word can wield the matter;
> Dearer than eyesight, space and liberty;
> Beyond what can be valued rich or rare;
> No less than life, with grace, health, beauty, honour;
> As much as child e'erlov'd, or father found[18]

The second daughter, Hemasundari, says, 'Whatever I wanted to say, my sister has already said it. I only love my father and love him a lot. I only wish to be born his daughter ever. I was born to serve and love him'. This is close to Regan's speech:

> I am made of that self metal as my sister,
> And prize me at her worth. In my true heart
> I find she names my very deed of love;
> Only she comes too short: that I profess
> Myself an enemy to all other joys
> Which the most precious square of sense possesses,
> And find I am alone felicitate
> In your dear highness' love.[19]

Gunasundari, however, says, 'I will not be able to say such sweet things as my sisters'. At this the king gets angry and reminds her of her duties as a daughter, to which Guna responds, 'I love my father as a daughter should. Neither less, nor more'. This echoes Cordelia's 'I love your Majesty/ According to my bond; no more nor less.'[20]

Ugrasena, like Lear, is incensed and rails at Gunasundari saying that he has brought her up, looked after her and cared for her. Guna says that she loves her father, respects him and will care for him. When the king wants to know who is important to her, she says that after marriage, the important person would surely be her husband. This angers the king who calls an end to the celebrations. He tries to force Gunasundari to change her stand. But she sticks to her convictions reiterating that she could not give all her love to her father since her husband would have equal claim. When asked to learn from her sisters, she says she is different from them and has spoken what she actually believes in. Unlike Lear, however, Ugrasena does not banish Guna but condemns her to a lifelong penance. When questioned whether she could love a deaf, blind and mute husband, she says that she will accept god's will and love him. To which the angry king says that it is not god but he who will chose a husband for her. He sends out word to get hold of a man of beggarly disposition and marries Guna off to a blind, lame, mute and deaf pauper, Daivadeenam.

It is from this point that the film moves into the realm of the folklore or *janapadam*. When it is discovered that Daivadeenam is in fact a prince under a curse, Gunasundari and Daivadeenam are banished from the kingdom. They live far away in a hut where Gunasundari reveals her devotion to her husband. The sad king is ill-treated by his two older daughters as in *King Lear*. He suffers a fall and is taken ill. When news of the king's condition reaches Gunasundari, she is upset and wants to alleviate his suffering. Only a precious gem, the 'Mahendra Mani', can save the king. So, the three sons-in-law set out on a quest for the gem, and Daivadeenam finds it. Haramati and Kalamati steal it from him, and the king is cured. Another curse hits Daivadeenam, who now turns into a bear. Pleased with Gunasundari's devotion, Lord Shiva and Parvati bless Daivadeenam, and he assumes human form again. The king, in great pain and agony, realises his mistake and crowns Daivadeenam the king. Unlike the Lear story, the resolution in *Gunasundari Katha* comes through miracles and magic.

Most of the actors rendered their own songs in the film, which were great hits, especially 'Sri Tulasi Priya Tulasi', a song dedicated to the auspicious household *tulsi* (basil) plant. According to legend the goddess Lakshmi was born as *tulsi* which is worshipped by pious women like Gunasundari. The soulful song reveals Gunasundari's loyalty to her husband and her ability to stand up for her beliefs, something for which she was cast away by her father. The audiences found the movie both entertaining and sentimental in parts. It was successful, and some theatres even had four shows running. *Gunasundari Katha* worked well because of its use of the popular formulaic features that appealed to the audiences – the song and dance sequences, curses redeemed, magical events, gods and goddesses and the two bumbling sons-in-law, one played by Relangi who was a popular comic actor in Telugu films. Vijaya Productions remade *Gunasundari Katha* in Tamil as *Gunasundari* with the same story and characters, six years after it was made in Telugu. This was directed by Kamalakara Kameswara Rao, but it did not do as well in Tamil as it did in Telugu.

Kasturi Sivarao was cast in the role of Daivadeenam in *Gunasundari Katha*. A versatile actor whose forte was not just comic roles, his rendition of the song 'Ore Ore Brahmadevuda' was one of the hit songs in the film. The song addresses the supreme god and voices Daivadeenam's surprise at the marriage of a disabled outcast like him to Gunasundari, a princess. The way Daivadeenam makes fun of Kalamati and Haramati during his journey to get the Mahendra Mani brought in a comic element into the film. The scenes of the snake and mongoose fight during one such adventure were extremely popular. There are scenes of sibling rivalry in the film, not just among the daughters but among Kalamati and Haramati too. The blind, impoverished Daivadeenam could be read as a fool figure who jumps around, causes quite a few laughs and is finally rewarded.

King Lear depicts a hostile universe in which the gods do not answer human pleas, and there is no alleviation of suffering. *Gunasundari Katha* is, however, framed by Shiva and Parvati's dialogue about a young woman's prayer, asking for divine intervention at a moment of crisis. This sets a different tone in the film in which divine intervention does come at the end and the good are rewarded. The magical elements which finally favour the good also combine to enhance the inherent folkloristic dimensions of the original tale, substituting a simple morality in place of Shakespeare's psychologising, more suitable for the popular form of the cinema.

The film appears to be faithful to the Shakespearean plot until the banishment of the youngest daughter. The characters and dialogues of the king and his daughters also follow *King Lear* closely. After Gunasundari's exile the film seems to move into the world of the folklore. However, elements from *King Lear* are strewn all over the film – the three sisters; the king who in a moment of anger makes a wrong decision; sibling rivalry; banishment; the youngest daughter's loyalty to the king; the older daughters' wickedness; the king's final repentance; and the fool figure in the person of Daivadeenam, whose character assimilates elements also from Poor Tom and Edgar. Daivadeenam's appearance as a blind, lame beggar is reminiscent of Edgar's disguise as the Bedlam Beggar, while his later transformation into a bear evokes shades of Lear's mad speech on seeing Poor Tom and realising that man is little more than a 'poor, bare forked animal', essentially bestial. The happy ending of the film is reminiscent of Nahum Tate's version of *King Lear* in which Cordelia does not die at the end of the play but gets married to Edgar.

Gunasundari Katha, I argue, is an example of a hybrid adaptation in which the nuances of the hybrid structure reveal a multilayered reading of the nature of intercultural exchange. The ease with which elements of the Shakespearean text and the Telugu folk format work reveals the dynamics of such exchange. The film appropriates a Shakespeare text within an indigenous art form and situates *King Lear* in an intertextual and intercultural literary and cinematic milieu.

Notes

1. www.desiretrees.com/baahubali-bahubali-total-worldwide-box-office-collections/. Accessed 15th September, 2015.
2. www.telangana.gov.in/about/history. Accessed 24th May, 2015
3. See S.V. Srinivas, *Politics as Performance: A Social History of the Telugu Cinema* (Ranikhet: Permanent Black, 2013) and S. Theodore Bhaskaran, *History through the Lens: Perspectives on South Indian Cinema* (Hyderabad: Orient Blackswan, 2009).
4. See Bhaskaran, *History through the Lens*.
5. M. Madhav Prasada, *Cine-Politics: Film Stars and Political Existence in South India* (New Delhi: Orient Blackswan, 2014), 62.
6. See Srinivas, *Politics as Performance*.
7. S.V. Srinivas, 'Telugu Folklore Films: The Case of Patal Bhairavi', *Deep Focus: A Film Quarterly* IX, no. 1: 45–50, referred to in Rachel Dwyer, *Filming the Gods: Religion and Indian Cinema* (London: Routledge, 2006), 52.
8. Ashis Rajadhyaksha, 'India's Silent Cinema: A Viewer's View', in *Light of Asia: Indian Silent Cinema 1912–34*, ed. Suresh Chabria (Pune: National Film Archives of India, 1994), 37.
9. Dadasaheb Phalke, 'Essays on the Indian Cinema, Bhartiya Chitrapat', in *Navyug*, Bombay: Nov. 1917 cited in Rajadhyaksha, 37.
10. Raja Ravi Varma (1848–1906), Indian painter whose lifelike paintings of Hindu gods and goddesses formed the basis of the presentation of mythological characters, gods and goddesses in Indian cinema.
11. Bhaskaran, *History through the Lens*, 40.
12. Narayana Rao, 'Coconut and Honey: Sanskrit and Telugu in Medieval Andhra.' *Social Scientist* 23:10/12 (October–December 1995): 24–40.
13. Gauri Viswanathan, *Masks of Conquest: Literary Study and British Rule in India* (New Delhi: OUP, 1989), 3.
14. List of Shakespeare translations in Telugu: *Antony and Cleopatra* by Lakshmikantamohan (Hyderabad: Sri Saraswati Book Depot, 1962); *Corialanus* by Lakshmikantamohan (Hyderabad: Sri Saraswati Book Depot, 1962); *Hamlet* by Durba Ramamurti (New Delhi: Sahitya Akademi, 1962); *Julius Caesar* by Vavilala Somayajulu (Guntur: Vijnana Manjusha, 1957); *Lear Raju* by Lakshmikantamohan (Hyderabad: Sri Saraswati Book Depot, 1962); *Macbeth* by Amarendan (Guntur: Maruti Book Depot, 1961); *Macbeth Anu Natakam* by O.S. Krishnamma (Madras, 1895), *Macbeth* by Lakshmikantamohan (Hyderabad: Sri Saraswati Book Depot, 1962); *Venus Vartakudu* by Lakshmikantamohan (Hyderabad: Sri Saraswati Book Depot,

1962), *Vanikupuravarta kodantamu* by Tallapragada Suryanarayanaravu (Suvarnarekha Series No. 3), both translations of *The Merchant of Venus*; *Othello* by Lakshmikantamohan (Hyderabad: Sri Saraswati Book Depot, 1962), *Virasenudu* by Cavali Laskhminarayana (Tenali: Sundaram & Sons, 1949), *Othello* by Jonnlagedda C. Satyanarayanamurti (Orient Publishing Co., 1960), *Pulindasusilamu* by C. Srinivasaru (Madras, 1909); *Tupanu* by Lakshmikantamohan (Hyderabad: Sri Saraswati Book Depot, 1962), *Sulapani Mahakavi Viracita Adbhuta sundari Leka Jhunjumarutamu* by Paramahamsa Vidyanandasvami (Madras, 1907), of *The Tempest*.
15 Sisir Kumar Das, 'Shakespeare in Indian Languages', in *India's Shakespeare: Translation, Interpretation and Performance,* ed. Poonam Trivedi and Dennis Bartholomeusz (Newark: University of Delaware Press, 2005), 71 n 23.
16 Salman Rushdie, *Imaginary Homelands: Essays and Criticism* (London: Granta Books, 1991), 14.
17 Thomas Cartelli, *Repositioning Shakespeare: National Formations, Postcolonial Appropriations* (New York: Routledge, 1999), 17–18.
18 *King Lear* ed. Kenneth Muir, Arden Shakespeare (London: Methuen, 1965), 1.1.55–59.
19 Ibid., 1.1. 69–75.
20 Ibid., 1.1. 92–93.

4 Shakespeare in Malayalam Cinema
Cultural and Mythic Interface, Narrative Negotiations

C.S. Venkiteswaran

Lineages of Shakespeare Translations

Keralam's encounter with Shakespeare begins in the middle of the nineteenth century, when the first Malayalam translations of his plays began to appear. The first play to be translated into Malayalam was Ummen Philippose's 1866 translation of *The Comedy of Errors*. By then, the spread of English education by Christian missionaries, and the study of English language and literature that gradually became an essential part of the new secular education of the region, had exposed the students to Shakespeare – either through his stories in abridged, 'retold' forms or as plays. At that time, in many colleges, Shakespeare plays or parts of them were also performed by students in their gatherings and festivals.

But translations had a different life and uses of their own. According to the noted Malayalam playwright and critic, N. Krishna Pillai (1916–1988), there were as many as forty-two Malayalam translations of sixteen Shakespeare plays. Plays like *Hamlet*, *Othello*, *A Midsummer Night's Dream* and *Merchant of Venice* have had several translations in the last century. Shakespeare's widespread influence drew even writers and traditional Sanskrit and Malayalam scholars. The legendary writer, poet and translator Kodungallur Kunjukuttan Thampuran (1868–1914), who translated the complete text of one lakh Sanskrit verses of *Mahabharata* in 874 days, also felt compelled to translate two Shakespeare plays – *Othello* and *Hamlet* – into Malayalam during the last decade of the nineteenth century. Lacking knowledge of English, he sought the help of his scholar friends. Obviously, the compulsions behind these translations were the fame that Shakespeare's plays had already achieved among the Keralam literati coupled with their literary felicity.

Krishna Pillai writes, 'Most of them [Shakespeare plays] were not translated by people who were associated with theatre. Among the Shakespeare translations, only a few have been performed on stage. Then and as it is even now, anyone who undergoes higher education in English cannot avoid Shakespeare. We received these translations from some such literary enthusiasts who got fascinated by this great playwright.'[1]

Though certain plays were staged in some cities – notable among them being *Othello* by Kainikkara Kumara Pillai – very seldom were translated plays adapted for performance. According to Pillai, during the first 100 years of Malayalam theatre, though about 3000 plays had been published, only around 300 were staged! This indicates that the predominant inspiration in translating plays was mainly literary rather than performative. As works of literature, these translations – including those of Ibsen, Chekov, Maeterlinck, Moliere, Strindberg, Sheridan, Galsworthy, Gorky and others, apart from several Greek classics – were avidly read and appreciated. And in some cases, like those of Ibsen, also inspired many distant Malayalam adaptations. Undoubtedly, these translations introduced the Malayalam audience and readers to the best of Western theatre and wielded a distinct influence on local theatre in terms of their thematics, narrative techniques and styles.

Apart from literary translations, Shakespeare was popularised through performative art forms like *kathaprasangam* – an indigenous storytelling form that originally dealt with mythical stories and *puranas*, and was later used by progressive movements, like communist parties, to propagate secular narratives. *Kathaprasangam* performers like Kedamangalam Sadanandan and V. Sambasivan addressed the masses through their scintillating storytelling abilities and were huge attractions at political rallies, processions and congregations. They narrated not only Malayalam stories and novels but also works translated from other languages like Maxim Gorky's *Mother*; Tolstoy's *Anna Karenina*; and Shakespeare's plays, like *Othello* and *Romeo and Juliet*. Poonam Trivedi describes *kathaprasangam* as an 'un-precedented success story of creating a "Shakespeare commons" in Kerala.'[2]

This gap between the presence and popularity of Shakespeare and world literature in Keralam's literary-cultural and educational scene, and the veritable absence of it on stage, continued in cinema too. Shakespeare's plays did not have a direct presence in Malayalam cinema for the greater part of the last century. This is surprising considering that during the 1960s and 1970s, when Malayalam cinema came into its own as an art form and a popular entertainment medium, it drew heavily from literature for its stories. But almost all of them were film versions of fiction and plays written in Malayalam rather than translations from other languages. This 'Shakespearean absence' in cinema may be explained by the fact that almost all the pioneers of Malayalam cinema – scenarists, actors, lyricists, music directors and others – came from theatre which lacked a tradition of Shakespeare productions. The theatre background of the practitioners was evident in the mise en scène and montage styles of early Malayalam cinema. The visual (and oral) influences of theatre in the acting styles and body language, set designs and costumes, music and dialogue rendering were also present. So, this absence of film adaptations of Shakespearean plays, despite available translations, can be attributed to the film industry's preference for local/Indian narratives, along with the challenges of recreating the 'period' setting of Shakespeare's plays and their related stage requirements. Moreover, it may be due to the film industry's positioning within the linguistic and performative boundaries of popular culture. In the Indian context, it was always a complex choice made from amidst the pull and push of three languages that any local expression, whether in literature, theatre or cinema, had to grapple with: first, the local language, which in Keralam is Malayalam; second, the classical language, Sanskrit; and third, the modern English. In this tussle, the industry, like the theatre of the period that was trying to free itself from the clutches of both Sanskrit classical theatrical forms as well as the 'vulgar' influences of the Parsi-Tamil popular theatre traditions, always tended to go with the vernacular idioms and literary/narrative sources.

Malayalam cinema, though it was inaugurated in 1928 with *Vigathakumaran* (Lost Child, directed by J.C. Daniel), found its own footing as an industry and art form only in the 1950s, when local productions and studios came up. Until then it was heavily dependent upon studios in Madras. But from the beginning, Malayalam cinema trod an independent path. Unlike other Indian cinemas, it never indulged in 'mythologicals' or '*sant*' (holy men) films; instead, 'socials' dominated its thematic terrain, realism was its aesthetic credo and literature was its predominant inspiration. In the next decades, especially from the 1970s, Malayalam cinema produced some of the finest auteurs, like Adoor Gopalakrishnan, Aravindan, John Abraham, K.G. George and others. Malayalam cinema was always open to trends in national and world cinemas, and its high aesthetic standard is evident from its overwhelming representation in the National Film Awards and in the Indian Panorama of the annual International Film Festivals of India.

Shakespeare in Malayalam Cinema

Though Shakespeare's plays were not directly adapted, there were passing references to the bard and allusions to his plays and characters in various Malayalam films. Many films incorporated key scenes from Shakespeare's plays, like Mark Antony's speech from *Julius Caesar* or Hamlet's soliloquy, which were presented as a performance within the film, either to underline a thematic point or as a caesura in the narrative. These scenes intensified the narrative conflict of the moment or were just enacted stage programmes in a college. One film also had a character like 'Shakespeare Krishna Pillai' (in *Kattathe Kilikkoodu*, directed by Bharathan, 1983) to depict pedantic persons who live in worlds of their own.

The first full-length adaptation of a Shakespeare play appears only at the end of the last century in *Kaliyattam* (1997) by Jayaraj, based on

Othello. It was followed by *Kannaki* (Jayaraj, 2001), an adaptation of *Antony and Cleopatra* and *Veeram* (Jayaraj, 2016) based on *Macbeth*. In 2012 V.K. Prakash directed *Karmayogi*, based on *Hamlet*. This essay will focus on these four films – all of which follow the Shakespeare text closely, though they are set in rural backgrounds and borrow heavily from the ritualistic and folk narrative traditions of Kerala. These films are not straight cinematic renderings of the plays but adaptations or 'transpositions'. The film narratives are placed within local social milieux and their folk culture, rituals, beliefs and customs. *Kaliyattam* and *Karmayogi* use local myths or legends existing among certain communities, regions and ritual performers in North Keralam as the background. These beliefs provide the narrative, a dramatic setting and a social context through which the narratives of the respective Shakespearean tragedies are elaborated and improvised on. *Kannaki* is set against the backdrop of cockfighting. The dramatic story of love, lust and machinations is woven into the local lore surrounding fighter cocks; the rivalries that feed them; and the beliefs, legends and rituals that express them. Such adaptations involve cultural negotiations between the Shakespearean dramatic elements and structure, and the mythical, storytelling and performative traditions of the local community creating new synergies, in which a local tragic idiom is rendered using a global/universal tragic template. This demands the foregrounding and sharper delineation of certain characters, situations and ethical dilemmas, and the marginalisation of others. Obviously, these choices have implications in terms of gender, culture and politics. The cultural dialogue and narrative engagement of these films with Shakespeare's plays unravel the complex power plays and emotional tensions contained in the texts. *Veeram* is based on folklore that are called 'Northern Ballads' and are part of the oral tradition in North Kerala. They are about the life and valorous exploits of men and women from the warrior castes in the region, who were experts in martial arts (*kalari*) and who fought in duels as mercenaries to settle scores between local landlords and chieftains.

Interestingly both Jayaraj and V.K. Prakash are film-makers who have experimented with various genres, forms and sources for their films. Both have made 'blockbuster' popular films and films that target international film festival circuits which have won critical acclaim both at home and abroad. Jayaraj, for instance, has attempted a series of films based on *nava-rasas* (the Nine *Rasas*), out of which he has already completed *Karunam* (Pathos, 2000), *Santham* (Peace, 2000), *Bibhatsa* (Disgust, Hindi/2002), *Adbhutam* (Marvellous, 2006) and *Veeram* (Valour, 2016). Why and how Jayaraj and Prakash have chosen to set their Shakespeare films not in contemporary Keralam but in ritual and folkloristic situations, and remote locations is a question this essay grapples with. Is it possibly because Shakespeare is still considered a 'period' piece, and despite Malayalam cinema's deep interaction with world cinema, the iconic English playwright remains unapproachable in contemporary terms?

Kaliyattam (The Play of God) – Universal Drama, Local Theatre

An adaptation of *Othello*, the narrative setting of *Kaliyattam* is a North Keralam village. The main characters belong to communities that perform *theyyam*, a popular ritual worship with a long history prevalent in the Malabar region of Keralam. This folk performance is related to the worship and invocation of spirits, ancestors, valiant heroes, ancient warriors and martyrs, and is linked to the worship of trees, animals, serpents and Mother and village Goddesses. In *theyyam*, the deity himself or herself manifests in the performer. Traditionally, the performers of *theyyam* belong to lower-caste communities like Malayans, Vannan, Velan and others. But when they perform *theyyam* such caste barriers are transcended as they are seen as personification of the deity by all the villagers, including those from the upper castes. While performing, they turn into live gods and have the power to bless and curse, invoke and condemn. The utterances and pronouncements of the *theyyam* performer are considered to be sacred, and people pour out their problems and miseries to these human deities when they perform.

The *kaliyattam* performance, from which the film draws its title, is one such ritualistic occasion which includes *theyyam* and *thira*[3] performances that are intended to propitiate a deity. The performer is custom-bound to observe sexual abstinence for a certain period before the performance in preparation for one of the most perilous acts in the performance – that of walking into fire. Once the massive headgear is placed on the head of the performer, he transforms himself into the divine character and goes into a trance; revering him as divine embodiment, people seek blessings from him. Along with such divine characters, *theyyam* performances also have comic characters, like Gulikan, Paniyan and Pootham, who can be identified from the spathemasks (made out of the sheath of the areca nut flowers) they wear.

The narrative of *Kaliyattam* transposes the characters and situations of *Othello* into this setting. Kannan Perumalayan (Suresh Gopi), who is a star *theyyam* performer, plays Othello, and his comic sidekick Paniyan (Lal) plays Iago. The film opens with a shot of flames rising from a burning pile of wood on the temple premises. This fire is a leitmotif that reappears at the end of the film and forms the centre of the *theyyam* performance; *theechamundi*, the main character, will go into trance and walk over it in frenzy to the awe of the audience, while the performance and the accompanying drum beats spiral into a climax.[4]

In this performance setting Paniyan plays the *komali* (buffoon) *theyyam*, the fool, providing a prelude to the entry of the spectacular *theechamundi* to be donned by Perumalayan, a well-known figure whose performances are admired by the villagers. Paniyan, who is deeply jealous of Perumalayan for his capabilities and fame, is yearning for a chance to play *theechamundi*. But that needs the blessings of Perumalayan and the removal of his more talented friend and competitor Kanthan (Cassio). While he is fooling around as *komalikolam*, Unni Thampuran (Roderigo) rushes in to inform Paniyan about the elopement of Thamara (Manju Warrier playing Desdemona), who is the daughter of the local landlord. This scene sets the tone and pace of the film. The rest of the narrative is driven by the insinuations and manipulations of Paniyan on behalf of himself and Unni Thampuran, the upper-caste rejected lover of Thamara. On the other side are Perumalayan and Thamara, whose love is gradually poisoned by suspicion and finally ends in tragedy.

The focus of the film is on two character trios: Perumalayan, Thamara and Paniyan (Othello, Desdemona and Iago) at the centre, with Kanthan, Cheerma and Unni Thampuran (Cassio, Emilia and Roderigo) in the background. Unni Thampuran's only mission in life is to possess Thamara, and Paniyan manipulates Unni Thampuran's blind desire to execute his own devious plans. Paniyan, who is a minor performer in *theyyam*, is also deeply jealous of his fellow performer and singer Kanthan, who is given more prominent roles. At one point in the play – the only moment when he seems to be true to himself – he tells his wife Cheerma, 'I want to play *theechamundi* at least once in my life and receive accolades from the chieftain'.

The narrative flow of the film is punctuated by Paniyan's machinations and Perumalayan's growing suspicion. Like the dramatic scenes in the play, most of the film scenes feature two characters at a time: Unni Thampuran/Paniyan, Paniyan/Perumalayan, Perumalayan/Thamara, Thamara/Cheerma and Thamara/Kanthan, and the dramatic tempo is structured around their increasingly tense relationships, riddled with yearning, envy, suspicion, desire, ambition and despair. It is taken forward by Paniyan who slowly but systematically plants, fuels and inflames suspicions in Perumalayan's mind, finally goading him to strangle Thamara to death.

All the other characters follow the characterisation of the play. If Paniyan/Iago is all vice, Thamara/Desdemona is all virtue. In the beginning, Thamara appears as a bold woman – one who dares her father and audaciously deposes before the local king and gives herself to Perumalayan. But gradually, she realises to her despair that her unconditional love is incapable of saving their relationship. She too falls prey to Paniyan's machinations despite her earnest efforts to allay her husband's unfounded suspicions and to stand by him against all odds. Her love and dedication are of no avail, and she is sacrificed in the end, but her death eventually causes the undoing of all.

As in the play, in *Kaliyattam*, Paniyan is evil incarnate, with the uncanny ability to turn 'trifles light as air' into 'proofs of holy writ' (3.3.94) by sensing the desires, anxieties and fears of those around him – Perumalayan, Thamara, Unni Thampuran, Cheerma and Kanthan – and to ruthlessly manipulate them to further his treacherous schemes. In the end, when his designs are revealed, he is mauled by Perumalayan in blind rage and left to a life of pain, suffering and humiliation as a cripple.

The sequences and the dialogues in the film closely follow the original, in some instances almost literally, as in the murder scene where Perumalayan addresses Thamara before killing her. One significant change is the use of *theyyam* fire at the beginning and end of the film, like visual quotation marks as it were. The fire in the beginning is the ritual fire lit for *kaliyattam*; in the end it turns out to be sacrificial: when Perumalayan realises the truth about Thamara/Desdemona and how he has been misled into committing a dastardly act, he walks into the fire in a final dance of death.

The setting of the film in the *theyyam* milieu opens visual possibilities in terms of spectacular night performances, masks, movements, orgiastic rhythms and colourful costumes. In the last scene where Perumalayan smothers Thamara to death, the painted serpent on his chest adds to the tragic and uncanny intensity of the moment. These *theyyam* figures also invoke various legends – stories about valour and sacrifice, kinship feuds and rivalry – that constitute the collective memories of the region.

The spirit of soldierly valour underlying the play is substituted in the film by the glory of donning key *theyyam* roles which turn humans into gods. The customs surrounding *theyyam*, which is both a ritual of invocation to village or community deities and ancestors, and an art form, and the ritual purity it demands from the performer and his wife; the rites and acts of penance that go with it; the awe that it inspires in its audience; the sacred space in which it is performed; and the elaborate process of facial make-up, costumes and preparatory rituals all constitute the visual and narrative elements in the film, portrayed through sensitive cinematography which lingers on the colours and contours without eroticising or sensationalising. The tragic drama of suspicion, jealousy, desire, violence and blind ambition is made more intense and poignant in the midst of the sacred rituals and verdant surroundings.

Most of the action in the film happens in open and liminal spaces like house-fronts, village paths and temple premises. Wide-angle shots frame the characters within the larger landscape, bringing in the sky, hilly terrain, rocky paths and forest vegetation to reflect and amplify the emotional ambience of the scenes. The expansive setting of the village seems to be charged with the moods of the characters, especially Perumalayan. Hills looming in the horizon, streams, Perumalayan's lonely house on the hill and the temple premises illuminated with night lamps and torches that come alive with *theyyam* all 'externalise' the tragic drama unfolding within Perumalayan's mind. Mostly shot outdoor, the only interiors are the houses of Thamara's father and Perumalayan. The latter's house is like his gullible mind, with its doors and windows vulnerably open. While the hills and streams resonate with Perumalayan's agonies, it is the tangled vegetation and shady jungle spaces that provide the spatial settings for the meetings of Paniyan and Unni Thampuran.

Fantasy sequences help to visualise Othello's state of mind caught in the web of suspicion. Huge *theyyam* figures appear before Perumalayan in the desolate landscape. In the first sequence, a single figure slowly emerges on top of the hill and then falls over the cliff. In another sequence, a group of figures, imposing in their masks, appear in a row standing on the hill, then they suddenly become still and walk away from him– it is as if Perumalayan's gods were deserting him.

The film uses evocative songs to punctuate the drama: they celebrate the erotic, underlying fears and anxieties, enact despair, evoke memories and also function as narrative pauses. In Act IV of the play, Desdemona recounts and sings the song of the 'willow' that her mother's maid used to sing remembering lost love for which she died. In *Kaliyattam* this song of death turns into a song from the past – one that she used to sing for Perumalayan when he lay in her house, recovering from the fatal burns he suffered during a performance.

Othello is one of the most frequently filmed Shakespearean plays. Many of its cinematic versions have explored the racial difference and the conflicts it engenders. *Kaliyattam*, despite the scope for such explorations in terms of caste divisions and hierarchies (Perumalayan belongs to a lower caste compared to Thamara), desists from pushing this too far. Instead it focusses on the emotional conflicts arising out of jealousy, suspicion, ambition and desire within the performative contexts and milieu of *theyyam* artists and their community. Paniyan's jealousy is driven by his frustrations at being denied bigger, more heroic roles and his greed for money and fame. His machinations dwell more upon fuelling suspicion in Perumalayan's mind by creating credible proofs and circumstances. If film versions of *Othello* have explored the spectacular and scopophilic possibilities of racial difference, especially in the Western context, in *Kaliyattam* a greater centrality is given to professional jealousy and marital distrust, marginalising caste or social divides. The social respect accorded to Perumalayan as an artist and the divinity accorded to him when he turns into *theyyam* complicate his lower-caste position. It is this caste-transcending element as *theyyam* that takes the edge out of the potential caste tensions and conflict inherent in Perumalayan's liaison with Thamara.

What makes *Kaliyattam* an interesting Shakespeare film is the way in which it is able to work its way through the local milieu-specific cultural and social elements to capture the resonances of the play. According to blogger and film critic Anuradha Warrier, 'Jayaraj imbued the

Shakespearean tragedy with local flavour and the Shakespearean tale of love and hate that was underlined by race became, in Jayaraj's hands, a love story torn apart by caste and class, jealousy and insecurity. By keeping to the spirit of the original but adding his own sensibilities, he turned the film from a mere "adaptation" to an almost-original work ... a tale set in Venice (and Cyprus) comes alive in the verdant climes and folk art of Keralam.'[5]

Kannaki – Cleopatra to Kannaki

Jayaraj's *Kannaki* follows the Shakespearean storyline and dramatic framework of *Antony and Cleopatra* while also transposing them into a Malayali milieu and ambience. The narrative of *Kannaki* unfolds in a remote village and revolves around local passions and rivalries surrounding cockfights, cockfighters and cock groomers. The film opens with the noisy scene of a cockfight near the village market with the villagers crowding around cheering the cocks. The prominent rivals who have their honour at stake are Choman and Gounder, but the star of the day is Manikkan, whose cock defeats Gounder's. Choman and Manikkan join hands and lead a victorious journey back home. Meanwhile Manikkan is invited by Kannaki, a mysterious woman with shamanic powers, who lives alone in a nearby village. Despite Choman's warnings, Manikkan accepts her invitation and goes to her house, where he confronts Gounder, who is her secret admirer as well as arch enemy. In their confrontation, he vows to side with Kannaki, being fatally attracted to her. Choman, in order to strengthen his bonding with Manikkan and to make him an ally in his fight against Gounder, fixes Manikkan's marriage with his sister (Kumudam). When this news is publicly announced, Manikkan is forced to agree half-heartedly. When Kannaki comes to know about it, she is shattered. Kumudam too is disappointed when Manikkan confesses to her that he regards her as a sister. She reveals this to Choman, and as a remedy, the community elder suggests that Manikkan should undergo a ritual penance that involves begging and paying obeisance at the famous temple of the Goddess at Kodungallur. Manikkan and Kumudam reach the temple where frenzied rituals follow, and they come to know of Kannaki's presence at the temple. That night, Manikkan leaves with Kannaki, leaving Kumudam behind. Both Kumudam and Choman are shattered by Manikkan's sudden change of mind. Even while Manikkan yearns to build a happy life, he is drawn out of domestic bliss by his rivals. He is challenged to participate in another crucial cockfight, in which he fails due to machinations on both sides: Kannaki wants him to fail so that he will return to her, and Choman wants to defeat him so that he is forced to come back to his sister. To create a rift between Manikkan and Kannaki, Gounder prompts Kumudam to lie to Manikkan that she is pregnant. However, Manikkan gears up for what he hopes will be his final fight; after winning this he would like to retire from cockfighting and return to a happy life with Kannaki. He leaves home, presenting Kannaki a wedding saree. But the fortune teller intervenes and misleads Kannaki that Kumudam and Manikkan are still in a relationship and later Kumudam herself lies to Kannaki that she is pregnant. So, Kannaki decides to leave Manikkan's life and shuts herself in the serpent house. She requests her lieutenant to ask Manikkan to marry Kumudam and live happily. After winning the fight Manikkan returns home to hear about Kannaki's decision. In a frenzy, he ties the knife to his fighter cock's claws and engages in a fight with it in which he is slashed to death. Finding him dead, Kannaki too commits suicide by serpent bite. The film ends with the shot of the two lovers lying dead, as if in final union.

In *Kannaki* Jayaraj takes only the basic storyline and emotional matrix of love within a power struggle from the original play and places it in a local village ambience and context. Manikkan, Choman and Gounder represent the triumvirate of Mark Antony, Caesar and Lepidus; along with Kannaki and Kumudam as Cleopatra and Octavia. The very name Kannaki evokes the legendary character of the Tamil epic *Silapathikaram*, who took revenge upon the Madura king and, in her rage, burnt the city to ashes. In the film she is a mysterious presence, a woman from nowhere with occult powers whom everyone in the village holds in awe and fear. The spoken language and the open landscapes ably transpose the love tragedy of *Antony and Cleopatra* to a Kerala setting. The high emotions of the cockfighters and the spectators that electrify fight scenes in village grounds aptly capture and substitute the rivalry of the Romans and Egyptians in the Shakespearean play. Manikkan, whose past is not elaborated, is actually an outsider who enters the scene, and with his prowess draws Choman's admiration and Gounder's jealousy; the latter two already have a very uneasy relationship. Manikkan becomes a weapon and also a prey to further their dreams. Jayaraj brings in local traditions and beliefs like cockfighting, serpent '*kalam*' drawn in temples of goddesses to propitiate snake gods, the religious pilgrimage to Kodungallur wearing red and observing penance and other rituals to add vibrant colour and mysterious complexity to the character of Kannaki. The film was appreciated for the performances of Lal as Manikkan and Siddique as Choman and had a fairly good run at the box office.

Karmayogi – From *Hamlet* to *Kelipatra*

V.K. Prakash's *Karmayogi* is an adaptation of *Hamlet* set in the traditions and customs of the yogi community from northern Keralam. The film begins with an invocation to Lord Siva followed by an introductory voiceover about Shakespeare and his relevance to the local community:

In the world of letters, William Shakespeare is considered immortal. For more than 400 years, his play *Hamlet* also lives amidst us. Here, *Hamlet* becomes the backdrop for a film in our language and is set within the rituals and customs of the Yogi community who live in north Keralam. For the sin of beheading a Brahmin, Lord Siva had to do penance by wandering as a beggar for 12 years. The figure of *kelipatra* commemorates that event. The duty of one who assumes the guise of *kelipatra* is to live a life of begging and silence. In Vedanta philosophy silence and begging have an important place. The chatter box called mind is buried in silence and begging eliminates the mind's ego. *Karmayogi* invokes man to act without hesitation, with firm belief in one's duty.

The narrative of *Karmayogi* is set in Ekarajya, where Chathoth is one of the leading families. The film begins on the wedding day of Bhairavan and Mankamma (Claudius and Gertrude). As the camera moves away from a group of young men practising *kalari* (martial art of Keralam) and enters the house, we see the newly married couple engrossed in love play. Outside, the wedding guests are chatting about the accidental death by snake bite of Rudran Valiyagurukkal (king), and the magnanimity of his younger brother Bhairavan in taking care of the family and marrying his elder brother's widow. The following day, Bhairavan *theyyam* (a fierce form of Lord Siva) is performed in front of the house, in which they recount the legend of Kelipatra and sing the virtues of the departed king. Rudran (Hamlet) makes his first appearance from amidst the crowd, and his presence unnerves all except Moonumani (Ophelia), who is in love with him. She is the daughter of Kidathan, a relative of the Chathoth family. Later, we find Rudran sitting pensively upon his father's burial mound. Bhairavan and his mother try to pacify him, but he is furious about their hasty marriage and the degeneration of the illustrious family. Kidathan has his own designs for usurping Chathoth properties and is upset about his daughter's love for the erratic Rudran. His son Kanthan (Laertes) leaves the village to acquire occult powers, and his journey is kept a secret from Bhairavan. Next morning, Rudran finds his friend Sankunni (Horatio) lying asleep near his father's burial mound. Sankunni tells him about a dream in which he saw Valiyagurukkal. Later, Rudran too has the same dream in which his father reveals the truth about his murder and urges him to take revenge. Though a deeply disturbed Rudran tells Sankunni about the dream he doesn't reveal the details. In an interesting turn, Rudran, instead of obeying his father's command, decides to become a *kelipatra*. In this way, while disregarding his father's call for vengeance Rudran also paradoxically follows his footsteps by taking on the guise in which his father spent his last days.

Meanwhile, Sankunni meets Komapanikker, the *poorakkali*[6] performer, and requests him to stage a performance at Chathoth house, in which they plan a scene that will reveal the truth about his father Rudran's murder and reveal Bhairavan's crime. During the *poorakkali*, the performers enact the murder scene, and an enraged Bhairavan asks them to stop. Though convinced of his uncle's crime, when the moment arrives, Rudran wavers again. Smelling danger, Bhairavan prepares to annihilate his enemies. But again, at the crucial moment, Rudran fails and the sword slips from his hand. Misinformed by Bhairavan that Rudran has killed Kidathan, Mankamma asks her son to leave. In the forest, Bhairavan's lieutenants, after being overpowered by Rudran, reveal the truth about Kidathan's murder and Bhairavan's wily schemes. Meanwhile Sahyan, the son of a rival family that Rudran's father had defeated, confronts Rudran, is defeated and joins Bhairavan's side.

Moonumani's descent to insanity and later death by drowning devastate both her brother and lover. Bhairavan conspires with Kanthan to annihilate Rudran and arranges a fencing match between them, where he poisons Kanthan's sword and prepares a deadly drink for Rudran. During the fight, Kanthan hurts himself with his sword and is killed. Mankamma too is poisoned by the drink, and before she dies she appeals to her son to avenge his father. Encouraged by all this, Rudran chases the fleeing Bhairavan. In the ensuing fight, Bhairavan is killed. A victorious Rudran offers all his possessions to Sahyan. Dressed as *kelipatra*, Rudran walks away towards the horizon, renouncing everything.

As this storyline shows, the film follows the characters, sequence of events and narrative structure of Shakespeare's play. In almost all scenes, Hamlet is present, and the events revolve around his filial duty to avenge his father, love for his mother and Moonumani and his inability to act decisively, like a 'man'. There are only a few major deviations from the play. For instance, Polonius/Kidathan in the film is killed not by Hamlet/Rudran but by Claudius/Bhairavan, a crime which he attributes to Rudran. While the sighting of the father's ghost opens *Hamlet*, the dead father appears later in the film and as a dream and not an apparition. Even before Rudran appears, the film presents Bhairavan and Mankamma engaged in love play, thus foregrounding Bhairavan's treachery and Mankamma's infidelity and unsettling the familial ethos. In the film, the family forms the site of dramatic events and encounters, while Rudran's internal dilemmas and struggles are played out in liminal spaces between home and the world or in the open, in temples, valleys or forest hideouts. If in *Hamlet*, it is the politics of power struggles between nations that provide the larger setting, in *Karmayogi* it is the simmering tensions within the family and the undercurrents of long-lasting feuds between Chathoth and other families as well as the community that constitute the context of the narrative. It is the repeated tributes paid to the departed Valiyagurukkal by Bhairavan, the villagers, Sankunni, Komapanikker and the house maid which fuels Rudran's guilt and goads him to act more than the inner call of conscience and filial responsibility.

Although many *Hamlet* film versions (like *Haider*, for instance) explore the sexual dimensions of Hamlet's relationship with his mother, *Karmayogi* doesn't touch upon this at all. It is family honour and his mother's vulgar haste in marrying Bhairavan that provoke his anger, and their interactions avoid any verbal or visual indications of sexual desire. Evidently, the intimacy and respect that Rudran has towards his departed father outweighs the love for his mother. But, on her part, there are several references to motherly affection, conveyed, for instance, through a strain of a lullaby that we hear in the background at emotional moments in their relationship like when he defies her, leaves home and becomes a *kelipatra* (Figure 4.1).

The film's use of the mythological allusion to *kelipatras* in particular, and the yogis in general, as Lord Shiva's descendants appears as a

Figure 4.1 Rudran/Hamlet as a *kelipatra* (yogi).

leitmotif. So, Rudran's vacillations receive a spiritual dimension in the film. It is not just a question of avenging one's father or of protecting family honour but also the need to realise one's inner potential. This self-realisation also generates the strength to transcend worldly desires and renounce everything. Through this conclusion, the film moves away from the play's tragic ending and finds a transcendental resolution of the hero's *dharmic* vacillations. This metaphysical dimension is evoked through invocations, in the background, to Lord Siva at crucial narrative points, especially when Rudran glimpses his real self or is about to realise his mission. The film, instead of emphasising Hamlet's tragedy, shows an internal transformation in him, which substitutes his tragic death in the play by his renunciation and self-exile.

Rudran's love for Moonumani is not as elusive as in the play. In the initial scenes, he actively responds to her overtures and sings a romantic and sensual song against a waterfall: 'Oh moon-faced darling, come hither to taste the honey of tender lips, like a bee towards a flower bunch'. The song's visualisation with erotically suggestive movements of the actors follows cinematic conventions of a love song. But Rudran starts avoiding Moonumani when overwhelmed by guilt at his inability to take revenge, he resorts to the *kelipatra* guise. But her memories haunt him: he tells Sankunni that he would meet her after accomplishing his mission. Failing to save her, he expresses deep regret for not having met her before she died.

The costumes in the film are neither 'indigenous' nor 'period'. Their stylisation appears theatrical and was probably intended as an alienation device that keeps the viewer aware of the 'enacted-ness' of the narrative. This stylisation, by resisting naturalist and realistic illusions, also discourages identification and helps foreground the emotional conflicts and ethical dilemmas at the heart of the play.

The scenes of Rudran's confrontation and conflicts with his mother and Bhairavan are shot indoors and focus on questions of infidelity and filial obligations. In these interior scenes Rudran appears uncertain and indecisive, whereas open spaces express the more positive sides of his personality. The love song, for instance, is picturised in the idyllic setting of greenery and cascading water, evoking a sensual ambience of fluidity and ecstasy. Rudran's life as *kelipatra* is shot in liminal spaces like the temple premises, forest paths, house fronts and roads he traverses during his itinerant life. His physical confrontations with Bhairavan and his allies happen outside, in jungles and in open spaces, as also his meetings with Moonumani. The ritualistic and the shamanic spaces are dark and ominous, neither inside nor outside, like ruins and desolate places. The state of being a *kelipatra* is linked to the undomesticated that lies outside the moral world of the family and society. Both Rudran and his father, once they adopt the guise of *kelipatra*, never return to the domestic/interior realm.

In both *Kannaki* and *Karmayogi* the drama is generated through transgression of the thin line between interior/domesticity/marriage and outside/nomadism/bachelorhood; in both films, the heroes, Manikkan and Rudran, undergo penance and follow ritualistic practices. Kannaki combines within herself the outside and the inside. She is a mysterious figure, a witch according to the local people, who falls in love with an outsider, Manikkan, for which she accepts the 'punishment' of death from the serpents. It is as if her desire to marry and settle for a family life itself is a transgression of sorts. Rudran in *Karmayogi* also moves within a dialectic of inside and outside, settling finally for an outdoor life of exile.

Karmayogi ends in a definite departure from the play. Unlike Hamlet, Rudran lives on. While the tragedy of the original is avoided to make the ending more palatable to Indian popular cinema audiences, it also indicates a discomfort with the ethical vacuum that it creates, where there are no victors or vanquished, no certainties, but only a terrifying moral void. So, the film takes an alternative route: the hero leaves the worldly realm as a *kelipatra*. After killing Bhairavan and thus fulfilling his father's wishes, Rudran gives away his land and his princely claims to Sahyan – this resolves another ancient family feud. Having settled his karmic debts as it were, he decides to become a *kelipatra*. Rudran is finally at peace within and without, having settled oedipal scores with his father, exorcised the haunting guilt from his past life and the demands of the world upon him. It leaves him free of worldly bondages and the lacerating conflicts of 'to be or not to be'.

In *Veeram* (Valour, 2016) Jayaraj returns to Shakespeare picking a very popular story from the 'Northern Ballads' (folk songs from North Kerala about the life and exploits of warriors). The story is about Chanthu, a *chekavan* (a warrior caste) who fought to settle scores between the local chieftains. Considering his valour, he is appointed the chief of the *kalaris* (the martial arts schools) by Aromal Chekavar of the legendary Putthooram family. Chanthu has once been spurned by Unniyarcha, sister of Aromal whom he loved. Chanthu is asked to accompany Aromal for a duel with his arch enemy Aringodar. Lured by the enemy camp, Chanthu agrees to manipulate the sword to be used in the duel by replacing its iron rivets with wooden ones. Even though the sword breaks, Aromal wins the duel by killing Aringodar with his broken sword. While returning from the duel, Chanthu murders Aromal while he is asleep. Enraged at Chanthu's betrayal, Unniyarcha vows to take revenge, which she later accomplishes through Aromal's son Aromalunni who challenges Chanthu to a duel and kills him.

The 'betrayer Chanthu' (as he is described in folklore and common parlance) is a popular figure and has appeared several times in earlier Malayalam films: *Unniyarcha* (1961) and *Aromalunni* (1972) by Kunchakko follow the traditional storyline with Chanthu as the villain and

Aromal as hero. *Oru Vadakkan Veeraghadha* (scripted by M.T. Vasudevan Nair and directed by Hariharan, 1989) recounted the story from the point of view of Chanthu, where he is misunderstood throughout his life and stigmatised as a betrayer.

Veeram follows the traditional storyline and is definitely the most spectacular of films in the 'Northern Ballads genre' in Malayalam cinema; Jayaraj has made marginal departures from the original and has added only a few situations and characters to embellish the story and to keep it in tune with the Shakespeare play. Like in the play, the film also begins at a point when Chanthu, fresh from a local victory, is made the chief of *Kalaris* by Putthooram House and ends where he is killed in the duel with Aromalunni, son of Aromal, whom Chanthu murders.

The main location where most of the action takes place – the Ellora Caves – gives the film a sort of timelessness, an epic ambience in which the protagonists automatically acquire larger-than-life dimensions. As characters are stylised and exaggerated thus, the nuances of expression are given less importance compared to the tableaux-like presentation of spectacular scenes of action.

There are three major duels in the film: one at the beginning introducing Chanthu, then the duel between Aromal and Aringodar where Chanthu plays the former's aide, and finally the one between Chanthu and Aromalunni. The murder of Aromal while he is asleep and the killing of Kelu and others are shot in a shady ambience, in dark places and, which is in sharp contrast to the duels enacted on raised platforms, in the sunlit exterior amidst jeering crowds, flying banners and royalty seated above.

Another spectacular aspect that assumes equal prominence in the film is the erotic scenes; one in the beginning, where Unniyarcha comes to visit Chanthu in the bedroom after his ascension to the new post; she inflames his old passion for her and urges him this time to protect the life and glory of her brother. The second one is between Chanthu and Kuttimani back home before he is about to go for the duel as aide to Aromal, where she adds fuel to his desires, both carnal and regal. In a way, the two women black magicians, one attired and the other nude, function as the counterpoints to these two women; they too appear twice in the film, once in the beginning and later, when Chanthu desperately seeks their advice.

Following the pattern of his other 'Shakespeare' films, here too the protagonist is faced with recurring nightmares: one that follows the play where he is startled at the feast by the apparition of Kelu, whom he had murdered. The other one is while he returns from the black magicians, when a crowd of oracles, all dressed in red and in trance, come running towards him, hitting their heads with their own swords and bleeding; among them are the bloodied faces of Kelu's murderers.

The epic proportions of the locales, the spectacular visualisation of the duels, the overcharged erotic scenes and the nightmares all add to the visual grandeur of *Veeram*. Many consider *Macbeth* to be the most 'fearfull' of Shakespeare plays, where 'we grow familiar with fear, learn to hear, taste, see, feel it on the backs of our necks, at the ends of our fingers and in the centers of our brains.'[7] For Jayaraj, the central theme of the film is 'valour', which also forms part of his series on *Navarasas*. *Veeram* tries to combine these two strands in the character of Chanthu, who is courageous and erotically charged on the one hand but gullible and fearful on the other. The larger narrative atmosphere and the folklore stories about Chanthu ideally fit the character of Macbeth, both in terms of the political climate of internecine feuds and the wasted valour of the warrior class who become prey in the larger political drama of acquisition and rivalries.

Conclusion

Any film adaptation from a literary work, especially, works as intricate and challenging and universal and elemental as Shakespeare's, is bound to be a complex interface between text and images, theatre and cinema, stagecraft and film conventions, Elizabethan age and contemporary India. It represents a cultural dialogue involving strategic choices of cultural, political and aesthetic dimensions as well as negotiations with commercial exigencies being a capital-intensive medium.

Interestingly, the films discussed, desist from any allusions to contemporary Keralam; instead, they explore the basic themes and dilemmas inherent in the respective Shakespeare plays. By placing them within a traditional milieu, its beliefs, customs and cultural practices, these dilemmas are given a mythic dimension. They are thus transpositions in narrative space and time, taking a text from one genre and delivering it to 'new audiences in cultural, geographical and temporal terms.'[8] Writing on Malayalam film adaptations of Shakespeare, Shyamala observes that *Kaliyattam* and *Karmayogi* do not only borrow the Shakespearean story, but they effect a cultural shift by 'incorporating the traditional folk culture and rituals of Keralam. Hence, these adaptations are transposition in type.'[9] This transposition could also be the tactical response of a 'regional' (or regionalised) cinema trying to find its distinctive place or voice within the global cinema where Shakespeare has more currency and acceptance. But as many Shakespeare scholars have reiterated, it must be the universality of the themes and the elemental drama of human emotions that the characters grapple with in all its complexity that makes such transpositions inviting and challenging. But placing the adaptations in a mythical past or in indigenous ritualistic traditions can also be read as a cultural strategy of placing and accounting for an author like Shakespeare who in a way embodies and represents colonial past, culture, and education.

Filmography

Kaliyattam, dir. Jayaraj, 1997, Malayalam, India, 130 Mins.
Kannaki, dir. Jayaraj, 2001, Malayalam, India, 127 Mins.
Karmayogi, dir. V.K. Prakash, 2012, Malayalam, India, 110 Mins.
Veeram, dir. Jayaraj, 2016, Malayalam, India, 100 Mins.

Notes

1 N. Krishna Pillai, *N Krishna Pillaiyude Prabandhangal – Sampoornam* (Complete Essays of N. Krishna Pillai, in Malayalam) (Kottayam: DC Books, 2014), 311–12.
2 Poonam Trivedi, 'Rhapsodic Shakespeare: V. Sambasivan's *Kathaprasangam/* Story-singing', in *Online Journal of Societe Francoise Shakespeare*, 'Shakespeare 450: A Jubilee in Paris', 33/2015, https://shakespeare.revues.org/2910. Last accessed 10 August 2016.
3 *Thira* is a popular ritual form of worship of North Malabar in Kerala, invoking Mother Goddesses through performance. The performers of *Theyyam* belong to the lower caste, and people consider Theyyam as personification of Gods and seek their blessings.
4 The many temples of Kerala have stories and legends of Gods attached to them. One such famous tale is that of Hiranyakashipu, the king of the *Asuras*. It is said that Hiranyakashipu was enraged with Lord Vishnu for having killed his younger brother, Hiranyaksha. He prayed to Lord Brahma and acquired special powers. Prahlad, his nephew, however, was an ardent devotee of Lord Vishnu. He was repeatedly plunged into fire by Hiranyakashipu and was finally rescued by Narasimha, the lion incarnation of Lord Vishnu, who killed Hiranyakashipu.
Theechamundi Theyyam is a ritual dance performance, an offering to Lord Vishnu's incarnation – Narasimhavathara – and the number of times the *Theyyam* enters into the fire corresponds to the number of times Prahlad is thrown into the fire. At the climax, the dancer wearing tender coconut leaves plunges into the bonfire and comes out safe, a sign how his arduous spiritual observances make him immune to burns.
5 Anuradha Warrier, *Conversations over Chai,* 'Kaliyattam (1997), 1 September 2014. anuradhawarrier.blogspot. Last accessed 10 August 2016.
6 *Poorakkali* is a ritual art form of northern Keralam in which men dance around the traditional lamp. The dance movements are closely related to martial art practice. The dancers usually observe a month of abstinence and undergo strenuous practice before the performance. Most of the songs sung are from the *Ramayana* or *Bhagavata*.
7 Carol Chillington Rutter, 'Introduction', *Macbeth* (Harmondsworth: Penguin Books, 2005), xxi.
8 Julie Sanders, *Adaptation and Appropriation* (London and New York: Routledge, 2006), 20.
9 C.G. Shyamala, 'Your Face ... Is a Book Where Men May Read Strange Matters', *Indian Journal of Comparative Literature and Translation Studies (IJCLTS)* 2, no.1 (February, 2014):112.

5 'Where art thou Muse that thou forget'st so long,/To speak of that which gives thee all thy might?'
Qayamat Se Qayamat Tak (1988) – A Neglected Shakespeare Film

Koel Chatterjee

Qayamat Se Qayamat Tak (*QSQT*) (From the End of the World to the Day of Judgement) is one of the best-known teen musicals to be made in Bollywood.[1] Its gross box-office takings in India were ₹10 crores.[2] It was a runaway success in 1988 and began to be termed a 'cult film' when it unexpectedly turned into the biggest film of the year, with some teenagers having watched it over a hundred times by the end of 1988.[3] In fact, the film won the National Film Award for Best Popular Film Providing Wholesome Entertainment in 1989, along with the Special Jury Award. It also won awards in seven of the main categories at the Filmfare Awards and eclipsed other contenders at Filmfare that year. *QSQT*, furthermore, marks a shift from the violent revenge dramas that dominated the industry in the 1970s towards the romantic comedies that characterised the 1980s and 1990s, and came to represent the 'typical' Bollywood film to the world.[4] The landmark status of the film and its cult following today makes it the most commercially successful Shakespearean adaptation in the Hindi film industry; however, its roots in Shakespeare's *Romeo and Juliet* have been curiously ignored, despite a growing interest in global/non-anglophone Shakespeares in contemporary times.

Influential critics of Indian Shakespeare, such as Rajiva Verma and Poonam Trivedi, who have written extensively on adaptations and appropriations of Shakespeare in Indian cinema, have not mentioned *QSQT* in their writings, despite it being one of the few commercial successes among Shakespeare adaptations on screen in India.[5] Recently, however, *QSQT* has found its way to several lists of Shakespeare adaptations, such as the British Universities Film and Video council database and compilations put together by universities, such as the Slippery Rock University of Pensylvania (SRU) list of feature-length films of Shakespeare's works assembled by Dr Derrick Pitard.[6] The first time that *QSQT* was evaluated as an adaptation of *Romeo and Juliet* was in 2010 (after Vishal Bhardwaj's global success with Shakespearean adaptations *Maqbool* and *Omkara*) in Courtney Lehmann's monograph, in which she devoted one page to this film while recounting a brief history of the play on screen.[7] Mark Thornton Burnett also touched upon the film in *Shakespeare and World Cinema* but did not give it as much importance in the scheme of his book as he did other adaptations.[8] Most Bollywood films are romantic musicals about doomed lovers, and a *Romeo and Juliet* story is often based on the legend of Romeo and Juliet or popular regional folklores of star-crossed lovers in India, such as Heer Ranjha or Laila Majnu rather than Shakespeare's *Romeo and Juliet*. Thus, Mansoor Khan's reference to the film's Shakespearean roots in interviews during the twenty-fifth anniversary of the film in 2013 excited curiosity in the wake of the renewed interest in Shakespeare among commercial film-makers in India. Nonetheless, to audiences familiar with Shakespeare, the references to the play are quite obvious.

The Shakespearean Influence

In *QSQT* hate is foregrounded in the backstory that we are given in the prologue. Honour feuds are a social reality in India and therefore, a context that Indian audiences are uniquely familiar with. When Ratan compromises Madhumati and refuses to marry her after she tells him that she is pregnant, she is forced to kill herself to save her family from disgrace. Her devastated brother, Dhanraj, carries her corpse to Ratan's wedding, shoots him and then goes to jail. There is thus ample cause for the feud between the two Thakur families; this is, by no means, unreasonable hate. Further, by interpreting the feud as taking place between individuals of the same Rajput Thakur caste, the film-makers have purposefully done away with all forms of otherness that may potentially make the hate seem unreasonable or impersonal; this feud is not a matter of race, colour or religion, as some Indian adaptations on stage and screen have chosen to depict it. Consequently, as Burnett argues, 'the film makes for a particularly intense and even introspective reading of the central players.'[9] Casting the two battling clans as Rajputs (Hindu warriors with noble blood) is of course a reference to the 'Two households, both alike in dignity' (The Prologue, 1) in *Romeo and Juliet*.[10] It is against this backdrop that Romeo/Raj (Dhanraj's son) and Juliet/Rashmi (Ratan's niece) accidentally meet each other, fall in love and reject the feud by eloping on the night of Rashmi's engagement to Paris/Roop Singh.

The depiction of Dhanraj as the impetuous Tybalt figure is important in the context of the transposition of the *Romeo and Juliet* story to Bollywood. In the prologue we find Jaswant Singh (elder, unmarried brother and head of the Montague/Thakur family) trying to restrain Dhanraj when together they go to confront Ratan, much like Capulet does at the ball when Tybalt tries to pick a fight with Romeo for daring to come to the Capulet masquerade. Since, as T.J. Cribb notes, 'Tybalt is hate', in recasting Romeo/Raj as Tybalt/Dhanraj's son, the vicious cycle of hate is amplified.[11] As Raj, unlike Romeo, is not a murderer and has in no way contributed to the feud, we ultimately find Raj and Rashmi paying for the sins of their fathers, a frequent theme in Bollywood, which underscores the futility and destructiveness of hate that is such an essential message of Shakespeare's play. Khan has therefore, quite ingeniously, used Bollywood themes and tropes to smuggle in the themes of Shakespeare's play. I will discuss more examples of this shortly.

It is, however, the tragic ending of *QSQT*, deviating as it does from the most important convention of an archetypal romantic musical in Bollywood, which undoubtedly makes this film a true adaptation of *Romeo and Juliet*. It is also paradoxically one of the reasons why the film has achieved cult status in the annals of the Hindi film industry. *QSQT* was scripted with a happy ending by the screenplay writer Nasir Hussein, Mansoor Khan's father; in fact the formulaic happy ending had been shot and canned when Khan decided to rescript it. In several interviews he claims that he was not convinced by the climax after filming the scripted ending and ended up rewriting the entire scene on set.[12] He had always been convinced that the lovers should die, but several people involved in the making of the film had had doubts about a tragic ending since Bollywood audiences typically do not support love stories with sad endings. Moreover, Hussein was known for his 'light-hearted, slice-of-life films.'[13] His only attempt at a tragic ending in the film *Baharon Ke Sapne* (1967) was not well received. Nevertheless, in an interview Khan says,

> Unlike Dad, I did not want a happy ending to the story, which would have been simplistic and unconvincing. The hatred was so intense that I had to show its futility with the death of the youngsters .... I liked the beginning of my father's script, but thought that I could add my own new take on a storyline inspired by "Romeo and Juliet" and similar stories even in Hindi films of lovers from warring families.[14]

Through this argument, Khan articulates one of the most important characteristics of Shakespeare's *Romeo and Juliet* – the 'profound sense of the tragic inevitability that fuels Shakespeare's play' – and effectively distinguishes *QSQT* as a Shakespearean version of *Romeo and Juliet* from the hundreds of 'wannabes' that seek access to the play's effective capital.[15] The tragic ending consequently, being more realistic in the context of the film, is what elevated *QSQT* above all the other films about young star-crossed lovers defying their parents and made Raj and Rashmi's love story legendary. The acceptance of the tragic ending by the audience, on the other hand, was preconditioned by the recent box-office hit *Ek Duuje Ke Liye* (1981) and the success and acceptance of adaptations which retained the tragic ending of the original play in traditional theatrical modes: for instance, Utpal Dutt's 1970 *Jatra* adaptation *Bhuli Nai Priya* (I have not forgotten, my love). Moreover, as I will discuss towards the end of this essay, Khan purposefully used intertextual references to *Ek Duuje Ke Liye* and *West Side Story* (1961), which were also popular culture appropriations of *Romeo and Juliet* on film aimed at younger audiences, to appeal to the largest portion of the film audience.

Although *Romeo and Juliet* is never directly quoted in *QSQT*, there are echoes of specific iconic scenes from the play that are identifiable. There is, for instance, a discreet homage in *QSQT* to the balcony scene and Romeo's departure after being exiled, though the contexts have been changed and the scenes have been conflated. When the lovers run away and set up house in an abandoned temple, Raj has to go to get wood to build a fire. As he tries to leave, Rashmi says, '*Kal chale jaana, abhi mat jao*' (Go tomorrow, don't go now) in a poignant echo of Juliet's 'Wilt thou be gone? It is not yet near day' (3.5.3). A similar sense of danger and foreboding characterising the lark and nightingale exchange between Romeo and Juliet at the beginning of Act 3.5 colours this scene, despite Rashmi's playful comment, because by now the audience is aware that the families are in pursuit of the lovers and that Rashmi's father has sent a contract killer after Raj. The scene plays out with Rashmi repeatedly calling Raj back, forgetting why she called for him and Raj patiently turning back every time, waiting for her to remember:

JULIET: I have forgot why I did call thee back.
ROMEO: Let me stand here till thou remember it.

(2.2.170)

The dramaturgical function of language in *Romeo and Juliet* has frequently been discussed by critics. Harry Levin, for instance, has claimed that the naturalness of the diction of the lovers is 'artfully gained through a running critique of artificiality', stylised expressions and attitudes.[16] In this context, I would like to highlight the use of language in *QSQT*, particularly the consistent use of Urdu in the dialogues and lyrics in the film. *QSQT* uses language and music for practical dramaturgical purposes throughout the film in a way that was unusual to film-making in Bollywood in the 1970s and early 1980s. Music constitutes a very important part of any Bollywood film, as is evidenced by the fact that the music of a film is usually released a few months before the release of a film. The box-office destiny of a film is also customarily dictated by how the songs of a film are received.[17] The soundtrack of *QSQT* was an instant 'hit' and played a crucial role in the success of the film. The songs are all unconventionally diegetic; audiences had become used to spectacular non-diegetic song and dance sequences in the 1960s and 1970s, with the sole purpose of showcasing the dancing talents of actors like Helen or Shammi Kapoor.[18] Each of the songs in *QSQT*, however, helps to move the plot forward, and the lyrics are conversations between the lovers; in fact, it has been commented on by critics that lyrics and dialogue are interchangeably used during the course of the film.[19] It is also noteworthy that the film begins with a *sher* (short four-lined Urdu poem) that has several functions:

Kya ishq ne samjha hain,
Kya husn ne jaana hain,
Hum khaaqnasheeno ki
Thhokar mein zamaana hain.

The poem can be loosely translated to mean 'the world does not understand love, but that never stops lovers from defying the world for love'. The most obvious role of the poem is to set the tone for the film and act as a prelude to the pre-credits sequence, an adaptation of the Prologue in *Romeo and Juliet*; it sets up love in opposition to hate and introduces the sense of inevitability that is characteristic of an adaptation of Shakespeare's *Romeo and Juliet*.

The specific use of an Urdu poem and the extensive use of Urdu poetry throughout the film are evocative of the Muslim social film and endow an aura of aristocracy to the characters that harks back to the Mughal era in India.[20] This is reinforced by the sequence in which Raj sneaks into Rashmi's birthday party, where the entertainment seems to consist, oddly, of *mujra*.[21] This reference to *nawabi* culture, in turn, has the further purpose of subtly bringing in the high culture associations that Shakespeare has in India and is thereby a method by which the director alludes to his Shakespearean source. As a film particularly aimed at younger audiences (accustomed to a colloquial blend of vernacular languages rather than chaste Urdu) and about two battling clans of Rajputs, however, the use of Urdu, usually associated with Muslim culture, has specific relevance.[22] Urdu is the language of love poetry in India; the extensive use of Urdu dialogues and lyrics in this film is meant, therefore, to make the whole film appear to be one long ode to love. This, I would argue, is meant to parallel Shakespeare's use of the sonnet and the Petrarchan model of love in *Romeo and Juliet*, which has been discussed at length by critics such as Levin, Black and Whittier.[23]

Language is manipulated in further ways in the film to discreetly allude to the Shakespearean play. Rashmi/Juliet consistently speaks in a very formal and stylised manner; she always refers to herself as *hum*, which is the Urdu equivalent to the 'Royal We' in English. This contributes to the poetry implicit in the dialogues of the film but has the additional purpose of referencing a theatrical tradition that Lynnette Hunter and Peter Lichtenfels refer to in which the Montagues are represented as aristocracy, and the Capulets are represented as merchants.[24] In this instance, however, Rashmi's family are portrayed as aristocrats, whereas Raj's family, though once on equal terms with Rashmi's family, have been reduced to the role of merchants as a consequence of the feud. The difference is portrayed in understated ways. For example, Raj is usually seen using a motorbike as his chosen form of transportation; when we see Rashmi first, she is riding a horse. This difference in status is also a subtle way to reference the rich girl/poor boy trope of forbidden love in Bollywood since both families are Rajputs, and there are no obvious obstructions to their love based on caste, religion or language, as is the case of other Bollywood films about star-crossed lovers. It lends greater intensity to the feud as well since the social and economic decline of Raj's family can directly be attributed to the misdeeds of Rashmi's family.

The most obvious allusion in *QSQT* to Shakespeare's *Romeo and Juliet* is, however, the characterisation of Rashmi/Juliet, which is a marked departure from female protagonists in Bollywood of the time and is therefore another departure from generic convention that is less frequently remarked upon as compared to the ending of *QSQT*.[25] The 1950s, 1960s and early 1970s saw actresses being cast as the *Sati Savitri* (Hindi equivalent of the Madonna role) or the *vamp* (the whore). Films such as *Mother India* (1957), *Madhumati* (1958) and *Kagaz Ke Phool* (1959) are illustrations of how film defined the characteristics of a 'good' woman for a society struggling to establish a modern Indian identity that straddled tradition and globalisation; most actresses chose to depict these 'positive' roles rather than being typecast as a *vamp*, which could potentially end their careers as leading ladies.[26] The late 1970s and 1980s led to a change in the characterisation of female protagonists: they were now cast as damsels in distress and often ended up as part of the mise-en-scène, while the male actors took centre stage, thereby reducing the status of the women from actresses to heroines.[27] Rashmi, coming at the end of the 1980s, therefore, was quite a change from the female protagonists that audiences had come to expect in this period.

The plot of *QSQT* closely follows the play text. Raj/Romeo secretly attends Rashmi's birthday party just as Romeo infiltrates the masquerade at the Capulets's house with his friends. Where in the text, Romeo's motivation was to catch a glimpse of Rosalind, in *QSQT* Raj has already seen Rashmi and is drawn to the party at her house to see her again. However, it is Rashmi who, like Juliet, actively pursues the man she loves, defying her family despite her fear of her father. She contrives ways to spend time with Raj, and eventually it is she who first declares her love, which in Hindi cinema was hitherto unheard of: '*Agar hum kisi ke liye deewane ho gaye toh yeh koi zaroori toh nahi ke woh bhi humare liye deewana ho jaye*' (If I have fallen madly in love with someone, it is not necessary that they too have fallen madly in love with me). This forthright behaviour goes against the usual depiction of the 'good woman' prototype. This particular exchange in the film, in fact, is reminiscent of Juliet's plainspoken lines to Romeo in the balcony scene (Figure 5.1):

> Thou knowest the mask of night is on my face,
> Else would a maiden blush bepaint my cheek
> For that which thou hast heard me speak tonight.
> Fain would I dwell on form, fain, fain deny
> What I have spoke, but farewell compliment.
>
> (2.2.85)

Figure 5.1 Poster for *QSQT* that was manually distributed by Amir Khan in Mumbai.

After the two-dimensional protagonists who played out their love stories according to convention in the last three decades, in *QSQT* an attempt to flesh out the lead protagonists is evident, and the audience is taken on a journey in which they observe the lead pair fall in love with a degree of realism through a series of artfully designed episodes that avoid formulaic scenarios. For instance, when Rashmi finds herself in trouble after her bus breaks down, she extricates herself from a situation that in most other Bollywood movies would be a cue for the hero to show off his fighting skills and machismo while the 'heroine' would play the helpless damsel. The hero does get to confront the bullies who were teasing Rashmi, but this happens the next day, and Raj is joined by his friends instead of single-handedly disposing of the gang as action heroes such as Amitabh Bachchan would usually do. Rashmi's character is, of course, based on Sapna, the spirited North Indian female protagonist of *Ek Duuje Ke Liye*, equally comfortable in a sari or a dress and more than capable of fighting her own battles.[28] Sapna, in fact, first meets Vasu while trying to lose her stalker at the beginning of the film; like Rashmi, she is no damsel in distress. However, Sapna frequently lapses into a Bollywood character type, unlike Rashmi. *QSQT*, therefore, surreptitiously changed the idiom of Hindi cinema, inspiring later film-makers to humanise their protagonists, as evidenced by the more complex delineations of female protagonists in the 1990s, such as in *Beta* (1992) (Son), *Dilwale Dulhaniya Le Jayenge* (1995) (The Braveheart Will Win the Bride), *Raja Hindustani* (1996) and *Hum Dil De Chuke Sanam* (1999) (I Have Already Given My Heart Away, My Love). The films of this decade are also notable for assigning equal importance to male and female protagonists in terms of screen time and action, and I would argue that *QSQT* had a large part to play in this development.

The major themes in *Romeo and Juliet* have also been neatly translocated to the context of *QSQT*. For instance, destiny, chance and the stars are referenced several times in the play. The Prologue refers to Romeo and Juliet as 'star-cross'd lovers'. At the beginning of the action when Romeo starts for the Capulet feast he says,' ... my mind misgives/ Some consequence, yet hanging in the stars,/ Shall bitterly begin its dearful date/ With this night's revels, and expire the term/ Of a despised life closed in my breast,/ By some vile forfeit of untimely death'. When Capulet forces Juliet to marry Paris she cries, 'is there no pity sitting in the clouds' and later, 'Alack, that heaven should practice stratagems' against her. In Act V, when Romeo learns of Juliet's supposed death he cries aloud, 'then I defy you, stars!' and when he decides to kill himself he says that death will 'shake the yoke of inauspicious stars/ From this world-wearied flesh'. Furthermore, critics such as J.W. Draper have argued how Shakespeare seems to indicate that 'astral influence actually governs the lives of these "star-cross's lovers."'[29] Destiny and chance are likewise referenced throughout *QSQT* using the cinematic vocabulary commonly seen in mainstream Bollywood. At the beginning of the film after their first meeting, Rashmi takes Raj's hand on the pretext of reading his palm and exclaims that their life lines are exactly the same.[30] This is simultaneously a reference to the exchange between Juliet and Romeo at their first meeting and their touching 'palm to palm' (1.5.99). Later in the film when Dhanraj, Raj's father, spots Rashmi at the hotel where both families happen to be staying, he tells Shyam/Benvolio that Rashmi is the kind of bride he wants for Raj underlining the fact that it is the feud that will separate the lovers. It is at this same hotel that Rashmi buys a decorative dagger as a present for Raj, which he first uses to build her a 'house' and then uses to kill himself. After learning Raj's identity almost halfway into the film, Rashmi remarks, *'Hone wali baat to hoke hi rehti hain'* (What is destined to happened, will happen). The protagonist of a later popular film sums up the popular aversion to tragic endings in Bollywood with the following lines:

Aaj mujhe yakeen ho gaya doston, ki hamari zindagi bhi hamare hindi filmon ke jaisa hi hai ... jaha pe end mein sab kuch theek ho jaata hai. 'Happies Endings'... Lekin agar end mein sab kuch theek na ho to woh the end nahi hain dosto ... Picture abhi baaki hai.[31]

(Today I am convinced that our lives are like our Hindi films, where everything ends on a positive note. Happy endings. And if everything does not turn out well in the end my friends, then that is not the end, there is more to the movie.)[32]

The calm, almost philosophical acceptance of a tragic fate by the protagonists of *QSQT* then, which is so alien to protagonists in Hindi films who always seem to be motivated by a naïve conviction in happy endings, is what, I would argue, marks this film as particularly Shakespearean. Nevertheless, the language used to express the Shakespearean motifs and themes is typical of Bollywood films.

By the same token, the 'death-marked love' that is referred to in the prologue of the play is also echoed in the 'setting sun' motif that characterises Raj and Rashmi's love story. This motif has been borrowed from *Ek Duuje Ke Liye* but used to greater effect as a recurrent theme underlining the doomed love of Raj and Rashmi. Rashmi first sees Raj through a camera while she is taking pictures of the sunset. When she uses the excuse of giving Raj copies of the pictures she has taken, he reminds her that Indian superstition holds that *'Doobte huyi suraj ke saath khichi huwe tasveerein paas rakhne se aadmi mar jaata hain'* (Keeping pictures of oneself taken against the background of a setting sun leads to the death of a person). Rashmi dismisses the superstition, and Raj accepts the pictures as a gift from her. Later, when acknowledging their feelings for one another Raj tells Rashmi, *'Iss hi doobte hue suraj ne hum mein pehli baar milaya tha ... dekhlena, yahi doobta huasuraj hummein ek din hamesha ke liye mila dega*' (The same sunset that first brought us together will one day unite us forever). Rashmi refers to this sentiment again while she lies dying in Raj's arms. The last tragic scene of the film, which has achieved iconic status in the history of Bollywood films, is of Raj, after having stabbed himself, falling across Rashmi in a parody of a loving embrace sharing one last kiss with her in imitation of Romeo's last embrace of Juliet ('thus with a kiss I die', 5.3.120), against the backdrop of the setting sun.

The popular motif of time in Hindi films providentially dominates the language and plot of *Romeo and Juliet*; critics such as G. Thomas Tanselle have attempted to list the numerous references to time in the play and examine them.[33] Benvolio and Romeo's first conversation, for instance, centres on hours and clock time; in 1.1.167, Benvolio tells Romeo that it is 'new struck nine'. At the end of the balcony scene there is a reference to clock time and hours by Juliet and Romeo; after the lovers have parted, Juliet calls Romeo back to ask him, 'At what o'clock tomorrow/Shall I send to thee?' (2.2.168). Most of the action, which is presumed to take place over a period of five days by most critics, is marked by days, hours, months and seasons. Both Romeo and Juliet struggle to maintain an imaginary world void of time in the face of the harsh realities that surround them. For instance, when Romeo swears his love to Juliet by the moon, she protests, 'O swear not by the moon, th' inconstant moon,/That monthly changes in her circled orb,/Lest that thy love prove likewise variable' (2.2.109). From the very beginning, the lovers are designated as 'star-cross'd', as I have discussed before, referring to an astrologic belief associated with time. Time is an equally important theme in *QSQT* and is couched in the familiar Bollywood motif of separated lovers anxiously waiting to meet; there is a sequence in the film with Rashmi counting the days before Raj comes for her against the backdrop of a song that goes '*Ay mere humsafar ek zaara intezaar, sun sadaye de rahi hain manzil pyaar ki*' (This is just a short wait, listen to love beckoning us to our destiny), which is further punctuated by the sounds of the ticking of a clock, and visuals of Rashmi physically crossing the days out on a calendar together with her friend and confidante Kavita (who takes over the role of the Nurse). The entire sequence is also reminiscent of Juliet's eager anticipation of Romeo and her wedding night at the beginning of Act 3.2: 'Gallop apace, you fiery-footed steeds,/ Towards Phoebus' lodging …' and, in turn, a reference to the setting sun motif in the film. However, this is a sequence that is not by any means unique in Hindi cinema. *Tezaab* (Acid) (1988) had the celebrated song sequence '*Ek, do, teen … terakaru din gin gin ke intezaar ajaa piyaaayi bahar*' (One, two, three, I count the days till we meet, come soon spring is here) and *Maine Pyaar Kiya* (1989), another cult film, had a similar sequence against the backdrop of the famous song '*Aaja shaam hone aayi*' (Come quickly, it will be evening soon) (Figure 5.2).

Figure 5.2 QSQT was one of the first few films that boasted on-screen kisses.

Khan has thus deftly woven the Shakespearean themes and motifs into the codified vocabulary and imagery of Bollywood films, while also challenging established Bollywood formulae. In discussions of filmed adaptations of Shakespeare, there has been much debate about how far the medium of film impinges on the transmission of the text and its meanings. Michael Pursell argues that 'Cinematic adaptation is necessarily a blend of the verbal and the visual, the ultimate aim being the integration of the visual realisation with the text so that each supports and enriches the other.'[34] In the case of a non-Anglophone adaptation, the film-maker is necessarily more dependent on a visual realisation of the text in order to capture the tone of the play without the words. Khan has thus successfully achieved 'the integration of the visual realisation with the text' when adapting *Romeo and Juliet* for the mainstream Hindi film market. Further, by using Bollywood formulae to comment on social realities such as honour feuds and gender stereotypes, Khan has extended critical discussions about the play itself. *QSQT* is therefore, I would argue, a particularly important film in the history of Bollywood Shakespeare films and should rightfully be considered a significant precursor to Bhardwaj's adaptations at the turn of the century.

Intertextualities

The first reworking of Shakespeare's *Romeo and Juliet* on screen in Bollywood was undertaken in the form of *Ek Duuje Ke Liye* (We Are Made For Each Other), which was the Hindi remake of the Telugu *Maro*

Charitra (1978). What is distinctive about these films is that they avoid the usual dichotomies that are available within the Indian context, such as religion or financial and/or social status, and locate *Romeo and Juliet* within an issue of contention that is rarely addressed – the differences that arise from identities related to specific Indian languages and cultures. Both films were directed by K. Balachander and had south Indian superstar Kamal Hasan playing the lead role of a Tamil Romeo; Saritha, who played the Telugu Juliet of *Maro Charita*, however, was replaced by Panjabi actress Rati Agnihotri in *Ek Duuje Ke Liye*. Both films were commercial successes (*Ek Duuje Ke Liye* earned a total of ₹100 million in receipts), and both were listed among CNN-IBN's 100 greatest Indian films of all time in 2013. Interestingly, however, while *Maro Charita* won several local awards, *Ek Duuje Ke Liye* won a National Film Award and three Filmfare awards.[35]

Ek Duuje Ke Liye was also the first post-independence Hindi film in a modern setting to reference Shakespeare's *Romeo and Juliet*. The source text is referenced several times as for instance when Sapna asks for Professor Munshiram's notes on *Romeo and Juliet* at a bookstore she frequently visits. Then, just after the sequence where we see Sapna and Vasu falling in love intercut with scenes of their parents fighting, Sapna reads out, 'What's in a name? That which we call a rose/ By any other word would smell as sweet' (2.2.43). This is a theme central to this film which deals with barriers of language and culture and personal identity. The repetitive scenes in which we see the names of the lovers inscribed on walls, in the sand, and in letters highlight the preoccupation that this film has with the concept of names as being part of a person's identity. The sequence that any audience familiar with the play would find most faithfully reflected in the film, however, is the one after Vasu is banished. His anguished cry, 'Why should I banished from this place? ... *Is sheher mein tumhe janne wale, nahin janne wale, janwar, panchhi, peddh, paude, yahan tak ki choti se choti chinti bhi dekh sakegi. Sirf main nahin dekh sakta?*' (Everyone in this town, people who know you, people who don't know you, animals, birds, trees, plants, even the tiniest of ants will be able to see you. Why should I be the only one not able to see you?), is a literal translation of Romeo's protest in the third act of the play: 'Heaven is here/Where Juliet lives, and every cat and dog/ And little mouse, every unworthy thing,/ Live here in heaven and may look on her,/ But Romeo may not' (3.3.29). Given the incredible popularity of this film, its influence on successive adaptations in popular culture would be unavoidable, and indeed, certain directorial decisions of Mansoor Khan – such as the setting of the lovers' union and death at an abandoned temple, Raj's bike, Rashmi's stalkers, and the assassins sent after Raj by Rashmi's father can be traced directly back to *Ek Duuje Ke Liye*.

However, a more direct intertextual relationship can be observed between *QSQT* and the American musical *West Side Story* (1961). *West*

Side Story reimagines the characters of *Romeo and Juliet* in Upper West Side New York City and the feud as between two street gangs – the Jets, comprised of white immigrants (Tony/Romeo is Polish-American), and the Puerto Rican Sharks. A decade after *QSQT*, Mansoor Khan adapted *West Side Story* to make *Josh*, but the influence of the American musical on *QSQT*, or, indeed, of *Romeo and Juliet*, was not acknowledged at the time of *QSQT*'s release. The most recognisable sequence that *QSQT* has borrowed from *West Side Story* is the one in which Tony and Maria pledge their troth before God. Their song 'One hand, one heart' is echoed in Raj and Rashmi's song *'Akele hain to kya gham hain'* (Alone but not sad) as they go on to sing *'Chahen to hamare bas mein kya nahin/ Bas ek zara saath ho tera/Tere to hain hum, kab se sanam'* (We can achieve anything/ As long as you are with me/ I have always been yours). Raj and Rashmi actually succeed in doing what Tony and Maria could not; they run away from home on the night of Rashmi's engagement to Roop Singh/Paris, and there is a charming sequence in the film in which the two lovers 'marry' in an abandoned temple and set up house next to it. Indeed the ending of *QSQT* shocks the audience even more because Raj and Rashmi seem to have finally outrun the hate surrounding them. However, Rashmi's eventual death is reminiscent of Tony's when she smiles at Raj and says, *'Ab humein tumse koi nahin juda kar sakta'* (Now no one can separate me from you). It is, of course, simultaneously a reference to Juliet's death and her refusal to be led away by Friar Lawrence when she wakes and finds her husband dead.

Khan, however, ultimately chose to return to the ending of *Romeo and Juliet* rather than of *West Side Story* or indeed, *Ek Duuje Ke Liye*. This latter film, which frequently quotes Shakespeare's *Romeo and Juliet*, is particularly remembered for the lovers' suicide at the end. There were several reports of lovers committing suicides after the release of *Ek Duuje Ke Liye*; the director was called in several times by authorities to appeal to young couples not to take their own lives. The growing incidence of suicides forced the director to modify the ending, but the change was instantly rejected by the viewers, who stuck to their demand for the original climax.[36] The ending of *Ek Duuje Ke Liye* has particularly influenced more recent adaptations and appropriations of *Romeo and Juliet* in Bollywood; *Ishaqzaade* (2012) and *Ram Leela* (2013), for instance, both end with the lovers killing themselves. Khan, however, had to avoid a death by suicide ending as his father's banner was traditionally associated with 'wholesome' films.[37] By ensuring that fate played a hand in the death of the lovers, Khan stayed close to the ending of *West Side Story* as well as to the original play text. Therefore, Rashmi gets shot in *QSQT* in an echo of Tony's death in *West Side Story* (which is an interesting conflation of these characters with that of Mercutio); however, whereas Maria does not die, Raj chooses to use the dagger that Rashmi had gifted him to kill himself, just as Juliet stabs herself with

Romeo's dagger: 'O happy dagger,/This is thy sheath;/there rust, and let me die' (5.3. 168). This scene is therefore a conflation of Shakespeare's text with *West Side Story* and justifies Khan's argument that the death of the lovers can be the only logical and acceptable ending to this story.

In his essay on Shakespeare in Hindi cinema, Verma had deliberated upon the commercial failure of most films based directly or indirectly on Shakespeare in Bollywood and the 'high-brow associations' that Shakespearean adaptations had for mainstream audiences which kept them away from Shakespearean adaptations.[38] Khan, in directing *QSQT*, adopted established narrative strategies in Bollywood, as well as intertextual references to mainstream Bollywood films and more importantly, to successful regional adaptations, to disguise the detailed translocation of Shakespeare's *Romeo and Juliet* on to a modern Indian setting. His ability to freely experiment with film-making at the beginning of his career and his decision to not adhere to a generic happy ending, however, was a surreptitious acknowledgement of his Shakespearean source, an acknowledgement that he made openly twenty-five years later when Shakespearean adaptations had become fashionable due to the recognition of Vishal Bhardwaj's Shakespearean films in the global arena. Furthermore, by drawing upon the social reality of honour feuds and challenging the gender stereotypes of the day, Khan gained the attention of the younger audience, which, as Paterson points out, is crucial to the success of many profitable films.[39] *QSQT* with its innovative marketing of the music of the film and the fresh faces of the actors playing the male and female leads succeeded, therefore, as a teen musical first, and a Shakespeare adaptation afterwards. As the first commercially successful mainstream Bollywood film, *QSQT*, nonetheless, paved the way for film-makers such as Bhardwaj to experiment with Shakespeare in succeeding years within the confines of the mainstream film industry and achieve global recognition for Indian Shakespeare films.

Notes

1 *Qayamat Se, Qayamat Tak*, Dir. Mansoor Khan and Nasir Hussain, Nasir Hussain Films, United Producers, 1988. The film is frequently listed as one of the top twenty best Bollywood romantic movies in popular opinion polls: see, for instance, The Internet Movie Database list of Top 50 Best Bollywood Romantic Movies of All Time *IMDb: Top 50 Best Bollywood Romantic Movies of all Time*, www.imdb.com/list/ls055035939/(11 December 2012), accessed 1 February 2015, the Rediff Movies compilation of the top 25 Love Stories in Bollywood *Top 25 Love Stories in Bollywood*, www.rediff.com/movies/slide-show/slide-show-1-top-25-love-stories-in-bollywood-over-the-years/20130702.htm#19(2 July 2013), accessed 1 February 2015 or the Pinkvilla list of Top 15 Most Romantic Bollywood Films of All Time *Top 15 most Romantic Bollywood Films of all Time*, www.pinkvilla.com/entertainmenttags/bollywood/top-15-most-romantic-bollywood-films-all-time(13 February 2013), accessed 1 February 2015.

Where art thou Muse that thou forget'st so long 107

2 *Box Office Collections for Qayamat Se Qayamat Tak*, http://ibosnetwork.com/asp/filmbodetails.asp?id=Qayamat+Se+Qayamat+Tak, accessed 22 March 2015. To put this in context, the Amitabh Bachhan starrer *Shahenshah*, directed by Tinnu Anand in the same year, had a box office collection of ₹16 crore according to *Box Office Collection for Shahenshah*, http://ibosnetwork.com/asp/filmbodetails.asp?id=shahenshah, accessed 22 March 2015.
3 See, for instance, an article about the unforeseen success of *QSQT* by Simran Bhargava, 'Teenybopper Heart-Throb', *India Today* (15 December 1988), http://indiatoday.intoday.in/story/bollywood-dreamboat-qayamat-se-qayamat-tak-makes-aamir-khan-a-teenage-sensation/1/330097.html.
4 James Monaco in *How to Read a Film Movies, Media, and Beyond: Art, Technology, Language, History, Theory* (Oxford and New York: Oxford University Press, 1981), 8–10, describes the 'staple of Indian cinema' as 'the lengthy, highly stylised musical'. For evidence of the watershed achievement of *QSQT* see, for instance, Madhu Jain's 'Return to Romance', *India Today*(1989), 132–39. Ajanta Sircar in her article 'Love in the Time of Liberalization: Qayamat Se QayamatTak', *Journal of Arts and Ideas* 32 (1999), 35–59, analyses the significance of *QSQT* as a 'new' love story of 80s/90s Bombay. She also refers to Sanjukta T. Ghosh's analysis of the film in *Celluloid Nationalism: Cultural Politics in Popular Indian Cinema* (PhD diss., Ohio State University, 1992) and Lalitha Gopalan's study of *QSQT* in *Wogs, Natives, Heroes: Examining Cinema and National Identity* (PhD diss., University of Rochester, Dept. of Foreign Languages, Literatures, and Linguistics, 1992) as evidence of the importance of *QSQT* as a landmark film.
5 See Rajiva Verma, 'Shakespeare in Indian Cinema: Appropriation, Assimilation, and Engagement', in *The Shakespearean International Yearbook: Volume 12: Special Section, Shakespeare in India*, ed. Tom Bishop and others, (Farnam and Surrey: Ashgate Publishing Ltd., 2012), 83–96 and Poonam Trivedi, '"Filmi" Shakespeare', *Literature-Film Quarterly*(1 April 2007), accessed January 2012.
6 The full link to the databases I have referred to here are British Universities Film and Video Council, *An International Database of Shakespeare on Film, Television and Radio*, http://bufvc.ac.uk/shakespeare/, September 2012 (13 June 2014) and Dr D. Pitard, *Shakespeare on Film*, http://srufaculty.sru.edu/derrick.pitard/shakespearefilms.htm, 7 October 2014 (1 March 2014).
7 Courtney Lehmann, *Shakespeare's Romeo and Juliet: The Relationship between Text and Film* (London: Bloomsbury, 2010), 97.
8 Mark T. Burnett, *Shakespeare and World Cinema* (Cambridge: Cambridge University Press, 2013), 206.
9 Burnett, 206.
10 All references to *Romeo and Juliet* are from Bantam Books edition, ed. David Bevington (Toronto and New York: Bantam Books, 1988).
11 Timothy J. Cribb, 'The Unity of Romeo and Juliet', *Shakespeare Survey*, 34 (Cambridge: Cambridge University Press, 1981), 99.
12 R. M. Vijayakar, '25 Years of 'Qayamat Se Qayamat Tak'. Taq', www.indiawest.com/entertainment/bollywood/years-of-qayamat-se-qayamat-taq/article_09e701b8-816d-5285-988f-27888c8e0302.html, 15 August 2014 (28 April 2013).
13 Sonil Dedhia, '*Why QSQT is Relevant Even after 25 Years*', www.rediff.com/movies/report/why-qsqt-is-relevant-even-after-25-years/20130429.htm, 15 August 2014 (29 April 2013).
14 Vijayakar, '25 Years of 'Qayamat Se Qayamat Tak'.
15 Lehmann, 97.

16 Harry Levin, 'Form and Formality in Romeo and Juliet', *Shakespeare Quarterly*11, no. 1 (1960): 3–11.
17 See Chapter 2 of Tejaswini Ganti, *Bollywood: A Guidebook to Popular Hindi Cinema* (New York: Routledge, 2013) for a more detailed explanation of how the music sells the Bollywood film.
18 For more information on Bollywood Music and its purposes see Heather Tyrell and Rajinder Dudrah, 'Music in the Bollywood Film', *Film's Musical Moments*(Edinburgh: Edinburgh University Press, 2006), 195–208, Anupama Chopra, 'Poetry in Motion (Music in Bollywood Films)', *Sight and Sound*13 (2003), 32, and Chapter 2 in Lalit M. Joshi, *Bollywood: Popular Indian Cinema* (London: Dakini Books, 2002).
19 See Vijayakar's interview of Mansoor Khan quoted earlier for a more detailed discussion of the music of QSQT and how it changed the way music was used in films in Bollywood.
20 The Muslim Social was a film genre in Bollywood that depicted Muslim culture and customs. It flourished in Bollywood in the 1950s and 1960s and lasted until the early 1980s. Presently, the typical Bollywood hero is Hindu; Bollywood superstars Shahrukh Khan, Salman Khan and Aamir Khan, for instance, have built their careers playing Hindu protagonists. To know more about Muslim characters in Bollywood, see Ira Bhaskar and Richard Allen, *Islamicate Cultures of Bombay Cinema* (New Delhi, India: Tulika Books, 2009).
21 *Mujra* is a form of dance originated by courtesans during the Mughal era which incorporated elements of the classical Kathak dance with music, such as *thumris* and *ghazals* or poems. The spectators are usually male due to gender segregation in the Muslim culture. This form of entertainment for the birthday celebrations of a teenage girl seems incongruous but plays into the *Nawabi* setting that Khan has purposefully constructed. It is also noteworthy that Khan himself was a young Muslim director making his first film in an era when the Muslim social genre was in decline and Bollywood was consciously constructing an Indian identity that was primarily Hindu.
22 The typical Indian speaks a blend of two or three different languages, and it is rare to speak pure Urdu outside of cultural engagements such as when Farhan Akhtar's character in *Zindagi Na Milegi Dobara*(2011) recites his poetry. Aparna Sen's new appropriation of *Romeo and Juliet*, *Arshinagar* (2015) reproduces this unique spoken language of Indians by getting her characters to speak a blend of Hindi, Urdu, Bengali and English that is typical of Indians living in Kolkata. The use of Urdu is also a reference to Chakram/Paris in *Ek Duuje Ke Liye* who is depicted as educated and comically pathetic in his devotion to Sapna/Juliet, and an ideal bridegroom in the eyes of her parents.
23 Read Harry Levin, 'Form and Formality in Romeo and Juliet', *Shakespeare Quarterly*11, no. 1 (1960): 3–11, Gayle Whittier, 'The Sonnet's Body and the Body Sonnetized in "Romeo and Juliet"', *Shakespeare Quarterly*40, no. 1 (1989): 27–41, and James Black, 'The Visual Artistry of Romeo and Juliet', *Studies in English Literature, 1500–1900*(1975): 245–56 for a more detailed description of Shakespeare's use of the sonnet and the Petrarchan model of love in *Romeo and Juliet*.
24 Lynette Hunter and Peter Lichtenfels, *Negotiating Shakespeare's Language in Romeo and Juliet: Reading Strategies from Criticism, Editing and the Theatre* (Farnham and Surrey: Ashgate, 2009): 6.
25 Read Sukanya Verma, *Getting Nostalgic about Qayamat Se Qayamat Tak*, www.sukanyaverma.com/columns-and-reviews/2013/getting-nostalgic-

about-qayamat-se-qayamat-tak (29 April 2013), accessed 15 August 2014 and Premankur Biswas, *25 Years of Qayamat Se QayamatTak: Why It's One of Bollywood's Best*,www.firstpost.com/bollywood/why-aamir-juhis-qayamat-se-qayamat-tak-is-one-of-bollywoods-best-736751.html (29 April 2013), accessed 15 August 2014, written on the twenty fifth anniversary of *QSQT* for an understanding of how the film changed the idiom of Hindi cinema.

26 Actresses such as Helen and Bindu are better known for their character actor roles, usually as *vamps*, than for the few leading lady roles they each played. The exception was Zeenat Aman who frequently played skimpily clad, anglicized leading lady roles which few Bollywood actresses of the time attempted.

27 This point is somewhat of a generalisation on my part as I am not referring to films by directors such as Guru Dutt, Basu Chatterjee or Govind Nihalani, who were exceptions to the rule, but to the majority of mainstream Bollywood films marketed to teenage and working-class audiences that depicted women in a certain way in this period where their objective in the film was primarily to support the 'hero'. See, for instance, Nidhi S. Tere, 'Gender Reflections in Mainstream Hindi Cinema', *Global Media Journal Indian Edition, Summer Issue/June*3 (2012), Keertana Sastry, *Comparing Bollywood's Portrayal of Women from Past to Present*,www.india.com/entertainment/comparing-bollywoods-portrayal-of-women-from-past-to-present-164384/ (12 May 2015), accessed 20 March 2016, and Priyanka Srivastava, *Depicting Women in Bollywood: The Mould Never Changes*, http://indiatoday.intoday.in/story/depicting-women-in-bollywood/1/395242.html (11 October 2014), accessed 20 March 2015.

28 *Ek Duuje Ke Liye*, Dir. K. Balachander, Prasad Productions Pvt. Ltd, 1981.

29 John W. Draper, 'Shakespeare's "Star-Crossed Lovers"', *The Review of English Studies*15 (1939), 16–34.

30 This is a conscious reversal of gender roles as in most mainstream Bollywood films it is usually the boy who takes a girl's hand on the pretext of reading their palm in a society where physical displays of affection are frowned upon.

31 *Om Shanti Om*, Dir. Farah Khan, Red Chillies Entertainment, 2007.

32 It is an interesting note on intertextuality that the character saying these lines is played by Shahrukh Khan, the same actor who played Max/Bernardo in Mansoor Khan's remake of *West Side Story*, *Josh* (2000), which had the formulaic happy ending so necessary for a typical Bollywood film, despite being an appropriation of *Romeo and Juliet*.

33 G.T. Tanselle, 'Time in Romeo and Juliet', *Shakespeare Quarterly* 15, no. 4 (1964): 349–61.

34 Michael Pursell, 'Zeffirelli's Shakespeare: The Visual Realization of Tone and Theme', *Literature/Film Quarterly*8 (1980): 210.

35 IMDb, *Highest Grossing Hindi Movies of 1981*, www.imdb.com/list/ls000028872/, 20 December 2014.

36 Read Jacinta Pilakkot, *Rati Agnihotri Still Nostalgic about Role in 'EkDujeKe Liye'*, www.outlookindia.com/news/article/Rati-Agnihotri-still-nostalgic-about-role-in-Ek-Duje-Ke-Liye/234855, 13 October 2014 (13 July 2004) and Bharati Dubey, *Happy Times for Sad Endings in Bollywood?*http://timesofindia.indiatimes.com/entertainment/hindi/bollywood/news/Happy-times-for-sad-endings-in-Bollywood/articleshow/20170928.cms, 14 October 2014 (22 May 2013). There is a further level of intertextuality in the choice of where the protagonists of the movie live – Dona Paula beach in Goa. The

place is named after Dona Paula de Menezes, the daughter of a viceroy, who committed suicide, when her father refused to marry her to a local fisherman, Gaspar Dias, whom she loved.
37 Vijayakar, 25 Years of 'Qayamat Se Qayamat Tak'.
38 Rajiva Verma, 'Shakespeare in Hindi Cinema', in *India's Shakespeare: Translation, Interpretation and Performance*, ed. Poonam Trivedi and Dennis Bartholomeusz (Delhi: Pearson Longman, 2005).
39 Ronan Paterson. 'Additional Dialogue by … Versions of Shakespeare in the World's Multiplexes', *Multicultural Shakespeare: Translation, Appropriation and Performance* 10, no. 25 (2013): 53–69.

Part II
Critical Innovations
Historiography of Silence and Poetics of Rasa

6 The Indian 'Silent' Shakespeare
Recouping an Archive

Amrit Gangar

> Shut your eyes and think of *King Lear*, if possible without calling to mind any of the dialogue. What do you see? Here at any rate is what I see a majestic old man in a long, black robe, with flowing white hair and head, a figure out of Blake's drawings ... wandering through a storm, cursing the heavens, in company with a fool and a lunatic. Presently, the scene shifts and the old man, still cursing, still understanding nothing is holding a dead girl in his arms.
>
> George Orwell[1]

Prologue

Strangely, but silently, Hamlet came to me at three different locations, at three different times, yet his serendipity I still do not find un-haunting! Being physically present deep inside the Kornberg castle in the Danish town of Helsingor, almost two decades ago, was like seeing, as put by Judith Buchanan, 'an excellent dumb discourse.'[2] Helsingor, as we know, has been immortalised as Elsinor in William Shakespeare's play *Hamlet*. The castle is situated on the extreme north-eastern tip of the island of Zelandat, the narrowest point of the Øresund, which interestingly interprets as the 'sound' between Denmark and Sweden.[3] It is unlikely that Shakespeare read Saxo's *Gesta Danorum*, but the story of the Danish prince who avenged his father was read and embellished throughout Europe in the 1500s. Around 1590, the dramatist Thomas Kyd gave the work the character of a revenge drama, which probably inspired Shakespeare to write *The Tragical History of Hamlet: Prince of Denmark* around 1600. And with this Saxo's legendary prince was made immortal. This immortality has even been reflected, time and again, in some of the 'silent', as well as the 'sound' or 'talkie', films that colonial and postcolonial India has produced.

Again in Denmark, at Nordisk Film, the world's oldest and still active studio, memory goes back to its actress, Asta Nielsen, who had impersonated Hamlet in female form in a 1921 German adaptation of this

Shakespeare play. A remarkable film, it more than proved Orwell's view that Shakespeare can be imagined as a puppet show, a mime, a ballet, a series of pictures. Part of the poetry of the play is inherent in the story and the characters, and is independent of its words. Shakespeare's 'voicelessness' was celebrated in as many as 250–300 early 'silent' films the world over.[4] And Indian cinema was not far behind.

More recently, standing at the French magician-silent film-maker Georges Méliès's tomb in Père Lachaise Garden Cemetery, Paris, I could hear the Hamletian memorial murmurs! As far back as 1907, Méliès had turned Shakespeare into a film, as noted by Kenneth S. Rothwell: 'George Melies, the inventor of trick photography, who put flying machines into space and showed people floating on air, performed the title role in a *Hamlet Segment* (1907), as well as a cameo William Shakespeare in *Shakespeare Writing Julius Caesar*(1907)'.[5] These filmic histories of 'silent' Shakespeare are fortunately still extant, inspiring others to retrieve theirs.

Drawing from these memories of mine, my attempt here would be to see whether we could recoup, if not all, at least some, traces of Indian 'silent' Shakespeare, either in the primary source of the film or the paper-based secondary or tertiary sources. Facing all kinds of absences, recouping an archive in India is a massive task, but there are efforts being made, though almost solitarily. Current evidence shows the presence of six silent Shakespeare films made in India: 1927 *Dil Farosh* (*Merchant of Venice*), 1928 *Khoon-e-Nahak* (*Hamlet*), 1928 and 1929 *Kusum Kumari* (*Cymbeline*), 1930 *Meetha Zahar* (*Cymbeline*) and 1930 *Khooni Taj* (*Macbeth*). Though all these films are irrevocably lost, this essay aims to redeem this archive and reconstruct it as far as possible from the time and circumstances that produced the films. It will also present new evidence of an additional, hitherto unknown, earliest silent Indian Shakespeare film: 1923 *Champraj Hado* (*Cymbeline*).

The Indian Silent Film 1913–1934: Swadeshi vis-à-vis Shakespeare

Though the first sound film or talkie, *Alam Ara*, was released in 1931, silent films in India continued to be produced until 1934. According to the most up-to-date and reliable Filmography of Indian Silent Cinema 1912–1934 prepared by the film historian-scholar Virchand Dharamsey, through his decades-long research, India had produced 1,338 silent films, including 1,290 full-length films and 48 short features.[6] Unfortunately barely two percent of these films exist in the National Film Archive of India based in Pune (Maharashtra), in which there is not a single Indian 'silent' Shakespeare!

Dhundiraj Govind (Dadasaheb) Phalke, who in 1913 made *Raja Harishchandra*, the first (silent)feature film in India, had a vision of creating

Indian images on screen which would be able to replace Western images, e.g. the first film he saw in 1910 was *Life of Christ*, and that inspired him to make films on Lord Krishna. This is how he expressed his feelings after watching the film: 'While the life of Christ was rolling fast before my physical eyes I was mentally visualizing the Gods, Shri Krishna, Shri Ramchandra, their Gokul and Ayodhya. I was gripped by a strange spell.'[7] Though the spirit behind Phalke's move was nationalist, he was primarily interested in developing an Indian film industry with Indian finance which would deal with Indian images exclusively. He was encouraged by his 'friends in the nationalist movement.'[8] Lokmanya Tilak's newspaper *Kesari* backed Phalke in every possible way and published reviews and news about him regularly from 1913 on. It hailed his first film as an 'entirely Indian production by Indians'; in other words, for *Kesari*, it was the first *Swadeshi* feature film.[9] In 1920, Suchet Singh directed *Shakuntala*, produced by Oriental Film Co., with lead stars Dorothy Kingdom and Sampson. The film was based on the play *Abhijnanasakuntala* (The Sign of Shakuntala) by Kalidasa (*c*. fifth century AD), widely regarded as the greatest poet and dramatist in the Sanskrit language and often referred to as the 'Shakespeare of India'. Later, this nationalist attitude might partially have led to Indianising Shakespeare on the silent screen in a manner that was found to be appropriate to attract larger audiences.[10]

Though both Western and Indian films were widely exhibited in British India, only certain types of Western films appealed to all classes and communities. Indian filmgoers liked spectacle and the films featuring Douglas Fairbanks, Harold Lloyd and Charlie Chaplin. The most popular film ever shown in India was *The Thief of Baghdad*, with Douglas Fairbanks in an Oriental setting. The taste of the Westernised Indian and the Indian who had some knowledge of English and acquaintance with Western ideas was akin to that of the European and generally the same films, whether social dramas, comedies or thrillers, which were popular in the West were also appreciated by this section of the Indian society. 'But', as the Indian Cinematograph Committee of 1927–1928 notes, 'the bulk of the population insufficiently acquainted with the English language and with Western ideas, enjoyed films with plenty of action, especially comic and adventure films, and found no attraction to social dramas.'[11]

Writer, director and film producer, J.B.H. Wadia, who had seen many silent films released in Bombay, recalled that many American films, including the Western silent comedies of Charlie Chaplin and Harold Lloyd, Fatty Arbuckle, Laurel and Hardy, and Keystone Cops, were shown in Bombay from 1914 onwards.[12] Some of the actors in early Westerns, including William Farnum, William S. Hart (with his wonder horse, Silver), Hoot Gibson and Harry 'Cheyenne' Carey, who continued playing character roles in the talkies for a long time would attract audiences. There were also serials, such as *Lucille Love*, *The Purple Mask*, *The Black Box* and *The Broken Coin*, starring Grace Cunard and Francis Ford, the elder brother of John Ford. Eddie Polo films were quite popular among cine-goers. Pearl White's *Perils of Pauline*, *Exploits of Elaine* and *The Iron Claw*, and the films starring Douglas Fairbanks, such as *The Mark of Zorro*, *The Black Pirate*, *The Thief of Baghdad*, *The Three* Musketeers and *Robin Hood*, were extremely popular in those days.[13]

Madan Theatres, India's largest film distribution and exhibition chain at that time, imported and exhibited a large proportion of American films, with a few British and Continental pictures. They also exhibited and distributed their own Indian productions and a few of the films of other Indian producers. Globe Theatres exhibited and distributed Western films exclusively. They specialised in British films, of which they were the largest importers. They also imported a large number of American films.

Shakespeare's Indianisation

As late as 1928, almost at the time when the silent film was about to speak and sing aloud, India had an extremely poor ranking in the number of cinema houses in the British Empire, as shown in Table 6.1.

Along with such dismal viewing paucity, there was widespread illiteracy, which meant that a large section of Indian audiences could not read intertitles on screen. In this situation, theatre was the major means of popular entertainment, and enterprising Parsi theatre owners took the opportunity of staging plays, creating a demand for more play texts, and Shakespeare came in handy. As many accounts mention, Parsi theatre blended realism and fantasy, music and dance, narrative and spectacle, earthy dialogue

Table 6.1 World's Distribution of Cinemas[a]

The distribution of picture theatres in the British Empire as compared with the U.S. is given as follows:

	Population	*No. of theatres*	*No. of persons per theatres*
Unites States	117,000,000	20,500	5,756
Great Britain and Ireland	47,000,000	3,760	12,500
Canada	9,000,000	1,000	90,000
Australia	9,800,000	1,500	4,633
India	**320,000,000**	**320**	**1,000,000**
South Africa	*60,000,000*	*150*	*400,000*

[Emphasis added.]
a The Report of the Indian Cinematograph Committee, 1927–1928, Volume 1.

and the ingenuity of stage presentation, integrating them into a dramatic discourse of melodrama. The Parsi plays also contained crude humour, melodious songs, music, sensationalism and dazzling stagecraft.

Ingenuous, Indigenous Translation

According to Sisir Kumar Das,

> the Parsi theatre followed a method of "translation" of its own. It was not the poetry of Shakespeare or the psychological conflicts that interested the Parsi theatre, which was keen to appropriate the story with its emotional turbulence and violence of action.[14]

Das tells us of the commonness of hearing Portia sing Indian songs, of the transformation of *Lear* into a comedy and the fusion of *King John* and *Richard III* into a single play. We also know of a *Hamlet* in which 'the Prince of Denmark is so thoroughly Indianized that his court is converted into a medieval Indian one where princesses performed *Kathak* dance around him.'[15] Considering such theatrical origins, what would these early Indian Shakespeare silent films have looked like? Such speculations would loom large on our research landscape.

Talking about the tastes of the popular audience at that time, theatre historian Somnath Gupt mentions that it was often impossible to perform a complete drama, be it a tragedy or a comedy. For this reason, perhaps, Shakespeare was not very popular. Only portions selected from his dramas were performed. To link the different scenes in a sequence, farces, music and other entertaining fare were inevitably added. The audiences liked them and preferred action and gesticulation to speechifying. They actually enjoyed an abundance of songs, exciting dancing and clowning. No matter whether the plot was well structured, the characterisation interesting or the stage design appropriate, the audiences wanted spectacle, demanding supernatural scenes and an element of romance, even in serious plays.[16] Interestingly, among a dozen hit dramas of the time that he lists, there is not a single Shakespeare.

Parsi theatre, however, did adapt about twenty-five Shakespeare plays in varying degrees of Indianisation.[17] The silent Shakespeare films, in the West too, were indebted to theatrical conventions of the time. Hence, an eyewitness account of the Parsi Shakespearean stage adaptations is particularly significant.

Khoon-e-Nahak and *Hamlet*

Writer Mulk Raj Anand (1905–2004), who had the privilege of seeing a performance of *Khoon-e-Nahak*, an adaptation of *Hamlet*, on stage, thinks that these plays were almost directly transferred to 'commercial films'. He adds, 'The professional drama in Bengali and the Madan Theatre's Hindustani plays, were to become the main inspiration for the cinema of the silent era'. He cites the specific example of the thespian Prithviraj Kapoor, who came into recognition through the Baliwalla Theatre in Calcutta: 'his entry into the film world of Bombay was almost a direct transformation, from the spoken theatre to the silent areas of celluloid.'[18] I think Anand's observations help us comprehend India's 'silent' (and early 'sound') film adaptations of Shakespeare better, particularly in the absence of the primary source – the film itself!

According to Anand, 'Agha Hashr being an Indian could not hold up the action too long and the members began to follow the 'doing away of Polonius with a rapier thrust. Soon Hamlet-Jehangir did away with Rosencrantz and Guildenstern and before long Ophelia drowned herself in the water. The turn of the Queen and King was not long in coming. Later I thought over this adaptation and have felt that Agha Hashr wanted to hold the audience throughout – the murder after murder had to follow, though for the sake of decency, the Indian author did something other than Shakespeare – the murder was shown half on the stage and half off stage.'[19]

Though Anand's description helps us understand the way Shakespearean play was adapted and staged, a correction needs to be made here that it was not Agha Hashr who adapted the *Hamlet* in question; it was, in fact, Hashr's contemporary Mehdi Hasan 'Ahsan'. Hashr was a prolific writer and had adapted the most number of Shakespeare plays for the Parsi theatres, being contracted to the Alfred Theatre in Bombay (1901–1905) and then (after 1916) to the Madan Theatres' Elphinstone and Corinthian companies in Calcutta and wielded considerable influence at the time. And as Dharamsey's Filmography clarifies, Madan Theatre did not produce the film *Khoon-e-Nahak*, the 1928 film; it was produced by Excelsior Film Co. and directed by K.B. Athavale. 7,353 feet in length, the non-extant Indian silent *Hamlet* was shot by the cameraman, Ambadas Pawar. Its lead players included K.C. Roy, Salvi, Yakbal and Rampiyari.[20] It was longer than the other known silent *Hamlets*: than Maurice by 3 minutes, Melies by 5 minutes, Hepworth by 59 minutes, and Rodolfi by 40 minutes.

The next *Hamlet* film, *Khoon-ka-Khoon* (Blood for Blood), a talkie which came soon after, in 1935, by Sohrab Modi was also very much a 'stage film' based on his long-running play of the same title. As Rajiva Verma mentions, among the tragedies, *Hamlet* has been 'the most popular, with as many as three screen versions, all of them in the Parsi theatre tradition'. The third was Kishore Sahu's *Hamlet* (1954).[21] And now we can add two more films to the list, viz. a Malayalam adaptation of *Hamlet* as *Karmayogi* (2012), directed by V.K. Prakash and Vishal Bhardwaj's Hindi film *Haider* (2014).

A revealing footnote to the popularity of *Hamlet* in colonial India and during the silent film era is to be found in the February 1904 issue of the *Hindi Punch* (previously *The Parsee Punch*), a popular cartoon journal, which had published a political cartoon with the caption *Hamlet at the Vice-regal Theatre, Calcutta* and the text 'The crime is out of joint: O! cursed spite,/That ever I was born to set it right!' Hamlet here is Lord Curzon, the British Viceroy in India, standing in front of rolls of papers with inscriptions such as 'Tibet Mission', 'Partition of Bengal', 'Universities Bill' and other knotty issues of the time. In a dilemma, he is panicking. As the cartoon pinpoints, Curzon had been subjected to a mass of adverse criticism at the hands of the press and the public.[22]

Indian Silent Cinema: *Cymbeline*, More Popular than *Hamlet*

However, from the available data *Cymbeline* seems to be more popular among production companies during the silent era. Out of seven silent films that we locate as Shakespearean, three had directly or loosely adapted *Cymbeline* and the earliest one, as the latest research by Dharamsey shows, was the 1923 *Champraj Hado*. This is a significant development as at this juncture of our study, *Champraj Hado* becomes the first Indian silent film that was influenced by a Shakespeare play. Let me briefly discuss these Indian 'silent' *Cymbelines*.

Champraj Hado and *Cymbeline*

The original play *Champraj Hado and Sona Rani* was written by Vaghji Asharam Oza, and he had staged it on behalf of the Sri Arya Subodh Natak Mandali (1878–1924), later renamed twice as Morbi Arya Subodh Natak Mandali and Navi Arya Subodh Natak Mandali. It was a pioneering Gujarati repertory in Morbi town of Rajkot district in the erstwhile Kathiawar. Established by Vaghji Asharam Oza and Moolji Asharam Oza, it had received the royal support from the Prince of Morbi State and Maharaja Sayajirao Gaekwad of Baroda. Eventually this theatre company closed down in 1924, living a fairly long life. Vaghji Asharam Oza knew the English language (he was also a teacher to the Prince of Morbi), and as such he was familiar with Shakespearean works in original English unlike many other Urdu/Hindi playwrights who had no direct contact with the English texts. The play *Champraj Hado* was staged in 1884 for the first time.

The 1923 'silent' film *Champraj Hado* was produced by Star Film Company and directed by Nanubhai Desai; it credits Vinod Kant as its storywriter. The Shakespearean inspiration through the play's Mughal settings is interesting. It has the Emperor Akbar's court and deals with Hada Rajpur of Bundi Kota and weaves a story about chastity and fidelity of a woman. As Dharamsey narrated to me the story traced through his research, Champraj (Posthumus) comes forward and presents the story of his virtuous wife Sona Rani (Imogen) when a courtier Sherbek (Iachimo) challenges him. The story, through its labyrinthine way, finally proves Sona Rani's innocence, and consequently Akbar adopts her as his daughter.

What is interesting here is the way in which Indian playwrights and 'silent' film-makers had Indianised Shakespeare by integrating a Rajput story and a Shakespearean play, no matter how partially. *Champraj Hado*, the play, and the 1923 film, both had retained all the Mughal court characters, whereas the 1932 talkie version of this play has different settings. Known as *Sati Sone* aka *Champraj Hado* aka *Sone Rani*, this 1932 talkie version was produced by Imperial Film Company and directed by Madanrai Vakil. Its story was written by Joseph David who had earlier scripted India's first talkie *Alam Ara* in 1931.

Interestingly, as Dharamsey told me, the playwright Vaghji Asharam Oza had taken the basic story of Sona Rani from Col. James Tod's *Annals and Antiquities of Rajasthan*, first published in 1829. Finding a resonance with the Shakespearean character of Imogen (*Cymbeline*), Oza then developed a plot that integrated the Mughal-Rajasthani story with Shakespeare's *Cymbeline* for his play. Such hybridity was quite common in the Indian plays adapting Shakespeare. *Champraj Hado*, the silent film (6,527 feet), was shot by the cameraman V.B. Joshi, and its lead players were Tara, Jilloo, Asooji, Elizer and Madanrai Vakil.[23] The 1932 talkie version changes the Mughal court scenario to the Rajput, still retaining the Shakespearean connection.

The Case of *Kusum Kumari* and *Cymbeline*

Besides the better-known *Khoon-e-Nahak*, another 'silent' Indian Shakespearean adaptation of interest is the film *Kusum Kumari* released twice with the same name in 1928 and 1929. Though no clear Shakespearean connection is established in the published Indian Filmographies, going by the traditional stage-screen symbiosis in the early phases of Indian cinema, these silent films could have a possible connection with the play *Kusum Kumari* which had been adapted from Shakespeare's *Cymbeline*.[24] Dharamsey's Filmography gives us some basic information: produced by Little Film Company, this *Kusum Kumari* (1928) was 6,451 feet long and was directed by Saki, having Elizer and the director himself as lead players.

The same title again appears in 1929, bearing no more information except its production company – Madan Theatres Ltd. In length, it was much shorter (3,710 feet) than its previous namesake. More interestingly, Greg Colon Semenza mentions a 1930 version of Indian silent film *Cymbeline*. He writes, 'India's creation of Shakespeare's films in the late 1920s and early 30s was the beginning of Shakespeare's increasing filmic presence outside the West: in addition to the 1927 *Merchant* and the 1928 silent *Hamlet*, India produced a 1930 silent *Cymbeline*, a 1932 silent (sic)*The Taming of the Shrew*, and a 1936 *King John* talkie of all things.'[25]

Cymbeline had been popular on stage; the production of an adaptation, *Kusum Kumari*, by Chandrakali Ghosh, is known to have been performed at the National Theatre, Kolkata, in 1874. It was also adapted to a Parsi theatre under the title *Meetha Zahar* (Sweet Poison) in 1900, which was much later turned into a silent film of the same name in 1930 by Sharda Film Co. Directed by A.P. Kapur, its story was written by M.R. Kapoor, and the film was shot by A.D. Pawar. Its lead cast included Nandram, Heera, Promoth Bose and Miss Salu.[26] Dharamsey's Filmography includes *Mitha Jahar* aka *She Wolf* in the year 1930 and clearly mentions that it was 'based on Shakespeare's *Cymbeline*'. Originally adapted by Narayan Prasad 'Betab', it was one of the most popular plays staged by the Parsi Theatre Company. While in his college days, A.P. Kapur, the director of the silent film, was actively involved in amateur dramatic activities.

Dil Farosh and *The Merchant of Venice*

Excelsior Film Co. also produced the 8,062-feet-long Indian silent film *Dil Farosh* (1927). Its scenario writer Gopalji Delwadakar is credited to have adapted it from Shakespeare's *The Merchant of Venice*.[27] Delwadakar, who had written several film stories earlier, was a popular Gujarati writer. The film's executive director Manilal Joshi entrusted its direction to M. Udwadia, and it was shot by D.D. Dabke. It had M. Udwadia, K.B. Athavale, Nargis and Saiyed Umer as lead players. Adapted freely from a Parsi stage play which was the original adaptation of *The Merchant of Venice* by Mehdi Hasan 'Ahsan' (1900), *Dil Farosh* has been considered to be the earliest and the most direct Indian filmic adaptation of a Shakespearean play in India. It was the most popular play staged by the New Alfred Co. which had Sorabji Ogra as Shylock. When staged at the Grant Road Theatre in Bombay an illusion of Venice was created, and the heroine was shown sailing in a boat.[28] This silent film too has been regretably lost. With the success of this film, Excelsior Film Co. produced *Khoon-e-Nahak* directed by K.B. Athavale (actor in *Dil Farosh*). Also called *Merchant of Hearts* after the Parsi theatre adaptation where the title *Dil Farosh* means 'stealer /seller of hearts'.

The Merchant of Venice was undoubtedly the most popular of all Shakespeare comedies in most Indian languages, but as Sisir Kumar Das maintains, it always lacked complete Indianisation: while 'Shylock has been, more or less, easily replaced by Indian money-lenders,'[29] it was not easy to find acceptable equivalents for the Christian-Jew antagonism.

However, going by what Sisir Kumar Das says, I would conjecture that the film, *Savkari Pash*, also called *Indian Shylock* (1925) to have been indirectly influenced by Shakespeare's Shylock of the *Merchant of Venice*. Directed by Baburao Painter for the Kolhapur-based Maharashtra Film Company, it was based on a novel, *Savkari Haak* (*The Call of the Sahukar*) by Narayan Hari Apte (1889–1971).

Much later, but still while the Indian sound film was in its first decade, J.J. Madan adapted *The Merchant of Venice* into *Zalim Saudagar* (aka *Merchant of Venice*), produced by the Calcutta-based Radha Film Company, in 1941. Pandit Bhushan wrote its screenplay.

Bhool Bhulaiyan, The Twelfth Night or The Comedy of Errors

In 1896, Ahsan is said to have adapted *Twelfth Night* into a play called *Bhool Bhulaiyan* (*Labyrinth*)which had run continuously for three years in Bombay.[30] Just after India's first sound film *Alam Ara* (1931) but still during its silent era that lasted until 1934 a talkie film *Bhool Bhulaiyan*, produced by Ranjit Film Company and directed by Jayant Desai was released in 1933, and was attributed to be an adaptation of Shakespeare's *The Comedy of Errors*; it was also known as *Comedy of Errors* and *Hanste Rehna* (*Laugh all the Way*).[31] Its lead players were Keki Adajania, Kamala, Shanta Kumari and Ghory, among others. Earlier on we find reference to the silent 1929 *Bhul Bhulaiya* directed by Vithaldas Panchotia produced by Sharda Film Company, in which Panchotia himself had played the lead role. This 2,933-feet-long film could have been inspired by a Shakespeare![32]

The earliest version of *Twelfth Night* that I had the opportunity to see was an American one of 1910. Produced by Vitagraph Company of America and directed by Charles Kent, it had four characters – Viola (Florence Turner), Malvolio (Charles Kent), Olivia (Julia Swayne Gordon) and Orsino (Tefft Johnson). Lasting over thirteen minutes, it is an ambitious film, considering when it was shot, including scenes of the ocean, and other exterior natural phenomena. It begins with an intertitle describing Viola's separation from her twin brother Sebastian and how she dresses herself as a boy. Shakespeare's comedy of shipwreck and lovesickness, mistaken identity and punctured pride, losing and finding, thematically has commonalities with *The Comedy of Errors*. This makes us wonder whether Jayant Desai's film *Bhool Bhulaiyan* (1933) was really an adaptation of *The Comedy of Errors* instead of *Twelfth Night*?

Abdul Alim Nami mentions that *Bhul Bhulaiyan*, composed by Ahsan, was based 'on the plot of Shakespeare's *The Comedy of Errors* as told to him by Sohrabji Ogra in 1901'. But Somnath Gupt disagrees: 'That play of Shakespeare', he says, 'hinges on the identical appearance of two brothers, whereas in *Bhul Bhulaiyan* it is brother and sister who are said to be identical. The error that occurs is on account of the brother-sister similarity, not that of two brothers. Thus Ahsan's play is not based on *The Comedy of Errors* but upon *Twelfth Night*, in which the similarity of a brother and sister is the source of the entire deception.'[33] Gupt also adds that though Ahsan wrote this drama on the basis of a work by Shakespeare, his play was quite different from the original, e.g. Ahsan's characters have Muslim names, and the play is set in a Muslim milieu. The events take place in the Tartar country, departing from Shakespeare. However, the main story resembles Shakespeare's.

Khuni/Khooni Taj and Pandurang Taligeri

Yet another early film that should add to the Indian 'silent' Shakespeare repertoire is *Khooni Taj* aka *All for the Crown* (1930), which was much longer than its predecessors. Produced by United Pictures Syndicate, it was, as Dharamsey's Filmography indicates, 12,542 feet long. Directed and shot by Pandurang Taligeri, this 'silent' adaptation of *Macbeth* had Wamanrao Kulkarni and Gangu in lead roles. Its Marathi title was *Raktacha Rajmukut*. Taligeri also wrote the scenario of the film. As an early filmic adaptation of *Macbeth*, this was a significant film. By 1930, film activity had spread to other parts of the country, including Poona, Punjab and parts of Southern India. B.D. Garga mentions Pandurang Taligeri, who showed his penchant for cinema early on and joined Ardeshir Irani's Star Films:

> In 1923, he formed a film unit, Deccan Pictures Corporation, in association with the famed Marathi playwright Mama Warerkar, who directed their first film, *Poona Raided* (1924). After one more film, *Prabhavati* (1925), Taligeri dissolved the partnership and set up United Pictures at Kirkee near Poona, which produced twenty-four films, many of them based on literary works.[34]

In Maharashtra it was K.P. Khadilkar who was deeply influenced by Shakespeare. Several of his characters, e.g. Anandibai in *Bhaubandki*, patterned after Lady Macbeth, were derived from *Macbeth*, *Hamlet* and *Richard III*.[35]

Epilogue: Recouping an Archive

In this context, one aspect that is to be noted is the unaccustomed length of the Indian silent film which was seen to be required to pull Shakespeare into its narrative fold, even though other silent Shakespeare films which had been made earlier were usually shorter. Dharamsey's 'Filmography', covering 1,338 silent films between 1912 and 1934, didn't show a single film until 1927, a timeline that now precedes to 1923 with *Champraj Hado* entering the Shakespearean Indian silent film canon. But the world's silent cinema had already adapted Shakespeare way back in 1899, almost from the birth of the moving image.

In the absence of the primary source, obviously, it becomes impossible to comment upon the quality of films, their production values and how theatrical they were, etc. Around the time the 'talkie' era had dawned with Imperial Film Company's feature film *Alam Ara* in 1931, there was a general anxiety prevalent about achieving higher standards for Indian films. Even the British, like Syd Lewis, who was connected with Madan Theatres Ltd. for several years when the company was considered almighty in the business, were of the opinion that methods of production in India were slowly and steadily improving. And in this context he refers to some film companies, such as Prabhat, Ranjit, Imperial, Krishna and Surya, including the Madan Theatres Ltd.[36]

Since Shakespeare has a long historical connection with Indian theatre and translations in various Indian languages and the Indian silent film (or even talkie) had been adapting/co-opting plays, there are possibilities of more silent films coming into the canon of silent Shakespeare, like *Champraj Hado*'s entry through Dharamsey's now published work. Towards further recouping the Indian 'Silent' Shakespeare Archive, I think it would be productive to explore and develop what the film scholar Ashish Rajadhyaksha calls the 'Likelihood' paradigm with reference to Virchand Dharamsey's Silent Cinema Filmography. This archive, sans the primary source of the film, would have to await deeper studies into India's literary traditions in different languages that had reproduced a large repertoire of the Shakespeare oeuvre in translations of either performative plays or non-performative texts. This essay is just an attempt towards indicating such a 'recouping'.

Notes

1 George Orwell, 'Lear, Tolstoy and the Fool', in *Shakespeare and the Critics*, ed. A.L. French (Cambridge: Cambridge University Press, 1972), 145–46.
2 Judith Buchanan, *Shakespeare on Silent Film: An Excellent Dumb Discourse* (Cambridge: Cambridge University Press, 2009). The title 'Of excellent dumb discourse' from *The Tempest*: 'I cannot too much muse / Such shapes, such gestures, and such sound, expressing – / Although they want the use of tongue – a kind / Of excellent dumb discourse' (3.3.36–39).
3 The Öresund or Øresund Bridge is a double-track railway and motorway bridge across the Øresund strait between Scania (southernmost Sweden) and Denmark. The bridge runs nearly 8km from the Swedish coast to the artificial island of Peberholm, which lies in the middle of the strait, and the crossing of the strait is completed by a 4km underwater tunnel.
4 Russell Jackson, *Shakespeare and the English-Speaking Cinema* (Oxford: Oxford University Press, 2014), 4.
5 Kenneth S. Rothwell, *A History of Shakespeare on Screen: A Century of Film and Television* (Cambridge: Cambridge University Press, 1999), 4.

6 Virchand Dharamsey, 'Filmography', in *Light of Asia: Indian Silent Cinema 1912–1934*, ed. Suresh Chabria (Delhi: Niyogi Books, 2013), 137–332.
7 Article by Phalke in *Navyug* (Bombay) November 1917 reproduced in *Phalke Centenary Souvenir*, The Phalke Centenary Celebrations Committee, 1970, 87–88.
8 Phalke Centenary Souvenir, 84–86.
9 Ibid.
10 *The Week*, Special Issue Shakespeare 400, November 2015.
11 The Report of the Indian Cinematograph Committee, 1927–1928, Volume 1, p. 117. The ICC, which was appointed to counteract American imports with censorship regulations, published its five-volume report in 1928. It refused to give British films preferential treatment and recommended a series of measures such as financial incentives to producers, the abolition of raw stock duty and the reduction of entertainment tax. The British administration ignored the report.
12 B.D. Garga, interview with J.B.H. Wadia, *Silent Cinema in India: A Pictorial Journey* (Noida: Harper Collins, 2012), 89–94.
13 Ibid.
14 Sisir Kumar Das, 'Shakespeare in Indian Languages', in *India's Shakespeare: Translation, Interpretation and Performance*, ed. Poonam Trivedi and Dennis Bartholomeusz (New Delhi: Pearson Longman, 2005), 50.
15 Ibid., 50.
16 Somnath Gupt, *The Parsi Theatre: Its Origins and Development*, trans. and ed. Kathryn Hansen (Calcutta: Seagull Books, 2005), 20.
17 Estimated by Poonam Trivedi, 'Parsi Shakespeare', *Rang Prasang* (13) January–March 2004.
18 Mulk Raj Anand, 'Performing Arts at the Turn of the Century', *Cinema Vision India, The Silent Era*, Vol.1:1, Mumbai (January 1980), 9.
19 Ibid., 9.
20 Dharamsey, 'Filmography', in *Light of Asia: Indian Silent Cinema 1912–1934*, 216. 1000 feet of 35mm film is about 11 minutes of running time; 24 frames per second. 1000 feet of 16mm film will run for about 27 minutes. But those days, I believe, 16mm film stock had not yet been introduced.
21 Rajiva Verma, 'Shakespeare in Hindi Cinema', in *India's Shakespeare: Translation, Interpretation and Performance*, ed. Poonam Trivedi and Dennis Bartholomeusz (New Delhi: Pearson Longman, 2005), 244.
22 *The Parsee Punch*, like the *London Punch*, contained 20–36 pages of comic illustrations. The weekly's name was later changed to *Hindi Punch* for a more pan-Indian identity and continued to be published until 1930.
23 Dharamsey, 'Filmography', in *Light of Asia: Indian Silent Cinema 1912–1934*, 158, and my personal discussion with him.
24 These filmographies mainly include B.V. Dharap's unpublished, *Silent Filmography*, National Film Archive of India; Firoze Rangoonwalla, *Indian Filmography: Silent and Hindi Films*, 1970, and B. Jha, *Indian Motion Picture Almanac*, 1986.
25 Greg Colon Semenza, 'The Globalist Dimensions of Silent Shakespeare Cinema', *Journal of Narrative Theory* 41, no. 3 (Fall 2011): Eastern Michigan University, 325.
26 Dharamsey, 'Filmography', *Light of Asia: Indian Silent Cinema 1912–1934*, 261. Filmography spells it as *Mitha Jahar*.
27 Ibid., 201.
28 Gopal Shastri, *Parsee Rangbhoomi (Parsee Stage)* (Mumbai: Published by the author, 1995, in Gujarati). In one of his appendices, Shastri provides

lyrics of a song from *Dil Farosh*, the play: *'Dil-e-nadaan ko hum samjane jayenge'* (*I will try to persuade the naïve heart*), 258.
29 Sisir Kumar Das, 'Shakespeare in Indian Languages', *India's Shakespeare: Translation, Interpretation and Performance*, 51.
30 Gopal Shastri, *Parsee Rangbhoomi*, 74.
31 *Encyclopedia of Indian Cinema*, ed. Ashish Rajadhyaksha and Paul Willemen (New Delhi: Oxford University Press, 1999), 584.
32 Dharamsey, 'Filmography', in *Light of Asia: Indian Silent Cinema 1912–1934*, 229.
33 Somnath Gupt, *The Parsi Theatre: The Origins and Development*, trans. and ed. Kathryn Hansen (Kolkata: Seagull, 2005), 87.
34 B.D. Garga, *Silent Cinema in India: A Pictorial Journey*, 165.
35 Ibid., 3.
36 'British Films in India: Interview with Syd Lewis', *Ruparekha*, Puja Issue, 1934, in *Indian Cinema: Contemporary Perceptions from the Thirties, A Celluloid Chapter* (Jamshedpur: Documentation, 1993).

7 Shakespeare, Cinema and Indian Poetics
Anil Zankar

The field of film studies has expanded a lot since the early days of cinema. Until the 1960s critical writing pertained mostly to film theories that explored the medium from within. Vachel Lindsay, Erwin Panofsky, Rudolf Arnheim, Hugo Munsterberg, Andre Bazin, Bela Balazs, Lev Kuleshov, Sergei Eisenstein, Vsevolod Pudovkin, Dziga Vertov and Siegfried Kracauer were the prominent theorists who attempted comprehensive theories of cinema from their own perspectives. The critical models to analyse cinema were mostly informed by the various concepts contained in the works of these theorists. In the 1970s, a new practice of critical study of cinema emerged, wherein the concepts from the other arts and human sciences began to be applied to cinema. The growth of cinema, reflected in the diversity of cultural expression and the wide accessibility of films through the international festivals and other means, such as the art-house cinema theatres, also encouraged this practice.

The ancient Indian concept of *Rasa-s*, articulated by Bharata in his *Natyashastra*, is a comprehensive theory in itself. There has been a sustained interest in critical writing in the various aspects of this theory but mostly in the field of drama and literature. To me, this theory, when applied to cinema, can yield insights into the process of adaptation (scriptwriting) and dramaturgy (mise en scène). Shakespeare provides very rich and complex texts for the film-makers to adapt and for the critics to probe the adaptation process by using the concept of *rasa-s*.

I

Rasa siddhanta *(The Theory of* Rasa-s*):* Rasa *as an aesthetic object*[1]

Rasa siddhanta (the theory of *rasa-s*), articulated by sage Bharata in *Natyashastra* (a treatise on theatre between 200 BCE and CE 200), is an important contribution of ancient India to aesthetic theory. *Rasa* literally means juice. It is associated with *charvana* (chewing), i.e. an enriched state produced after testing the *rasa-s*. Though initially elaborated in the

Natyashastra, the concept of *rasa* was later adapted in *Sahityashastra* (Indian Poetics).

Rasa exists potentially in the text (*Kavyartha*) but is manifested during the performance of a drama (*Natyartha*), leading to an aesthetic experience. Nine *rasa-s* have been identified as the most universal in nature and are described accordingly. Further, some emotions which are held to be permanent are identified with each *rasa* specifically. These can be shown as follows:

Rasa	Sthayibhava (Permanent emotions)
Shringara	Love
Veera	Valour/fervour
Bibhatsa	Disgust
Raudra	Anger/cruelty
Hasya	Laughter
Adbhuta	Wonder
Karuna	Pathos
Bhayanaka	Fear
Shanta	Repose, tranquillity

Out of these *Shringara, Veera, Raudra* and *Bhayanaka* are considered to be the principal *rasas*, and *Hasya, Adbhuta, Karuna* and *Bibhatsa* are considered to be subsidiary (*Anuchara*) *rasa-s*. The *rasa-s* are perceived to exist in dynamic relationship to each other. *Hasya* is considered to be obverse of *Shringara, Adbhuta* of *Veera, Karuna* of *Raudra* and *Bibhatsa* of *Bhayanaka*. *Shanta* is repose and the attainment of tranquillity.

The emotions and feelings associated with *rasa-s* are considered to be means to evoke a particular *rasa* and are not synonymous with the experience of *rasa*. Thus, the *rasa-s* are clearly distinguished from emotions, feelings and sentiments. Therefore, *rasa* is neither to be understood in psychological terms, nor is *rasa* epistemic in nature since it is not inferred but directly experienced. In this sense *rasa-s* are a unique category. They are not ideal types and have no classificatory role in defining or explaining human nature. *Rasa-s* are those in the absence of which we will not be in a position to explain the nature of human beings, in whichever condition they live.

Rasa *as a Transcendental State*

According to Bharata, *Natyashastra* is a *kriyakalpa*, i.e. a text primarily concerned with the technique and embodiment of a stage performance. It is mostly instructive in nature. Abhinavagupta (CE 950) made an epochal contribution by composing *Abhinavabharati*, which is an extensive commentary on the text of *Natyashastra*. Abhinavagupta not only clarified many issues that had been debated since Bharata's time, but he added more dimensions to *rasa siddhanta*. He looks at *rasa* as an aesthetic object from the viewpoint of the spectator and explains the process of the attainment of *rasa-s*. He also defines a *Rasika* (meaning a qualified spectator) as someone who is capable of savouring *rasa* from a work of art. A *Rasika* has a capacity to ruminate over the experience, and thus he finds his self in a pure form. Abhinavagupta calls this person a *Sahrudaya* (compassionate). A *Sahrudaya* is one who has (a) an inborn taste for literature/arts, (b) a capacity to identify himself with the situation at the imaginative level, (c) a capacity to visualise and identify with the focus of the situation and (d) a contemplative habit. Thus, Abhinavagupta places the onus of the attainment of *rasa-s* on the spectator.

The Dramaturgy Involved in Creating Rasa-s

Natya (drama) is manifested through the performance of the actors and is witnessed by the audience as an integrated experience. If the drama fails to invoke *rasa-s*, then it is of no significance. Creation of *rasa* is a fairly elaborate process involving many factors. The process can be paraphrased in terms of its constituent factors as follows.

Drama expresses *Lokadharma* (the social nature of the experience) through the presentation of *Pravruttis* and *Vruttis*. *Pravruttis* are the significant details of costumes, language, behaviour and customs; hence they are social in nature. *Vruttis* are mental and physical processes, and therefore, they are individual. Drama presents the *Lokadharma* through *Natyadharma* (techniques of theatrical language).

Natyadharma is expressed through *Abhinaya* (acting), which consists of speech, physique, costumes, properties and a concentrated mind. However, acting alone will not be sufficient. It has to be supported by credible situations with a human focus (*Vibhava*); the physical changes brought about by emotions (*Anubhava*); and the expression of transient emotions, such as suspicion and annoyance (*Vyabhicharibhava*).

These constituents are not the products of nature but creations of art that reproduce poetic vision. *Vibhava* stands for the dramatic situation, which is not the cause but only the medium through which an emotion arises in an actor. *Vibhava* has two aspects: (i) *Alambana*, the object primarily responsible for the arousal of the emotion, and (ii) *Uddipana*, the environment and the spatio-temporal factors. *Anubhava* are all the physical changes that are brought about due to the rise of emotion and seen in the performance. *Bhava* is used in the sense of mental state. *Bhava* has two aspects: *Vyabhicharibhava* are transient emotions, and *Sthayibhava* are permanent emotions. The creation and persistence of permanent emotions (*Sthayibhava*) leads to *rasa*.

II

This process of realisation of a dramatic act in *Natyashastra* would probably be the world's first codified articulation of a mise en scène in theatre. This is also the point at which *rasa* theory can invite comparison between itself and the theory and practice of mise en scène in cinema that was developed in the twentieth century. The concept of mise en scène in theatre, as it emerged in Europe and America, was a historical development in the nineteenth century. It was related to the emergence of the theatre directors after the era of actor-managers. It denoted the arrangement of actors on stage. It was not synonymous with staging, i.e. the whole process of theatrical production, but simply meant the positioning and movement of actors within the space created by sets. Taking this as the starting point, Sergei Mikhailovich Eisenstein propounded the theory and practice of mise en scène in cinema extensively. In cinema the concept was amplified by Eisenstein to mean not only the staging but the total design of scene in terms of acting, cinematography, sound, setting and possibilities of editing. In his scheme the stress is on planning the scene in its entirety as if in an empty space and then designing it in the language of cinema in terms of individual shots. Through an analysis of the various factors employed in creating a scene, he lays down a directorial method. In *Natyashastra* too, the essential components are analysed and discussed as a part of the harmonious whole. But the discussion is focussed on the patterns of human behaviour: the emergence of feelings and their orchestration leading up to a dramatic structure. Thus, it is process centric and not method centric.

In the background of this brief overview I wish to analyse the opening scenes of Shakespeare's *Macbeth*, Vishal Bhardwaj's film *Maqbool* (an adaptation of *Macbeth* in Hindi, 2004) and Akira Kurosawa's film *The Throne of Blood* (Japanese, 1957) using the concepts of dramaturgy from the *Natyashastra*. I also want to illustrate how these concepts are realised through mise en scène in cinema.

The Scenes in Macbeth

The prelude with three witches sets the tone of the narrative and is prescient. The witches speak in riddles: 'when the hurly burly is done, when the battle is lost and won; where fair is foul and foul is fair and hover through fog and filthy air'. They announce that they are heading to meet Macbeth at the blasted heath. This is the beginning of *Alambana* as it creates a focus on Macbeth, the character who will generate feelings. The next scene at a camp at Forres, wherein upon listening to the valorous tale of Macbeth defeating the rebels in a battle, the King (Duncan) confers on him the title of Thane of Cawdor. These scenes sustain and build the interest in Macbeth, although he is yet to appear in person, and in the next scene the witches reappear to meet Macbeth and Banquo at the blasted heath.

These scenes contain harsh elements of nature and the grotesque imagery of killing swine and cutting off the pilot's thumb. Macbeth's first line as he enters the scene is 'So foul and fair a day I have not seen'. Through these dramatic devices, the disquieting spatio-temporality is established. This is *Uddipana*. At that point, Ross and Angus enter to confirm the first part of the witches' prophecies, leaving Macbeth and Banquo elated, suspicious and bewildered, and with these dominant transient emotions (*Vyabhicharibhava*) they head to meet Duncan.

The vision of the witches corresponds to *Bibhatsa (disgust)*, and their action or what they hint at corresponds to *Raudra (anger)*. The vision of Macbeth and Banquo is of the brave warriors confronting the evil boldly (*Veera/valour*), and it changes to them acting bewildered due to the fantastical prophesies (*Adbhuta/wonder*).However, Shakespeare chooses to plant the seed of suspicious fear in Macbeth at this stage. The same grows embryonically within him until he is settled in his mind at the end of the first act, when he resolves to remove Duncan from this world. Macbeth is poised for a major transition, and after denuding the self of the noble qualities, he can no longer be considered brave; hence *Veera rasa* will not be associated with him anymore in the play.

The Opening Scene of Maqbool

Vishal Bhardwaj's opening scene is dominated by the two corrupt policemen Pandit and Purohit, who are his version of the evil witches. They execute a young criminal with sadistic delight on the stroke of midnight after toying with him.

This sequence (*Vibhava*) begins with a graphic visual of the *kundali* (Indian horoscope that is composed of geometrical forms and is striking in appearance) being drawn on a vaporous windshield by a finger. The dialogues about their own evil deeds introduce *Pandit* and *Purohit* as the corrupt cops and sadists, who revel in vulgarity. Once the *kundali* of Mumbai is drawn, Pandit announces that the future crime lord of the city will be Maqbool. And immediately we see a close-up in black and white of Maqbool wearing a white cap, praying with his eyes closed. This image is followed by the title of the film in red colour (Maqbool). Thus the focus is established on the other main character. His boss Abbaji has already been referred to in the dialogue earlier (*Alambana*– creating a focus and interest in a situation and a character/s).

The drama is created on a rainy night in the closed confines of a police patrol vehicle. The scene is shot entirely from within the van. The midnight hour, rain, vapour, the anonymity of a city, the dimly lit interior in which we see the characters semi-silhouetted do create a claustrophobic and cavernous atmosphere (*Uddipana*– establishing the spatio-temporality). The perverse delight the cops take in their evil acts definitely makes their vision *Bibhatsa*. Fear is also touched upon through the pleadings of the victim as he begs for mercy and feels the naked fear. These are the *Vyabhichari bhava*. All of these lead to the premeditated and cold-blooded murder. The shot that depicts murder is a close-up of the same *kundali* with red blood spattered over it and creates a strong and lingering image of the cruel act (*Raudra*).

The Opening Scene in The Throne of Blood

Kurosawa opens the film with the camera travelling over the hazy images of mountains and fog, while a chorus sings the dirge '*Behold, this desolate spot! Where stood a proud castle*'. No supernatural element appears here; no characters either; instead as the fog clears slightly, graves and a monument to the dead become visible. Kurosawa foreshadows a tragedy through this prologue.

The scene of Washizu (Macbeth) and Miki (Banquo) who are riding through the forest and lose their way amidst rain, thunder and lightning follows. They attribute this to an evil spirit and decide to ride on challenging the evil power with their weapons. Their gallop stops abruptly, when they encounter a bamboo hut with a thatched roof. Inside is an old woman sitting on the ground slowly turning a spinning wheel with one hand. They charge ahead and interrupt her. Unperturbed, she answers their queries about being an evil spirit through her prophecies that astonish them. Then she gets up and vanishes suddenly into thin air, along with the hut.

The *Alambana* begins with the memories of the castle. Then it brings into focus the principal character who will be the lord of the castle along with his peer and friend. Their brave defiance of the evil spirit and hostile conditions of nature that these men face establishes their character. The entire forest environment and miraculous changes within it due to the presence of the supernatural element are the *Uddipana*.

The energy and the bravado of the rider are supplemented by the moving camera, and a dynamic soundtrack consisting of music, natural sounds, incidental sounds and human cries creates the fervour of the *Veera rasa*.

In total contrast is the sequence of their encounter with the old woman. It creates a sudden and dramatic pause in the narrative. The evil spirit's extraordinary appearance, stylised manner of speaking, fantastic revelations and sudden disappearance are magical. This persistent feeling of wonder produces *Adbhuta*.

The first sequence is a dynamic action sequence, while the second one is a dialogue sequence that takes place in the magically quiet surroundings.

The use of contrasting techniques in the mise en scène produces the shift from *Veera* to *Adbhuta*.

III

Scripting (Creating Kavyartha) as the Basis of Creating the Potential of Rasa-s in Adaptation

If mise en scène is the microstructure of a film unfolding from scene to scene on the screen, script is the macrostructure that defines the spatio-temporal order of scenes. Script being the blueprint of the mise en scène assumes critical importance in studying the changes made during adapting a work for the screen.

Although the narratives have become far more complex since the days of *Natyashastra*, the *rasa siddhanta* can help explore the relationship between the original and the adapted work at the script level. Usually in an adaptation, the definition of the characters, cultural and historical context, spatio-temporal form of the narrative and the form of the narrative in another medium get redefined. However, I wish to argue that the thematic references of the principal *rasa-s* of the original work may or may not continue as a lineage in the new work. Scripting becomes a key element here and plays the essential role in defining the emerging film. The configuration of *rasa-s* will, accordingly, be guided by the script. I wish to cite two examples in this context – *Haider* (2014) by Vishal Bhardwaj and *Rashomon* (1950) by Akira Kurosawa.

Fatema Kagalwala says the following about Vishal Bhardwaj's adaptation of *Hamlet* (*Haider*, 2014):

> Based on *Hamlet*, Shakespeare's much revered, intense and moody play, *Haider's* central motif is not the problem of Hamlet's chaotic inner landscape but the "the rotten state of Denmark" (*Hamlet*, 1.4, Marcellus to Horatio). Here the Danish setting has been replaced by the reality of brutalized Kashmir .... Much like Akira Kurosawa's adaptations *Ran* (*King Lear*) and *Throne of Blood* (*Macbeth*) that take place in 15th century Japan, using the then contemporary Noh theatre style, Bhardwaj applies the Indian political landscape, Indian language -- mostly in prose, Kashmiri street theatre elements (in Bismil, the song) a smattering of Bollywood conventions to localise *Hamlet* making it applicable to a contemporary audience. He further puts an original spin by switching from realistic to black comedy to pastiche, and mixing it all up to tell the story of Kashmir. In doing so, he forfeits Hamlet's interiority for dystopian Kashmir, with Haider and his quest becoming a metaphor for Kashmir's dilemma.[2]

The script of *Rashomon* has evolved from two independent stories *Rashomon* (Rasho Gate) and *In A Grove* of the same author (Akutagawa). Kurosawa discards the plot but retains the location of the first story (Rasho Gate) and integrates it into the main plot which derives from the second story (*In A Grove*). In the first story the horrifying and disgusting details of the dead bodies abandoned dominate the story. A discharged servant who has taken shelter beneath the gate decides to be a thief and robs an old woman of the robe she is wearing to keep him warm. He leaves after knocking her down. The story ends there. The story evokes *Raudra*, *Bhayanaka* (*fear*) and *Bibhatsa*. In *In A Grove* a death of a samurai has occurred in a horrific manner. There are many versions of the same event: some by the actual participants and some by the witnesses. None of them tally; hence again there is no closure to this story that evokes *Raudra* and *Bhayanaka*. Kurosawa has discarded the plot of the first one and consequently these *rasa-s* that are associated with that story. He also transforms the location Rasho Gate as a peaceful shelter eliminating the dead bodies and other references.

Donald Richie presents this analysis of Kurosawa by tracing the path his script has taken:

> Kurosawa's most significant addition (beside that of the abandoned baby in the last scenes) is the introduction of the character of the commoner, a cynical yet inquisitive man, whose questions and disbeliefs act as a comment upon all the various versions of the story. The commoner ... in a way acts as a moral or (amoral) chorus. It is through his questions that the film evolves ... Akutagawa is content to question all moral values, all truth; Kurosawa obviously is not. Neither anarchist, nor misanthrope, he insists upon hope, upon the possibility of gratuitous action. Like the priest he cannot believe that men are evil- and, indeed if Kurosawa has a spokesman in the film it is probably the priest: weak, confused but ultimately trusting.[3]

Thus Kurosawa has been able to alter the perspective of the story and is able to lead it to compassion (*Karuna*) through a positive world view of men in contradistinction to Akutagawa. By imposing the viewpoint that each story is only a version of someone he has been able to give positive qualities to each of the three principal characters by turn invoking *Veera* rasa in some parts of the film.

Using the understanding that script is the macro composition of a film and mise en scène (direction) is the micro composition, we can continue the comparison between *Macbeth* and *Maqbool* and add to it Akira Kurosawa's adaptation of *Macbeth*, i.e. *The Throne of Blood* as another example.

Shakespeare's Macbeth – *Characters and Context*

Natyashastra says that plot is the body of a play and an intelligent writer should treat plot in a binary manner. The main plot should alternate with the incidental plots. The main plot is defined as the one that will be strong enough to reach a result and the rest are to be treated as incidental ones.

Shakespeare's plot is linear and mostly stays focussed on Macbeth. In his scheme *Raudra* becomes the defining tendency of Macbeth. *Shringara (love)*, *Hasya (humour)* and *Shanta (peace)* are precluded. *Veera* is alluded to in the beginning but only for a short period. The fantastical prophesies and their impact do bring in *Adbhuta*, but that is overshadowed by *Raudra*. In the acts and images of the witches and later of Macbeth, *Bhayanaka* and *Bibhatsa* find expression. *Raudra* can give rise to *Karuna* (pathos), but since the play is so strongly centred on Macbeth, the plight of the others is seen as the result of his acts. Hence, there is not much identification with the anguish of the vanquished and no space for *Karuna*. This lack of counterbalance in the dramatic structure makes *Raudra* more concentrated. Therefore, Macbeth becomes a larger-than-life figure without any warmth. And through his journey we perceive *Raudra* to be the dominant *rasa* of his narrative overshadowing the other ones.

Maqbool – *Context, Plot, Characters and the* Rasa-s

Vishal Bhardwaj's *Maqbool* is a Mumbai underworld story told in the tradition of Hindi mainstream films. The stereotypes of this kind of a story have been well set by predecessors like *Nayakan* (Mani Ratnam, 1987). Some of these features have been influenced by American gangster films especially *The Godfather* (1972) of Francis Ford Coppola.

Abbaji (Duncan) dominates the film more than Maqbool (Macbeth) does. The crucial thing that precipitates the key act in this drama is the weakness both Abbaji and Maqbool have for Nimmi (Lady Macbeth). Nimmi is Abbaji's wife to begin with, and after his murder she becomes Lady Macbeth. These are the major departures from Shakespeare that redefine the relationship between the three main characters.

Killings in the opening scenes of the film set *Raudra* as the keynote. In the beginning (*Alambana*) Abbaji's absolute power over everyone is established, so any dramatic event that occurs in the story – like the overnight transfer of the police officer– is hardly a surprise. *Shringara* is manifested in the sequences between the lovers – Nimmi and Maqbool and Guddu and Sameera. However, both these subplots remain muted as they are clandestine and overshadowed with the fear of exposure and its consequences. The cops mostly speak in an informal comical language, but that humour is cynical, sadistic and vulgar, and therefore tends towards *Bibhatsa*. When the killings become anticipated, the sense of fear expressed by characters reinforces *Bhayanaka*. Strangely, when Maqbool is cornered and all have turned against him, and as Nimmi deteriorates *Karuna rasa* finds an expression. The end of the film is also somewhat unexpected, given the pattern of the narrative throughout. Maqbool (after Nimmi's death) goes to the hospital to eliminate his young rival, Guddu. But the vision of Guddu and Sameera with the new born has an unexpected effect on him. He looks at them – a picture of a happy family – from a distance through the glass with wistful eyes and perhaps a recognition coming over him that this is what he shall never be. Nimmi is already gone. He acknowledges his loss, his final defeat and walks away abdicating his revolver and walks out of the hospital aimlessly and listlessly. He is an easy kill for Boti, who has been stalking him. When Boti calls him out at close range, he does not respond, does not even turn to face him and just keeps walking ahead. Obviously, he is resigned to his fate. This death scene has a strange gentleness to it, especially in the way he falls to ground in slow motion and finds tranquillity in death. This evocation of *Karuna* leading to *Shanta* is dramatically opposite to the beginning and most parts of the film dominated by *Raudra*.

It is interesting to see the transference of *Raudra* that occurs in the film. Cops set up the keynote much like the witches do in *Macbeth*. Once Abbaji is established and becomes the prime mover of the narrative, his acts and aura sustain the dominant *rasa* (*Raudra*). Then cops and Maqbool and his rivals take over after his death. All the other *rasas* are evoked alternately as described above. Thus despite the major changes affected in the script, the film stays close to the basic keynote of Shakespeare, except at the end.

Pankaj Kapur as Abbaji creates this stodgy personality on the screen. His slow deliberate speech, heaviness of movement, the cruel opacity of his gaze, the mock politeness, the complete lack of tenderness and the icy glares as disapproving reactions are remarkably intense. His performance helps sustain and underline the presence of *Raudra* implicitly, although he seldom explodes into rage or indulges in physical violence. By comparison Maqbool (Irfan Khan) is restless, always drawing upon the support of Nimmi (Tabu). He also gives the impression of being conscious of not being big enough to fit into Abbaji's shoes. Their romantic moments are always overshadowed by it being a clandestine affair in Abbaji's realm. And after Abbaji's killing Maqbool's and Nimmi's lives are under threat. So, *Shringara* always remains muted.

The Throne of Blood – *Context, Plot, Characters and* Rasa-s

Kurosawa's story is set in medieval Japan. He follows the *jidai-geki* (period film) genre in Japanese cinema that creates the historical reality through spectacle. The two most prominent features of Kurosawa's mise en scène are an adoption of Noh theatre style and turning the poetic lines of Shakespeare into flamboyant visuals. The idiom of Noh is very compressed. Noh performers are storytellers who present the essence of the narrative through the use of masks and other visual symbols. The characters are not 'enacted' by the actors in the way they are in the Western theatre.

Kurosawa makes some major changes to the plot. He drastically reduces roles and the presence of the other Lords. Hence, many subplots like the slaying of Macduff's family also get eliminated. The discussion of the state of the land (Scotland in Shakespeare) and the external help (England) is excluded too. Consequently, the narrative gets more densely Washizu [Macbeth]-centred. Lady Asaji (Macbeth) conceives and then has a miscarriage leading to her death in his film. The evil character [Old Woman] is the opposite of the three weird sisters in Macbeth. A witch in the Western sense is incompatible in Japanese tradition; hence her iconography undergoes a change. When asked as to how she can be so sure of the future of the others? She replies, 'You humans are mystifying. You want something and behave as if you don't'. This is Kurosawa's insightful interpretation of Macbeth.

Kurosawa opens and closes the film with the same solemn song, thus reiterating the prologue as the epilogue that conveys a sense of a cyclical closure. Thus he invokes pathos, bracketing the film with *Karuna rasa*.

Kurosawa precludes *Shringara*, *Hasya* and remarkably *Bibhatsa*. He has very strongly evoked *Veera* rasa with Washizu in the beginning. Then, as his character changes and he leans towards deceit and destruction, *Raudra* is manifested. But Kurosawa's evocation of *Raudra* through Washizu is unique. In his moments of tumultuous anger Washizu loses control over himself. Lady Asaji is the opposite. While Washizu remains agitated and unsure of himself, Asaji is always steady and guides him in action. She is the deeper vision of *Raudra*, and acts of Washizu are the manifestation. *Adbhuta* is not limited to the witch's scene only. All the birds suddenly flocking in the night to the castle and the Cobweb forest on the move have the sense of extraordinary happenings. Towards the end when Washizu is feeling isolated and threatened, his acts of riding out to the Cobweb forest to seek the reassurance of the evil spirit are apparently a bravado but really express the felt fear, as do many of his actions in the later part of the film.

But his death scene is remarkable for the transference of *Raudra*. Washizu's death occurs not at the hands of his opponent but of his own soldiers. Washizu is unable to command his army as they have lost respect for him. As he begins raving and ranting, as arrows start flying towards him, fear seizes him, and he moves about like a wounded beast. The death sequence is elaborate, ritualistic and ends on the extreme visual of an arrow piercing his throat. After this horrific *Raudra* image we see him walk agonisingly towards his army and fall down to the ground. His fall to the ground is gentle and watched in silence by his army.

This is followed by the epilogue. The same funeral dirge is heard over the images of fog, and *Karuna* balances *Raudra*. Although Kurosawa does create *Raudra* through Washizu, his realisation of the same is different. He sees all the destructive acts of Washizu as the acts of a person, who is trying to rise to a commanding position but is inadequate. Washizu is definite and brave in the beginning, but when his character shifts his inner weakness begins to drive him. The very formally composed scenes in the castle have a melancholy about them. Thus *Karuna* is subliminally present.

IV

A Variation

What I have presented so far is a focussed study of the adaptations of *Macbeth* by two film-makers from the perspective of *rasa siddhanta*. Before concluding, I want to comment on two more cinematic adaptations of Shakespeare by Roman Polanski (*Macbeth*) and Vishal Bhardwaj (*Haider/Hamlet*) as an extension of my argument.

Polanski follows Shakespeare's text closely in terms of the language, location, time period and the characters in his *Macbeth* (1971).He emphasises the cruelty, the lack of compassion, in characters a great deal. He sees the narrative as the drama of the tyrants and the victims. His characters are intense, merciless and vulgar, and they express these traits in an uninhibited manner. At the end of the scene at the blasted heath, one of the old witches mocks Macbeth and Banquo by lifting her dress to expose her genitals to them before disappearing into the den. The slaying of Macduff's family is shown in detail, every individual being methodically quartered. The final fight between Macbeth and Macduff is similarly gory. It is a prolonged one with long pauses in between ugly falls and recoveries. Instead of being a skilled fight between the warriors, it has been presented as raw fight of survival between two beasts. The climactic visual of Macbeth's head being severed and falling down the steps along with his torso has the imprint of *Raudra*. Similarly his landscapes are bleak, rain soaked and rough. Interestingly towards the end of the film he returns to the location of the blasted heath as if stressing the continuation of the evil. The film is devoid of any compassion (*Karuna*), and *Bibhatsa*, *Bhayanaka* and *Raudra* dominate it.

Vishal Bhardwaj's *Haider* (2014) is his third adaptation of Shakespeare. In this one he follows the principal plot, situations and characters of Shakespeare closely, yet the film emerges more autonomous as compared to his earlier adaptations. He has effected some daring mutations to Shakespeare's characters and locations. *Haider* is not limited to a castle or any such close establishment, but it locates itself in the real, historical and turbulent landscape of Kashmir. Kashmir of the 1990s does not form a mere backdrop to the story; instead *Haider* becomes the story of Kashmir. Also this Kashmir is not the romantic paradise full of sunshine that Hindi films have depicted over the years but a severe, snow-clad landscape in the dead of winter. The Indian army has a dominating presence in this landscape and precipitates action. Haider's (Hamlet's) angst has been externalised and politicised. It leads him to defiance and to seek the truth of his own predicament and also of his community's. Hamlet's motive for vengeance is transformed into a strong quest for personal, sociopolitical truth, changing the perspective of the narrative. It is also a journey to find hope and truth through ambiguities. Thus his link to the collective is contemporary and strong.

We can see this as redefining of *Pravruttis* (the significant details of costumes, language, behaviour and customs; social in nature) and *Vruttis* (mental and physical processes; individual in nature). We can see as to how it changes the character of Hamlet and more aspects of his personality come out in the film.

It can be seen that while recreating their versions of *Macbeth*, both Bhardwaj and Kurosawa tend towards *Karuna* and *Shanta* after depicting violence, but Polanski does not. This leads one to believe that it is the interpretative world view of the scriptwriter/film-maker with respect to the original work that forms the basis of the mutations and consequently the configuration of *rasa-s*. As can be seen from these examples, we are in a position to say that the study of macro and microstructures of a film can be linked to the dynamic operation of the *rasa-s* in cinema. And, in the process, it lends fresh interpretative insights.

Notes

1 Since *Rasa* is to be experienced it is an object of experience. One experiences a particular *rasa* in the sense that the particular *rasa* is an object of one's own experience. It is a special kind of object not to be confused with a material object.
2 Fatema Kagalwala, 'World's his stage,'twas ever thus/ A Bard's Eye View', *Lensight, Quarterly Journal of Film and Media*, Film and Television Institute of India (January–March 2015), 59–60.
3 Donald Richie, *The Films of Akira Kurosawa* (Berkeley: University of California Press, 1998), 71.

Part III

Between the Global and the Local

8 *Such a Long Journey*
Rohinton Mistry's Parsi *King Lear* from Fiction to Film

Preti Taneja

Such a Long Journey (1991)[1] by Rohinton Mistry draws deeply on Shakespeare and particularly on *King Lear* to explore the 'janus faced' psychological dilemma of the male Parsi postcolonial subject, 'looking forward and yearning backward'[2] to a time in India when the British were in charge, 'the Bard' was revered and life was good for a privileged few. Shakespeare's tragedy is a primary organising device for the novel, acting as meta- and intertext, the medium through which Mistry writes a political critique of life in 1970s Bombay.[3] And yet the novel is curiously nostalgic, infected with a diasporic sense of longing, making the Parsi community it focusses on seem preserved in aspic. As Nilufer Bharucha speculates,

> Although Parsis are among the most Westernized group in India, Mistry is likely to have experienced a kind of ancestral diaspora even in India (his Persian ancestors being exiled from Iran), together with the general feeling that the Parsis have become downgraded in the economic upheaval following the retreat of the colonial forces in the 1940s.[4]

Paul Brians calls Sturla Gunnarsson's 2002 cinematic adaptation of *Such a Long Journey* 'beautiful, entertaining and remarkably faithful'[5] and finds that in screenwriter Sooni Taraporevala's script, 'almost every line of dialogue [...] comes directly from Mistry's novel.'[6] However, several important cuts are made: Taraporevala and Gunnarsson expunge almost completely explicit references to Shakespeare and particularly to *King Lear* from their narrative. This chapter examines Mistry's appropriation of Shakespeare as a key site of postcolonial negotiation and contrasts this with the approach taken by Gunnarsson and Taraporevala to this theme. My aim is to understand how an idea of 'India' is created for a global marketplace in two different kinds of artistic media: an intertextual literary work by a writer of the Indian diaspora whose debt to *King Lear* has thus far been underappreciated and a Western art-house film about which there has been a dearth of critical thinking to date, perhaps partly because of its 'silencing' of the Shakespeare *ur*-text. This erasure also means the film has so far gone unlisted in major bibliographies of Shakespeares on screen.[7]

Despite their differences in approach to Shakespeare, I also highlight one major similarity of novel and film. While Shakespeare writes Goneril, Regan and Cordelia a complex, important agency, in Mistry's novel women's lives are absolutely elided, even beyond the misogyny Lear as a character expresses. Taraporevala/Gunnarsson exploit this, visualising a reassuringly backward India in which female sexuality and agency are safely confined. A patriarchal social prudishness met with concern over representing 'India' to the West comes to the fore, fuelled, I suggest, by a strong sense of diasporic nostalgia shared by the author, screenwriter and director.

In critical terms, these choices have been 'successful'. Mistry won a Canadian Governor General's Award for *Such a Long Journey*; the book was also shortlisted for the Man Booker Prize. Gunnarsson is an Oscar-nominated director, and Taraporevala was also writer on Mira Nair's Cannes-nominated, Oscar-winning, *Salaam Bombay!* (1988). The Gunnarsson/Taraporevala adaptation of Mistry's novel was nominated for twelve awards by the Academy of Canadian Cinema and Television, and was distributed internationally, including in key North American and UK territories. The nexus of endorsement around the novel and film could hardly be more gilded; their similarities and differences in approach to Shakespeare (the West's most canonical marker of high culture) are therefore overdue fresh critical attention.

'Diaspora' Film

The idea of 'diaspora film' in relation to Indian stories exercises intricate authority over its audience and critics. The term might be applied to films that focus on the particulars of diaspora lives lived entirely abroad, such as Sangeeta Datta's Bengali-British *King Lear*-inspired *Life Goes On* (2011). It can also be used to refer to English-language films made by Indian diaspora directors that are also set in whole or in part in India and deal with the experiences of transnationalism: for example Nair's *Monsoon Wedding* (2001) or Gurinder Chadha's appropriation of *Grease* (1978) by way of Jane Austen in musical *Bride and Prejudice* (2004). Perhaps the U.S.-set *The Mistress of Spices* (2005), directed by Chadha's husband Paul Mayeda Berges, with a screenplay adapted by Chadha from the novel by diaspora writer Chitra Banerjee Divakaruni, might also have a place in the genre by dint of its author, screenwriter and themes. The term might also be used for work by non-Indian/diaspora directors that is set in India, again dealing with the difficulties of transnationalism: for example Michael Winterbottom's *Trishna* (2011).[8]

Are films made by diaspora directors which are set in India but do not deal directly with diaspora experience (Deepa Mehta's 'Elements' trilogy, *Fire* (1996), *Earth* (1998) and *Water* (2005), for example) to be considered 'diaspora films'? If not, it becomes clear that the thematics of a piece are more important than the director's geographical background (or 'homeland') and/or nationality: Taraporevala and Gunnarsson's *Such a Long Journey* can therefore be classed as a 'diaspora' film. That the word itself describes the dispersion of people commonly belonging to one nation or culture, or the concentration of those people as a minority in a particular locale supports this: much of the film is set in Khodadad Building, an enclave where Bombay's decimated Parsi population huddle as if under siege from the forces of cultural entropy and a future over which they have little control.

Nevertheless biography does seem to infer authority, and the production team behind *The Mistress of Spices* serves as example. Like that film, *Such a Long Journey* is by a diasporic screenwriter and is an adaptation of a diasporic author's novel. Like Mayeda Berges (director of *Mistress*, an American of Japanese and Basque ancestry), Gunnarsson (a Canadian born in Iceland) has strong emotional ties to the Indian diaspora and to India via his wife. As he explains,

> I've travelled often and extensively throughout India, am married into a big Indian family [...] I've lived in India and made a film there [...] and experienced how challenging and, on the face of it, impossible, everything can be there. [...] And despite this, in every photograph I've seen of myself in India, I have a big smile on my face. It's just something about the place, and especially the people, that makes me feel that, in spite of all the obstacles, things are possible.[9]

The author and screenwriter lend this affirmation weight. Mistry was born in Bombay in 1952 and immigrated to Canada in the 1970s. *Such a Long Journey* was written twenty years later as his debut but is set in 1971 in the city he left behind. His cultural and religious identity as a Bombay Parsi lies at the heart of this novel. Taraporevala is also Parsi; she left India to train in New York before returning to Bombay (now Mumbai). As well as writing Parsi characters into film, she has documented their lives in India via her own photography, displayed in galleries and published in books. Both Mistry and Taraporevala articulate a deeply felt personal commitment to bear witness to the fate of their people, whose numbers are inexorably diminishing in India.[10] This sense of connection and 'insider'/'outsider' knowledge encourages an assumption of authority; authenticity; and, importantly, affinity between the film's makers and their intended western diasporic audiences. The very first frames of

146 *Preti Taneja*

Such a Long Journey promote this, offering background 'knowledge' (in a highly stylised idea of a Persian font) to introduce the epic history of the Parsis:

> 1200 years ago, the Persian Empire was conquered by Arabs. Forced to choose between Islam and death, a small band of Persians fled by sea to India. Taking with them their ancient religion of the prophet Zarathustra.
>
> In India they prospered and became known as Parsis. Under British Rule, they prospered and were the architects and administrators of the city of Bombay. This is the story of one Parsi called Gustad Noble. It takes place in Bombay in 1971, twenty-four years after Independence. Indira Gandhi is Prime Minister. India and Pakistan are still in conflict. Now, the issue is Bangladesh.[11]

The film follows the novel's lead to represent 'the dailiness of postcolonial life that is at once bigger and more trivial than we usually credit.'[12] The tone is set for an immersive work successfully aimed at a global audience of receptive non-specialists looking to be moved, entertained, and, as a by-product, educated about Parsis and 'India' by people who can be trusted by dint of their 'diaspora' credentials – offering historical 'truth' based on personal testimony.

The well-documented Parsi history of trade with the British and the 'divide and rule' strategy which marked the community out for a special relationship with the colonisers[13] can be summed up by the Parsi maxim to be 'loyal to the British, friendly to the Indian.'[14] In the film this is evoked through sepia-tinted flashbacks of a Lutyens-style bungalow meant to be Gustad's childhood home. A mysterious Maharani floats through the scene, bizarrely dressed in full wedding lehenga. We hear jazz and see it being played on a sophisticated Western gramophone. The music becomes non-diegetic, segueing into Indian classical string and tabla: these two soundtracks represent both Parsi status under the British and the film's Western/Eastern binary. Later, when things get particularly ugly, dirty, overtly sexual or physically disgusting on screen (when characters cover their noses against the smell of open sewers, for example), the Indian classical music swells, underlining the base sensual and spiritual foreignness. When the jazz returns, it is for scenes of jaunty hope and happiness: a child is well again (thanks to Western medicine); Gustad rips down blackout paper and lets in light; the jazz that references his childhood closes the film with a sense of progress, and the music mix moulds the narrative to the Hollywood norm of a resolved happy ending. The novel's ending is more fragile and ambiguous: 'as the first sheet tore away, a frightened moth flew out and circled the room' (339).

The realisation, sound and editing of the film's opening scene also emphasise exotica and the idea that positive spiritual salvation is to be found underneath all the dirt in 'India'. It begins (like the novel) with

Gustad Noble at prayer in the dawn, with birds chirping around him. The film uplifts with this chirping but does not end on a warning note as Mistry does: 'Always the sparrows were first, the cawing of the crows came later' (1). This signals that the director is no Nair, making *Salam Bombay!* with a documentarists' eye. Instead, Gunnarsson's Bombay satisfies a global audience's imagination of a 'solid, sordid, smelly' (301) but picturesque India in which streets are colourful but not garish: Gustad's home, the Khodadad Building, is charmingly dilapidated. The whole is filmed with an eye for the local, romanticised colour of 'old' India or, as *The Times of India* put it, full of

> A list [of images] straight off the *Lonely Planet* guide to India, with colourful Islamic celebrations, paanwallahs describing 'bedbreaker paans,' Chor Bazar gee-gaws, Kamathipura [the redlight district of Bombay] and pavement artists who paint gods on walls-turned-urinals.[15]

The 'outsider' eye here is Mistry's and Gunnarsson's; the aforementioned images are written into Mistry's novel. But where Mistry has Gustad taking the bus from Victoria Terminus (referencing Queen Victoria's empire and, perhaps, its end) Gunnarsson shoots Gustad on the inevitably overcrowded Indian train, that enduring symbol of the Empire's positive but, as such images suggest, sadly ill-kept legacy. The choice also references the brutal Partition history of interethnic violence in which train carriages became containers for the mass killing of people travelling from India to the new Pakistan or vice versa.[16] The emphasis is on native difference, rather than Mistry's more careful attempt to make human connections across various histories of violence.

Aesthetically and thematically Taraporevala/Gunnarsson's *Such a Long Journey* aligns itself with the most canonical of 'diaspora' films: those of Ismail Merchant and James Ivory. *The Householder* (1963), *Shakespeare Wallah* (1965), *Bombay Talkie* (1970) and *Heat and Dust* (1983) were scripted by Ruth Prawer Jhabvala, a Jewish woman born in Germany in 1927 who lived in India in the 1950s, was married to a Parsi and finally settled in New York. The films imagine India through a veil of heightened passions, exotic music and intrigue,[17] and Gunnarsson takes a similar approach. But Dan Venning notes that Merchant Ivory's *Shakespeare Wallah*

> Replicates and perpetuates [...] cultural imperialism by situating the viewer's sympathy with the British troupe members, not the newly liberated Indian culture, but simultaneously calls this imperialism into question by subtle irony aimed at perpetrators of this imperialism – both the troupe leaders and their devoted Indian audience members, and thus, by extension, the film's audience who sympathize with the troupe. The viewer is encouraged to understand that

the loss of "Shakespeare" is natural and even necessary, even as she or he mourns the passing.[18]

Mistry's use of Shakespeare in *Such a Long Journey* is nuanced in this way, appropriating, quoting and deliberately misquoting the plays throughout the book to interrogate the Parsi relationship to the Raj and to argue against it for a strong return to 'pure' Parsi tradition.

However, in Taraporevala/Gunnarsson's film, which exists in diluted lineage with work such as *Shakespeare Wallah* and other diaspora films, only one scene directly references Shakespeare. This elision depoliticises the film, further enhancing the nostalgic, exotic tone.

Shakespeare in the Novel and Film

An almost primary claim to Shakespeare in India is woven into Parsi identity, given the early adoption of the plays by the Parsi theatre during British rule. With this history in mind Mistry's use of Shakespeare as 'architect and administrator'[19] for his novel adds poignancy; it also serves as a political statement on British influence on India, on the situation of male Parsis as caught between two majority forces, and on his own writing. The erasure of Shakespeare and the elisions and omissions of context in the film demonstrate a bias that shores up its soft-focus reassurance that it offers no difficult postcolonial critique. It is instead a voyeurs' retrospective view of a once-proud Parsi civilisation now in the grip of an unstoppable but apolitical decline that only a few heroic men, such as Gustad Noble, might stem.

One of Mistry's explicit Shakespeare references comes when Gustad is in the Chor Bazar (Thieves Market), looking for a specific copy of *The Complete Works of Shakespeare*, which he has been told will be 'displayed prominently' for him to find. The book contains a coded message from his friend Jimmy Bilimoria, a member of Indira Gandhi's secret service, RAW (Research and Analysis Wing) who tells Gustad,

> To be absolutely certain if it is the right one, open the book to *Othello*, end of act 1 scene iii, where Iago gives advice to Roderigo. The line, 'put money in thy purse' will be underlined in red.
>
> (91)

Evoking misplaced trust, betrayal, corruption, misdirection, manipulations and racial tension, *Othello* here references, evokes and critiques a historical context in which Shakespeare was used as civilising tool by the British in India as well as the complex impact this has on Indians. Mistry pre-empts this scene with a veiled reference to Macaulay's 1835 Minute on Indian Education, with its insistence that he (Macaulay) could not find 'one among them [Indians] who could deny that a single shelf of a good European library was worth all the literature of India and Arabia.'[20] Gustad goes in search of Shakespeare, bypassing 'mainly paperbacks, westerns and romances' (102) in the market until he reaches a 'selection of books more respectable than any he had seen so far' (102). He scoops up three of Western civilisation's finest tomes that when taken together construct a single shelf of what it means to be a man: 'The *Great Dialogues of Plato*', one of Western philosophy's keystone explorations of the conscious self, 'volume seven of the *Encyclopedia of Religion and Ethics*, edited by James Hastings', a keystone of Western understanding of the spiritual/social self, and 'Henry Gray's *Anatomy of the Human Body*', Western medicine's Bible of the physical self, (102) and thinks,

> What was six rupees for three classics. Must visit Chor Bazaar regularly from now on. One or two books and eventually I will have enough to fill that bookcase. It's all a family really needs. *A small bookcase of the right books* and you are set for life.
>
> (103, my italics)

The Complete Works of Shakespeare (the ultimate all-round guide to civilised self) is given to Gustad for free; he takes the books home.

This essential context is absent from the film. The link between the British as colonisers-of-minds and the implication of the book being in the 'thieves market' (and therefore up for appropriation) is also downplayed. Instead the film shows Gustad picking through the bazaar until he finds Shakespeare and, as per the novel, shows how 'He opened the volume to *Othello* [...] Yes, there they were, underlined in red, all five repetitions. 'Put money in thy purse' (104).'

An exhortation to Indian/Indian corruption and betrayal is highlighted above all else, and *Othello* is pressed into service in the film only for this particularly useful line.

In the novel, *King Lear* plays a much more subtle and central role. Peter Morey argues that it is better to think of Mistry's texts 'as subtle enactments of the postcolonial injunction to reiterate and subvert colonial categories, from the inside, as it were, through echoes and mimicry, rather than aggressive opposition.'[21] This neatly describes Mistry's appropriation of *King Lear* in *Such a Long Journey*, which (as the film's opening text explains) takes place against the splitting of East and West Pakistan and the creation of Bangladesh. The hereditary nature of Indian politics and the sociopolitical backdrop to the novel is described via Lear's relationship with Cordelia:

> The country's beloved Panditji, everyone's Chacha Nehru [...] the great visionary, turned bitter and rancorous. From now on, he would brook no criticism, take no advice [...] he no longer had any use for defenders of the downtrodden and champions of the poor, [...] . His

one overwhelming obsession now was, how to ensure that his darling daughter Indira, the only one, he claimed, who loved him truly, who had even abandoned her worthless husband in order to be with her father - how to ensure she would become prime minister after him.

(10–11)

Nehru is Lear turned obsessive with the disappointment of betrayal. Indira Gandhi is imagined as a Cordelia who has abandoned France to come to her father's aid. The corruption, sycophancy and poverty which Lear rails against within his own world are sketched in as they might be in the programme note to a theatrical production of *King Lear*, except here the description is for India. While I recognise the challenge of visualising such backstory in film, the omission of this idea from Gunnarsson's work marks the first major elision of Shakespeare I want to highlight here.

The novel's strategy to show the legacy of Empire connected to elite Parsi culture declining against a new India which believes in economic supremacy at any cost is seen through the prism of that central dynamic of *King Lear*: the wrestling between an old age and a new one or age verses youth. In the novel, high literary culture must give way to a better focus on technological progress. The age reference is explicit: the 'proudest moment' for Mistry's Gustad comes in the early days at Khodadad Building, when his son Sohrab entertained the whole compound with a 'homemade' production of *King Lear*, 'Sohrab of course was Lear, producer, director, costume designer and set designer. He also wrote an abridged version of the play' (66).But as Sohrab reaches adulthood, priorities shift for his father, as Sohrab muses, 'Daddy never [...] dreamed dreams of an artist-son [...] No, it was always: my son will be a doctor, he will be an engineer, he will be a research scientist' (66). Gustad desperately wants Sohrab to attend the prestigious Indian Institute of Technology (IIT), marked by Prime Minister Jawaharlal Nehru as representing 'India's urges ... India's future in the making.'[22] Sohrab's securing of a place there comes as a cause for celebration: it will restore his family's financial and social status.

For Gustad and his family are Parsis in a state of decline: they were once furniture makers and bookshop owners, whose livelihoods succumbed to a cultural shift in emphasis towards technological and economic 'progress'. Gustad's feelings are persuaded by mainstream Hindu Indian discourse of the period; his desires for Sohrab's future and how that reflects on his own sense of self enact the traditional Parsi value for learning that must give way to the new national imperative.

Though Gunnarsson does utilise flashback, the first of these signals that Gustad's family was rich not via intellectual pursuits or craftsmanship but by the fact they can afford to have live chickens brought by servants from the market to the Noble kitchen. As an adult Gustad must now buy the expensive chicken himself and bring it to the dilapidated apartment in Khodadad Building, expecting his wife Dilnavaz to kill and prepare it in celebration of Sohrab's IIT achievement. The sense of the audience as voyeurs of the exotic strangeness of an unindustrialised world that *still* kills, cooks and eats chickens in the home is played up as the camera lingers over the flashback birds clucking in the basket and then via a jump cut to the present day, closes onto the chicken dhansak Dilnavaz obediently stirs as a witch might mix her brew.

Though this moment of civilisation mixed with implied barbarism is a minor and somewhat misdirected means of demonstrating some of the themes of the novel, it is lovingly included. Meanwhile the scene in which the young Sohrab produces and stars in his own version of *King Lear* is not. The childhood re-enactment serves both as critical refraction of key sociopolitical and personal themes and also underlines the importance of *Lear* to Mistry's body of work.[23] Since the scene also acts as plot demonstration of the boy Sohrab's inherited bookish nature and foreshadows his later clash with a father who feels forced to deny that inheritance, its omission is therefore a striking one.

Will Sohrab go to IIT? 'Speak', Gustad commands him, 'Becoming mute helps nothing'. Here is a version of Lear's warning to Cordelia: 'nothing will come of nothing, speak again' (1.1.90). To explicitly include Sohrab's childhood *King Lear* might have undermined the film's focus on the exotic specificity of Parsi lives, narrowing the difference between the international audience and those 'others' apparently still stranded in the old world. The scene's absence was not Gunnarsson's choice: it was never filmed, perhaps never even scripted, so it was not cut in the edit.[24] Perhaps then, the choice was Taraporevala's. Because her script strays only a little from its dependence on Mistry's novel any echoes of Mistry's Shakespeare relegate him to the same presence he has in contemporary mainstream English-speaking consciousness – the ghost in our mouths and syntax, whose phrases are woven into our discourse almost unknowingly.

Missing Pasts and Futures

Perhaps the most serious of erasures that the film makes is to gloss over the local, specific present and future threat that Parsis and other minority communities face: the grip of the Hindu right wing political party, Shiv Sena on the psychogeography of the people. Such is the strength of Mistry's critique of their divisive tactics in *Such a Long Journey* that the novel was removed from the syllabus of Bombay University in 2010 following pressure from the group.[25] As Gustad and his Kent/'lovable' Fool Mr Dinshawji discuss 'the bastard Shiv Sena leader who worships Hitler and Mussolini' (73). Dinshawji bemoans its '"Maharashtra for Maharashtrans" nonsense' (i.e. the state, of which Bombay is the capital), believing, 'They won't stop until they have a complete Maratha

Raj' (73). For Dinshawji the renaming of the streets from English into Marathi negatively links the Shiv Sena's tactics to those of the British but also erases his life's history, 'So what happens to the life I lead? Was I living the wrong life, with the wrong names?' (74) he asks. Referencing Shakespeare's *Romeo and Juliet*, Gustad argues, 'What's in a name?' Not only is this line absent from the film, which instead has Gustad say, 'What does it matter?' but Dinshawji's repost is kept to the personal, with no mention of the links between the Shiv Sena and the Raj so important to Mistry's analysis.

The novel's consistent, direct critique of Indira Gandhi's Congress Party as 'Congress Party crooks' (69) is curtailed to 'crooks' in the film, and Dinshawji's most violent outburst blaming Indira Gandhi for the violence that took place in 1960 via her encouragement of Shiv Sena 'demands for a separate Maharashtra' is cut, even though Mistry writes, 'How much bloodshed, how much rioting she caused. And today we have that bloody Shiv Sena, wanting to make the rest of us into second class citizens. Don't forget she started it all by supporting the racist buggers (39).' It's a damning authorial indictment that stands out in a novel that depends for its success on the depiction of its fictional world as 'real'.

Later, when Gustad visits Jimmy Bilimoria on his deathbed in jail, Jimmy's disclosure of Mrs Gandhi's corruption and theft of money she promised to Mukti Bahini,[26] his allegations that 'everything is in her pocket, all will be covered up', that the money went to, 'her son, his Maruti car factory' (279), are diluted in the film to one accusation against Mrs Gandhi and a rant about politicians in general. The Parsi dictum is therefore one that Taraporevala/Gunnarsson seem to have taken to heart to appeal to a Western, touristic idea of India *and* appease a conservative Indian 'home' audience. It suppresses Mistry's use of Shakespeare, which forms the bedrock of his 'janus faced' critique of Parsi nostalgia for the British Empire and the terror of the contemporary Hindu right wing, with its communally divisive, silencing agenda.

The Depiction of Women in Novel and Film

Much has been written about the misogyny of Lear as a character: his overblown curses express his disgust and fear of female sexuality, and he struggles against his sorrow as a 'mother' (2.4.62) within who must be supressed. Another important focus of the play is its dissection of the impact on women of life under a stifling patriarchy and as objects of material exchange: Goneril, Regan and Cordelia's attempts to break from this or mimic its practices power the play to its devastating end. In *Such a Long Journey* however, even this agency is absent. Mistry instead takes Lear's misogyny to heart: it is not expressed in the way the male characters treat women but in his authorial choices. Women are stereotypes limited to 'perfect wife and mother', 'delicate, submissive daughter' or 'ridiculous, meddling spinster'. They are therefore in line with the most conventional critical readings of Goneril and Regan – selfish, or, as traditionalists argue, evil by nature – or Cordelia – a goddess who sacrifices herself for her father.[27]

Mistry's writing asks readers to collude with him in mocking his female characters' frustrated responses to their passivity. The novel's appropriation of Goneril's line, 'Pluck out his eyes' (3.7.6) to Regan, and the rest of the scene in which Regan takes part in the blinding of Gloucester remove any mention of masculine involvement to highlight the 'amusing' selfishness and superstition of women. At Miss Kutpitia's instigation, Dilnavaz, worried about her sick daughter Roshan, performs a spell and throws a pan of hot curry from a window over old Mr Rabadi, the dogwallah. Rabadi rails, 'Blinded! Blinded completely! Look, you shameless animal! Whoever you are! Look at me! Eyeless in the compound! [...] Dimple pranced and leaped around him, enjoying his unusually animated state (275).' In this passage, a link is made between dogs and women, similar to the one made by Lear in the hovel, remembering the love test as he acts out a trial of his three daughters: 'The little dogs and all,/Trey, Blanch and Sweetheart, see they bark at me' (3.6.60–1).[28] In the play, the blinding quickly follows the trial; here Mistry meshes them, with the caveat that Dilnavaz and Miss Kutpitia (whose name makes a cut-pity demand on monolingual English readers) behave this way because their socially circumscribed lives lead to circumscribed imaginations. However, though Parsi culture is strongly patrilineal,[29] Parsis were 'more inclined to adopt the European education system for both men and women than were the Hindu community since ... (unlike in Hinduism) the need was felt for women to be intellectually on a par with their husbands.'[30] By 1971, many 'had gone to college or better,'[31] yet this is education seems absent in Dilnavaz ('soothing to the heart') and Roshan ('ray of light'), whose nomenclature evokes the feminine ideal of purity and nurturing.

While the temptation is to understand them as Cordelias, for Mistry they are only so in name: men usurp their role as agents of truth and change. In *Such a Long Journey* the real Cordelia is not Roshan, who for much of the novel exists in darkness, as Lear imagines Cordelia, like a bird 'i'the cage' (5.3.10).[32] Instead it is the boy Sohrab who opens the novel in the Cordelia role. Despite his father's wish that he take up his place at IIT, he refuses: he wants to become an actor. He is exiled from the home and from Gustad's affections in Lear-like terms: 'My son is dead ... Now he is nothing to me [...] . Out of my house, out of my life!' (52). And as Sohrab disappears from the narrative for a time, another male Cordelia takes his place. Enter the intellectually challenged Tehmul, reminding us that the same male actor often played Cordelia and the Fool on Shakespeare's stage.

154 *Preti Taneja*

As Lear loves his Fool, so Gustad loves and protects Tehmul and, in turn, is adored by him. When Tehmul is killed in a riot, the annoying wailing of women is silenced, as 'without a word, Gustad slipped one arm under Tehmul's shoulder, and the other under his knees. With a single mighty effort he rose to his feet, cradling the still warm body' (335). The action evokes Lear, who 'enters with Cordelia in his arms', a stage direction often included in editions of the play.[33]

The poignancy and pain of the moment are emphasised as Gustad carries Tehmul's corpse through the throng of silenced onlookers and lays him on his bed, reciting Parsi prayers over his body. In this moment, Gustad realises he must tear down his own defences and reconcile with Sohrab. So, Gustad is allowed two Cordelias – the one who effects his canonisation among the community, and the actual child he can be reconciled with in his lifetime – which is Lear's fantasy made real. The Lear-like father both achieves catharsis and gets his living Cordelia: furthermore both are boys. Here is a happy rewriting of a tragic end in which the hero, in a culture that honours male children over female, triumphs.

Because the film follows the novel almost scene for scene but omits the important Shakespearean skeleton, the film visualises this moment as I have described. However, the emphasis on heroic male agency and its closing focus on a trinity of men[34] is even more forcefully realised, as is the exoticisation of women as models of self-sacrificing, Indian femininity, signifiers of the goodness of the nation.

The only female sexuality allowed in novel and film belongs to the Indian Christian Laurie Coutino, secretary in the back office of a bank where Gustad also works. In the novel, her person 'is as impeccably ordered as her desk', with Gustad pruriently noticing that 'the short skirt had hiked a fair but controlled distance' (72). In the film, the short skirt is denim, worn with a skintight, hot-pink sleeveless vest, an outfit that would be considered remarkable in any office of the period (and perhaps even today), inevitably making Laurie fodder for the male gaze in any public space in India. Her overtly Western clothing denotes her religious, social and (by inference) moral difference to her modest Parsi female counterparts and insidiously suggests a justification for her consistent sexual humiliation by Dinshawji (whose own wife exists in the novel but not in the film, an omission one critic describes as making him 'somewhat more sympathetic').[35]

Laurie is not a 'Bad Girl' – in fact she is quite innocent. From this perspective, which pits whiteness (in Laurie as manifested by her Christianity) against brownness in women, and brown men against women in general, the depiction of the Fool/Tehmul as a sexually repressed, intellectually challenged mascot with an uncontrolled masturbatory habit who nevertheless 'on the whole got on well with children' (3) takes on problematic proportions. In both the novel and the film, women complain about Tehmul's nakedness in childlike euphemisms:

Muà lutcha knew perfectly well what his parts were for, never mind if his head was not right – what with a big packet like that, and no underwear even to keep it all in place, it was shameful to have him wandering around dingle-dangle.

(31)

The writing undermines any real sense of threat from Tehmul that women might feel, focussing instead on a cultural and sexual shame that is directed at them via social mores. Whereas they must dress modestly, Tehmul does not have to – he is male and physically and mentally challenged; the first licences him to roam, and the second generates pity and immunity. As Goneril must stomach the Fool's childish innuendos, Parsi women must live alongside Tehmul's unmediated, sexualised, free-ranging presence while monitoring their own bodies as the laws of shame dictate.

In his gibbering, Tehmul also echoes Poor Tom, particularly also in the care and concern Lear shows him as a 'naked wretch' (3.4.32). But while Tom's nakedness is not sexualised, Tehmul's is – and violently so. Before the denouement of the novel, Gustad approaches Tehmul's room, concerned by the 'panting, heavy breathing' (302) he can hear. Gustad surprises Tehmul having sex with Roshan's life-size, blue-eyed, white-skinned doll, which he has stolen from Gustad's apartment. This white plastic figure is adorned in wedding attire, which Tehmul has learned to handle by spying on Dilnavaz, who undressed the doll to keep its clothes clean. Now Mistry's descriptions of Tehmul shift from the effeminate, childish register of 'packet' and 'dingle-dangle' to describe 'an enormous erection', a 'rampant penis' (302). Even where Lear's masculinity is re-calibrated on being reunited with Cordelia, and the Fool and Poor Tom eventually evoke a more equal humanity as 'poor, bare, forked' (3.4.115) animals, Tehmul's rampant masculinity and Gustad's remain intact. The doll is a silent, passive victim, synecdoche for her obedient mistress, the child Roshan.

The scene is realised on film with a candid, almost full-frontal gaze that underlines the bestial, sexual nature of Lear's world and hints that the Indian social world is the same. The scene brings alive an intricate chain of colonial/postcolonial injunctions: the 'look but don't touch' status of white women (precious dolls) over brown men; the hierarchy of brown men over brown women; and the white doll won at school by a young brown girl, where this winning marks the end of her school career for the duration of the novel and film. Winning whiteness is not accepted, possessing it results in theft and symbolic (and real) rape by brown men. When Tehmul dies, Gustad lays the doll alongside him as his bride, a warning perhaps of what happens when men desire outside their race. In this scene the weight of sympathy remains with Gustad as he forgives and takes pity on poor, lunatic Tehmul; in novel and film, women lie passively, waiting for their fate to happen to them. To return

156 *Preti Taneja*

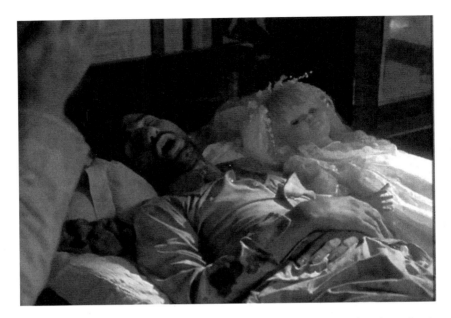

Figure 8.1 When Tehmul dies, Gustad lays him down on the bed with Roshan's white-skinned bridal doll.

to my earlier point, this charge certainly cannot be levelled at Cordelia, Goneril or Regan for all their apparent other faults (Figure 8.1).

Is Mistry's myopia about women perhaps because he writes as a first-generation immigrant, recalling a childhood thirty years ago? In an interview he claims his mother, who 'supported her husband and nurtured her family [...] was happy in that role, [...] doing the miracle that all mothers perform of making what was barely enough seem like abundance.'[36] This public avowal, and his depiction of such a figure in his novels,[37] is perhaps all we will ever know of the real woman. Angela Lambert notes that Mistry's fiction is 'exilic' marked by its 'reinvention of the past, seen through the sharp eyes of a child and then filtered through veils of nostalgia,'[38] this seems to have most effected his female characters. Meanwhile Bruce Westwood, Mistry's Canadian literary agent, notes,

> Rohinton [...] has lived [in Canada] for longer than he lived in India, but his books are still set in the Bombay of his youth, reinvented with perfect recall. At times he seems to have idealised it into a childhood paradise, like Nabokov's Russia.[39]

Can 'perfect recall' go hand in hand with an idealised vision? The sleight of mind such an idea contains is the absolute purview of the cinematic medium; the trick of 'seeing is believing'. A warning against falling for this, which can be read with surprisingly contemporary ramifications for the global marketplace, is contained within *King Lear* itself: 'I stumbled when I saw. Full oft 'tis seen | Our means secure us and our mere defects | Prove our commodities' (4.1.21–23).

Conclusion

Because of its erasure of Shakespeare, the film might be described as an example of 'Diaspora-pudding', a term I coin from film criticism's 'Euro-pudding'. Mariana Liz writes, 'there is no systematic study on the meaning of Euro-pudding; yet this is a key concept in contemporary European cinema.'[40] As well as embodying certain co-production financing criteria with an (apparently) art-house sensibility, and transnational themes explicated by casting the highest affordable level of recognisable stars, they are shot in English and focus preferably on historical subjects.[41] Randall Halle notes that Euro-pudding has also been used 'to denounce such productions whose good intentions so often yielded such bland results. Even if the films aspired to art film status, they appealed to the lowest common denominator of cultured interest with little hope for broad social or political resonance,'[42] and this seems a fair summation of Taraporevala/Gunnarsson's approach. Diaspora-pudding must work even harder than Euro-pudding to gloss over any difficult contemporary politics, crossing two continents and seeking to reach an audience of global exiles whose memories are sacred, but that will also include people who have general interest in the locale of the film or its family themes but not necessarily any link to Parsi history. The film's DVD cover makes this clear, setting out its mission to present, 'A country on the brink of war .../ a family torn apart .../ a man caught in the middle'.

Yet, given that Shakespeare's 'universal' human themes have been lauded for their seeming ability to cross boundaries of culture and language, the omission of Shakespeare made by Taraporevala/Gunnarsson seems even more surprising. It might either be down to cinematic contingency – to include Shakespeare would have made the film longer, its global marketing more complicated – or because it would have repointed the work as one deeply critical of past, present and rising regimes. The terrible, hollow ghost of *King Lear*, the legacies of Empire and the pernicious, insidious rise of the Shiv Sena is exorcised, brown women are in the home; the audience can rest assured that Parsi culture will endure unchanged because Gustad Noble has reconciled with his son.

This narrative of filial reconciliation (denied to Lear) seems the real 'long journey' the film is organised around. This is far from the journey evoked by Mistry's troika of opening epigraphs: from the Parsi sacred text, the *Shah-Nama*, T.S. Eliot's *Journey of the Magi*, and Rabindranath Tagore's *Gitanjali*, framing the novel as Parsi, Western Modernist and Colonial/Postcolonial Indian, underlining the importance of its commentary on the cycles of violence that marked the origination of Bangladesh. Instead, in its amorphous representations of India, the film avoids any implication of culpability of those living in former colonising nations either for the effects of colonialism or the hardening of far-right responses that the novel, via its use of Shakespeare, attempts to make.

Of the novel, Bahri notes that the 'politics of representation makes the example exemplary, the representation representative.'[43] The cover image of the 2006 Faber paperback of *Such a Long Journey* shows, in sepia, a reproduction of a photograph by Marilyn Silverstone of a dirty, barefoot boy holding a black umbrella evocative of the type used by Western businessmen as the monsoon keeps up its 'dreadful pudder' (3.2.49). He also appears to be eating a banana. Though 'authentic' because its American photographer lived and worked in India during the period in which the book is set, the image itself has no connection at all with the novel. Instead the cover perfectly captures 'India' in its Diaspora-pudding soft-focus depiction of the contradiction of civilisation and barbarism, its poor, wise children and the lost legacy of the civilising, protective Empire-as-shelter.

Here the representation is made representative. Mistry and Taraporevala's creative decisions, crowned with Gunnarsson's 'love' of India, do little justice to Parsi lives and particularly to women in a period of seismic social and political change (overseen by a woman as prime minister) that meanwhile affects the men around them deeply. For readers and audiences alike, *Such a Long Journey* ultimately cements an idea of India both quaint and good, whose menace and silencing in terms of real politics and gender issues are wrapped in jolly word play and where kindly, kingly father figures are always on hand, struggling, suffering, essentially 'noble'. In the praise heaped upon both by literary and film critics there is little to no mention of the elisions I have discussed here: a testimony to the global marketplace and its grip on popular imagination by two works that eventually cannot offer any lasting 'truth', despite their carefully constructed claims to do so.

Notes

1 Rohinton Mistry, *Such a Long Journey* (London: Faber and Faber, 1991). All further references are to this edition, and page numbers shall be listed in brackets in the text.
2 Rohinton Mistry, *Swimming Lessons and Other Stories from Firozsha Baag* (New York: Vintage, 1987), 258.
3 Renamed Mumbai in 1995 following pressure from the Shiv Sena.
4 Jaydipsinh Dodiya ed., *The Fiction of Rohinton Mistry* (New Delhi: Prestige, 1998), 24.
5 Paul Brians, *Modern South Asian Literature in English* (London: Greenwood Publishing, 2003), 156.

6 Ibid.
7 For example, Yvonne Griggs, *Screen Adaptations, Shakespeare's 'King Lear'* (London: Methuen, 2009).
8 This film is based on Thomas Hardy's *Tess of the D'Urbervilles* (and includes references to Atul Kumar's concurrent stage production, *Hamlet, the Clown Prince*).
9 'An Interview with the Director', www.monsoonmovie.com/about/, accessed 2 March 2015. While Gunnarsson describes his wife as 'Indian', the *Times of India* notes that she is 'a Canadian of Sikh origin' and describes the director as a 'foreigner without Indian roots'. Meenakshi Shedde, 'It's not exotic, it's Indian', *Times of India*, 24 January 1988, accessed 2 March 2015, www.soonitaraporevala.com/media/indian.html.
10 *The Zarathushti World, a 2012 Demographic Picture*, Compiled by Roshan Rivetna, accessed 12 May 2016, http://fezana.org/downloads/Zoroastrian-WorldPopTable_FEZANA_Journal_Fall_2013.pdf.
11 Sturla Gunnarsson, *Such a Long Journey* (The Film Works, 2002). https://openaccess.leidenuniv.nl/handle/1887/19459
12 Deepika Bahri, *Native Intelligence: Aesthetics, Politics, and Postcolonial Literature* (Minneapolis: University of Minnesota Press, 2003), 132.
13 Tanya M. Luhrmann, *The Good Parsi: The Fate of a Colonial Elite in a Postcolonial Society* (Boston: Harvard University Press, 1996), 1, and Luhrmann, 'The Good Parsi: The Postcolonial 'Feminization' of a Colonial Elite', *Man* 29, no. 2 (1994):338. Also, Leisbeth Rosen Jacobson, *We Must Hunt with the Hounds, the Changing Nature of Parsis in India and Abroad*,(unpublished MA Thesis, Lieden University, 2012) accessed 5 March 2015, https://openaccess.leidenuniv.nl/handle/1887/19459.
14 Sooni Taraporevala, *Parsis, The Zoroastrians of India* (London: Overlook Duckworth, 2004), 19.
15 Shedde, 'It's not exotic, it's India'.
16 See, for example, Kushwant Singh, *Train to Pakistan* (New Delhi: Penguin India, 2007).
17 Although I would argue that, in fact, many of these Merchant Ivory films include far more 'grit' and critique of nostalgia than Gunnarsson's, a full discussion of this is beyond the scope of this chapter.
18 Dan Venning, 'Cultural Imperialism and Intercultural Encounter in Merchant Ivory's *Shakespeare Wallah*', *Asian Theatre Journal* 28, no. 1 (2011): 149–67, 152.
19 The introductory screen to the film *Such a Long Journey* reads: 'In India, over the centuries, they became known as Parsis. Under British rule, they prospered, and were the architects and administrators of the city of Bombay'. I borrow the wording here.
20 Thomas Babington Macaulay, 'Minute on Indian Education, 1835', accessed 2 March 2015, www.columbia.edu/itc/mealac/pritchett/00generallinks/macaulay/txt_minute_education_1835.html.
21 Peter Morey, *Rohinton Mistry* (Manchester: Manchester University Press, 2004), 14.
22 IIT Website, accessed 3 April 2015, http://web.archive.org/web/20060708041546/http://www.iitkgp.ernet.in/institute/history.php.
23 Rohinton Mistry's *Family Matters* (2002), relies heavily on *King Lear*.
24 Sturla Gunnarsson, email to author, 13 April 2015.
25 Jason Burke, 'Mumbai University Drops Rohinton Misty Novel after Extremists Complain', *Guardian*, 19 October 2010, accessed 2 March 2015, www.theguardian.com/world/2010/oct/19/mumbai-university-removes-mistry-book.

26 Muthiah Alagappa notes, 'the Mukhti Bahini liberation force was composed of Bengali troops who had revolted against Pakistan, as well as youths who were recruited later'. Muthiah Alagappa, *Coercion and Governance: The Declining Political Role of the Military in Asia* (Stanford: Stanford University Press, 2001), 212.
27 See AC Bradley, *Shakespearean Tragedy* (London: Macmillan, 1908). The category witch/spinster is not in Lear. The novel follows the immersive techniques, authorial moralising and slapstick elements of nineteenth-century writing by Charles Dickens or William Thackeray. Miss Kutpitia is the 'ubiquitous witch of fairy stories come to life' (2). She is the suspicious spinster, appearing in line with '19th and early twentieth century literature as an embattled figure, often the subject of ridicule and scorn', as Dipesh Chakrabarty notes in *Contemporary Postcolonial Theory, a Reader*, ed. Padmini Mongia (London, New York: Arnold, 1996), 234.
28 William Shakespeare, *King Lear*, ed. R.A. Foakes (London: Arden, 1997). All further references are to this edition.
29 Jenny Rose, *The Traditional Role of Women in the Iranian and Indian (Parsi) Zoroastrian communities from the Nineteenth to the Twentieth Century* (unpublished MA Thesis, SOAS, University of London, 1986), accessed 2 April 2015, www.shapworkingparty.org.uk/journals/articles_88/8_Rose.pdf.
30 Ibid.
31 Luhrmann, 135.
32 Though this image might affirm father-daughter intimacy, it can also be read as Lear's wish fulfilment, a final attempt to possess the daughter who keeps trying to escape, and whose final line attempts to stall the inevitable imprisonment: 'Shall we not see these daughters and these sisters?' (5.3.8).
33 Shakespeare, *King Lear*, 385.
34 The play also closes on Kent, Edgar and Albany; however in the context of comparison with Mistry, Sohrab can only be understood as Cordelia.
35 Paul Brians, *Modern South Asian Literature in English*, 156.
36 See also Angela Lambert, 'Touched with Fire', *Guardian*, 27 April 2002, accessed 20 March 2015, www.theguardian.com/books/2002/apr/27/fiction.books.
37 E.g., *Family Matters* (2002).
38 Angela Lambert, 'Touched with Fire'.
39 Ibid.
40 Marianna Liz, 'From European Co-Productions to Euro-Pudding', in *The Europeaness of European Cinema: Identity, Meaning and Globalisation*, ed. Mary Harrod, Mariana Liz and Alissa Timoshkina (London: IB Tauris, 2015), 74.
41 Ibid., 75.
42 Ibid., 76.
43 Bahri, 131.

9 Cinematic *Lears* and Bengaliness
Locus, Identity, Language

Paromita Chakravarti

In recent times, the distinction between 'regional' cinema produced in the local languages of the Indian states and Hindi cinema with a pan-Indian market and mode of address is being challenged. While Tamil and Telugu cinemas are producing films like *Baahubali* (2016), which transcend regional borders and target national and international distribution circuits, Bollywood, perhaps in a bid to capture smaller, regional markets, is showcasing local cultures and identities. This is evident in the Bollywood Shakespeare films too: the detailed evocaations of the Mumbai underworld in *Maqbool*, the badlands of Uttar Pradesh in *Omkara*, Kashmir under insurgency in *Haider*, the colours of Benaras in *Issaq* and the North Indian small town in *Ishaqzaade* help to root Shakespeare in the rich diversity of Indian regional cultures. This careful creation of the local for global consumption is also a mode of producing and maintaining difference in an increasingly homogenising international market. In diasporic and anglophone Shakespearean cinema too there is now a closer examination of ethnic identities and the particular histories of their engagement with Western modernities and Shakespeare. This essay explores how Shakespeare's *King Lear* has become a productive site for cinematic explorations of 'Bengaliness' in English-language films made both in India and in the United Kingdom for global audiences. Focussing on Aparna Sen's *36 Chowringhee Lane* (1981); Jon Sen's two-part television drama made for Channel 4 TV, *Second Generation* (2003); Rituparno Ghosh's *The Last Lear* (2006); and Sangeeta Datta's *Life Goes On* (2009), the essay will examine how these films deploy *King Lear* to construct a Bengali identity, poised between the West and the East, tradition and modernity, colonial and postcolonial legacies, enlightenment values and popular prejudices. While *Lear* in these films provides a tragic template of lost worlds, disintegrating families and rejected patrimonies, it also supplies possibilities of reconciliation and recovery through an acceptance of change, otherness and hybridities. In this context the essay will discuss how the genres of these films and their engagement with the Shakespearean legacy and modernity map the categories of the global, regional, local, national, postcolonial and diasporic as well as their mutually constitutive relationships. Finally, the essay will briefly discuss the recent films on Shakespeare's plays made in and around the quatercentenary of his death in the regional Bangla film industry and their explorations of a changing Bengali identity.

Shakespeare and 'Our Modernities'

The introduction of Shakespeare to Indians as part of the colonial government's modernising mission has been examined in the context of the Indian Education Act (1835), which promulgated English education for Indians in order to create a native elite educated in Western ideas who would be co-opted to consolidate British rule.[1]

Considered the acme of Western culture, Shakespeare's plays became the cornerstone of English education in India, a conduit for diffusing Enlightenment ideals of liberalism and humanism against the 'regressive' tendencies of native life, the '*mantra* for the new India in its fight against obscurantist traditionalism,'[2] and played an important role in a colonised people's early encounters with modernity.

While the new learning created a servile *baboo* class it also constructed a modern, liberal identity for the young urban Indian male and augmented his confidence in himself and his own culture. Paradoxically, English education helped to forge a nationalist consciousness and fuelled cultural revivalist movements like the nineteenth-century Bengal Renaissance.

The Indians' introduction to Western modernity involved complex negotiations. The native urban elite demanded an education which would challenge orthodoxies without upsetting the traditional, social and religious hierarchies which ensured their privilege. This is reflected in the naming of the new college of modernisation as Hindu College.[3] Thus Indian modernity shaped under colonial rule is an amalgam of mimicry of and resistance to Western paradigms.[4]

Partha Chatterjee points out the ambiguous ways in which 'the history of our modernity has been intertwined with the history of colonialism', leading to the complicity of 'modern knowledges' with 'regimes of power'. Indians' attempts in the nineteenth century to 'nationalise' Western sciences should be seen within the larger endeavour of pursuing knowledge which was both modern and national.[5] However, Swapan Chakravorty argues that the quest for literary modernity in Bengal traversed a different route. Despite calls to nationalise literatures by focussing on the Bengali language, Tagore tended towards a more universalist position. In the essay 'World Literatures' he apprehends that we might fail to understand literary works if we reduce them to narrow considerations of Time and Space. Chakravorty suggests that perhaps Tagore had anticipated that the ideals of a nationalist literature could breed 'provincialism', even parochialism.[6] Thus unlike in the sciences, literary modernity in Bengal, inspired by thinkers like Tagore, has been associated with an internationalism which was not seen as contradictory to cultural nationalism.

The nineteenth-century translations of Shakespeare represent the Bengali colonial subject's early attempts to fashion an Indian self through encounters with Western modernity, constructing a Bengaliness which would transcend the region to attain a national and international valency. The legacy of these identity constructions continues to define our postcolonial Shakespearean transactions, receiving a particular articulation in diasporic cultures. The following sections will explore how four English-language films based on *King Lear* and produced in the twentieth and the first decade of the twenty-first centuries frame Bengali identity through the vexed questions of colonial modernity, global cultures and the changing conception of the nation.

King Lear, Calcutta and Bengali Modernity: *36 Chowringhee Lane* (1981) and *Last Lear* (2006)

King Lear has not been frequently translated or adapted on the nineteenth-century Bengali stage or screen and has figured rarely in criticism. However, in twentieth-century Marxist Shakespearean scholarship *Lear* regains importance as a play exemplifying a dialectical conflict between a declining feudal aristocracy and emerging bourgeois values in an age of transition. This is best demonstrated in the critical writings of Bengali actor, playwright-director, theatre scholar and Shakespearean actor-translator Utpal Dutt.[7] Dutt's 1985 play *Aajker Shahjahan* (Shahjahan Today), although not directly connected to *King Lear*, uses its plot. Borrowing its historical frame from an older Bengali play based on the last days of the Mughal emperor Shahjahan, incarcerated by his son and cared for by his daughter Jahanara, Dutt's play's parallels with the Lear story are obvious.

In *Aajker Shahjahan*, a retired stage actor, Kunja, inhabits a theatrical wasteland littered with old stage props and re-enacts scenes of old plays he had once performed. Scenes from old Bengali drama and the murder scene from *Othello* are both part of a common repertory of performances that remain stored in his archival memory. Kunja demonstrates the unique character of Bengali modernity, moving easily between English and Bangla, Western and indigenous, colonial and nationalist cultures.

Yet this smooth traffic of English-language theatre and the popular vernacular stage appears to have been lost in Rituparno Ghosh's 2006 English film *The Last Lear*, which is loosely based on Dutt's *Aajker Shahjahan*. The film erases all traces of the Bengali stage tradition – none of the characters are identifiably Bengali. The indigent, out of work Kunja is reincarnated as the gentrified Shakespearean actor Harish Mishra (a North Indian Brahmanical name, shortened to the anglicised

Harry), who speaks with an elite English accent. Living reclusively in an old mansion, drinking scotch on the rocks, disdainful of philistine journalists who cannot distinguish between a Robin Hood and a Robin Goodfellow, Harry represents an Anglophiliac bardolatry, which is at odds with Dutt's revolutionary indigenisations of Shakespeare in Bengali folk theatre (*jatra*).[8] Ghosh's film misses the spirit of the Bengali Shakespearean negotiations by associating Dutt's play and Shakespeare's legacy with an exclusively English theatre practice and with cultural and class privilege.

Although the characters in Ghosh's film represent a generalised middle-class Indian rather than a specifically Bengali identity, the focus on the city of Calcutta brings in a distinctive regional flavour.[9] While Shakespeare's other tragedies are given a specific locus – Denmark, Venice and Scotland –*King Lear*, associated with the bleak generality of the heath, is perhaps the least localised. Yet Calcutta appears in the two English-language Indian cinematic representations of *Lear* as an inalienable aspect of their Shakespearean engagement. In Aparna Sen's *36 Chowringhee Lane* (1981), a paean to Calcutta's disappearing Anglo-Indian community, the ageing protagonist, Violet Stoneham (Jennifer Kendal), recites Lear's line in the final scene as she sits rejected in front of the Victoria Memorial, the legacy of Calcutta's imperial past. The image, the lines and the scattered Shakespeare allusions provide an idiom of a lost past for the city – its colonial and cosmopolitan history, which lingers in nostalgia. The film's name describes more than Miss Stoneham's address – it evokes the '*Saheb paara*', the 'white city' where the British lived and where the colonial architectural past of the city still exists in old offices, clubs, museums, markets and particularly the crumbling apartment houses where the dwindling Anglo-Indian community still lives. The Chowringhee Road, Calcutta's iconic artery and its neighbouring streets also housed many theatres, including the fashionable Chowringhee Theatre (1813–1839) and *Sans Souci* (1839), which staged Shakespeare plays. It was Chowringhee Theatre which gave Theatre Road its name, which is now renamed as Shakespeare Sarani (Figure 9.1).

The hybrid Anglo-Indian culture struggles to keep alive the memory of a city which was syncretic in its love for Western culture, particularly Shakespeare. Contemporary Calcutta is impatient for this imperial past, exemplified in the film by Violet's bored students who read popular novels in her *Twelfth Night* classes. The young Bengali couple who exploit Violet's generosity also represents the growing amnesia and parochialism of a new Bengali identity, insensitive to the city's diverse cultural legacy. They shut out Violet from their home, and she wanders as an outcaste on empty streets, at night, befriending a bewildered dog to whom she recites the lines from *Lear*.

In *The Last Lear* Calcutta and its history are linked to the film's central concerns of identity and culture. The director, Ghosh, stated that

Cinematic Lears and Bengaliness   165

Figure 9.1 36 *Chowringhee Lane*: Miss Stoneham reciting *Lear* to a dog.

the setting was meant to evoke the empire and its erstwhile capital as well as its English theatre tradition and the Bengali love of Shakespeare: 'the city itself is one of the characters in the film.'[10] In an interview, Ghosh said, 'I grew up meeting Shakespeare on the streets of Kolkata. Theatre Road was renamed Shakespeare Sarani. Shakespeare is lodged permanently in Kolkata.'[11]

Although Kolkata (the Bengali name for the anglicised Calcutta) is a character in the film *Last Lear*, it is a city remotely viewed, a collage of soundscapes and images, which Harry observes, amusedly, through a CCTV (close circuit television) camera from atop his house, protected from the grime and dust of everyday city life. Contemporary Calcutta appears as grainy black-and-white surveillance images transported into Harry's secluded room, suffused by memories of his Shakespearean performances, interrupting the film's grand interiority. Young film director Sidharth and veteran actor Harry spend hours on the digitally reproduced sights and sounds of the bustling city, so alien to the time and space that Harry inhabits. They try to guess the professions of people going about their business, embarrassing them with questions and Shakespearean quotations, ironically evoking Lear's fantasy of being imprisoned with Cordelia, playing 'God's spies' to courtiers and worldly men (5.3.8–17). Significantly, Violet recites this very passage at the end of *36 Chowringhee Lane*, staring at an indifferent cityscape. In both films, Lear's story becomes a vehicle for narrating the city and its Shakespearean legacy, both its brooding past and its forgetful present. The play helps to articulate the dilemma of a postcolonial Bengal whose modernity, nationalism and cosmopolitanism are derived from the experience of colonisation and tied to the privileges of class, education and community. These films use *King Lear* to examine the vexed question – is there a way of being a modern Bengali or even a Calcuttan without acknowledging an imperial past? The colonial programme of limiting Western education to a privileged class has ensured that these questions will linger and fracture our identities long after the British have left (Figure 9.2).

Harry's and Violet's gazes on images of contemporary Calcutta remind us of the opening sequence of Satyajit Ray's[12] *Charulata*. Based on Tagore's novella, Ray's 1964 period film depicts the loneliness of a nineteenth-century Bengali housewife, Charulata, whose English-educated, upper-class husband has no time for her. The film opens with Charulata on a lazy summer afternoon, looking down from the window of her mansion at the city streets and the passers-by, at a life she cannot be a part of. The black-and-white CCTV city images observed from an old house in *The Last Lear* transport us to an older Calcutta, seen through Charu's opera glasses. The cinematic citation is a tribute to both Ray and Tagore, icons of Bengali modernity who represent a literary gentility increasingly under erasure in postcolonial times. Yet Bengali identities continue to be defined by nostalgia for this lost modernity which haunts diasporic cultures.

The Quest for Bengali Identity: *Life Goes On* (2009)

Sangeeta Datta's 2009 film *Life Goes On*, another intertextual version of *King Lear*, set in the Bengali diaspora in the United Kingdom, uses the triad of Shakespeare, Tagore and Ray to articulate the yearning for a Bengali modernity which is both nationalist and cosmopolitan.

Figure 9.2 The Last Lear: Harry and Sidharth watch CCTV images of Calcutta like 'god's spies'.

Generically, the film is in the tradition of middle-of-the-road, realist cinema. Datta had assisted Ghosh, maker of *The Last Lear*, whose films, influenced by Ray, on upper-middle-class Bengali lives and loves have influenced Datta. Ghosh's films also have a generic affinity with those of Aparna Sen, director of *36 Chowringhee Lane*, which looks back at Merchant Ivory's *Shakespeare Wallah* through its theme and production history.[13] Datta's *Life Goes On*, a diasporic film set in London, has close links with this tradition of nostalgia movies, characterised by a love of high culture (represented by Shakespeare, Tagore and Ray), Kolkata and Bengaliness.

In Datta's film, after the sudden death of Manju, a middle-aged Bengali woman in London, Manju's three daughters struggle to understand their relationships with their father; their homes, both in England and India; and the Bengali culture that their mother stood for and which they are only tenuously connected to.

Days after Manju's death, her youngest daughter, Diya, a drama student, appears as Cordelia in a performance of *Lear*. Her father, Sanjay, attends the play and finds succour in it, as he does in the works of canonical Bengali poets and authors. Sanjay recites Jibananda Das's romantic poem 'Bonolata Sen' to Manju on their wedding anniversary and recounts to his granddaughter, Upendra Kishore Raychowdhury's tale of Goopy and Bagha, later made into a classic children's film by his grandson Satyajit Ray. Datta's film is replete with references to the cinema of Ghatak[14] and Ray. Diya mentions the boatman's song in Ghatak's film, and in a poignant homage to Ray's cinema, Sanjay pulls out a cigarette to calm his nerves after Manju's death only to find a handwritten message by his dead wife on the packet saying: 'Only one a day, you promised'. This echoes the young bride Aparna's warning, scrawled on her newly married husband's cigarette packet, in Ray's 1959 film *Apur Sansar* (The World of Apu). Significantly Aparna, who like Manju dies suddenly, leaving behind a devastated husband, was played by a fourteen-year-old Sharmila Tagore, who plays Manju in *Life Goes On*. These cultural references along with Tagore's music resonating through the film constitute markers of a sophisticated Bengali identity. In the diasporic consciousness, Shakespeare shares space with Bengali high culture, constituting a continuum of good taste. But unlike the easy traffic between the popular vernacular and the Shakespearean stage in Kunja's memory in Utpal Dutt's *Aajker Shahjahan*, for the protagonists of *Life Goes On*, Shakespeare remains a British icon, rendered through the English accents of students trained at the Royal Academy of the Dramatic Arts as they rehearse scenes from *King Lear*. When Diya, a RADA student, feels unable to go through with her role as Cordelia after her mother's death, it is her father Sanjay (a Shakespeare aficionado who is teased by Manju for his Lear-like love for Diya) who insists that the show must go on. Her sisters also encourage her. This is in contrast to their outrage when Tuli, Diya's older sister, desperate to become a sports journalist, gets an opportunity to cover an important football match during the morning and decides to take it. The sports-loving lesbian daughter, reprimanded by Diya as a 'footie and lager girl' who betrays her ignorance of Bengali culture by wondering how sandal paste is made, is clearly the 'black sheep'. She lets down her Rabindra *sangeet*-singing mother and her father who recites Jibananda and Shakespeare with equal ease (Figure 9.3).

Access to Shakespeare signifies the cultural privilege of the English-educated Bengali elite who are ideal diasporic subjects because they blend in well. In *Life Goes On*, Alok, Sanjay's friend describing his friendship with Manju, says, 'I used to take her to the theatre, to movies, Stratford-upon-Avon, Wordsworth's House—everything that you Bengalis must do'. The reclusive stage actor Harry, and the successful NRI doctor Sanjay, Lear figures in *The Last Lear* and *Life Goes On*, are both inheritors of a common legacy of colonial education. Jigna Desai points out,

> The English speaking classes first imagined by colonialism and reformulated by anti-colonial nationalism are most frequently the constituents who seek the metropolitan center that they have been taught to desire. Hence colonialism and nationalism have engendered transnationality in postcolonial migration.[15]

It is this desire for the metropolitan centre which manifests itself in the love for Shakespeare. But while Shakespearean theatre evokes nostalgia for a now-lost and marginalised British past in *The Last Lear*, in *Life Goes On*, *King Lear*, paradoxically, represents a yearning for the home left behind and the values of the Indian family, however flawed, living together. But these values are contested as conflicts erupt.

Figure 9.3 Life Goes On: Diya rehearses Cordelia's role in *King Lear*.

The opening scene in *Lear* is echoed in Sanjay's decision to settle his property on his daughters which upsets Diya who considers these discussions inappropriate during mourning. Tensions escalate when Diya reveals her love for Imtiaz, a Bangladeshi Muslim doctor whose child she is pregnant with. Sanjay cannot accept this relationship because of his deep-rooted hatred for Muslims, who had, during the 1947 Partition of India, burnt his home and forced his family to become refugees. Argument between father and daughter climaxes in the Learesque scene of Sanjay's homeless wanderings over London on a stormy night while the lines 'Blow winds' (3.2.1)[16] play in voiceover. He is found at dawn by Imtiaz (the Edgar/Kent figure) and returns to ask Diya's forgiveness: 'Pray do not mock me' (4.7.60). A reconciliation scene follows, creating space for an intergenerational dialogue at Manju's funeral where the family presents a united front.

In *Life Goes On*, the longing for familial togetherness is evoked through Shakespeare because his plays, like the traces of Bengaliness preserved in Manju's songs or Sanjay's poetry, symbolises an ideal which is at odds with the popular British culture represented by Tuli's love for football or the fusion rap which plays in London pubs. Whatever gestures that the film might make towards these popular expressions, it remains committed to the 'pure' art of Shakespeare shored up by the classic Bengali canon of Tagore and Ray as in Ghosh's *The Last Lear*.

Significantly, in 1996, the Indian High Commission installed Tagore's statue in the garden of Shakespeare's Henley Street 'birthplace' in Stratford-upon-Avon. It was inscribed with Tagore's English translation of his poem 39 from *Balaka*, a tribute to the bard. Swapan Chakravorty wonders why the Indian government felt the need to have Tagore's bust in Shakespeare's birthplace and shows how this move 'throws many interesting sidelights in the politics of high culture, on the process of canon formation and the relationship of former colonies to Western Metropolitan centres.'[17]

One of these 'interesting sidelights' is provided by the Indian bureaucrats who translated Tagore's poem into Hindi for the commemorative volume of the event. By rendering Tagore's poem in the Indian national language they were perhaps seeking to 'nationalise' the poet's Bengali cosmopolitanism. In *Life Goes On* too, Datta attempts to produce a Bengali identity which is not just regional or international but also national. The character of Alok, Sanjay's friend who reminds us of Lear's fool, is a Hindi-speaking North Indian whose presence tempers what might otherwise appear as Bengali parochialism. On his demand, the two Tagore songs used in the film appear in Hindi translations, and he makes fun of stereotypical Bengali traits, like sentimentality. When Lolita, the oldest daughter speaks of her failing marriage, he says, 'No more Bengali melodrama, no *ronaa dhonaa* (crying)'. The film's mixed cast including Bengali and non-Bengali actors with varying *Bangla*-speaking competences also stretches the idea of Bengaliness. While Sharmila Tagore who plays Manju is Bengali, Sanjay's role, initially written for Soumitro Chatterjee, veteran Bengali actor of many Satyajit Ray films, was undertaken by Girish Karnad, an acclaimed artiste of Kannada and English theatre and art-house Hindi cinema of the 1980s. Although his snatches of Bengali dialogue sound awkward his presence imparts a pan-Indian quality to the self-conscious construction of Bengaliness in the film.

Datta points out how certain regional identities have come to represent Indianness in diasporic cinema, indicating the preponderance of Punjabis and North Indians in the films of Gurinder Chaddha or Deepa Mehta.[18] In Bollywood films too, whether set in India or in the West, North Indian customs and the Hindi language constitute national identity. It is only recently that the diaspora is being pluralised. Crossover films like *The Namesake* or *Brick Lane* based on novels on Bengali lives are generating a new interest in Bengali identities. In trying to delineate Bengaliness through the Lear story, Datta was attempting to focus on a community which rarely represents the face of Indian diaspora.[19] Could this be because the middle-class, educated Bengali, historically designed to be 'English in tastes, in opinions, in morals, in intellect' is so well assimilated in the culture of the host nation that its specificities do not stand out? Or, despite its cosmopolitanism Bengali culture remains too obscure to be legible in the idiom of popular cinema?[20] Datta has therefore tried to portray a Bengali identity which is accessible through the national and international languages of Hindi and English. Migration, diaspora and globalisation have created hybrid and transnational identities which have challenged the hegemony of the nation state and the racialised and exclusionary formations of national identity. However, through nostalgic articulations of a homeland and the desire for a pure, timeless originary location and belonging, diasporic imaginings also help to construct and reinforce the logic of the nation. In fact, diasporic and national identities are mutually constitutive, producing each other through cultural discourses and material practices.[21] Just as the homeland is not an '*apriori* given'[22] but emerges through diasporic constructions of an idealised past before exile in a foreign land, the homeland also imagines itself and its diasporas as being linked through a mythical, unchanging, shared culture of a common nation.

In *Life Goes On* the Bannerjees appear to be well integrated in British society. Sanjay has an OBE (Order of the British Empire) and is an 'Asian achiever' and a community leader, while Manju and the daughters have successful lives and careers in the United Kingdom. Yet the question of cultural difference is insistently evoked particularly in times of crisis. Although Lolita's British husband is accepted in the family, as soon as there is a possibility of a marital breakdown, Sanjay remarks, 'There is such a thing as cultural difference'. Tuli's desire to live alone and follow her sexual and career choices are regarded by Manju as being against 'our custom'. The most intense and anxious articulation of a Bengali Hindu identity comes from Sanjay when Diya announces her decision to marry Imtiaz. Like the irate Lear when Cordelia refuses to speak, Sanjay takes this as a personal affront: 'I have a reputation in this community'. Manju too asks Diya, 'What happens to us, our values, our culture, our family?' The veneer of sophisticated liberalism crumbles, and the myth of *bhadralok*[23] modernity lies exposed. Yet this modernity in its colonial formulation was always already inflected by the privileges of class, majoritarian religion and nationalism. In its diasporic *avatar* these fissures are accentuated. Instead of weakening the nation state, the transnational spaces created by migration have provided a site for consolidating religious nationalisms.[24] In the post-9/11 world prejudices against Muslim immigrants have intensified creating further divisions between 'good' and 'bad' migrants within state ideologies of Western multiculturalism. The educated, professional Asian migrant like Sanjay is promoted as a 'model minority' subject who is assimilated in the host country, contributes to its economy and is worthy of its citizenship, while poor Muslims like Imtiaz's brother who insists on asserting his Islamic identity are marked as being misguided, susceptible to radicalisation and resistant to integration. Poised to make a life for himself in the United Kingdom and marry into a Hindu family, Imtiaz is careful to avoid such identifications. He reminds his brother, who on the Maulvi's advice, decides to give up 'anti-Islamic' music: 'Music is in our blood, in our culture … Islam teaches you to be a good human being—don't confuse culture with religion'.

The relationship of Bengali culture and religion is a running theme in the film. Sanjay locates his hatred for Muslims in his traumatic displacement during the Partition, an event seen as a historic caesura, a rupture which divided two communities who had always lived in harmony. However, these communal prejudices have a longer history. Sanjay's outburst about Diya's Muslim boyfriend is not a momentary fracturing of an otherwise modern Bengali self but a manifestation of a modernity in which literary cosmopolitanism coexists with entrenched class, race and religious biases. The modern Bengali self is always already marked as Hindu and Indian. Bangladeshi Muslims have had to struggle to claim their right to the Bengali language and identity.[25] Imtiaz's defence of music suggests that the claim to a common Bengali culture can be made perhaps only by erasing the demands of an Islamic identity.

In *Life Goes On*, Datta provocatively asks, how can we think of Bengaliness more inclusively and transnationally? Although it has historically defined itself through its dual allegiance to Western education and nationalist thought, to Shakespeare and to Tagore, it has failed to transcend the boundaries of religion and class. For Sanjay, despite the commonalities of language and culture of the two Bengals,[26] Imtiaz's religion is an insuperable barrier. He finds it easier to accept the obvious 'cultural difference' of his British son-in-law, John, partly also because of his class. While John is a banker of financial and social standing, to Sanjay, Imtiaz represents the 'bad migrant'–Diya's marriage to him would compromise Sanjay's own status within the diasporic community. To justify his own prejudices, Sanjay evokes the worst stereotypes of Muslims as failed subjects of modernity – illiberal, irrational and violent. He asks Diya, 'Do you want to get involved in terrorist activities?'; 'Are you going to spend the rest of your life wrapped up in a *hijaab*?'

As in colonial times, the tradition and modernity debate is played out on the woman's body. In Sanjay's imagination the *hijaab*-wrapped woman embodies the regressiveness of Muslim migrants and is defined against the modernity of Diya and the women in his family. Yet Manju, despite her integration into British society, continues to be identified with Hindu Bengali tradition, the Mother figure who represents Indian culture. She wears sarees, sings Tagore songs, plays the sitar, offers flowers at the feet of Gandhi's statue and creates a 'home' in a foreign land. Desai argues, 'diasporas maintain and consolidate connections and imaginings of the homeland by performing national identities through gender and sexual normativities.'[27] Manju's normative femininity performs the Nation. When she dies, tensions erupt, particularly around 'deviant' sexualities which threaten not just the family but also the community and the nation maintained through heteronormative constructions of birth, lineage, race and caste. Gayatri Gopinath shows how the 'queer diaspora' challenges nationalist ideologies by recuperating 'those desires, practices and subjectivities that are rendered impossible and unimaginable within conventional diasporic and nationalist discourses.'[28]

In British diasporic cinema from *My Beautiful Laundrette* (1985) to *East is East* (1999) or *Bend it Like Beckham* (2002), sex and gender deviances threaten migrant nationalisms. In *Life Goes On*, Tuli's lesbianism and love of sport challenges the gender-sexuality norms which construct cultural nationalism. She says, 'I want a different life, different from your culture'. The other daughters too resist love and marriage within the community. Even Manju's status as the ideal wife is questioned when Alok hints at a past moment of adulterous passion between them. By the end of the film, the narratives of family, Bengaliness and Nation lie disrupted and must be renegotiated through rebuilding relationships.

The Sanjay-Diya reconciliation does not automatically bring resolution. The ending remains ambiguous. Although Sanjay gestures to Imtiaz to join the group of friends and family, father and daughter walk arm in arm in exclusive intimacy while 'Come let's away to prison' (5.3.8–17) plays in Sanjay's voiceover.[29] One wonders whether the Nahum Tate like ending[30] with Cordelia/Diya marrying Edgar/Imtiaz which is hinted at can even begin to heal the historic breach of the Indian Partition.

Globalising Bengali Modernity: *Second Generation* (2003)

A two-part film, *Second Generation*, produced in 2003 by Channel 4 Television and directed by Jon Sen also uses the template of *King Lear* to construct a diasporic Bengali identity. The title hints at a narrative about second-generation migrants. But in the context of video or audio recording 'second generation' refers to copies which are not true and of poorer quality having suffered degeneration of the original master tape.[31]

The two-part serial is an unabashed celebration of the second generation's take, albeit impure and declaredly hybrid, on their parents' culture. Here Bengaliness does not bear the legacy of colonial modernity but is like takeaway chicken *korma* or the pickles made by the factory owned by Sharma, the Lear protagonist, suited to British tastes and unapologetically inauthentic perhaps even deliberately so. The film starts in Kolkata with iconic shots of the Howrah Bridge, a dead woman on a pyre, and floating images of letters from the Bangla script. Like these random alphabets, Bengaliness in the film is not rooted to any larger cultural meaning but is a bricolage of citations culled from touristy stock shots of Kolkata, references to the Calcutta University, Durga *puja* and snatches of Tagore songs, trying, through familiar images to evoke a milieu at several removes. They appear like a collage of the first generations' memories of a past life, filtered through the incomprehension of the second generation to whom these sights and sounds are empty and free-floating signifiers. Yet the aura of the Bengali identity is deployed as a mark of sophistication, pride or even secrecy when Heere (Cordelia) and her childhood sweetheart, Samir Khan (Edgar), start talking in public in Bengali. Sam tells Heere in front of her uncomprehending British boyfriend, Jack (Albany), that the latter would never be able to love her as he does because they do not share the same language. Ironically, the supposedly Bangla sentences that Sam and Heere exchange would sound alien to native speakers because of their awkward syntax and stilted accent. Like the underground South Asian fusion music which is a leitmotif in *Second Generation* (as in *Life Goes On*), Bengaliness is something of a remix and a mashup, a potpourri of cultural references drawn from various sources, not all of them Bengali. In fact rather than any recognisably Bengali Hindu or Bangladeshi Muslim experiences which they are supposed to reflect, most of the aural and visual allusions are derived from the dominant Punjabi and North Indian diasporic cultures and their mediated forms in Bollywood and diasporic cinema. The names of the Bengali characters are patently North Indian, like Sharma, the patriarch with three daughters. Cordelia's name, Heere, is unfamiliar even to the characters within the film who speculate whether it is Punjabi or Gujrati, only to be told proudly that it is Bengali. The *puja* held to celebrate Sharma's (Lear) recovery from illness is performed with the Hindi song, '*jai jagadish hare*', familiarised by Karan Johar's North Indian extended family melodramas like *Kabhi Khushi Kabhi Gham* (2001). From the 1990s, these Bollywood films, popular among diasporic audiences, established globally circulated iconic images of an elite Hindu life style which became synonymous with a generalised notion of Indianness. *Second Generation* deploys these tropes, legible markers of a hybridised British-Indian or diasporic South Asian identity inflected by Bollywood and diasporic cinema to construct an ambiguous notion of what it insistently labels as Bengaliness.

In *Second Generation*, the roles of first-generation Bengali migrants are enacted by North Indian Bollywood actors like Om Puri and Anupam Kher who struggle to speak Bangla. The presence of actors like Om Puri (lead actor in *My Son the Fanatic* and *East is East*) who plays Sharma/Lear and Parminder Nagra (of *Bend It Like Beckham* fame) as Heere/Cordelia help to locate the film within South Asian diasporic cinema with its small budgets and edgy narratives of violent intergenerational conflict. In fact successful diasporic films like *Bend It Like Beckham* and *East is East* have established the now-familiar plot comprising an intransigent patriarch, the transgression of gender and sexuality norms by his children and cultural contestations threatening to break up the family, the ultimate marker of South Asian identity.[32] This structure, uncannily close to the Lear story, frames *Second Generation*, although Shakespeare's play is not referred to self-consciously as a cultural product and an aspect of Bengali modernity as it is in *Life Goes On*.

Despite distinctions in the class positions of the families and in attitudes to culture and identity, the narratives of *Second Generation* and *Life Goes On* have parallel trajectories. Both use the *Lear* plot to tell the story of a Bengali Hindu patriarch and his three transgressive daughters, of whom the Cordelia figure insists on marrying a Muslim boy. In *Second Generation* Sharma's objection to Heere's initial decision to marry the white music critic Jack is far more intense than his reaction to her later relationship with Sam Khan, the son of his Muslim business associate of many years. This also distinguishes the Sharmas from the Bannerjees in *Life Goes On* who welcome their white son-in-law – not only does his presence in the family signify their own successful integration into British society, but it also underlines their modernity marked by their openness to Western culture. The Sharmas are from a less educated and rooted Bengali background and appear to be more easily threatened. Both films revolve around the memory of the dead mother who represents a nostalgic yearning for the home left behind. While in *Life Goes On*, Manju is a central figure, animated through frequent flashbacks, Sonali, Sharma's wife in *Second Generation*, is only glimpsed in fleeting images and heard through a refrain, chastising her husband for selling out to an alien country: '*Ei deshtaa ki korechhe tomaake*' (what has this country done to you!). Ironically, this moral condemnation for the loss of cultural identity is delivered in accented, second-generation Bangla, in which sound undermines sense.

Notwithstanding the hybridised and 'impure' expressions of Bengali identity in *Second Generation*, it articulates a cultural nationalism inflected with an anti-capitalist, even moralistic disapproval of deracinated diasporic subjects. Despite the powerful evocations of and hegemonic status accorded to Bengali culture, *Life Goes On* valorises assimilation into British society, and the possibility of return is never considered. Sharma, Heere and Sam, however, abandon the greed, individualism and selfishness of their families and associates in Britain and return home, to Kolkata, as the mother, Sonali, had so desperately wanted. Heere gives up her white boyfriend and chooses Sam, fellow Bengali and childhood sweetheart, who speaks her language and understands her filial responsibilities. In *Second Generation*, Sam's religion (Islam) is less of an impediment than Imtiaz's is in *Life Goes On*. Heere and Sam's relationship is located in a timeless, originary oneness untroubled by the historical tensions of Partition. Assisted by the Kent figure (Roshan Seth), Heere and Sam rescue Sharma from the psychiatric hospital to which his two older daughters had committed him so that they could take over his company and property.

Heere's journey to Kolkata with her father and Sam signifies a flight from a rapacious, alien society to the comfort of home – an idyllic, almost pre-capitalist, premodern space suffused with memory, symbolised by images of the mother. At the end of the film, Kolkata provides the quiet haven of intimacy, a refuge in which father and daughter can sing 'like birds in a cage' and comment detachedly on the bustling world going by. In a final aerial shot, Heere and Sam look out from a terrace at the Kolkata skyline and comment ambiguously: 'It is not London'. Does the return then signify a retreat from the modern metropolis, a 'not-London' space emptied of any other significance? Does *Lear* then provide the emotional context for this withdrawal and the recuperation of a lost Bengali identity, an idealised simplicity and the values of the traditional extended family? Does the film, despite its celebration of the hybrid lives of the second generation, ultimately reinforce an Indian cultural nationalism upheld paradoxically by Shakespeare?

When asked whether the ending confirmed the regressive and racist demand for immigrants to go back home, Jon Sen said,

> I think it's a positive statement ... It turns on its head that whole traditional view of immigration, that it's a one-way traffic from India or the subcontinent to England ... India in the last 20 years ... has revolutionized its economy, there's Bollywood, the telecommunication

industry ... This idea that young British Asians can make a life for themselves back in India with an equally good standard of living, is a positive thing because it reverses the kind of automatic suppositions.[33]

Sen suggests that rather than marking a flight from modernity and cosmopolitanism, the end of the film affirms a new globality in which traditional constructions of home and the world, of the diasporic and the national, of the British-Asian and the Bengali can be redefined. In this reformulation of multiculturalism, not sponsored by the British state but negotiated against the twenty-first-century Kolkata skyline, Shakespeare continues to be relevant, not in the self-conscious way of *Life Goes On* but as an influence so well integrated that it does not require citation. Although Shakespeare's play refuses to offer any sense of reconciliation, in both *Life Goes On* and *Second Generation* the ending hints at Cordelia's marriage to Edgar indicating a new beginning. In both films, although Shakespeare appears to uphold Bengali traditions, the changed ending also anticipates a new dispensation signified by the possibility of a Hindu-Muslim union. Whereas in *36 Chowringhee Lane* and *The Last Lear*, Shakespeare is more of a cultural relic upholding a Bengali modernity evolved through an inequitable colonial education, in the two diasporic films there is a gesture, ever so slight, towards a new Shakespearean negotiation and the forging of a more inclusive Bengali identity.

Afterword: *Bangla* Shakespeares and Millennial Kolkata

The recent spate of regional Bangla films based on Shakespearean plays articulate a more syncretic and contemporary Bengaliness, rooted in a rapidly changing Kolkata cityscape. These films try to move away from the template of middle-class, realist cinema based on literary themes with a predominance of dialogues which constituted the 'Bengaliness' of Bangla cinema since its inception, setting it apart from the action, dance and spectacle of popular Hindi films. Working within this paradigm and drawing from world cinema, the films of Ray, Ghatak and Mrinal Sen put Bengali cinema on the international map. But from the 1980s, changing audience demographics created a demand, particularly in rural Bengal, for a less cerebral cinema which could approximate to popular Hindi films. This gave rise to the work of Shakti Samanta and Anjan Chowdhury. Rituparno Ghosh, Aparna Sen and Anjan Dutt continued to direct films on *bhadralok* Bengali lives in the mould of Ray for an urban audience. However, in recent times these directors and some younger ones are exploring other kinds of lives and experiences in a globalising Kolkata, perhaps to woo newer and younger audiences. The recent Shakespeare films represent this shift.

No longer an icon of the empire nor of an elite colonial modernity, Shakespeare's plays become sites of real estate gang wars in Aparna Sen's *Arshinagar* (Mirror City, 2015), a take on *Romeo and Juliet*; film industry intrigues in Anjan Dutt's *Hemanta* (2016), a version of *Hamlet*; or dockyard crime in Srijit Mukherjee's *Zulfiqar* (2016), based on *Julius Caesar* and *Antony and Cleopatra*. Not only do these films depict a new Kolkata of sky scrapers and malls, slum evictions and political corruption, consumerism and the glamour industry, but they also construct a new Bengaliness. Moving away from the English-educated, Hindu, middle-class protagonists of the English *Lear* films, they focus on actors, rock singers, hackers, land sharks, mafia dons and their molls and narrate stories of classes and communities often underrepresented in serious Bengali cinema. In *Arshinagar*, Juliet/Juli comes from an upper-class Awadhi Muslim family who intersperse their Bengali with chaste Urdu words, while the docklands in *Zulfiqar* represent a melting pot of Muslim, Christian and Hindu cultures expressed through a potpourri of languages, accents and dialects. While the English *Lear* films explore a cosmopolitan and diasporic Bengali identity caught up in colonial legacies, the new Bangla Shakespeare films manifest an irreverent zestfulness towards traditional notions of Bengaliness as well as the bard. Unlike the 1965 Bengali film *Saptapadi* (dir.Ajoy Kar) which self-consciously cites *Othello*, none of these films underline their deployment of Shakespeare and do not expect their audience to notice it. Here Shakespeare is not a signifier of a culture or an identity but merely a resource to be used to narrate the story of millennial Kolkata and its denizens. Interestingly, whether in Bollywood, diasporic or regional cinema, Shakespeare provides a medium for articulating local identities and paradoxically, it is through these increasing forms of localisation that Shakespeare's universality survives.

Notes

1 The aim was to create 'a class of people Indian in blood and colour but English in tastes, in opinions, in morals, in intellect' serving as 'interpreters between us and the millions whom we govern'. See Thomas B. Macaulay, *Minute on Indian Education*, 1835. Reprinted in *Selected Writings*, ed. J. Clive and T. Pinney (Chicago: Chicago University Press, 1972), 729.
2 J. Bagchi, 'Shakespeare in Loin Cloths: English Literature and the Early Nationalist Consciousness in Bengal', *Rethinking English: Essays in Literature, Language, History*, ed. Svati Joshi (New Delhi: Trianka, 1991), 151.
3 Ibid., 149.
4 Homi Bhabha, 'Signs Taken for Wonders: Questions of Ambivalence and Authority under a Tree outside New Delhi—May 1817', *Critical Inquiry* 12, no. 1 (1985):162.
5 Partha Chatterjee, Our Modernity (Rotterdam and Dakar: Sephis and Codesaria, 1997), 14.
6 Swapan Chakravorty, *Baangalir Ingreji Sahitya Charchaa* [English Literary Studies by Bengalis] (Kolkata: Anushtup, 2006), 38.

178 *Paromita Chakravarti*

7 Utpal Dutt (1929–1963) was a foremost Indian Shakespearean. For his views on Indian theatre and cinema, see *On Theatre* (Kolkata: Seagull Books, 2009); *On Cinema* (Kolkata: Seagull Books, 2009). See overview of his career by Samik Bandyopadhyay in Nemai Ghosh, *Dramatic Moments; Photographs and Memories of Calcutta Theatre from the 60's to 70's* (Kolkata: Seagull Books, 2000). See Dutt's interview with Samik Bandyopadhyay in Rajinder Paul ed. *Contemporary Indian Theatre: Interview with Playwrights and Directors* (Delhi: Sangeet Natak Akademi, 1989).
8 See Tapati Gupta, 'From Proscenium to Paddy Fields: Utpal Dutt's Shakespeare *Jatra*' in *Re-playing Shakespeare in Asia*, ed. Poonam Trivedi and Minami Ryuta (New York and London: Routledge, 2010), 157–77.
9 The colonial name Calcutta is used to evoke a history relevant to these films. In 2001 in an act of postcolonial reclaiming, the city was renamed Kolkata, thereby readopting its precolonial name.
10 www.rediff.com/movies/2007/sep/19ab.html. Accessed 12th September, 2015.
11 www.realbollywood.com/news/2007/09/rituparno-ghosh-last-lear.html. Accessed 13th September, 2015.
12 Writer, musician, artist Satyajit Ray (1921–1992) was also a leading Indian film-maker whose *Pather Panchali* (Song of the Road, 1955) established Indian cinema in the international arena. Ray won awards at Cannes, Berlin, Venice and Moscow film festivals, thirty-two national film awards and an honorary Oscar in 1992. He directed over thirty feature and short films and several documentaries most of which were in Bengali.
13 The film was produced by Shashi Kapoor, lead actor of the Merchant Ivory *Shakespeare Wallah* and Violet was played by his wife, Jennifer Kendal, daughter to Geoffery Kendall and member of his itinerant theatre group celebrated in *Shakespeare Wallah*.
14 Ray's contemporary, Ritwik Ghatak (1925–1975) was a Bengali film-maker renowned in Indian cinema for the depiction of social reality and the impact of the Bengal Partition.
15 Jigna Desai, *Beyond Bollywood: The Cultural Politics of South Asian Diasporic Film* (New York and London: Routledge, 2004), 11.
16 All references to the play are from *The Norton Shakespeare*, ed. Stephen Greenblatt et al. (New York: W.W. Norton and Co., 1997).
17 'Words on a Pedestal', *The New Straits Times*, 18 June 1997.
18 In a personal interview to the author March 2015.
19 Ibid.
20 Recently Bollywood cinema has been creating caricatured or stereotypical versions of Bengali culture and of Kolkata in films like *Kahani*, *Byomkesh* and *Piku*.
21 Desai, 17–19.
22 Ibid., 19.
23 The Bangla term *bhadralok* literally means gentleman and refers to the caste, class and religious privileges associated with Bengali modernity.
24 Desai, 15.
25 The 1951 language movement in the then 'East Bengal' (under Pakistan's dominion) demanded Bangla rather than Urdu as their official language.
26 West Bengal in India and Bangladesh.
27 Desai, 29.
28 Gayatri Gopinath, *Impossible Desires: Queer Diasporas and South Asian Public Cultures* (Durham and London: Duke University Press, 2005), 11.

29 This passage also recited by Violet and Harry links *Life Goes On* with the films discussed earlier in an intertextual matrix.
30 Nahum Tate's 1681 adaptation of *King Lear* is a tragicomedy with Lear regaining his throne and Cordelia marrying Edgar which was popular on the English stage for over a century.
31 Sukhdev Sandhu, 'Its Asian Life but Not as We Know It', accessed on 12 January 2016, www.telegraph.co.uk/culture/tvandradio/3602568/Its-Asian-life-but-not-as-we-know-it.html.
32 See Desai, 48.
33 'Homeward Bound', 19 September 2003. Rashmee Z. Ahmed's interview with Jon Sen, accessed on 15 January 2016, http://timesofindia.Indiatimes.com/home/Sunday-toi/all-that-matters/Nobody-owns-a-nations-culture/articleshow/4093742.cms?referral=PM.

10 Shakespeare and Indian Independent Cinema
8×10 Tasveer and 10 ml Love

Varsha Panjwani

For those who have been following India's millennial filmic adaptations of Shakespeare, it is quite certain that they would have come across Vishal Bhardwaj's trilogy: *Maqbool* (*Macbeth*), *Omkara* (*Othello*) and *Haider* (*Hamlet*).[1] It is also likely that they would not know about *10 ml Love*, Sharat Katariya's 2012 take on Shakespeare's *A Midsummer Night's Dream*,[2] or *8×10 Tasveer*, Nagesh Kukunoor's 2009 reworking of *Hamlet* as a murder mystery.[3]

These Shakespeare adaptations have been overlooked because they are independent (henceforth indie) Indian movies,[4] and they remain largely unnoticed. Rachel Dwyer, one of a handful of scholars to give Indian indie cinema any attention, admitted in 2011 that 'there is little scholarly research on these films as yet,'[5] and this continues to be the case today, even though the Indian indie is at least twenty years old. Director Kaizad Gustad says that 1998 was a 'watershed year' for the Indian indie. His indie film *Bombay Boys*[6] and Kukunoor's movie *Hyderabad Blues*[7] were released in this year, and 'what became clear was that you could make a commercially viable project that wasn't mainstream Bollywood.'[8] If the projects were not 'mainstream Bollywood', they were not parallel or art-house cinema either. Both these movies feature young, middle-class, transnational, urban protagonists; are shot in real city locations; employ the language of the Indian cosmopolitan youth – Hinglish (a mixture of Hindi and English) mixed further with vernacular languages: Telugu in *Hyderabad Blues* and Marathi in *Bombay Boys*; and are made on a very small budget. It was clear that a new type of cinema had emerged. Around 2001, Gustad recognised that the indie movement in India was underway and drew up a manifesto for these films:

> Our manifesto is a simple one: set after 1947 (partition); director of Indian origin or content of Indian origin, no Bollywood, parallel or arthouse, no gratuitous songs, dances, or foreign locations.
> Fiction: short or long contemporary. Original. Any medium. No script, no shoot. No slow pans, and the director retains final cut. Currently the filmmakers are Dev Benegal, Anuradha Parikh-Benegal, Kaizad Gustad, Elaphe Hiptoolah [*sic*], Nagesh Kukunoor,

and we keep our doors open to other filmmakers who share the ideals of our manifesto.

... The idea is to develop, produce, promote and acquire films that create a new culture of cinema in India that is independent of the mainstream and parallel ideologies.[9]

Today, many more directors have joined their ranks (including Anurag Kashyap, Onir, Dibakar Banerjee and Shonali Bose), and the Indian indie can be sampled in various genres and styles. These movies do not necessarily conform to all the tenets laid out in the manifesto but remain true to its spirit in that 'the cinema is independent of the mainstream and parallel ideologies'. The declaration of difference is usually encoded in the films themselves. For instance, Gustad's *Bombay Boys* is not about the nature of the Indian indie per se, but it nevertheless satirises Bollywood, thereby calling attention to its own status as a film which occupies a different niche in Indian cinema. Similarly, Kashyap's latest offering, *Ugly*,[10] is about the perversity of human emotions and the monetisation of relationships. The story kicks off when a little girl disappears from her father's car. As her relatives begin to look for her, they get caught up in settling scores and fraudulently obtaining money from each other instead of concentrating on their search. Unlikely as it might sound, this movie includes a pastiche of the infamous 'item song' trope used in Bollywood and takes this opportunity to declare its difference from a Bollywood film.

As indie film-makers are interested in promoting their markedly different sensibilities in the films themselves, self-referentiality has become a prominent characteristic of an Indian indie, no matter what the content. Perhaps it is because of the self-reflexivity of Shakespeare's plays that Indian indie directors have been attracted to them. It is telling that the Indian indie's first forays into Shakespeare are *Hamlet* and *A Midsummer Night's Dream* (henceforth *MND*). With a play-within-the-play and rehearsal scenes, these two are the most metatheatrical of Shakespeare's plays. Just as Shakespeare uses his plays to comment upon the theatre industry and the playwright's craft, Katariya and Kukunoor use Shakespeare's plays to draw attention to the Indian indie industry and the director's craft in working within the available resources. It is this very stance that is responsible for the uniqueness of their approach to Shakespeare. The films' obsession with talking about the Indian indie's limited means translates into an incisive materialistic reading of Shakespeare's plays. As a result, these films merit consideration by scholars of both Shakespeare and Indian indie cinema, and this essay is the first to give them the critical attention that is their due.[11]

8×10 Tasveer

In an email exchange, Kukunoor explains that the idea for *8×10 Tasveer* came out of [him] staring at a photograph that hung on the wall opposite [his] bed. A lot of times [he] would wonder what the people in the photo were thinking about at the exact moment the shutter (pre digital days, of course) was snapped ... it suddenly hit [him] that [he] should write a whodunit using that premise.[12]

Kukunoor does not even claim Shakespeare as an influence, and *8×10 Tasveer* does not advertise its Shakespeare connections anywhere on its posters or publicity material. Despite Kukunoor's reservations, it is tough not to see *8×10 Tasveer* as a freewheeling adaptation of *Hamlet*. A summary of *8×10 Tasveer* is essential to trace the parallels between the movie and the play.

The story revolves around Jai (Akshay Kumar), who has the psychic ability to delve into anyone's past by looking at their *tasveer* (photograph), but this comes at a price because every time he uses this power, he requires a blood transfusion, and if he employs it for more than one minute, he is likely to die. Early on in the film, Jai's father, Jatin (Benjamin Gilani), dies in a mysterious accident. Jai does not 'doubt some foul play' (1.2.254),[13] but his father's spirit is not yet at rest and haunts Jai in a dream, calling out *'meri madat karo beta'* ('help me, son'). Aided by a loyal Horatio-like confidante, Happi (Jaaved Jaaferi), who convinces Jai that his father's death was not an accident, Jai sets out on a whodunnit quest to discover his father's killer. Jai's first suspect is his mother, Savitri (Sharmila Tagore), as she is the sole beneficiary of her dead husband's substantial property. However, Jai dismisses her as a prime suspect when he travels to the past with the help of a photograph which was taken minutes before his father's death. He discovers that, in fact, it was his uncle who 'poisoned' his father by mixing a fatal dose of a blood pressure medicine in his drink. When his uncle is found hanging by a noose in his house, Jai realises that his uncle was not the only Claudius in this story. Jai's next suspect is Anil (Girish Karnad), his father's family friend and lawyer, who has always been in love with his mother. In a scene which recalls the Hamlet-Gertrude dynamic, Jai shows up at his mother's house only to find his mother and Anil in an embrace. Jai is enraged and tells his mother in no uncertain terms that he finds her behaviour 'disgusting' and that he suspects her and Anil of plotting the murder of his father. He finally leaves but not before telling his mother that he intended to stay with her but cannot do so because 'it's overcrowded'. So, this is a film which includes a father who dies in an accident and solicits his son's help in a dream, a mother who inherits the property, and two suspects – an uncle who 'poisons' his father and his father's friend, who had a motive since he loved Jai's mother (Figure 10.1).

The similarities do not stop here as the language itself is replete with echoes from *Hamlet*. At one point, Jai's best friend and his dead father's protégé, Adit (Rushad Rana), advises Jai that *'tu bhooton ka peecha*

Figure 10.1 Jai/Hamlet finds his mother embracing his uncle.

karna band kar de' ('you should stop chasing after ghosts'). Moreover Jai is charged throughout the movie with madness caused by excessive grief. Adit tells Jai that it is his 'emotional breakdown' over his father's death which has led to '*paagalpan*' (madness), and his mother chides him when she says that '*iss photo ke chakkar ne tumko bilkul pagal kar diya hai*' ('this photo affair has driven you insane'). Finally, Hamlet-like, Jai is acutely aware of his lonely position, and he confesses as much to his friend, Adit, when, over a drink, he says, '*na mein kissi pe bharosa kar sakta hon, na mujpe koi yakeen*' ('neither can I trust anyone, nor will anyone believe me').

In this *Hamlet*-with-a-twist, it emerges that the real killer was Jai's long-lost identical twin, Jeet (also played by Akshay Kumar), whom the family had believed dead after a childhood incident. Jai and Jeet were playing football during a family picnic in the mountains, and Jai was responsible for holding Jeet as he went to retrieve the ball from an awkward spot on the cliff; Jai lost his hold, and Jeet, the family supposed, fell to his death. Jeet, who miraculously survived, holds Jai responsible for this accident and comes back to exact his revenge chiefly upon his brother; the movie both deepens the play's sibling rivalry between Hamlet senior and Claudius by multiplying the brother-kills-brother pairs and reproduces the double-revenge structure of *Hamlet* as Jai is both the revenger of his father and the (supposed) killer of his brother. Jeet, however, is more like Hamlet than a Laertes; Jeet's similarities with Shakespeare's Hamlet are to do with his position as a playwright-director. Hamlet's writerly bent is most explicitly exhibited when he composes a 'speech of some dozen or sixteen lines' for the players (2.2.477). He then proceeds to direct the production of the 'mousetrap' by giving detailed instructions to the players on their gesture and diction (3.2.1–43). Jeet too is an obsessive writer-director and has a 'mousetrap' of his own: his plan is to rewrite his destiny by killing his brother and replacing him as the heir to the family fortune and business.

While Kukunoor's film can be seen as an intriguing remake of *Hamlet* as a murder mystery, what is really interesting to anyone studying the Indian indie is the way in which *8×10 Tasveer* references the plight of the indie film-maker. Jeet can be seen as an indie film-maker as most of them are both writers and directors of their films. His rewriting is not textual but extremely cinematic. He secretly spies on his brother by filming and photographing him. A shot of Jeet's house reveals several tapes and photographs, and he learns his brother's mannerisms by playing and replaying these tapes, so he can eventually replace his brother as the heir of the family. Also, characteristic of an Indian indie director, Jeet has a script but does not have the money, so he is forced to collaborate with Jai's 'friend', Adit, because the movie makes it clear that *'har plan ko financing ki zaroorat hoti hai'* ('every plan requires funding'). Moreover Jeet enlists the help of his lover, Sheila (Ayesha Takia), to spy on his brother. In this version, it is not Polonius but the aspiring Hamlet who uses his Ophelia as a honey trap to learn more about the supposedly rightful heir. Thus Jeet uses every means and resource available to him to make his project a success. Also, he has to change his script a number of times because of money matters. He reveals that he never intended to murder his father but was forced to do so because his father was planning to donate all his money to his elder son Jai's organisation. Jeet changes his plan again when he stabs his mother because she decides to fulfil her late husband's wishes. Finally, however, the changing fancies of his parents and the different agendas of his collaborating partners – Adit (who escapes with a substantial amount of money when his secret is out) and Sheila (who is upset when Jeet seems momentarily persuaded by his elder brother that they need not quarrel over money) – lead to his death. Like Hamlet, he dies, but unlike Hamlet, he does not have his revenge, and his plan goes completely awry. Through Jeet's bleak fate, Kukunoor exemplifies what happens to the ambitious ideas of a writer-director when he is forced to rely on those who can finance the project. No matter how carefully executed and directed, plans are bound to prove futile and be perceived as failures under these circumstances.

Uncannily, this was exactly the trajectory followed by *8×10 Tasveer*. To begin with, Kukunoor had a reasonable budget and cast megastar Akshay Kumar in the lead role. The movie was shot in Canada and boasts stunning cinematography, and the verdant landscape is beautifully captured. In addition, the action scenes, such as Jai jumping off a cliff to procure incriminating evidence and an underwater sequence in which he rises to the surface after freeing himself, are deftly executed, giving the movie a slick and polished feel. The film also set benchmarks in visual effects. The creative team at Prime Focus who worked on it

Shakespeare and Indian Independent Cinema 185

explain that techniques like shooting in several layers are common practice for movies that involve double roles, but for this movie, they used a frame-by-frame rotoscoping: 'all of Akshay's shots were shot twice in two different layers using a dummy character in front of him. Later, the dummy character was rotoed out from each frame and was replaced by Akshay shot in a separate layer.'[14] These innovations were extended to scenes on a boat in which a particular incident is seen from various camera angles and perspectives. As he begins to unravel the mystery, Jai repeatedly visits the scene of the crime on the boat via the characters in the photograph. In each of these scenes, the audience shares the field of vision of the characters as if they were investigating the crime scene themselves. In other words, the audience enters the film through camera work just as Jai enters the scene through the photograph. Despite the inventive screenplay and the accomplished shooting, the movie was a critical and commercial failure. While he is never one to shy away from being self-critical, Kukunoor staunchly defends this film, which, he asserts, 'turned out exactly the way I intended ... the script and the story were what I intended'. Instead, he says that 'what didn't work was the process of making it.'[15] The production problems he faced as an indie film-maker started early. The newspaper *Mid-Day* reported that finances were a major part of the problem as 'the money wasn't flowing in and the deposits on locations hadn't been paid. When they wanted to shoot in a $20 million mansion, they couldn't pay the $25,000 deposit'. The line producer also confirmed that there were 'money problems' and elaborated that 'the Canadian crew needs to be paid every week. We have shot over 40 films in Canada and USA, and we've rarely had such problems.'[16] Such hiccups continued right until the film's release, which was in jeopardy when the production company defaulted on a payment to T-series, which held the music rights.[17] Although this issue was swiftly tackled, all these incidents cumulatively meant that 'a film that should have been neatly wrapped up by the end of 2007 dragged on for another 18 months or so and it shows.'[18] When asked about the negative reviews of the film, Kukunoor sardonically remarked that 'it's a non-Bollywood film. That's its flaw.'[19] *8×10 Tasveer* did not lack ideas, talent or even star-power, yet the process of indie film-making was largely responsible for its failure. Kukunoor's remarks prove that he was acutely aware of his difficult position as an indie film-maker while directing *8×10 Tasveer*, and Jeet's trials and tribulations mirror the production reality of the film, intentionally or unintentionally.

In 2007, just one year before Kukunoor's film, Margreta de Grazia published *'Hamlet' Without Hamlet*,[20] and Dympna Callahan applauded it as 'a dazzling interpretation of the play that deftly reprises the history of *Hamlet* criticism.'[21] What de Grazia's book does for *Hamlet* scholarship, Kukunoor does for *Hamlet* production. De Grazia's reading was revisionist because it emphasised the materialist aspects of the play which are often overlooked. Kukunoor's reframing of the play is no less dazzling and no less material. De Grazia argues that Hamlet's biggest complaint is that 'at his father's death, just at the point when an only son in a patrilineal system stands to inherit, Hamlet is dispossessed.'[22] One of the two Hamlets in *8×10 Tasveer*, Jeet, has precisely this problem as he does not wish to lose his inheritance. In order to appreciate the refreshing nature of this interpretation, it is important to register just how different this is to the mainstream portrayals of Hamlet. Post-Sigmund Freud, who developed his theory of the Oedipus complex using Hamlet as a template, the prince has usually been depicted as fixated on his mother. In Anglo-American criticism and performance, *Hamlet* has often been read as a domestic drama 'with some productions to this day omitting Fortinbras and most of the play's politics (this happened, for example, when John Caird directed Simon Russell Beale at the National Theatre in London in 2000)'. In other parts of the world, however, 'notably in eastern and east-central Europe during the dominance of the Soviet Union and the Cold War, *Hamlet* has been primarily a political play enacting the possibility of dissent from various forms of totalitarianism.'[23] The most recent Indian adaptation, *Haider*, masterfully fuses these parallel performance traditions. Haider (Hamlet, played by Shahid Kapoor) has both revolutionary and oedipal tendencies. The film is set in the fraught territory of Kashmir at the peak of militancy in the mid-1990s, and Haider is as stifled by Kashmir as he is troubled by his mother Ghazala's (Gertrude, played by Tabu) infidelity. The chemistry between Haider and Ghazala is as crackling as it is uncomfortable to watch, and Haider's psychological troubles erupt in a scene where he smashes everything in sight when Ghazala admits to harbouring feelings for his uncle. In *8×10 Tasveer*, while Jai's supposed madness results from loneliness and betrayal, Jeet's psychopathic killing spree is set off when he realises that there is no other way to protect his assets and property. While Jai simply wants to avenge his father's death, Jeet's sole motivation is to prevent the loss of his inheritance. Kukunoor offers the viewers two Hamlets: one framed by modern criticism as beleaguered with psychological problems and the other more material in his approach as it is the loss of his rightful claim to his father's property that has caused his anguish. Thus *8×10 Tasveer* both recalls and then provides an alternate reading of the play by zooming in on the materialistic aspects of the play in an unprecedented manner.

10 ml Love

If Kukunoor had to deal with the production challenges faced by an indie director, then Katariya had an even bigger trial on his hands as his budget for *10 ml Love* was extremely small – a fact that was frankly, and at times proudly, shared by Katariya. Like Kukunoor's film, the production context of *10 ml Love* seeped into the interpretation of its content. For his debut film, Katariya wanted to make a movie about aphrodisiac sellers who line the streets of Mumbai. Only when he had decided upon this subject matter, did he recall that *MND* too revolves around love potions, so he decided to use Shakespeare's play as a framework.[24]

A Midsummer Night's Dream is an attractive play to set in an Indian context as the text itself includes references to India. Oberon and Titania argue over the 'Indian boy', and Titania describes how 'his mother was a votaress of my order, /And in the spicèd Indian air by night/Full often hath she gossiped by my side, /And sat with me on Neptune's yellow sands/Marking th'embarkèd traders on the flood' (2.1.123–27).[25] As Sukanta Chaudhuri points out, 'this is the only passage in Shakespeare where, in one of his characteristic brief vignettes, he depicts what purports to be an Indian setting' but to Shakespeare 'what matters is not India as India, but India as not-England, not-Europe: something strange, something other'. Chaudhuri elaborates that 'there is nothing localized or distinctively perceived about the scene ... the passage affords us the mere sense of an exotic, lyrically presented otherness' or 'undifferentiated exoticism.'[26] In a radical break with Indian theatrical adaptations of this play which focus on the 'Indian boy' or at least find a vocabulary to realise the 'spicèd Indian air' of Shakespeare's imagery,[27] Katariya eliminates any mention of either and sets the first half in the far-from-exotic streets and houses of cosmopolitan Mumbai and the next half in a forest-farmhouse such as those owned by the urban elite in India. The result is that the play is indigenised but not orientalised so that India is not viewed through Shakespeare's gaze as 'something strange, something other'; rather Shakespeare is viewed through an urban Indian gaze.

The characters are as cosmopolitan, modern and as Indian as the setting. In an echo of stage productions of the play since Peter Brook, Theseus and Hippolyta are also Titania and Oberon. The actors Tisca Chopra and Rajat Kapoor do not merely double the roles – they combine them; Roshni is an amalgam of Titania and Hippolyta, and her husband, Ghalib, is a combination of Theseus and the extremely 'jealous Oberon' (2.1.61). The couple are neither Duke and Duchess nor King and Queen of the fairies; Ghalib sells quack medicines and assorted aphrodisiacs at a makeshift roadside stall, and Roshni specialises in bridal henna designs. The two pairs of lovers are retained, and their plot is closely followed. Hermia becomes the upper-middle-class Shweta Rai (Tara Sharma Saluja), and Helena becomes Minnie Mehta (Koel Purie Rinchet). Shweta is in love with car mechanic Peter Perriera (Lysander, played by Neil Bhoopalam), but she is to marry globetrotter Neel Bhatia (Demetrius, played by Purab Kohli). For Shweta, this is a typical Indian 'arranged' marriage, but for Neel it is something more as he has always had a childhood crush on Shweta. Meanwhile, Neel's long-time

188   *Varsha Panjwani*

and long-suffering girlfriend Minnie is saddened by this and looks for ways to prevent the marriage and convince Neel that Shweta does not care about him as she does. Minnie finds an opportunity when, in confidential girl-to-girl chat, Shweta tells Minnie that she loves Peter. Minnie searches for Peter and convinces him to elope with Shweta on the day of the wedding. Minnie, Shweta, Neel and Peter thus gather at Shweta's house during the wedding celebrations. Roshni too joins this gathering as she has been hired to apply henna on the would-be bride Shweta's hands, and her suspicious husband follows her with one of his most potent aphrodisiac and love potions, *josh-e-jawaani* (passion-of-youth). Apparently only a little bit (10 ml) of this potion in water is enough to make the person drinking it fall in lust and love with whomsoever they see immediately after consuming the potion. The usual mayhem ensues when Neel and Peter both drink the potion by mistake and see Minnie, whom they start desiring immediately. Finally, instead of the mechanicals, it is the servants employed by Shweta's father who are rehearsing a play and are beset with disruptions. Roshni, after drinking *josh-e-jawaani* herself, lusts after their leading actor Chand (Bottom, played by Manu Rishi) and spends the night with him in the forest-farmhouse.

Such everyday locations also put a strain on Katariya's budget, and he describes how one of his biggest challenges was shooting the nighttime forest scenes, even though he had anticipated this. Katariya had reserved a sizeable portion of his budget for this shoot; he did not mind 'cheap locations' for the entire film because he wanted 'to save the money for that part'. Luckily, his production designer found a 'good eucalyptus farm' which 'looked great'. On reaching the venue he discovered to his dismay that 'lighting this place would take seven days' if they 'wanted good lighting'. He explains that 'it takes huge budgets to light places like this otherwise it will just be a patch of light and it looks very odd in films' so creative ways to shoot had to be found.[28] Even this seemingly individual difficulty aligns Katariya to a specific film industry context because indie directors always mention lighting as their stumbling block. Kashyap, for instance, relates how his entire film was marred by this. His 2008 release, *Gulaal*, was written in 2000–2001 but was made over eight years because Kashyap would 'shoot it around every Diwali [an Indian festival] because [they] didn't have money for production and Jaipur is all lit up around Diwali. It was beautiful and it gave [him] enough light to shoot in. That's why all the night shots you see from beginning to end are shot on Diwali'. While the light was 'beautiful', this destroyed the film because it was 'set in the immediate future then but by the time it was released, the future was the past.'[29] Onir maintains that if there is one thing he wishes he could have done differently about his film, *My Brother ... Nikhil*, it is the 'night sequence in the film which [he] had to shoot with no lights because [they] didn't have the money and whenever [he] look[s] at it now, [he] always feel[s]

[he] could have just shot the scene during the day and it would not have affected anything.'[30]

Katariya's solution was to shoot the night-time scenes during the day in a 'day for night' format. This meant shooting in broad daylight using filters to kill excess sunlight and 'boosting' light on faces, with the result that the night-time forest scenes are bathed in bright blue light.[31] Katariya's position here was not unlike that of Shakespeare who was writing for the Globe and Blackfriars where lighting was largely inflexible. Just as Shakespeare employed theatrical resources such as language and gesture to distinguish between day and night on his stage, Katariya found a relatively inexpensive way to make the night-time forest scenes work for his film. Rather than impede the quality of the scenes, it turned out to be an advantage for the adaptation. When I first saw the movie without being aware of the context, I associated it with the 'magical' and 'enchanted' quality of the forest where anything can happen. The blurry quality of light gave the scenes a dreamy and moonlit quality. This unexpected success is an example of how the smallness of budgets need not be a limitation. Kukunoor, for one, is a firm believer that 'what happens when there is too much money is that you don't have any fear, so you don't force yourself to do your best work.'[32] For Katariya, the limited funding became a blessing and enhanced the aesthetic quality of the film.

If Shakespeare used conventions such as language and gesture to indicate darkness, he also mocked these tropes in the very play in which he used them.[33] For instance, in *MND*, Oberon and Puck indicate the time of the day and state of lighting in their extended dialogue in 3.2.354–95. This convention, which is used earnestly here, is mined for comic value in the same play when Bottom bursts upon the stage as Pyramus reciting, 'O grim-looked night, O night with hue so black, /O night which ever art when day is not! /O night, O night, alack, alack, alack' (5.1.167–69). The lack of money which forced the use of alternate resources produced good comic scenes in Katariya's film too. For example, when Shweta and Peter are discussing eloping, they are shown sitting inside a car, and heavy rain is splashing against the windshield. This is reminiscent of a number of Bollywood movies. As soon as there is either a romantic moment or a scene where conversation takes a serious or depressing turn in Bollywood, it starts raining heavily,[34] and Katariya makes us believe that the same trope is being employed in this film. At first, it feels as though this is a concession to the mainstream style, but minutes later, the viewers learn that it is not the rain that is splashing on the windshield but the water-jet from a car wash! This realisation simultaneously gets a laugh, sends up the Bollywood convention and points to the fact that in the ordinary lives of car mechanics, romance and tragedy can only have banal backdrops. However, the car wash scene not only lends realism to the world of the film but is also a production reality. Katariya simply did not have the budget to produce artificial rain on set nor did he have the money to shoot in the rain. Whether the quality of light in the forest scene or the comedy of the car wash scene, what is apparent is that material realities touched every aspect of this adaptation.

Katariya's interpretation of the play also takes its cue from this production concern as money is at the centre of *10 ml Love*. It does not take long for money to explicitly enter the discourse of the film. While Shakespeare's play is silent about why Egeus prefers Demetrius over Lysander, Katariya's script makes abundantly clear the social distance between the two suitors is great. Neel is from a well-to-do family, his parents live in America, and, while teasing him, Minnie reveals how he has never had to struggle for anything in his life. Shweta too belongs to an upper-middle-class family and is a bit of a spoilt brat, so their arranged marriage fits within the conventional pattern of Indian marriages between people from a similar social background. Meanwhile, Shweta's love, Peter, is a working-class car mechanic who can never hope to win the approval of her family. As Peter sits brooding over Shweta's marriage to Neel, his friend explains to him that love is a luxury: '*dekh, ye love-vove apunke liye haich nai. Ye sab bade logon ka chochla hai saala. Jeb mein maal hain tho pyaar karneka, nai tho gupchup saala kholi mein kadi marke baith jaaneka*' ('look, this love is not for the likes of us. It is the preserve of the upper class. If you have money in your purse, you can afford to love otherwise you should lock the door and sit still in your house'). This stark reminder of the power of money to open doors makes a deep impression on Peter, so much so that when Shweta suggests they should elope he, at first, loses his nerve and tells Shweta that he is afraid her father would use his influence, and '*voh police ko phone karega aur yeh kahega ki mechanic Peter Perriera ne meri beti ko kidnap kiya hai. Phir kya karenge hum?*' ('he will call the police and tell them that mechanic Peter Perriera has kidnapped his daughter. Whatever shall we do then?'). Besides fearing Shweta's father, Peter worries that he will not be able to provide Shweta with the luxuries she is used to. When an exasperated Shweta tells him, '*Peter, mein ghar chod ke tumhare paas aayihoon*' ('Peter, I've left home for you'), he sullenly corrects her and tells her that '*chodke nahi, sab pack karke suitcase le aayiho*' ('you've not left home, you've packed everything in a suitcase and brought it along'). In this regard, Peter is very different from Lysander who can assure Hermia of a comfortable existence when he tells her that 'I have a widow aunt, a dowager, /Of great revenue; and she hath no child. /From Athens is her house remote seven leagues; /And she respects me as her only son. /There, gentle Hermia, may I marry thee' (1.1.157–61). While Shakespeare briefly brings up financial considerations, Katariya anchors one of the play's ambiguities on money and uses it to explain why Peter and Shweta's love is forbidden. Only when Shweta follows Peter to the forest is he convinced that she is serious about adjusting her lifestyle to his means. Towards the end of the film, even the very last lines that Shweta and Peter exchange pertain to money. Peter proposes to Shweta, but Shweta is annoyed, not only because Peter has spent the night chasing Minnie but also because he has forgotten to get her a ring. Peter then makes her a ring out of leaves and grass and promises her that he will buy one for her once his friend returns his money next month. Shweta is placated and pleased with this and, as long as they are in the forest, material inequality does not seem to bother either of them.

If this strand of the plot maps the connections between money and the freedom to love, then the mechanicals' play makes links between money and artistic freedom. Whereas *MND* begins with the aristocrats, Theseus and Hippolyta, *10 ml Love* opens with the mechanicals or the army of domestic servants employed by Shweta's father. It is important to note the differences between the mechanicals in *MND* and the performers in *10 ml Love*. To begin with, there is an alteration in the social status between the mechanicals and the domestic servants. Whereas the mechanicals in Shakespeare's play are artisans (Quince is a carpenter, Bottom is a weaver, Flute is a bellows-mender, Snout is a tinker, Snug is a joiner and Starveling a tailor) and free to ply their trade, the domestic servants are worse than even apprentices as they are 'unskilled' labour.[35] Moreover, these servants are not intending to perform the tragedy of Pyramus and Thisbe at the wedding; rather they are rehearsing for the *Ramlila*. *Ramlila* (literally Rama's play) is a dramatic representation based on the central Hindu epic, the *Ramayana*. It is performed according to the annual Hindu calendar around the festival of Dusehra and as such is both a religious and a theatrical performance.[36] This opens a gap between Shakespeare's play and Katariya's film. In Shakespeare's play, the wedding is an employment opportunity for the mechanicals and therefore something to look forward to. In direct contrast, Shweta's wedding is an interruption for these amateur actors. As one of them remarks, '*shaadi ke chakkar mein Ramlila ka tho banta dhaar hogaya*' ('this wedding affair has destroyed the Ramlila'). From the first few sentences itself, it is clear that their rehearsal time is extremely limited. Ghanshubhai (Peter Quince played by Brijendra Kala) has to convince his troupe that Shweta's wedding preparations will not interfere with their rehearsal schedule. However, even while distributing roles, they are shown to be working constantly, chopping vegetables and arranging furniture. Also, they are able to carve out time for rehearsal with great difficulty; before the rehearsal they appear in various scenes and are shown following complicated instructions for the wedding preparations. For instance, they are shown putting up a marquee for the wedding, they are rudely instructed on the pattern of the lights which they arrange for the wedding, and finally Shweta's father himself comes to check on the catering and food supplies and has to be assured that the wedding preparations are indeed complete.[37] It is only after all these chores have been completed that they find rehearsal time and space. This space is not the forest but the backyard of Shweta's house. Even then, it is not 'a marvellous convenient place' (3.1.2–3) for their rehearsal as they are disturbed by the loud music that the wedding guests are dancing to. While the aristocratic wedding in Shakespeare fosters the artistic ambition of the mechanicals which, they hope, will lead to praise and monetary reward, in *10 ml Love*, the wedding disrupts the artistic ambitions of the servants and eats up the time that could have been devoted to profitable activity (Figure 10.2).

In each of the scenes with the mechanicals, Katariya's film comments on the relationship between money and art. In a hilarious opening sequence, Chand implores Ghanshubhai to give him the role of Ravan (antagonist of Ram in the *Ramayana*) or alternatively that of Ram (the protagonist). Bottom never quite manages to convince the audience that he will make a good Thisbe in a 'monstrous little voice' (1.2.48) or will be well cast as Lion either with a roar that 'will do any man's heart good' (1.2.67) or a roar as gentle as 'any sucking dove' (1.2.77). In contrast, when Chand performs snippets of Ravan or Ram, he is surprisingly good. Nevertheless, Ghanshubhai decides that the role of Ravan should go to one of the other servants who is hard of hearing. He then hands out the role of Ram to another servant with a pronounced stutter. As the opening credits roll, Chand is told that he would have to play the role of the monkey god, Hanuman, with no speaking lines. Chand protests because he has been playing Hanuman for a number of years and now wants to try something artistically ambitious. Ghanshubhai, however, is immovable on this point, and Chand is offered no alternative. When the servants gather at the back of the house for rehearsals, the scene ends

Figure 10.2 Mechanicals carving out time for rehearsal between chopping vegetables.

in chaos. To begin with, Chand, who is always eager to carve out more stage time for himself, performs the prologue. He does it brilliantly, his fellow actors are moved, and there is no doubt that Chand is the best performer among them. Ghanshubhai, however, decides that Chand should not try to be too different. Rather, he wants Chand to perform exactly the way he did in the past. When Chand objects that he has outgrown his role, which seems only to consist of jumping around like an ape, he is reminded that it was this very role that made him famous throughout the community. It is then that one of his fellow actors chimes in that it was this jumping around that led to them receiving a donation of ₹(INR) 501. The viewers are explicitly told that this is a big amount for them because one of the actors has just (somewhat erroneously) overheard that the Henna artist, Roshni, is about to receive ₹(INR) 5000 and is flabbergasted by this information. He reveals this information slowly, with gestures to emphasise the amount and the troupe share his incredulity at what seems to them an unbelievable sum and declare that '*kya dimaag kharaab kar raha hai!*' ('it is enough to drive one nuts!'). By now, it is clear that these servants have little power to be inventive or to take risks. While Shakespeare's mechanicals give the meatiest role (Pyramus) to their best actor (Bottom), here Ghanshubhai wants Chand to perform exactly the same part in exactly the same manner as it might net in a donation as it had done earlier. In utter frustration, Chand picks a fight with Ghanshubhai who reveals that he was not able to follow his own artistic ambitions as he had to raise Chand as a single parent when Chand's own parents had died. Significantly, the rehearsal is disrupted, not because Chand turns into an ass but because he is frustrated that the troupe would value monetary donations above artistic growth. The film's scenes with the mechanicals, therefore, deepen Katariya's materialistic critique.

The frustrations presented here are a reflection of some very real problems facing *Ramlila* troupes in India today; lack of funds is leading to their gradual decline.[38] The predicament of the *Ramlila* performers (both within the film and in India at large) parallels that of the Indian indie director trying to offer an alternative to Bollywood on a miniscule budget. One of the posts on the Facebook page dedicated to promoting the film (social media publicity was the only affordable option) states that 'Rajat Kapoor helped us in keeping the film within budget by having black coffees. We saved a lot of money on sugar and milk. That money went into hiring one more assistant for the film.'[39] The statement (obviously exaggerated and tongue-in-cheek) performs several functions – it draws attention to the shoestring budget on which the film-makers were operating, it uses this for comic value, and finally deploys this fact in the service of its publicity. This joke provides a template for understanding the film. Money (or the lack thereof) was not only a production reality of this movie but also, as this section has demonstrated, the key to understanding this adaptation. It was the mirroring between the material circumstances of production and the material circumstances of the world within the film that produces the most potent insights into both the Indian indie film industry and Shakespeare's play.

10 ml Love's achievement in shedding new light on the play can be fully grasped by comparing it to another millennial screen version of the play which centres around class divisions: the BBC's TV adaptation of the play (part of BBC's *ShakespeaRetold* series in 2005).[40] In this adaptation, the mechanicals are lower-class security guards. These guards decide to put on a variety entertainment show for Hermia's wedding but are completely unsuited to the task. For instance, the performer who decides to present a magic show practices throughout the film but cannot present a single trick and Bottom bumbles through the film desperately trying to amuse with his unconvincing impressions and unfunny stand-up routines. Ultimately when these guards perform at the wedding, they are rescued by the benign fairies who make the magic trick work and induce laughter in the audience when Bottom performs. As Carol Thomas Neely observes, the mechanicals 'crucially catalyse the comedy's happy ending', even though their 'lack of talent is irredeemable.'[41] In direct contrast, *10 ml Love* cuts the mechanicals' final performance altogether and ends on a bittersweet note. The film opens with a talented actor Chand petitioning for a role and ends with him waking up semi-naked in a boat. He quietly picks up his clothes as the closing credits roll on the screen. While the couples in the movie receive their happy endings, the *Ramlila* troupe never gets to perform. The film emphasises that artistic endeavours which are not well funded have to struggle hard to survive and might die out no matter how gifted the performers might be. In showing how lack of resources can lead to love problems and failed performances, *10 ml Love* provides the most sustained materialist take on the play to date.

Conclusion

Recognising the potential of the Indian indie, Dywer writes that 'their importance as a new type of cinema and the films' formations of new film-makers and audiences must be recognized.'[42] An even more positive endorsement of their artistic quality comes from Thierry Frémaux, the artistic director of Cannes Film Festival, where India was one of the invited countries in 2013 and Indian indie films featured prominently. Enthusiastic about these movies, Frémaux said, 'today, I feel that a third voice has emerged and young directors and producers those who grew up with films of Martin Scorsese are taking this further. Therefore I firmly believe that this new generation can bring a fresh air not only to Indian Cinema but also to World Cinema.'[43] As my analysis has shown, these films not only reflect the frustrations, trials, tribulations and joys of making an Indian indie but also, owing to their unique perspective, offer fresh insights into Shakespeare's plays. In her book on Jacobean drama on screen, Pascale Aeibisher complains that there is a tendency, 'in criticism of screen Shakespeares, to ignore the films' imbrication in a larger body of work and a film industry context that determines not only what can be filmed, but *how* it may be filmed.'[44] As the case of *10 ml Love* and *8×10 Tasveer* proves, where Indian indie is concerned, it would be negligent to ignore the industry context and the material conditions that indeed dictate not only the 'what' and the 'how' of the films being produced but also influence the content of the movies. The directors' concern with their own production milieu where they have to make the best of limited resources and compete against Bollywood and parallel cinema allows them to interpret Shakespeare's plays materially. The Indian indie Shakespeare adaptations are thus poised to revitalise both world cinema and Shakespeare studies.

Notes

1 *Maqbool* (2003), *Omkara* (2006) and *Haider* (2014) all three directed by Vishal Bhardwaj.
2 *10 ml Love*, directed by Sharat Katariya (2012). The movie has not been released on DVD, but it is available, at the moment at least, in its entirety on YouTube: www.youtube.com/watch?v=hp12Wi83Gkg accessed July 2016. I am profoundly grateful to Hemant Shetty who directed my attention to this movie and insisted that I should watch it because he was convinced that I would enjoy it; he was right!
3 *8×10 Tasveer*, directed by Nagesh Kukunoor (2009; Delaware: Cornerstone, 2009), DVD.
4 My criterion for claiming that these are indie films is simple: they are acknowledged as such by their directors. Katariya asserts that *10 ml Love* 'is a true indie film as it is independent of the star system, the usual grammar of normalized feature film writing, and all other cliché elements of a regular comic entertainer. There is also no big producer backing it' (Sharat Katariya, interview in *Pandolin*, n.d.: http://pandolin.com/desperate-times-disparate-skills/). Kukunoor has famously maintained that he can 'never make a hardcore commercial film'. Citing the case of this film, he says, 'I can work with commercial actors, but they would still have to work in my space, like John (Abraham) did with *Aashayein* or Akshay (Kumar) did with *8×10 Tasveer*' (Nagesh Kukunoor, interview quoted by *NDTV*, 5 February 2015:http://movies.ndtv.com/bollywood/nagesh-kukunoor-can-never-make-hardcore-commercial-film-737205).
There is still some confusion over terminology when referring to these films. Rachel Dwyer refers to them as *hatke* ('different') films, and she explains that they are so called because 'people say a film is "*hatke*/different" from other films'. Besides indie and *hatke* they are also referred to as multiplex films as they appeal to an urban audience and are usually screened at multiplex cinemas as multiple screens allow for the screening of movies which might not attract a huge cross section of the audience. Although Dwyer distinguishes between *hatke* which, she explains, are more 'experimental' films and 'multiplex' movies which are 'more realist than Bollywood' but

'share some features of Bollywood cinema', she agrees that these categories 'overlap'. As she makes a distinction between these movies, she argues that Bhardwaj's adaptations are closer to this cinema than to Bollywood as 'these films feature major stars, big-budget production values and Bollywood music, but they have social and political references and often subordinate melodrama to realism in the manner of the multiplex' (Rachel Dwyer, 'Zara Hatke ('Somewhat Different'): The New Middle Classes and the Changing Forms of Hindi Cinema', in *Being Middle-class in India: A Way of Life*, ed. Henrike Donner (London: Routledge, 2011), 198, 199). Garcia-Periago agrees that *Maqbool*'s place 'within the so-called Bollywood cinema is somehow ambiguous' as it both 'deconstructs and broadens Bollywood conventions' (Rosa M. Garcia-Periago, 'The Ambiguities of Bollywood Conventions and the Reading of Transnationalism in Vishal Bhardwaj's *Maqbool*', in *Bollywood Shakespeares*, eds. Craig Dionne and Parmita Kapadia (New York: Palgrave Macmillan, 2014), 65). Though *Maqbool* is closer to the Indian indie, Bhardwaj's *Omkara* is closer to Bollywood. See Brinda Charry and Gitanjali Shahani, 'The Global as Local/Othello as Omkara', in *Bollywood Shakespeares*, 107–24. *Haider* too aligns more with Bollywood than Indian indie due to its lavish budget.
5 Rachel Dwyer, 'Zara *Hatke*', 198.
6 *Bombay Boys*, directed by Kaizad Gustad (1998; Mumbai: Eros International, 1998), DVD.
7 *Hyderabad Blues*, directed by Nagesh Kukunoor (1998; Eagle Home Entertainment, 2010), DVD.
8 Kaizad Gustad in Tula Goenka, *Not Just Bollywood: Indian Directors Speak* (India: Om Books International, 2014), 263.
9 The manifesto is reproduced in full in Jigna Desai, 'Bombay Boys and Girls: the Gender and Sexual Politics of Transnationality in the New Indian Cinema in English', *South Asian Popular Culture* 1, no. 1 (2003): 52. She uses yet another label for the Indian indie films and refers to them as 'New Wave' cinema in India. For further implications of this label, see endnote 11.
10 *Ugly*, directed by Anurag Kashyap (2013 at Cannes Film Festival, 2014 in India).
11 In their rejection of mainstream Bollywood tropes, the directors of the Indian indie movement and their Shakespeare adaptations share similarities with the Danish 'Dogme brethren' who advocated an anti-Hollywood aesthetic and published a group statement against Hollywood in 1995. Their Shakespeare adaptations, like the Indian indie's, are as much about Shakespeare as about their anti-Hollywood stance in film-making. See Amy Scott-Douglass, 'Dogme Shakespeare 95: European Cinema, Anti-Hollywood Sentiment, and the Bard', in *Shakespeare, The Movie, II: Popularizing the Plays on Film, TV, Video, and DVD*, eds. Richard Burt and Lynda E. Boose (London: Routledge, 2003), 252–64. However, while the Dogme manifesto explicitly rejects technological advances and urges a return to the technology of the past, no such restrictions are mentioned in the Indian indie manifesto. Moreover, the Indian indie directors poke fun at Bollywood and critique it but do not vehemently hate it as Dogme directors abhor Hollywood and all it stands for.
The Indian indie Shakespeare adaptations can also be studied in the context of 'new wave' Shakespeare on screen as defined by Thomas Cartelli and Katherine Rowe. Cartelli and Rowe explain how the work of these 'new wave' film-makers is different from 'Hollywood directors on the one hand, and, on the other, from stage-to-screen directors'. While the Indian indie fits

within the general paradigm of 'new wave Shakespeare' defined as a 'large subset of recent screen Shakespeares' which 'share a propensity for visual and narrative experiments that conspicuously diverge from more classical modes of adaptation', it does not have access to the big budgets of some of these film-makers, such as Julie Taymor, Baz Lurhmann and Peter Greenaway (Katherine Rowe and Thomas Cartelli, *New Wave Shakespeare on Screen* (Cambridge: Polity Press, 2007), 1, ix).
12 Nagesh Kukunoor, e-mail message to author, 21 July 2015.
13 William Shakespeare, *Hamlet*, eds. Ann Thompson and Neil Taylor (London: Bloomsbury, 2006). All quotations of the play are from this edition, and the act, scene and line numbers are incorporated within the body of the essay.
14 Money Sharma, 'The Trick behind Akshay's Double role in *8×10 Tasveer*', *Bollywood Hungama*, 22 April 2009: www.bollywoodhungama.com/movies/slideshow/type/view/id/341. Accessed May 2016.
15 Nagesh Kukunoor in Tula Goenka, *Not Just Bollywood*, 251.
16 Upala KBR, 'Jinxed to the Core', *Mid-Day*, 1 October 2007: http://archive.mid-day.com/entertainment/2007/oct/442213.htm.
17 Agencies, 'Percept denies stalling release of *8×10 Tasveer*', *The Financial Express* (Mumbai, India), 27 March 2009: http://archive.financialexpress.com/news/percept-denies-stalling-release-of-8x10-tasveer/439778.
18 Nagesh Kukunoor in Tula Goenka, *Not Just Bollywood*, 251.
19 Nagesh Kukunoor, interview by Harshikaa Udasi, 'Bollywood Blues', *The Hindu*, 10 April 2009: www.thehindu.com/todays-paper/tp-features/tp-cinemaplus/bollywood-blues/article3021352.ece. Accessed May 2016
20 Margreta De Grazia, *'Hamlet' Without Hamlet* (Cambridge: Cambridge University Press, 2007).
21 Dympna Callaghan, '"Hamlet" Without Hamlet (Review)', *Renaissance Quarterly* 60, no. 4 (2007): 1467.
22 Margreta De Grazia, *'Hamlet' Without Hamlet*, 1.
23 Ann Thompson and Neil Taylor, 'Introduction', in William Shakespeare, *Hamlet*, eds. Ann Thompson and Neil Taylor, 26, 29.
24 Sharat Katariya, interview by Andrew Dickson, 2012. I would like to express my deepest gratitude to Andrew who generously gave me a copy of this unpublished interview.
25 William Shakespeare, *A Midsummer Night's Dream*, ed. Stanley Wells (London: Penguin, 1967). All quotations of the play are from this edition, and the act, scene and line numbers are incorporated within the body of the essay.
26 Sukanta Chaudhuri, 'Shakespeare's India', in *India's Shakespeare: Translation, Interpretation, and Performance*, eds. Poonam Trivedi and Dennis Bartholomeusz (Newark: University of Delaware Press, 2005), 159, 160–61. For the view that the references to India in this play were actually references to America, see Henry Buchanan, '"India" and the Golden age in *A Midsummer Night's Dream*', Shakespeare Survey 65 (2012):58–68.
27 For examples of such performances, see Poonam Trivedi, 'Shakespeare and the Indian Image(nary): Embod(y)ment in Versions of *A Midsummer Night's Dream*', in *Re-playing Shakespeare in Asia*, eds. Poonam Trivedi and Minami Ryuta (New York: Routledge, 2010). Also, see *The Magic Hour* performed by Arjun Raina in which he invokes the Indian boy and relies on Kathakali. For more details about this performance as well as the argument that Raina is not simply exoticising, see Ania Loomba, 'Shakespeare and the Possibilities of Postcolonial Performance', in *A Companion*

198 *Varsha Panjwani*

to *Shakespeare and Performance*, eds. Barbara Hodgdon and W.B. Worthen (Oxford: Blackwell Publishing, 2005): 121–37. I am comparing the film to Indian theatrical (as opposed to Indian film) adaptations because, despite its popularity on the stage, Katariya's is the first Indian *MND* on screen. Notice the absence of *MND* in the accounts of Shakespeare in Hindi cinema: Rajiva Verma, 'Shakespeare in Hindi Cinema', in *India's Shakespeare: Translation, Interpretation, and Performance*, eds. Poonam Trivedi and Dennis Bartholomeusz (Newark: University of Delaware Press, 2005) and Poonam Trivedi, '"Filmi" Shakespeare', *Literature-Film Quarterly* 35 (2007).

28 Katariya, interview by Andrew Dickson.
29 Anurag Kashyap in Tula Goenka, *Not Just Bollywood: Indian Directors Speak*, 284.
30 Onir in Tula Goenka, *Not Just Bollywood: Indian Directors Speak*, 311.
31 Katariya, interview by Andrew Dickson.
32 Kukunoor in Tula Goenka, *Not Just Bollywood*, 247.
33 See Alan C. Dessen, *Elizabethan Stage Conventions and Modern Interpreters* (Cambridge: Cambridge University Press, 1986).
34 Random examples of rain during serious and depressing moments include the downpour that begins at the very moment when Rahul tells Anjali (his best friend who is in love with him) that he loves someone else in *Kuch Hota Hai*, directed by Karan Johar (1998; Mumbai: Yash Raj Films, 2003), DVD, or the torrential rain which begins and continues to beat on the windshield of Akash's car as he heads back home after bidding what seems like a final farewell to Kiara in *Anjaana Anjaani*, directed by Siddharth Anand (2010; Mumbai: Eros International, 1998), DVD, or the ceaseless rain on the witch-police's car as they are making their dire predictions in the opening shot of *Maqbool*. Examples of romancing in the rain are plentiful: perhaps the most famous example of this is the song *pyaar hua* ('love happened') where the romantic leads share an umbrella in *Shree 420*, directed by Raj Kapoor (1955; India: Yash Raj Films, 2001), DVD. For a more modern instance, see *1942: A Love Story*, directed by Vidhu Vinod Chopra (1994; India: Eros International, 2003), DVD.
35 For the class tensions in London society in Shakespeare's time, see Paul S. Seaver, 'Apprentice Riots in Early Modern London', in *Violence, Politics, and Gender in Early Modern England*, ed. Joseph P. Ward (Hampshire: Palgrave Macmillan, 2008).
36 For more information on *Ramlila*, its performance conventions and its place in the Hindu tradition, see Anuradha Kapur, *Actors, Pilgrims, Kings and Gods: The Ramlila at Ramnagar* (India: Seagull Books, 1990).
37 The imagery of the big fat Indian wedding with flowers, rich colours, beautiful dresses, and endless parties is often used in Bollywood as well as diasporic cinema and is usually a song opportunity. For instance, see *Hum Aapke Hain Koun*, directed by Sooraj R. Barjatya (1994; India: Eros International, 2003), DVD and *Monsoon Wedding*, directed by Mira Nair (2001; India: Channel 4, 2008), DVD. Katariya satirises this trope by stressing the labour and cost of putting on such a wedding.
38 Sample revelatory newspaper headlines such as Priyangi Agarwal, 'Break in non-stop Ramleela as SP govt stops funds', *The Times of India* (Lucknow, India), 3 April 2013: http://timesofindia.indiatimes.com/city/lucknow/Break-in-non-stop-Ramleela-as-SP-govt-stops-funds/articleshow/19354131.cms, or Amber, 'Inflation takes toll on Ramleela Celebrations', *The Daily Pioneer* (Ranchi, India), 7 October 2013: www.dailypioneer.com/state-editions/ranchi/inflation-takes-toll-on-ramleela-celebrations.html. All accessed May 2016.

39 '10 ml Love', *Facebook.com*, last modified 22 November 2012, www.facebook.com/10MLLOVE/timeline. Accessed May 2016.
40 *A Midsummer Night's Dream* (BBC's *ShakespeaRetold* series), directed by Ed Fraiman (2005, UK: Acorn Video, 2006), DVD.
41 Carol Thomas Neely, '*A Midsummer Night's Dream* at the Millennium: Performance and Adaptation', *Shakespeare Survey* 65 (2012): 156, 167, 164.
42 Rachel Dwyer, 'Zara *Hatke*', 201.
43 Thierry Frémaux, interview by Nandita Dutta, 'New Gen Indian Directors Can Bring Fresh Air to World Cinema', *Dear Cinema*, 8 May 2013: http://dearcinema.com/interview/thierry-fremaux-cannes-indian-cinema/2301.
44 Pascale Aebischer, *Screening Early Modern Drama: Beyond Shakespeare* (Cambridge: Cambridge University Press, 2013), 6.

11 'Singing Is Such Sweet Sorrow'
Ambikapathy, Hollywood Shakespeare and Tamil Cinema's Hybrid Heritage

Thea Buckley

India's southern state of Tamil Nadu has an ongoing passionate love affair with the film song. The state's capital city of Chennai (formerly Madras) is the regional[1] production centre for 'South Indian cinema—embracing Tamil, Telugu, Kannada and Malayalam cinema'[2]—and it is also the world's largest producer of film music.[3] Recorded Tamil film songs 'blare from horn speakers and cassette players at weddings, puberty rites, and temple and shrine festivals.'[4] These regionally produced and immensely popular songs hint at Indian cinema's unsuspected and complicated hybrid cultural heritage. In one popular lullaby from *Aalayamani* (1962), S. Janaki croons the tender refrain '*Thookkam unn kangalai thazhuvattum! Amaithi unn nenjil nilavattum! Andhath thookkamum amaithiyum naanaanaal.*'[5] These lyrics replicate Romeo's rhyming couplet in the balcony scene (2.1.231–32): 'Sleep dwell upon thine eyes, peace in thy breast./Would I were sleep and peace, so sweet to rest.'[6] The lyrics' Shakespearean origins, however, are several generations removed, inherited through the reworked Tamil film dialogue from the 1937 hit *Ambikapathy*.[7]

This essay regards *Ambikapathy* as a critical point in the evolution of regional Indian film and its inheritance of Shakespeare on screen. Superficially, this historic collaboration between Kollywood[8] and Hollywood was a successful intercultural experiment, resulting in the technical and thematic progress of Indian cinema. However, *Ambikapathy* represents a subversive national tradition in which Indian cinematic Shakespeare appropriates the British playwright to speak back to the colonial master in multiple voices. Hybridising Shakespeare's *Romeo and Juliet* with a Tamil love tragedy, *Ambikapathy* uses the central theme of forbidden love as a lens to explore tabooed themes of sexual and political autonomy. In an era of Tamil revivalism,[9] *Ambikapathy* appropriates and reinvents symbols of Western culture, employing lyrical and musical metaphor as a form of cultural resistance.

With the advent of cinema sound and music in pre-Independence India, adaptations of 'India's own love legends' and 'historicals'[10] established indigenous cinema as a carrier of national culture and identity.[11] Cinema had arrived in India in 1896 via the British.[12] While British Madras held only twelve cinema theatres for a population of around 750,000,[13] families 'would travel ten miles or more by bullock cart to sit on the ground under a tent with their babies and would eat food out of their picnic baskets, while viewing the featured film.'[14] In the 1930s, Tamil film distributor N.R. Desai noted that local cinema 'gives us musical entertainment which even the best Hollywood pictures cannot.'[15] Despite British attempts to 'stifle'[16] the indigenous film industry by importing Hollywood musicals and censoring regional pictures,[17] the local population asserted their independent preference.

Successful South Indian films appropriated foreign elements selectively, borrowing themes from Hollywood imports like George Cukor's *Romeo and Juliet* (1936).[18] Here, Norma Shearer played Juliet opposite the dreamy Leslie Howard, supported by theatre stars Basil Rathbone (Tybalt) and John Barrymore (Mercutio). When Cukor's film reached Madras, it was viewed by his 'long-time friend'[19] and visiting American film director Ellis R. Dungan. Dungan decided to model selected scenes and dialogue from *Romeo and Juliet* in his next project, *Ambikapathy* (1937).[20] Based on the star-crossed love story of the legendary Chola princess Amaravathi and Ambikapathy, son of the twelfth-century Tamil poet Kambar, Dungan's Tamil-language film mingled Western romance with Eastern myth and music in a successful intercultural formula; *Ambikapathy* ran at Madras' Gaiety Cinema for months, 'breaking all records.'[21] The triumph of this Shakespearean hybrid led to a 1957 remake and established cinema as a new vehicle for Tamil culture, despite the leads' daring 'Western' on-screen kiss.[22]

In exploring this hybridised inheritance, this essay discusses adaptation as a thematic and textual evolution from 'telling' to 'showing'—from script to song, stage to screen—using Linda Hutcheon and Siobhan O'Flynn's theory of cinematic adaptation.[23] *Ambikapathy* employs cinematic techniques, set elements and imagery to translate the narrative of 'telling' into 'showing', transcending linguistic distinctions for a polyglot Indian audience.[24] *Ambikapathy*'s singing lovers begin in discretion and end in open passion as Ambikapathy and Amaravathi's romance progresses from the first love message to the balcony scene and bedroom kiss, an evolution that further illustrates the complex negotiation between the private and public representation of romance in Tamil cinema. *Ambikapathy*'s theme of transgressive union and its 'Hollywood-style' gender dynamics stretch the prevailing narratives and romantic tropes in both Tamil love legends and colonial cinema.

This essay also considers the intertextual use of Shakespearean dialogue and songs to highlight 'telling' through 'singing', using music as a unifying language of emotion that 'replaced the presumed visual universality of silent films with a new aural universality.'[25] Tamil cinema music also often 'performs the task of encoding the blending of cultures and ideals,'[26] and in a time of colonial censorship, Shakespeare was transformed into a subversive subtext of musical propaganda celebrating Tamil culture.[27] Here, the lovers' union acts as a metaphor for the ideals of the liberation of the Tamil motherland and the abolition of caste-based hierarchies. The 1937 film's post-Independence legacy includes a 1957 *Ambikapathy* remake and a 1962 hit film song. These linger in collective cultural memory with an enduring popularity in a complex generational phenomenon that sheds light on the local production and reception of Shakespeare.

Star-Crossed Lovers: Parallel Cultural Perspectives

Films based on Shakespeare's plays often 'exist at a meeting point between conflicting cultural assumptions,'[28] and intercultural versions add another set of intersections. *Ambikapathy* (1937) appropriates thematic elements from Shakespeare's tragic love story to connect with a common cultural concern. It highlights relational dynamics between lovers who transgress socially sanctioned boundaries, setting up a conflict between individual and collective needs. Patricia Tatspaugh underlines this dual focus by suggesting that Cukor's *Romeo and Juliet* shares a common aim with other filmic versions, engaging our sympathies by making the 'young lovers attractive to the cinema audience' and providing a realistic portrayal of their societies.[29] For audiences in independent India, indigenous film became 'an agent of a much wider social change, of making a new country from a very old one.'[30] Accordingly, Tamil cinema reflected contemporary societal conflicts of caste and colonial hierarchy, often encapsulated in personal tragedy.

The trope of lovers' suffering is common to both Shakespearean and Indian narratives. Paralleling Shakespeare's Desdemona, Hermia and Juliet are Rukmini, Subhadra and Usha of the Hindu epics *Mahabharata* and *Ramayana*, heroines who marry secretly against familial, societal or astrological opposition.[31] Such tales are woven into the fabric of the typical South Indian household.[32] Modern-day romantic relationships remain complicated by the patriarchal institution of arranged marriage, which is based on rigid social hierarchies of class, religion and caste. Conversely, the majority of complicated love stories end happily; when a princess falls in love with a poor hero, he turns out to be a prince in exile or disguise.

There was no such happy ending for Amaravathi, the eleventh-century Chola princess who fell in love with the commoner Ambikapathy. In the historic legend, which the 1937 film retains, the titular hero is the talented son of the court poet Kambar.[33] After Ambikapathy wins Amaravathi's heart through his love songs, their affair is discovered, and he is imprisoned by her father, King Kulothunga Chola. The king is willing to marry the lovers if Ambikapathy can prove his poetic prowess. He must spontaneously compose and sing one hundred songs that describe the joys of war and government (*puram*) without once mentioning romantic love (*aram*). In the ensuing public trial, as Amaravathi tallies the songs for her lover, she mistakenly includes the traditional opening invocation, or *kadavulvaazhthu*, in the list. She announces victory prematurely on the penultimate song, whereupon Ambikapathy bursts into an exultant composition praising his lover's beauty. As he is promptly executed for his temerity, his beloved collapses and dies of grief.

In this tragic love story, *Ambikapathy*'s American director saw Shakespearean echoes. Dungan writes that his audience favoured the reworked romance, incorporating dialogue and 'a balcony scene similar to the one in *Romeo and Juliet*.'[34] Broad shared themes of tragic love and poetic legacy can be traced between the Chola legend and *Romeo and Juliet*. However, the former fits into a comparatively rare Tamil tradition of tragic couples that mainly comprise Kovalan and Kannaki, the hero and heroine of the epic *Silappatikaram*.[35] Yet their tragedies evade concrete cultural parallels. *Ambikapathy* (1937) can be termed an early Indian Shakespeare appropriation, demonstrating 'a more decisive journey away from the informing source into a wholly new cultural product and domain.'[36] By incorporating Cukor's cinematic Shakespeare into a Tamil love tragedy, Dungan reset Shakespearean elements into a narrative, medium and culture with different assumptions (Figure 11.1).

Text versus Spectacle – Telling versus Showing

Ambikapathy (1937) fits into the tradition of Indian cinema directors borrowing Shakespearean elements to 'show off' their indigenous

Figure 11.1 Amaravathi and Ambikapathy singing a love duet.
Source: Courtesy NFAI

offerings.[37] In adapting Cukor's 1936 film, Dungan astutely chose a version of *Romeo and Juliet* that foregrounded spectacle over dialogue. Like the best Bollywood films, Cukor's adaptation features dramatic fights, showy love songs and dances, lavish sets and costumes, and emotional close-ups mixed with large crowd set pieces. While Cukor's film follows Shakespeare's narrative, the text of *Romeo and Juliet* is cut by more than half to accommodate a carefully choreographed Capulet ball and intertextual Shakespearean love songs.[38] The film even starts with a wedding, a theme beloved to the Indian audience.[39] The result was panned by home critics: 'it is frequently saved—by Shakespeare—from becoming a bad film', observed Graham Greene.[40] Yet with over half of the English text replaced by song and dance, Cukor's *Romeo and Juliet* arguably appealed to Tamil audiences that typically expected 'high paid stars' and 'good quality music.'[41] Indeed, *Ambikapathy* was the first film to advertise its music director, Papanasam Sivan. The 'context of reception' is crucial to a film adaptation's success, Hutcheon and O'Flynn stress,[42] and Tamil audiences are especially receptive to the musical medium.

Ambikapathy was poised at the crest of heightened public interest in Tamil film music. If the hero cheerfully rejoined, 'Sing a hundred songs; is that all?' it was no joke, for *Srinivasakalyanam* (1934), the first Madras-made Tamil film, had recently incorporated fifty.[43] Film historian S. Theodore Baskaran credits Dungan with streamlining the industry by cutting down songs per film from '30 or 40 to 6–8.'[44] In the context of these drastic song cuts the 1937 film's impressive popularity indicates that the director remained respectful of the South Indian sensibility while relocating Shakespeare into Tamil literature and culture. *Ambikapathy*'s positive reception resulted in stardom for both Sivan and its budding lead actor, Mayavaram Krishnamurthy Thyagaraja Bhagavathar (M.K.T.). Ironically, it was a film adaptation of Shakespeare that was to exert a major influence on the developing Tamil film industry.

For a love story about singing, *Ambikapathy*'s scriptwriter Thanigachalam (pen name Elangovan) exploited the intrinsic musicality of the Shakespearean verse. Subsequently, the poet revolutionised Tamil cinema dialogue with his 'flowery lines in chaste Tamil, studded with literary allusions.'[45] Elangovan and Dungan saw Cukor's film 'several times', the scriptwriter taking 'notes as he watched the picture', and then together they 'designed the dialogue and action for the balcony love scene.'[46] Here, Romeo's parting couplet 'Sleep dwell upon thine eyes, peace in thy breast' (2.1.231) was translated broadly into lyrical Tamil for Ambikapathy's leave-taking after the secret balcony assignation: 'Uṉ kaṇkaḷil tūkkam taḻuvaṭṭum, hrutaiyattil cānti alaipāraṭṭum, Āhā! Anta tūkkamum cāntiyum nāṉākayiruntā...' The director felt that 'Elangovan's poetic dialogue helped to make the film a great success.'[47] Throughout, Elangovan referred to an English text of *Romeo and Juliet* given to him by Dungan, with passages marked for incorporation in the Tamil script, effectively bypassing Cukor's cuts and resulting in comparatively unmediated textual fidelity.[48]

This fidelity to the Shakespearean text is most evident in *Ambikapathy*'s balcony scene. In lines that parallel Juliet's 'if they do see thee, they will murder thee' (2.1.112), Amaravathi expresses a fear of the danger latent in their assignations. In turn, Ambikapathy assures her that the only danger he fears lies in her eyes, mirroring Romeo's 'Alack, there lies more peril in thine eye/Than twenty of their swords' (2.1.113–14). Other scenes translate textual telling into cinematic showing. The lovers' shared sonnet is replaced by a palm leaf scroll bearing the princess' love poetry, which she sends to Ambikapathy through her maid, Sundari. In a convention that replicates Juliet's use of the nurse as an emissary, Sundari functions as a typical Indian *sakhi* or female confidante who often acts as a romantic go-between. Receiving the princess' love letter, Ambikapathy kisses the parchment, substituting the lovers' initial touch of lips with a visual approximation of Shakespeare's 'palm to palm is holy palmer's kiss' (1.5.99). After returning to her mistress' bedchamber, Sundari's dialogue mirrors the conversation between Juliet and her nurse; Sundari even breaks off from listing her aches and pains to ask, 'Where is your mother?' (2.5.50). Throughout the film, this deployment of Shakespearean-verse-based Tamil dialogue, with its intrinsic musicality, reduced the need for actual song.

'If music be the food of love, sing on'

Ambikapathy (1937) avoided the excessive use of songs by using lyrical Shakespearean dialogue as a happy medium between singing and telling. However, the film retained a vital number of songs since in Tamil cinema the 'songless film is a freak.'[49] In the 1930s and 1940s, before sound dubbing, a Tamil actor's ability to sing was a precondition for hire[50]; producers employed talented Carnatic musician-actors like G.N. Balasubramanyam or 'India's nightingale' M.S. Subbulakshmi.[51] Early Tamil talkies merely duplicated the popular stage musicals of the company drama.[52] Randor Guy writes of Tamil actors 'standing in a row, or a semi-circle, and reciting—shouting—their lines, gesturing and gesticulating [...] . "Show, don't tell", the essential principle of Cinema [sic], is more honoured in the breach than in practice.'[53] Thus, the Tamil public was used to films where songs and music were integral to the entertainment experience. Film-makers borrowed dramatic conventions, aiming to achieve emotional impact through 'appropriate music'[54] and songs that reworked classical Carnatic *raga* and *tala*. Film theatres broadcast musical excerpts from external speakers,[55] functioning much as an Elizabethan trumpet prologue, with the aural preceding visual reception.

Hutcheon and O'Flynn[56] describe musical drama as a textual script brought to life, not merely told but also 'shown' in embodied sound, and the same applies to Tamil cinema in the new talkie era where 'an essentially visual medium tended to be predominantly aural.'[57] As in the company drama, at intense moments film characters 'often broke into song' to 'underline the emotional significance of a scene.'[58] William Beeman suggests that this blurring of telling and singing has greater acceptability in Indian film culture, because of the closer 'psychological distance between speech and song.'[59] Alternatively, Baskaran views this reversion to song as the 'continuation of a literature-oriented aesthetic where versification or poetry is considered superior to conversational or prose Tamil.'[60] *Ambikapathy*'s characters break from poetry into song in moments of intense sorrow, wonder or joy.

The first song in *Ambikapathy* occurs after the rare gap of nearly half an hour. This strategic distillation perhaps rendered the film's comparatively fewer songs more popular. Composer Papanasam Sivan adapted the *raga* and *tala* of devotional classical Telugu hymns by Purandara Dasa and Thyagaraja. Sivan reworked hymns such as '*Nenenendu vedha kudura*' and '*Mokshamu galada*'[61] into film songs like '*Chandrasooriyar*' ('Sun and moon ...' – raga *mandu*), '*Ulaginil inbam verundo*' ('Is there any greater joy in the world?' – raga *simhendra madhyamam*) or '*Bajanai seivai maname*' ('Oh heart, sing in worship ...' – raga *behag*).[62] *Ambikapathy*'s songs were clearly non-essential to the narrative, for when the film's eleventh reel went for emergency re-splicing on debut, the film ran for a week without critics or audience noticing the loss of two songs from the imprisoned hero's repertoire.[63]

The genesis of these flowery Tamil love songs can be traced to the early Indian stage musicals, influenced perhaps by translations and adaptations of *Romeo and Juliet*. Dating from 1877, these were staged all over the Madras state including performances by touring Urdu and Marathi theatre groups.[64] In the preface to his 1908 translation of *Romeo and Juliet [Ramyanum Jolitaiyum]*, S.V. Srinivasiar decries the incongruous musical convention of the Tamil stage that ruins the performance of Shakespeare, including 'dancing in season and out of season.'[65] R.K. Yajnik records similar conventions in the Marathi five-set musical tragedy *Juliet/Salini*: 'After the orthodox prayer, the two "*Rasas*"[66] of the drama, love and pathos, are emphasised in a song'.[67] And *The Fatal Banquet* is 'a crude tragi-comedy in three acts' where 'Instead of the garden-scene, the lovers meet before marriage in Juliet's private apartment and sing duets of amatory verse.'[68] This Urdu musical's court setting, the singing lovers and nurse, and the scene in the princess' private apartment are all seen in *Ambikapathy*. This similarity suggests that while some elements in the 1937 film may have been lifted directly from the Hollywood film version, others were retained from Indian musical stage versions of Shakespeare with conventions appealing to the local audience.

'Singing Is Such Sweet Sorrow' 207

Successfully, *Ambikapathy* (1937) translates *Romeo and Juliet*'s romance richly into Tamil music, song and dance.[69] Songs provide an excuse for the visualisation of the lyrics, such as a lotus that doubles as a metaphor for Amaravathi's blooming face. Dialogues between the lead pair become duets, often pictured against pastoral Tamil scenery, or the stock river gushing with metaphorical romantic passion. Moonlit riverbank meetings evoke both the celestial imagery in Shakespeare, as well as the trope of the mythical Krishna romancing and dancing with the *gopis* or milkmaids. Interweaving Shakespeare's love story and poetry, the film showcases the beauty of Tamil language, land and legend. The Tamil poet Ambikapathy's yearning for his beloved Amaravathi, a union forbidden by the ruler, becomes a metaphor for Tamil cultural and political emancipation, as the next section examines.

The Politics of the Love Song and the Balcony Space

Ambikapathy (1937) fits into a tradition of colonial Tamil literature that blends Shakespearean translation with political subversion. In an age of Civil Disobedience and censorship, 'Script and songwriters became adept at indirect reference to Indian nationalism and British tyranny.'[70] *Ambikapathy* was perfectly placed to glorify Tamil sentiments, its release coinciding with the loosening of censorship laws in 1937, when C. Rajagopalachari became the prime minister of the new Madras Presidency[71] and allowed films to include 'patriotic songs' and 'symbols of nationalism.'[72] The film's scriptwriter Elangovan was associated with the literary Tamil magazine *Manikodi* and a group of writers who saw the propagandist potential of film to communicate local sentiment.[73]

Incorporating the balcony scene from Cukor's *Romeo and Juliet*, *Ambikapathy* (1937) foregrounds a famous setting for forbidden love that here further symbolises sociopolitical transgression.[74] Amaravathi's balcony represents several levels of demarcation. As a patriarchal boundary, it reflects Indian purdah architecture, screening the modesty of the cloistered royal female while allowing her to observe the common scene below. The balcony also marks the margin between love and death. In a departure from *Romeo and Juliet*, the heroine falls in love as she first spies Ambikapathy from her balcony. She laughs as the returned war hero spars below and humiliates his rival, the army chief Ugrasenan, who later falls to his death from the balcony while trying to spy on the lovers. The balcony is soon transgressed for several secret assignations in the princess' bedchamber; Ambikapathy mounts to it on 'love's light wings' (2.1.109) or arrives there through a secret underground passage. Ten years later, a poster for the (lost) 1947 Hindi film version advertises the 'famed balcony scene', clearly still a selling point for the Indian audience (Figure 11.2).[75]

208 Thea Buckley

Ambikapathy's balcony scene occurs at a point of intertextual and intercultural overlap. Latha K. remarks that for a Tamil audience raised on Hindu epics, there are unmissable textual parallels;[76] Amaravathi/Juliet's laugh at Ugrasenan/Paris evokes Draupadi's legendary laugh that humiliated her husband's rival, sparking the war between two royal families in the *Mahabharata*.[77] Amaravathi's balcony can also be taken to represent the barriers of caste and class in Tamil society.[78] The lovers' household heads are unequal in dignity: while the poet Kambar represents the Tamil nation, King Kulothunga represents the unjust ruler-state. As film-maker K. Hariharan explains, in this scene between the princess up high and the poet below, he sees the moment at which the lower-caste man must gain the courage to both physically and metaphorically rise and grasp his romantic destiny.[79] In colonial India, this pivotal scene in *Ambikapathy* therefore also represented wider Tamil aspirations, to transcend class and caste distinctions and to gain political Independence. The next section examines how scenes from *Romeo and Juliet*, mediated through the conventions of Hollywood romance, represented a means of transgressing not only political censorship but also cultural taboo.

'You kiss by the book': The Politics of Romance

While Hollywood's music and spectacle were welcome on the Tamil screen, the local audience was unprepared for its scenes of physical intimacy. S.V. Srinivasiar explains the difficulty of adapting Shakespearean

Figure 11.2 The balcony scene.

social codes for a Tamil audience, as 'the greeting of women by men with kisses in public, the liberty of the fair sex and the equality of the sexes are strange and perhaps in some cases repulsive to the Hindu mind [...] this [difficulty] is especially so in the case of "Romeo and Juliet" [sic] which is wholly a love play.'[80] If the Marathi Romeo and Juliet in *Salini* could 'touch but not kiss'[81], in Srinivasiar's translation 'the reference to kissing has been omitted to suit the Indian taste.'[82] Thus Romeo and Juliet's bedroom kiss caused a sensation when reproduced in *Ambikapathy* in what Dungan recalled as 'the first on-screen embrace between a man and a woman in the history of the Tamil cinema.'[83] Tamil film historian 'Film News' Anandan remembered 'audiences coming back repeatedly for the kissing scene!'[84] *Ambikapathy* was the rare Tamil film to show an on-screen kiss before the implementation of new censorship laws, which were repealed only in 1986.[85] The artistic milestone saw Shakespeare deployed to transcend cultural taboos in colonial India.

Ambikapathy's central balcony scene remains faithful to the Shakespearean original in terms of its dialogue, yet the scene's position in the plot trajectory alters its romantic dynamics. When the scene unfolds, the princess above is still unattained, intensifying her lover's longing to reach her. Unlike Shakespeare's or Cukor's lovers, who kiss at their first meeting, Ambikapathy and Amaravathi's first kiss is deferred to their bedroom assignation, which is effectively a private 'marriage.'[86] Their physical intimacy is delayed in accordance with Indian cultural codes, which enjoin couples to kiss only after marriage. The lovers' private union also hints at the Tamil drive to break caste hierarchies through the 'self-respect' marriage.[87] This first kiss therefore carries great significance, symbolising an on-screen consummation of forbidden love when a mere screen wink was considered scandalous. It was a scene of 'unthinkable' intimacy for a Tamil film with Ambikapathy laying Amaravathi on her back in bed to kiss her, in an 'obscene'[88] position, 'making the audience gasp with visions of what would follow after the fade out'![89] The scene's eroticism is only heightened when the camera coyly cuts to a statue of the divine lovers Radha and Krishna, sculpted in an embrace.[90]

Ambikapathy's lead actors M.K.T. and M.R. Santhanalakshmi modelled their love scenes on Howard's and Shearer's, after Dungan had the Tamil actors watch Cukor's film. However, in the balcony scene, the director's implicit confidence in the cultural translatability of Hollywood's romantic codes was exploded promptly by Santhanalakshmi's pragmatism. When Dungan coaxed her, 'You know what it's like to be in love. After all, you are married and have three kids', the actress responded, 'Director Sahib, a woman doesn't have to know anything about love in order to be able to have kids!'[91] Even if Tamil love films encourage the 'singing of romantic songs' and a 'great, if often unfulfilled, desire for romance', arranged marriage continues to be the cultural norm.[92]

Notably, *Ambikapathy* (1937) was not the first Indian motion picture to show a screen kiss. Colonial Indian cinema featured the occasional titillating kiss.[93] With its bold screen kiss and its outspoken female protagonist *Ambikapathy* also challenged the gender dynamic of Tamil cinema and its stereotypical passive and silent heroines.[94] Amaravathi is unashamed of her love and openly reciprocates the hero's overtures; when her father eventually spies her kissing Ambikapathy, she declares in Tamil, 'I'm happy; we haven't done anything wrong'. Amaravathi's forthright defence of her lover before his unjust execution further aligns her with literary notions of Tamil womanhood and nationhood.

There are clear intertextual parallels between the tragedies of Amaravathi and Kannaki, the legendary heroine of the Tamil verse epic *Silappatikaram*.[95] In this tale of love and loss, Kannaki curses the king of the realm after he unjustly executes her husband, Kovalan, for suspected theft. Her curse causes the king's symbolic regal parasol to fall suddenly, an inauspicious omen signifying impending disaster; Kannaki then burns down the kingdom in her righteous wrath. The identical sequence of a collapsing royal parasol appears at the end of *Ambikapathy* (1937), a visual device that further orients the film towards the familiar Tamil epic with its literary tropes of tragic love and righteous rage against the state.[96] The 1957 remake of *Ambikapathy* retains the Kannaki link; after her lover's execution, a grieving Amaravathi curses her unjust father: 'Let this kingdom come to ruin'. The Kannaki legend and *Ambikapathy*'s forthright heroine are both connected to the rebirth of Tamil Nadu,[97] reflecting the 1930s Tamil political era when 'female emancipation' came to be 'tied to the idea of national regeneration and liberation.'[98] Thus Amaravathi's kiss could be seen as a marker of female sexual agency that symbolises political Independence, leading to the birth of a new society.

Ambikapathy Remade Post-Independence

Directed by local film-maker P. Neelakantan, the 1957 version of *Ambikapathy* proudly emphasises a newly independent Tamil cultural identity over Shakespearean intertextuality.[99] The remake of the 1937 film was produced during a period of social reform, ten years after Independence and the legal abolition of caste-based discrimination. *Ambikapathy* (1957) retains the original film's overarching theme of class war and echoes the 'radical anti-caste message'[100] of the new Tamil political party *Dravida Munnetra Kazhakam* (DMK).[101] The 1957 film radicalises the binary proposed by Craig Dionne and Parmita Kapadia, who question whether Indian films use Shakespeare as a vehicle to assert postcolonial identity or to advance colonialist fantasy.[102] The film affirms postcolonial identity by privileging Tamil poetry over translated Shakespearean verse and by erasing traces of the Hollywoodised *Romeo and Juliet* while foregrounding regional culture. For example, the opening spat occurs at a village festival, intercut with extended sequences of Tamil folk dance; classical *Bharatanatyam* in court replaces the Capulets' ball; and romantic scenes are trimmed to accommodate Tamil songs.

In *Ambikapathy* (1957), the ancient grudge revolves around Tamil poetry, based on a feud between Ambikapathy (Sivaji Ganesan) and the poet Ottakoothar (M.N. Nambiar), who discovers his rival's love affair and reports it to the king. A third historical figure, the late court poet Pukazhenthi, is introduced through the character of his daughter Kannamma (Rajasulochana), the bosom companion of Princess Amaravathi (P. Bhanumathi). Kannamma forms the third wheel in a love triangle, in a role that combines the stock *sakhi* with the character of Rosaline and Paris.[103] This interpolation of an additional tragic heroine gives further scope for extended laments, sung against a backdrop of scenic Tamil fields, rivers and temples.

With the 1957 film's focus on the rural Tamil countryside, the Shakespearean balcony fades into the background – here, the hero mounts it by moonlight nearly two hours into the film. Instead, Tamil literature is foregrounded as Amaravathi falls in love with her ears rather than her eyes, hearing Ambikapathy's eloquent court arguments regarding his father's translation of the *Ramayana*.[104] In Sivaji Ganesan's films, Randor Guy argues, the 'technique of "tell, don't show" [...] became more evident' since the actor was famous for his 'high-flown Tamil.'[105] *Ambikapathy* (1957) further links Tamil literature and politics by featuring comedian and DMK activist N.S. Krishnan as a poet, playing (real-life wife) T.A. Madhuram's lover.[106] Krishnan's scene of island shipwreck clearly references *Parthiban Kanavu* (1942), Kalki Krishnamurthy's popular Tamil novel.[107] The novel itself is a circular reference to the 1937 *Ambikapathy*, and possibly *Romeo and Juliet*, featuring a Chola prince who unwittingly falls in love with the daughter of his enemy.

In *Ambikapathy* (1957), even G. Ramanathan's love songs gain a literary intertextuality, using classical Tamil poetry to inform rather than merely illustrate the action. This shift is visible in a key scene where Ambikapathy's rival Ottakoothar schemes to expose the lovers to the king by arranging an 'accidental' palace reunion. When Amaravathi enters the room to serve her father's guests, including Ambikapathy, her smitten lover bursts into an impromptu love song with a verse from the Tamil *Ramayana*: 'Ittaardi novu, edutthaadi koppalikka' ('Bearing a dish in hand, she enters on feet so tender they will blister upon touching the ground'). Ambikapathy's horrified father prays to goddess Saraswati, the muse of letters and music, who promptly intervenes and provides him with a literary pun that saves the situation.[108] While the 1937 film references this legendary incident, it omits the episode and the vernacular *Ramayana* lyrics.

Like the 1937 film, the 1957 remake continues to focus on romantic union, articulating the desire for social equality and secularism in the new Indian democracy. Here, after Ambikapathy's imprisonment and execution, the princess stabs herself with his dagger, joining in his fate. If the king had attempted to silence his daughter, and to force the hero to sing one hundred compositions on the virtue of *pēriṉpam* (higher pleasure) as opposed to *cirriṉpam* (lower pleasure), in the end the pair gain poetic revenge by joining in an eternal love duet beyond his jurisdiction. They sing together happily in a cloud-filled studio heaven, far above earthly restrictions of class and caste.

In its erasure of Shakespearean traces in favour of Tamil themes, the later *Ambikapathy* (1957) represents a post-Independence desire to reassert Tamil taste and control over the popular mass medium. Now films placed an 'emphasis on Tamil linguistic pride, and the associated pro-Tamil, anti-Brahman, anti-North political sentiments.'[109] After the 1950s, local film-makers returned to indigenous narratives and 'the Hollywood narrative style petered out.'[110] Colonial Shakespeare, whether visual or aural, was subsumed in the assertion of a new regional and national identity.

Postscript

Traces of both *Ambikapathy* (1937) and *Romeo and Juliet* resurfaced in K. Shankar's *Aalayamani* (1962). In the film, Elangovan's rhyming couplet from the balcony scene was reshaped as playback singer S. Janaki's aforementioned lullaby: '*Thookkamun kangalai thazhuvattum! Amaithiun nenjil nilavattum! Andhath thookkamum amaithiyum naanaanaal*' or 'Sleep dwell in thine eyes, peace in thy breast/Would I were sleep and peace, so sweet to rest' (2.1.231–32). The lullaby, in turn, is overtly linked to the 1937 film by the heroine Prema (R. Vijaykumari). She offers to soothe the film's bedridden hero, Thyagarajan (S.S. Rajendran), with a song from their college days, 'when they once acted Amaravathi and Ambikapathy.'[111] This episode further refers to the Tamil film trope of the hero and heroine as college mates who enact a Shakespeare play, reflecting the contemporary practice of amateur Shakespeare performances in college festivals. In Tamil films, these 'one-act Shakespeare college festival plays' include other tragedies: 'Hamlet' in *Rajapart Rangadurai* (1973) and 'Othello' in *Ratha Thilagam* (1963).'[112]

In contemporary Tamil cinema, however, little remains of these early Shakespeare appropriations of *Romeo and Juliet*.[113] Today, regional, national and foreign cinema remain interconnected in their influence on cinematic Indian Shakespeares. Yet the 1937 and 1957 films indicate the centrality of Shakespeare in the development of Indian popular cinema.[114] In adapting Hollywood Shakespeare for South Indian cinema in a successful fusion of literature and love lyric, the new audiovisual

'Singing Is Such Sweet Sorrow' 213

medium came into its own. Tamil cinema's singing Shakespeare left a lasting legacy through films and film music, as part of the intercultural inheritance that saw Indian cinema evolve from playing metaphorical second fiddle to first violin.

Notes

This piece is dedicated to Lizz Ketterer in gratitude for the inspiration behind her memorial trust that supported my research for this piece.

1. Sara Dickey, *Cinema and the Urban Poor in South India* (Cambridge: Cambridge University Press, 1993), 51. Dickey defines 'regional' as the label given to films in any language besides Hindi or English.
2. Yves Thoraval, *The Cinemas of India (1896–2000)*, trans. Veena Kilan and T.K. Gopala (Delhi: Macmillan, 2000), 35.
3. Joseph Getter and B. Balasubrahmaniyan, 'Tamil Film Music: Sound and Significance', *Global Soundtracks: Worlds of Film Music*, ed. Mark Slobin (Middletown: Wesleyan University Press, 2008), 120.
4. Dickey, *Urban Poor,* 3.
5. *Aalayamani*, dir. K. Shankar, perf. Sivaji Ganesan and B. Saroja (P. S. V. Pictures, 1962). Kannadasan's song can be seen here: http://youtu.be/D-VfDf2NTk accessed 31 May 2015.
6. William Shakespeare, *Romeo and Juliet*, in *The Oxford Shakespeare Complete Works*, 2nd ed., ed. John Jowett, gen. eds. Stanley Wells, Gary Taylor, et al. (Clarendon: Oxford University Press, 2005).
7. *Ambikapathy*, dir. Ellis R. Dungan, perf. M.K.T. Bhagavathar and Santhanalakshmi (Salem Sankar Films, 1937). The film's title is alternatively spelt *Ambikapathi*, as on the 1937 film poster.
8. 'Kollywood' is the Tamil cinema industry based in Kodambakkam, Chennai.
9. S. Theodore Baskaran, *History through the Lens: Perspectives on South Indian Cinema* (Hyderabad: Orient Blackswan, 2009), 62.
10. C.R.W. David, *Cinema as Medium of Communication in Tamil Nadu* (Mysore: The Christian Literature Society, 1983), 23.
11. Ibid., 22.
12. The *Madras Mail*, 8 December 1896 records that that month, T. Stevenson, proprietor of the Madras Photographic Store, offered the first 'cinematograph or animated photograph' shows. In Stephen Putnam Hughes, 'When Film Came to Madras', *BioScope: South Asian Screen Studies* 1, no. 2 (2010) 165, footnote 10.
13. Ellis Roderick Dungan, *A Guide to Adventure* (Pittsburgh: Dorrance, 2001), 53.
14. Ibid., 56.
15. Quoted in B.D. Garga, *So Many Cinemas: The Motion Picture in India* (Mumbai: Eminence Designs, 1996), 80. Tamil talkies brought local cinema production houses a new financial security; see Dickey, *Urban Poor,* 51.
16. S. Theodore Baskaran, *The Eye of the Serpent: An Introduction to Tamil Cinema* (Chennai: Westland Ltd., 2013), 24.
17. Hughes, 'Music in the Age of Mechanical Reproduction: Drama, Gramophone, and the Beginnings of Tamil Cinema'. *Journal of Asian Studies* 66, no. 1 (February 2007), 11–12.

18 *Romeo and Juliet*, dir. George Cukor (Burbank: Warner Home Video, 2007 [1936]). The film, starring producer Irving Thalberg's wife Norma Shearer and Leslie Howard, was by all accounts a box-office failure in the U.S.
19 Dungan, *Adventure*, 66.
20 Ibid.
21 Ibid., 67.
22 Ibid., 66.
23 Linda Hutcheon and Siobhan O'Flynn, *A Theory of Adaptation* (London: Routledge, 2013), 38.
24 Ibid., 1.
25 Hughes, 'Music', 13.
26 Joseph Getter and B. Balasubrahmaniyan, 'Tamil Film Music: Sound and Significance', *Global Soundtracks: Worlds of Film Music*, 147.
27 Baskaran, *Lens*, 14.
28 Russell Jackson, ed., *The Cambridge Companion to Shakespeare on Film*, 2nd ed. (Cambridge: Cambridge University Press, 2007), 8.
29 Patricia Tatspaugh, 'The Tragedies of Love on Film', Ibid., 142.
30 Mihir Bose, *Bollywood, a History*, 2nd ed. (Stroud: Tempus Publishing Limited, 2007), 127.
31 The episode of Rukmini's elopement during her arranged wedding was reworked for Desdemona/ Dolly's elopement with Othello/Omi in Vishal Bhardwaj's film adaptation *Omkara*.
32 Dickey, *Urban Poor*, 184.
33 Alternatively known as Kamban, 'Kambar' is the honorific plural name for the Tamil poet revered for translating the Sanskrit *Ramayana* into Tamil.
34 Dungan, *Adventure*, 66.
35 Kannaki is also the heroine of the titular 2001 Malayalam film adaptation of *Antony and Cleopatra* directed by Jayaraj. For the translation of Tamil passages, explanation of local customs and elucidation of Kannaki's curse on the regal umbrella, I am indebted to Latha R.
36 Julie Sanders, *Adaptation and Appropriation* (London: Routledge, 2006), 26.
37 This is evidenced by the multilingual Indian Shakespeare filmography appended to this volume.
38 Among these, Tatspaugh identifies *The Tempest*'s 'Honour, Riches, Marriage, Blessing' and *Twelfth Night*'s 'O Mistress Mine', while the latter play's 'Come Away Death' is also incorporated; see 'Tragedies', 143.
39 The opening Capulet-Montague quarrel here takes place among pomp and circumstance as the twin retinues wind through the streets to a wedding. *Ambikapathy* (1937) has a similar opening as the triumphant Chola army returns, complete with a royal retinue of horses, elephants and trumpeters.
40 *Spectator*, 23 October, quoted in Russell Jackson, *Shakespeare Films in the Making: Vision, Production and Reception* (Cambridge: Cambridge University Press, 2007), 157.
41 Kalki Krishnamurthy, *Ananda Vikatan*, 3 January 1937.
42 Hutcheon and O'Flynn, *Adaptation*, 149.
43 Dungan estimates that early Tamil talkies incorporated thirty to forty songs in four hours; see *Adventure*, 66. Hughes calculates similarly that these films devoted 'two hours out of a total running time of three hours to accommodate fifty or sixty song sequences'; see 'Mechanical', 3.
44 Ibid., 31; 'Dungan the director', *Frontline* 10 January 2014. www.frontline.in/arts-and-culture/dungan-the-director/article5492566.ece accessed

'Singing Is Such Sweet Sorrow' 215

31 March 2015. Joseph Getter and B. Balasubrahmaniyan write that films today 'generally adhere to the convention of including about a half-dozen or more songs'. See their article 'Tamil Film Music: Sound and Significance', *Global Soundtracks: Worlds of Film Music*, 116.
45 Baskaran, *Lens*, 63.
46 Ibid.
47 Ibid. Indebted to Arani Ilankuberan for refining the translation.
48 Randor Guy, 'Wordsmith', *The Hindu* 28 August 2011.
49 Kobita Sarkar, *Indian Cinema To-day: An Analysis* (New Delhi: Sterling Publishers, 1975), 103.
50 Getter, 'Tamil Film Music' 123; Dickey, *Urban Poor*, 52.
51 Baskaran, *Lens*, 14, 104, 150.
52 Hughes, 'Music' 4.
53 Randor Guy, *Starlight, Starbright: The Early Tamil Cinema* (Madras: Amra Publishers, 1997), 177.
54 S. Theodore Baskaran, 'Persistence of Conventions: '*Company Drama*' and the Tamil Cinema', *STQ* 31 (September 2001): 95.
55 *An American in Madras*, Dir. Karan Bali. Alex Anthony, 2013.
56 Hutcheon and O'Flynn, *Adaptation*, 34.
57 Baskaran, 'Persistence', 95.
58 Baskaran, *Lens*, 125.
59 William O. Beeman, 'The Use of Music in Popular Film: East and West', *India International Centre Quarterly* 8, no. 1 (March 1981): 83.
60 Baskaran, *Lens*, 130.
61 Randor Guy, 'Man with the Midas touch', *The Hindu* 18 March 2010 www.thehindu.com/features/cinema/man-with-the-midas-touch/article257173.ece accessed 30 March 2015.
62 'MS Tribute'; Baskaran, *Eye*, 24.
63 Dungan, *Adventure*, 67.
64 R.K. Yajnik, *The Indian Theatre* (New York: Haskell House, 1970), 199.
65 S.V. Srinivasiar, *Romeo and Juliet [Ramyanum Jolitaiyum]* (Madras: Srinivasa Varadachari and Co., 1908), xi.
66 *Rasas* are emotional tones or states. See Anil Zankar in this volume.
67 Yajnik, *The Indian Theatre*, 199.
68 Ibid., 202–3.
69 Dungan records the challenges of shooting in Calcutta's East India film studio in a pre-dubbing era. Songs and dances had to be recorded live; shooting ceased whenever it rained, as the music would be drowned out by the din on the studio's tin roof; see *Adventure* 56.
70 Dickey, *Urban Poor*, 53. Censorship came into force with the British Cinematograph Act of 1918.
71 Priya Jaikumar clarifies that 'Censorship in colonized India was not centralized in one board but housed in the provinces of Bombay, Madras, and Calcutta, which were also the chief ports of film import'; see *Cinema at the End of Empire: A Politics of Transition in Britain and India* (Durham: Duke University Press, 2006), 245.
72 Baskaran, *Lens*, 39.
73 Guy, 'Wordsmith'.
74 *An American in Madras* includes a discussion of this issue.
75 Andrew Dickson, *Worlds Elsewhere: Journeys around Shakespeare's Globe* (London: Penguin, 2015), 225; see 214 for the *Romeo and Juliet* poster image.
76 Latha K., telephone interview, 7 May 2015.

77 Indian stage adaptations commonly included characters from the epics such as the *Ramayana* and *Mahabharata*.
78 Preminda Jacob, *Celluloid Deities* (Plymouth: Lexington Books, 2009), 86.
79 K. Hariharan, in *An American in Madras*.
80 Srinivasiar, Ramyanum Jolitayum (*Romeo and Juliet*), xi–xii.
81 ibid., xiii.
82 Ibid.
83 Dungan, *Adventure* 100. While the twenty-first century has seen the Indian screen kiss become mainstream, kissing in public is still largely taboo. See M. Madhava Prasad, *Ideology of the Hindi Film: A Historical Construction* (Delhi: Oxford University Press, 1998).
84 Karan Bali, 'Found in Translation', *IQ The Indian Quarterly* 25 December 2013 http://indianquarterly.com/ found-in-translation/ accessed 29 March 2015.
85 Dickey, *Urban Poor*, 55.
86 The Indian chivalric code recognised several types of marriage, including the private pact.
87 The 'self-respect' marriage, championed by reformers like E.V. 'Periyar' Ramasamy, abjured the need for Brahmin priests.
88 S. Theodore Baskaran, in *An American in Madras*.
89 Randor Guy, 'Full of Technical Innovations', *The Hindu*, 17 December 2004. Tamil cinema convention appropriated the bedchamber scene quickly, as can be seen in a still from the film *Madhurai Veeran* (1938). This image is reproduced in S. Theodore Baskaran's 'Persistence of conventions: "company drama" and the Tamil cinema', *STQ* 31 (September 2001): 94.
90 Among the 'unthinkable' scenes that are missing in the restored version is one where the hero winked suggestively at his lover, yet the only wink that survives is in a still of Ugrasenan teasing his own lover. Apparently, M.K.T.'s wink became his trademark.
91 Dungan, *Adventure*, 66.
92 Dickey, *Urban Poor*, 99.
93 These films included *A Throw of Dice* (1929), directed by Franz Osten, featuring an eloping royal couple, and John Hunt's *Karma* (1933), the Bollywood tale of a disobedient princess in love. See Madhulika Varma's 'Obituary: Devika Rani', *The Independent* 26 March 1994 www.independent.co.uk/ news/people/obituary-devika-rani-1431657.html accessed 27 March 2015 and Priyanka Dasgupta's 'India's longest kissing scene clips in Paoli film', *Times of India* 30 April 2012 http://timesofindia.indiatimes.com/entertainment/bengali/ movies/ news/Indias-longest-kissing-scene-clips-in-Paoli-film/articleshow/12934783.cms? accessed 28 March 2015.
94 Sathiavathi Chinnaiah writes that the conventional celluloid heroine, like an ideal Tamil woman, is 'chaste' and assumes 'a subordinate position within the narrative', in 'The Tamil Film Heroine: From a Passive Subject to a Pleasurable Object', *Tamil Cinema: The Cultural Politics of India's Other Film Industry*, ed. Selvaraj Velayutham (Abingdon: Routledge, 2008), 38.
95 Selvaraj Velayutham, ed., 'Introduction'. *Tamil Cinema: The Cultural Politics of India's Other Film Industry*, 9. Velayutham writes that Kannaki is the symbol of ideal Tamil womanhood in her chastity, intelligence, motherliness and divinity.
96 Latha K., interview.

97 K. Chellappan, *Shakespeare and Ilango as Tragedians: A Comparative Study* (Thanjavur: Tamil University Press, 1985), 126.
98 Kumkum Sangari and Sudesh Vaid, eds., *Recasting Women: Essays in Indian Colonial History* (New Brunswick: Rutgers University Press, 1990), 9.
99 *Ambikapathy*, dir. P. Neelakanthan, perf. Sivaji Ganesan and P. Bhanumathi (A.L.S. Productions, 1957).
100 Jacob, *Deities*, 92.
101 Chinnaiah, 'The Tamil Film Heroine', 32.
102 Craig Dionne and Parmita Kapadia, eds., *Bollywood Shakespeares* (London: Palgrave Macmillan, 2014), 6.
103 Kannamma and Ambikapathy had been intended for one another by their poet fathers, yet she yields him to Amaravathi. While aiding the pair's foiled elopement, Kannamma is mistakenly stabbed by the king in the dark, a fate resembling that of Kamala, the *sakhi* in D.A. Keskar's 1908 translation *Tāra-Vilas*. Here, Kamala/Rosaline 'has to marry Tybalt; but remains enamoured of Romeo. She is a boon companion of Juliet'. See Yajnik, 157–58. Kamala precipitates triple tragedy when she delays delivering the letter to Romeo, fakes her death, hides in a temple, and is assaulted and killed there.
104 Guy, 'Ambikapathy'.
105 Ibid.
106 In the 1937 version, Krishnan romances married woman Madhuram in a bawdy *Merry Wives of Windsor* style comic subplot, evading her husband's multiple attempts at detection.
107 Latha K., interview.
108 The goddess' blessing is also visible in the final scene, where the executioner's axe turns into flowers, momentarily saving the hero until the king himself stabs him.
109 Dickey, *Urban Poor,* 54.
110 Baskaran, *Lens*, 32.
111 Latha K., interview.
112 Guy, *Starbright,* 279–80. These films all starred Sivaji Ganesan, who also played Ambikapathi in the 1957 remake.
113 The 1957 film's leads Bhanumathi and Sivaji Ganesan later reunited in *Arivaali* (1963), A.T. Krishnaswami's Tamil remake of *The Taming of the Shrew*. Yet this pairing was arguably due to their talent rather than any Shakespearean association. See A. Mangai's essay in this volume.
114 See this volume's essays on Tamil cinema and on Indian film versions of *Romeo and Juliet*.

Part IV
Reimagining Gender, Region and Nation

12 Gendered Play and Regional Dialogue in *Nanjundi Kalyana*

Mark Thornton Burnett

This essay understands the highly popular Kannada-language film *Nanjundi Kalyana* (dir. M.S. Rajashekar, 1989) in terms of its rewriting of Shakespeare's *The Taming of the Shrew*. Crucially, *Nanjundi Kalyana* places a regional gloss on its adaptive procedures, continually citing cultural practices and gendered attitudes germane to southern parts of India and to Karnataka in particular. The film functions both as an adaptation and as an intervention in a discussion about regional identity, as evidenced in a dialectic that places rural and urban locales in opposition, in an interplay between the old and the new, in a localising procedure (comprised of images and references) and in specific deployments of mythological allusion. *Nanjundi Kalyana* takes many of the premises of Shakespeare's play – namely a concern with shame, the taming of the 'shrew' and ideas of home and domestication – so as to invest them with meanings and resonances particular to a Kannada-language milieu. In this sense, it seeks to steer a path between notions of obedience central to the Shakespearean narrative and ideals of family, marriage, reciprocity and honour more familiar to Karnataka cinematic audiences. As a result, *Nanjundi Kalyana* presents itself as a rich fusion of traditions and constructions, one which, in the same moment, testifies to the variety of cinemas in India and to a vibrant history of adapting Shakespeare to different languages and environments.

Shakespeare came early to Karnataka. As Vijaya Guttal notes, the first loose translation of *The Taming of the Shrew* into the Kannada language was in 1897, other translations of the play following in 1910 and 1920, respectively. A more 'faithful' translation was published in 1936. Adaptations and translations went side by side, and a healthy tradition of translating and performing the play has been in evidence in the state for at least the past 120 years.[1] The aim, as with other translation and performance practices in India, was to 'indigenize the alien text to the native context.'[2] At roughly the same time that *The Taming of the Shrew* was being recast in local guise, the Kannada-language film industry, sometimes known as 'Sandalwood', was being inaugurated. A number of 'talkies' in the 1930s announced the coming into being of the industry (these were melodramas in the main), and, after lulls and setbacks, the production of mythological and historical films in the 1950s testified to a particularly prosperous phase. A period characterised by fewer films and a slower production rate followed before the emergence, in the 1970s and 1980s, of a more diversified film output (popular films and 'art-house' films being released together) and so-called 'parallel cinema' works. Currently, there are 950 single-screen theatres in Karnataka, and over a 100 films are made each year.[3] Interestingly, in the film industry of India as a whole, *The Taming of the Shrew* has repeatedly attracted filmic treatment. As Rajiva Verma notes, the '*Shrew* theme has easily been the most popular on the Indian screen', adaptations such as *Chori* (dir. Anant Thakur, 1956), *Ponga Pandit* (dir. Prayag Raj, 1975) and *Betaab* (dir. Rahul Rawail, 1983) reflecting a widespread deployment of the play's ideas and motifs.[4] If we understand translation as a potential mode of resistance, and, moreover, as a practice that elevates, in order to underscore the significance of, the 'indigenous', then a film such as *Nanjundi Kalyana* might be seen as affirming the distinctiveness of Kannada culture and language. As I argue in this essay, the film goes beyond itself in terms of its importance, registering not simply an individual engagement with Shakespeare but also the endeavours of a local film industry to establish a uniquely crafted identity.

Shakespearean Variations

Released in 1989 and set in the present day, *Nanjundi Kalyana* quickly established itself as a hit romantic youth film. Part of its impact was due to the friction between the central leads, Ragu/Petruchio and Devi/Katharina, but additional appeal surely inhered in the modern slant placed on the history of 'shrew'-taming films in Indian cinema. Although the play is not directly referenced as a source of inspiration, *Nanjundi Kalyana* clearly functions as an adaptation, as witnessed in the plot line; the combative relationship between a male wooer and an independent woman; and scenes of taming, humiliation and resistance. The basic situation – two friends love two sisters, but the eldest (third) sister has to marry first – resembles that of *The Taming of the Shrew*, while parts of the dialogue instance the play specifically. Devi/Katharina's complaint of Ragu/Petruchio – 'Truly, this is a mental case' – echoes that of Katharina when she states, 'a mad-brain rudesby ... a frantic fool' (3.2.10, 12), suggesting a degree of linguistic commerce between film and text.[5] Parallels are also implied in film/stage business. For instance, both Devi and Katharina display a penchant for slapping servants, the idea being that the physical horseplay of *The Taming of the Shrew* functions as a practical point of reference. Even the framing structure of *The Taming of the Shrew* might be said to be internally imitated in *Nanjundi Kalyana* for the induction with the players is recalled when Ragu/Petruchio hires actors to impersonate his mother and father in an episode that imbues the film with a pronounced theatrical self-consciousness.

While *Nanjundi Kalyana* follows the Shakespearean narrative arc, it is distinguished by plot details and developments that lend it a unique complexity. As the film makes clear, Shankrappa, a wealthy landowner married to Sita, has argued with his brother-in-law, Puthooru, a city dweller married to Suthooru (who is Shankrappa's sister). The conflict is a source of continual emotional stress for Shankrappa, to the extent that Ragu/Petruchio, son to Shankrappa and Sita, offers to woo and marry Devi/Katharina, the eldest daughter of Puthooru and Suthooru, thereby healing the rift. In order to expedite this plan, and remain under cover, Ragu takes on the identity of Nanjundi, a brother to Shankrappa who, believed dead, has magically reappeared. From this brief rehearsal emerges a fundamental Shakespearean departure. Whereas, in *The Taming of the Shrew*, Petruchio is represented as a bounty hunter or man-on-the-make, stating that his mission is 'Happily ... to wive it wealthily in Padua' (1.2.53, 72), *Nanjundi Kalyana* discovers Ragu as motivated by a sense of filial duty or *dharma*. The film re-envisions Petruchio to suit contemporary South Indian *mores* and in such a way as to play up the importance attached to a principle of familial unity. It is the division between the father and the brother-in-law that shapes and impels the action, and that the fatal argument occurred on a festival day lends the episode a religious if not sacrilegious cast. The audience is never allowed to forget the rift, and the need for reconciliation, making *Nanjundi Kalyana* a youth film centred around themes of family responsibility and commitment, and giving a logic to the ways in which characters are elaborated (daughters and sons are realised in terms of professions and parentage).

Localising Procedures

But, as the film suggests, these types of values are under pressure. Continually, the film maps social relations in a process of flux, as conjured in sequences that set against each other urban pastimes and rural ways. For example, Ragu/Petruchio is represented very much as a product of a farming community; he drives family members and farm workers to a village festival in a tractor, while the surrounding conversation centres on crops and the harvest. When Devi/Katharina arrives with Ragu/Petruchio at his house (a lowly shed designed to convince her that he is a servant), the camera's focus upon the dwelling's tools and utensils – pots, pans, farm implements and baskets – not only points out the fact that a rural setting underpins the action but also demonstrates how, in any move from city to country, issues of class come to the fore. The urban/rural dialectic in *Nanjundi Kalyana* is highlighted in the contrasts the film engineers between the old and the new. Hence, as implied by his yellow, open-necked shirt, short-sleeved top, neck-chains, and penchant for loud colours, Ragu/Petruchio stands as a figure for the modern; for her part, Devi/Katharina, not least because of the badminton racket she wields and her fashionable stripy dress, sunglasses, bomber jacket, trainers and love of jogging, is imagined as a contemporary sportswoman characterised by quasi-European sophistication. The house in which she lives – a creamy residence in a wealthy suburb adorned with knick-knacks and an interior fountain – is the very manifestation of bourgeois aspiration fulfilled. The idea of Devi/Katharina as a cosmopolitan late twentieth-century Indian woman is maintained throughout, and it is most obviously expressed in her reliance on English terms such as 'You!' and 'Scoundrel!' (Interestingly, these terms have long been markers of the 'modern' in Indian film, suggesting that, at another level of its fabric, *Nanjundi Kalyana* flirts with the 'spoilt young woman' stereotype.)[6] However, at the moment when she smashes up her room in a fit of distemper, destroying the television set, an abuse of the bourgeois ideal (and a desecration of the material contentment the family has worked to achieve) is implied. M.K. Raghavendra notes of *Nanjundi Kalyana* that 'rural life and the village ... are extraneous and have little significance' and that the 'city is ... simply a glamorous space', yet, on close inspection, each of these locales emerges as symbolically coded, connoting, variously, concerns of morality, work, ambition and youth identity.[7]

What distinguishes *Nanjundi Kalyana* from any number of seemingly similar 'Bollywood' or Hindi-language Shakespeare adaptations is a carefully worked localising representational procedure. Such a mode of representation functions, moreover, to stamp *Nanjundi Kalyana* with a specific sense of itself, to characterise it as possessing a particular regional attachment. It is no accident that the city in the film is Bangalore, the capital of Karnataka; this is the hub to which much of the action, even if intermittently, is drawn. Cities loom large in the fabric of the dialogue, invariably to underscore an idea of Karnataka as a state with its own cultures and traditions. The scene in which Ragu/Petruchio takes on (successfully) a wrestler (sent against him by Devi/Katharina) is a case in point. Here, it is announced that Ragu/Petruchio 'won in Bombay' and that his next fight is to take place in 'Mavalli'. The equation between Mumbai, in the state of Maharashtra, and Mavalli, a village in the southerly part of Karnataka, is a telling one, reinforcing the idea that Ragu/Petruchio is loyal to his state, that, despite success, he never loses sight of the particularity of his affiliation. Not surprisingly, then, Ragu/Petruchio is described by the master of a martial arts school as having 'brought fame to our land', 'land' substituting in this formulation for Karnataka and pointing to a region-specific sense of pride. (Of course, the romance between a 'salt of the earth' young man and a rich and cossetted woman is a recurring trope in popular Indian cinema, the difference being that *Nanjundi Kalyana* suggests a specifically local engagement with the theme).[8] The film is even capable of ironising its own procedures, not least when we learn that Devi/Katharina's birthday and 'Karnataka Freedom Day' share the same date. If only sub-textually, a parallel is drawn between a key political event and Devi/Katharina's speeches of fiery independence. Beyond these popular culture references, *Nanjundi Kalyana* establishes itself as embracing a discrete demographic via strategically devised scenes and images. There are several shots, for example, of the 'Hotel Ashok', a hotel in Bangalore that, because it is frequently instanced in Kannada-language cinema, has become a byword for sumptuousness and luxury. It is to this hotel that Shashidhara, suitor to Devi/Katharina and a version of *The Taming of the Shrew*'s Gremio, gravitates; the detail that he is a doctor from Mysore, the third-largest city in Karnataka, works to suggest a network of professional interrelations spanning the state's urban conurbations. Professionalisation and education are invariably regionally delineated. The 'J. C. College of Science and Commerce', which Devi/Katharina attends as a student, is a fiction, an amalgam of several similarly titled colleges in Karnataka, but its presence in the film testifies both to a long-standing commitment to education in the state and to a generalised idea of modernity.

Typically in *Nanjundi Kalyana*, regional detailing is underpinned by a subscription to ritual. It is not accidental that, at the start, the framing *puja* to which Ragu/Petruchio and members of his family are bound is the *Gauri Ganesha* festival, an occasion on which the elephant deity Lord Ganesha is worshipped as a bringer of good luck and a remover of obstacles (the festival holds a particular place in the Karnataka religious calendar). Judging by the mise en scène, the film takes pains to establish the authenticity of its festive representation for the clay figurine of the white elephant god is carried with due reverence, and appropriate decorative accoutrements are spotlighted (including banana stem and mango leaf flourishes). Interestingly, a *puja* recurs after the wedding; Ragu/Petruchio and Devi/Katharina sit down in the servant hut to enjoy a celebratory meal, a key moment for newly married couples. The foods themselves are evocative; 'betel leaves', 'Mysore leaves' and the 'malenadu areca nut' are referenced, all of them natural products of different parts of Karnataka. Significantly, Devi/Katharina's refusal of the local food in this scene illuminates a larger and more dangerous form of resistance. In Karnataka, betel leaves are offered, and then consumed, as a sign of respect and good fortune. When lovers chew the areca nut, combined with the betel leaves, an auspicious union is affirmed (the male nut and the female leaves are symbolic). *Nanjundi Kalyana* is imbricated in local ideologies and attitudes; it also finds in these an index of Devi/Katharina's departure from the principles, as they are enshrined in the philosophy of Hinduism, of a marital ideal.

Gendered Resistance

The inclusion in the film of a college, the 'J. C. College of Science and Commerce', anchors in a regional mode what is perhaps *Nanjundi Kalyana*'s most unsettling type of resistance – Devi/Katharina's flouting of gendered norms. It is at the college, in a revealing flashback, that Devi/Katharina's particular mode of 'shrewishness' is first realised. Arriving for her class in Western denims and a fast car, Devi/Katharina finds that a satirically minded male student has posted a cartoon in which she is drawn with a moustache, the abusive term 'Terrorist' decorating the picture's margins. At once here, 'Terrorist' suggests a figure of terror and a political dissident, arguably one who endangers the organic identity of Karnataka as an Indian state. All around, Devi/Katharina encounters laughing students and, of course, the gleeful moustachioed cartoonist: they join in an amused response to the representation of a Devi/Katharina who becomes aberrant because she is viewed as male. 'Are you going to tease me by drawing a moustache on my picture?' Devi/Katharina demands and punches the hapless cartoonist across the classroom in an explosion of rage. The sequence is of interest for the contrasts it engineers (the appearance of the other women students in *sarees*, for example, offers a counterpoint to Devi/Katharina's Western-style dress), but it is also striking because it serves to inaugurate the film's much larger concern with the pervasiveness and extent of Devi/Katharina's dereliction of the ideal woman's standards. For instance, her alterity and lack of convention are suggested in the scene in which the mother, Suthooru, and Devi/Katharina's seemingly demure sisters, Lakshmi and Saraswati, versions of Bianca, are represented leaving a temple; Devi/Katharina is conspicuously absent from their devotions. Elsewhere, she is seen reading a book entitled *Devil*, an indication of an infernal disposition, or reclining on her bed underneath a poster showing Cassius Clay crowing over the broken body of Sony Liston in their infamous 1965 boxing bout; her points of identification, it is implied, are with brutal battles and male victors. Indeed, the martial character of Devi/Katharina's contests with men is continually stressed. One suitor is hit over the head with a guitar, an instrument associated with female accomplishment; another, who appears on a horse and wearing armour, finds to his chagrin that Devi/Katharina scares the animal away, thereby derailing the wooing process. Devi/Katharina, then, is discovered as no hapless maiden at home in an epic adventure.

Beyond Devi/Katharina's gendered unorthodoxy is a tangled web of historical determinants. In the late nineteenth century in India, particularly in Bengal, the emergence of the so-called 'modern' woman resulted

Gendered Play and Regional Dialogue in Nanjundi Kalyana 227

in a series of vernacular satires. Such expressions of criticism singled out for treatment an imagined man-woman influenced by Western mores, a type dressing inordinately and judged unnatural. Cartoons sometimes accompanied the portrayals, suggesting a link with *Nanjundi Kalyana*'s similar deployment of ironic pictorial material. As Partha Chatterjee notes, the satires ridiculed 'the idea of a Bengali woman trying to imitate the ways of a *memsāheb*' via a focussed targeting on such elements as 'manners ... clothing ... [and] the use of Western cosmetics and jewellery', the underlining anxiety being that 'the Westernized woman ... cared little for the well-being of the home.'[9] Various social and political elements can be identified in these developments, and, at a juncture when concepts of the nation were in a process of flux and change, there were attendant attempts to reinstate a seemingly besieged patriarchy and to protest against class differences exacerbated by the foundation of colonial institutions. Part of *Nanjundi Kalyana*'s richness inheres in the fact of its allusiveness, its capacity for taking energy from discussions relating both to the here-and-now and to periods of a much earlier moment.

For example, at the same time as Devi/Katharina's behaviour is imbricated in Victorian satire, so does it recall a key debate about the so-called 'man-woman' from the seventeenth century. In the anonymous pamphlet, *Hic Mulier* (1620), women who act as men, in 'attire, in speech, [and] in manners', are branded 'base, in respect it offends man in the example and God in the most unnatural use; barbarous, in that it is exorbitant from Nature and an Antithesis to kind, going astray with ill-favoured affectation.'[10] Devi/Katharina is elaborated within such a schema of transgression and, crucially, the racial epithets at work in the *Hic Mulier* description resurface in the film. Several remarks testify to Devi/Katharina's inordinate appetite ('She can eat men', opines Kittu, Ragu/Petruchio's friend, while Ragu/Petruchio himself declares that he is not going to be 'prey' for the 'lioness'), and these are crystallised in the expression 'She is a wicked cannibal'. Bringing *Othello* to mind, but also the *Hic Mulier* association of the 'man-woman' with Barbary, Africa and all that is barbarous, the statement momentarily pitches Devi/Katharina out of a Southern Indian milieu into an early modern colonial realm in which the woman is 'other' because incompatible with European notions of normalcy. More generally, distinctive in these delineations of Devi/Katharina's discontent is the inventiveness of the Shakespearean translation. Thus, Ragu/Petruchio's animal epithet points up a recasting of the play's reference to Katharina as a 'wildcat' (1.2.191); the *Devil* book over which Devi pours underlines a filmic response to the idea, in *The Taming of the Shrew*, that Katharina is 'a devil, the devil's dam' (3.3.29); and, when Devi smashes the guitar, a parallel is suggested with Katharina's similarly destructive wielding of her lute. If Devi/Katharina's mode of resistance is rooted in a locally situated evocation of education, then it is also indebted to the descriptors and actions characteristic of

Shakespeare's play. The 'man-woman' is objectionable, according to *Hic Mulier*, because he/she is 'unnatural', and an additional area of concern in *Nanjundi Kalyana* is the way in which Devi/Katharina reverses the order of things, emasculating men via assertions of emotion and will. Her physical domination over the cartoonist, and forced removal of his paintbrush, signals the dissolution of his phallic authority. By the same token, when he finds himself, thanks to Devi/Katharina's superior battle skills, without his moustache (she has shaved it off), he is reduced to hiding his lip with his shirt; as he becomes a veiled woman, so is Devi/Katharina elevated to the position of teacher, director and vengeful barber.[11] The motif of male-female inversion is consistently comically rendered. A 'rowdy' hired by a suitor who wishes to impress Devi/Katharina is himself vanquished through a well-placed kick in a sensitive area, and Kittu and Puttu, suitors to the sisters, Lakshmi and Saraswati, summarise the situation pithily. Asked by Devi/Katharina, 'Are you male?', they reply, 'We don't know what we are in front of you'. Such is Devi/Katharina's effect on men, it is implied, that the presumed solidity of male identity discombobulates, men being reduced to an amorphous and indeterminate state that robs them of customary potency.

Epic Parallels

The central conflict between Ragu/Petruchio and Devi/Katharina takes on an epic dimension in that it is repeatedly realised in mythic terms. In many respects, the confrontation between the two leads is envisaged as a larger-than-life struggle between heroic forces. A measure of his morality, Ragu/Petruchio has a tendency to reference Indian mythology, as when he alludes to the episode in the *Ramayana* in which Rama breaks the 'Shiva bow' to win his consort. Associating himself with Rama, Ragu/Petruchio places himself within a key narrative of valour and self-assertion, and takes on, as a consequence, wisdom beyond his years. (Raghunath is another name for Rama, meaning King of the dynasty of the Raghuvanshi: hence, Raghu is synonymous with Rama in a literal and figurative sense.) Elsewhere, Ragu/Petruchio alludes to Rama's fifteen-year exile, again as it is described in the *Ramayana*; the idea here, which is consistent with the narrative of the film, is that he will eventually come into his own, that he will recover a status previously eclipsed. As Ragu/Petruchio himself declares, confirming the connection, 'That Rama is me'. For Devi/Katharina, there is no equivalent paradigm of elevation. For, in her case, the mythological backstory is a pejorative one. 'She is too arrogant' to be obedient, we learn, 'like Chandi, Chamunda or Shurpanakhi' (either female demons or destructive versions of the mother goddess), the very range of the comparisons pointing out a corresponding effort to approximate the extent of Devi/Katharina's difference.[12] Interestingly, these are all mythic figures that have been,

Gendered Play and Regional Dialogue in Nanjundi Kalyana 229

in Indian engagements with Shakespeare, used as correlatives for the 'shrew', an indication of their dangerousness inhering in the insignia or accoutrements with which they are associated – sharp nails or a black appearance.[13] On another occasion, and in keeping with the particular mythic focus placed on Devi/Katharina, she is labelled as 'Durga Devi'; as Nilima Chitgopekar notes, this is the 'war goddess' and 'buffalo trampler' possessed of a 'violent energy', and she serves therefore as an apt cipher for Devi/Katharina's own brand of aggressiveness.[14]

But there is one female goddess with whom Devi/Katharina is indelibly associated. One of the sisters reflects that Devi/Katharina is 'just like Kali' (the female consort of Shiva whose 'dread appearance', in Alain Daniélou's words, 'is the symbol of her boundless destruction'), and it is in the episode centred on the celebration of the engagement that the identification is rendered explicit.[15] As Ragu/Petruchio and his male friends gather, the refrain of their song is heard, the chief cause for jubilation being that the 'arrogance' of Devi/Katharina (apparently, at least) has been broken. Among the dancing crowd can be glimpsed a *hijra*, the transvestite figure, thought to possess divine powers, who traditionally accompanies social gatherings to bestow blessings. (The *hijra* is a devotee of a further mother goddess, Bahuchara Mata, who, after having been attacked, cut off her breasts and was subsequently elevated to the Hindu pantheon). Gradually during the dance, the *hijra* is unveiled, but this is presented as no instance of gender confusion or inversion; instead, the happy participation of the *hijra* suggests his/her approval of Devi/Katharina's 'taming', while the spectacle of bodies dancing in unison points up an idea of men having assumed control. Moreover, in the place of the earlier cartoon of a moustachioed Devi/Katharina, now the camera's focus is on a placard showing a crude picture of Devi/Katharina and Ragu/Petruchio side by side. 'Happily Married' is the message that supersedes 'Terrorist', the change of caption indicating a switch in the gendered arrangement of things, and the fact that Devi/Katharina is here represented without a moustache implies that her anomalousness has been rectified. In the song's lyrics, Ragu/Petruchio's triumph is equated with the heroic exploits of Arjun (the central protagonist and hero of the Indian epic, the *Mahabharata*) and Shiva; indeed, such is the general confidence of the assembly that the former suitors, who form part of the group, now feel they have the confidence to 'fight with Devi'. Yet, in a countermove that is so characteristic of the film's procedure, and via a development that demolishes the male mythic/heroic parallels the episode has invoked, the show of confidence is exposed as transitory and insubstantial. For, immediately afterwards, Devi/Katharina appears, dressed in the guise of Kali and bearing a trident. The mise en scène does not discover Devi/Katharina in Kali's full regalia (that is, archetypally the goddess holds a sword and severed head and wears a garland of skulls), but the identification is there nonetheless.[16] Quickly the heroic postures evinced in the song crumble, not least because a female mythological figure challenges the occasion's discursive conjuration of Arjun and Shiva and breaks up the proceedings. Specifically, Devi/Katharina as Kali routs the celebrants and crushes the placards under her feet, suggesting that she rewrites classic narratives according to her own priorities and executes the mother goddess' vengeful role. Contrary to how the sequence is introduced, a reversal of the male-female order is again prioritised. Of course, none of this should necessarily strike audiences as surprising. Even without the film's mythological echoes, Devi's name is sufficient to bring ideas of female power to the fore. 'Devi', meaning goddess, suggests the woman's *shakti*, energy or divine capacity. Furthermore, the association of Devi with the dark forces of a range of mother goddesses belongs with the characterisation and is in keeping with the discovery, in the play, of Katharina as a type of 'devil' (3.3.29). What is distinctive is the local cast of the mythic construction. For example, in her South Indian manifestation, Durga, the war goddess, as Nilima Chitgopekar notes, is constituted as a 'dangerous ... murderous, bride' who 'takes ... energies, strength and potency ... from the male gods in order to perform her own' deeds; such a figuration is of a piece with *Nanjundi Kalyana*'s depiction of processes of emasculation and also accords with the conceptualisation of Devi more generally.[17] A further local-mythic idea is at work in the film's title. *Nanjundi Kalyana*, or the wedding of Nanjundi, references the area (Nanjangud) in Karnataka where, according to a regional variation of the legend, Shiva (or Nanja or Nanjundeshwara) drank poison. At one point, Ragu/Petruchio even prays to his local namesake. A local habitation for a mythic narrative is suggested here as well as the notion that the title character, Nanjundi/Ragu/Petruchio, is a player in a story of epic proportions.

Shameful Spectacles

The wedding itself suggests Devi/Katharina's determination to continue in an assertive role. Although, at the ceremony, she is represented wearing traditional garb, her submission to male power is illusory only; as she states in an aside, 'there is no love ... I married him to take revenge'. Much of the subsequent action takes its impetus from *The Taming of the Shrew*. For example, as in Shakespeare's play, the move to Ragu/Petruchio's village from the city entails class reorganisation, while the forced conditions in which Devi/Katharina finds herself (she is unable, in that order, to wash, eat or sleep) are precisely those rehearsed in the original 'shrew' narrative. The scene in the temple, to which Devi/Katharina is drawn in a vain attempt to find food, seems prompted by Shakespearean references to 'beggars' (4.3.4) and 'charity' (4.3.6). Meanwhile, Ragu's relentlessly chirpy philosophising recalls Petruchio's similarly *faux* buoyant reflections. In the play, 'shame' (3.2.8) is linked most obviously to Katharina's reductive experience. By contrast, in *Nanjundi Kalyana*, 'shame' is registered as a more widely felt phenomenon, one that is related to the resentment of Puthooru, brother-in-law to Shankrappa (the former claims that the latter gave evidence against him, thereby leading to a loss of 'respect' in the 'public court') and also to a series of predicaments in which Devi/Katharina finds herself. As she complains, having to walk in the street in her 'swimsuit' is an 'embarrassment'. (In terms of the representation of women, this is a particularly uncomfortable and gratuitous moment.) At issue here is not simply an emphasis on notions of female pride and family honour. Key, too, is the theme that shame is galling precisely because it is visible. Perhaps the most extended and involved elaboration of the idea is reserved for the sequence in which, in order to 'shame' Ragu/Petruchio in the eyes of the community, Devi/Katharina elects to leave the servant hut and get drunk, becoming, contrary to her plan, a figure of shame herself. The sequence is premised on ideas of contrariness and inversion; the flashback photonegative images of Devi/Katharina that inaugurate the episode, for example, reinforce a theme of opposites and opposition even as they pave the way for her conversion. Incidental business confirms these associations, as when Devi/Katharina buys a bottle of alcohol in a local shop, eliciting shocked reactions on the part of the customers. Engaged in a demeaning transaction, it is implied, Devi/Katharina has exceeded the bounds of the *domus*. A sense of indecency is additionally conjured in Devi/Katharina's appearance; with midriff showing, and hair loosened, she is represented as particularly scantily attired. Typically, motifs of male-female confusion recur. 'When a girl is drunk, she becomes a he-man', Devi/Katharina sings, showing her muscles in a display of conventional masculinity and recalling both Victorian satire and the *Hic Mulier* tradition of women gone awry. The whole is elaborated as a nadir of unseemliness, not least because, in this extra-domestic display of disobedience, Devi/Katharina is spectated upon in the street by all and sundry, including appalled lower classes. Admittedly, as the lyrics suggest, at another level the song admits to the challenges facing Indian women in contemporary society (as Devi/Katharina sings, 'It's difficult to find the path with so many twists and turns'), but, even here, the dominant impression is of a woman who has failed to live up to expected standards. And, so as to broaden the scope of its applications, *Nanjundi Kalyana* takes the instance of Devi/Katharina's derelictions and uses it to make a political point. Bringing to mind Indira Gandhi, who served as prime minister of India in two separate terms (1966–1977 and 1980–1984), the song continues: 'Tomorrow, if I became Prime Minister, the arrack shop would be my capital'. Invoking a well-known alcoholic beverage, the song is both retrospective (recalling well-known women-led movements against arrack, which has historically been seen as a trigger for gambling and domestic abuse) and anticipatory, looking forward to Karnataka's banning of the drink in

2007. Functioning in these dual capacities, the song marks Devi/Katharina as a markedly transgressive political construction. So is Devi/Katharina brought down still further via a comic invocation of a place of trade substituting for government institutions.

Domestic Ideals

In the musical interlude that makes up the shaming ritual, Devi/Katharina's voice is prioritised. But as a way of taking spoken authority away from the characters and stressing the importance of a general perspective, the final song, which sounds over the scene of Devi/Katharina's humiliation at her husband's hands followed by illness, is given to no speaker in the filmic action. Rather, an omniscient voice is heard in keeping with the official philosophy being espoused. *Nanjundi Kalyana* does not enact in dialogue the classic 'obedience' (5.2.140–83) speech of the play, but it does analogise and reconceive that speech's statement of principles in a song concerned with the need in marriage for reciprocity. Notably, then, the lyrics draw attention to forms of 'harmony': husband and wife, the song argues, 'come close with friendship', they 'walk together', and 'are like two eyes of a family'. Emphasised here are the equal contributions of husband and wife to the marital institution, the idea being that union works best if seen as an arrangement in which both partners honour jointly shared responsibilities. In this connection, matching the instructive bent of the lyrics, the mise en scène discovers Ragu/Petruchio tending to Devi/Katharina, feeding her and performing domestic tasks. It is such an execution of husbandly *dharma* that provokes in Devi/Katharina a final crumbling of will and the onset of her reformation; as she states, 'Please forgive me'.

Underpinning the process of Devi/Katharina's conversion is a subscription to an ideal of 'home'. In the reciprocity song, and as a key philosophical tenet, the following notion is espoused: 'When a wife is like a goddess, then the home is like a temple'. And, as a result of her shaming Ragu/Petruchio, Devi/Katharina is thrown out of the servant hut, a move that confirms her alterity. The battle between husband and wife on the threshold is multilayered, and, in being rejected and forced back onto the street in the wake of her drunken escapade, Devi/Katharina is excluded in gender, class and institutional terms, occupying a non-category. As Ragu/Petruchio exclaims, instancing the 'home' as ideological measure and device, 'You crossed your limit ... You don't have a place in my house'. The storm that ensues upon his climactic announcement, as well as ramping up melodramatic excess, serves to indicate the seismic shift of Devi/Katharina's imminent embrace of conformity. Although, elsewhere in the film, mythology and sociality are used to mitigate the patriarchal drift, the move at this point is an entirely typical one in Indian popular cinema and points up the ways in which *Nanjundi Kalyana*

Gendered Play and Regional Dialogue in Nanjundi Kalyana   233

legitimises and sanitises the masculinist trajectory of film and play. But the 'home' is telling in *Nanjundi Kalyana* not just at the level of the central characters. Its prominence in the film's philosophical fabric is such that it operates, too, as the instrument of a larger familial reconciliation. (In this connection, the film enacts one of the 'specific solutions' for the problem of the Victorian Westernised woman, investing in a set of practices that dispels the threat posed to 'home and family' as institutions.)[18] When, for example, in the wake of Devi/Katharina's coming into consciousness of conformity, Shankrappa seeks the forgiveness of Puthooru, and is welcomed back into the fold, he reflects: 'By calling me inside, he saved his respect in the house'. Notions of inside and outside, and shame and honour, are dramatically rehearsed in a moment of new-found accord. These suggestions reverberate in what is the film's final reconciliation scene. In a reversal of the play's movement, *Nanjundi Kalyana* brings the family to Devi/Katharina (rather than the other way around), thereby pointing out the importance attached to rural ways. 'Come in', the smiling and 'tamed' Devi/Katharina announces to her father and mother, gesturing them into the servant hut; her gorgeous white *saree*, flecked with blue, enacts in a visual register the note of connubial content. (The garish and 'modern' clothes of before are no more.) 'We are not here to come into your house', replies a surprised Puthooru, adding, 'we are here to take you to our house ... where you were born and grown'. Under the impression that his beloved daughter has been deceived and stolen away by an imposter (a servant using the alias of 'Nanjundi'), Puthooru is represented as anxious to reinforce paternal authority, as this is expressed in the domestic establishment, and to reinstate Devi/Katharina's status as daughter rather than wife. Once the confusions have been resolved, and the identity of Nanjundi is revealed (he is, as the audience has always known, Devi/Katharina's cousin), an all-embracing coming together of the family unit can be facilitated, and key to that development is a rethinking of where the 'home' resides. Devi/Katharina's observation, 'Now, this is my only house', is a resonant one, and it encompasses not simply her own acceptance of a wifely role but also a bigger *rapprochement* between locations, generations and modes of thought (Figure 12.1).

The Taming of the Shrew closes on a note of doubt and ambivalence. ''Tis a wonder, by your leave, she will be tamed so' (5.2.193), observes Lucentio in a remark that has been used to undergird an extended debate about the performativity of Katharina's acceptance of wifely obedience.[19] An echo of that debate sounds in *Nanjundi Kalyana* at the moment where, faced with the reconciled members of their families, Devi/Katharina and Ragu/Petruchio playfully nudge each other. But such a gesture, I suggest, amounts to no more than a teasing reference to stage and film adaptations in which the 'taming' of Katharina is left open. Instead, because of the ways in which *Nanjundi Kalyana* concludes, the emphasis of its closing moments would appear to reside far more with the multiple elements with which this regional rewriting of *The Taming of the Shrew* has been preoccupied. Bringing the title of the film to mind, the final stages revolve around the wedding's symbolic functions.[20] Clearly, the reinstatement of the family is a crucial concern here, but so too is the sacramental dimension of Devi/Katharina and Ragu/Petruchio's union. In showing how a family might be reconstituted, and in representing Devi/Katharina ushering into the 'house' her mother and father with all due formality, *Nanjundi Kalyana* harks back to the broken *puja* of the start and highlights again the importance of a local culture. Implicitly in this manoeuvre, the city is rejected as a place of positive interaction, and in this film's vision of the state of Karnataka, it is the country that is foregrounded, the village operating as an ideological destination-point.[21] With the rifts opened by the rupture of the *puja* healed, the action can point out a further localising feature. That is, because of the familial link between Devi/Katharina and Ragu/Petruchio, the virtues of endogamy are alluded to; bonding and integration are made possible because the two belong to a community based on consanguinity.[22] The restitution of the *puja* is significant in another way, for, as Alain Daniélou notes, the image of Lord Ganesha traditionally adorns a house's entrance, while the appearance of the deity (his elephant ears resemble winnowing trays) invokes the harvest.[23] Bringing back so as to re-enact this *puja* in particular affirms not only the place of 'home' but also its positioning in rural (as opposed to urban) environs. Beyond the resonances of locale, the concluding montage is of interest

Figure 12.1 Devi/Katharina, reformed, greets her parents.

Gendered Play and Regional Dialogue in Nanjundi Kalyana 235

for the ways in which it reintroduces the film's mythological subtexts. In being 'tamed', Devi/Katharina can no longer be identified as a type of Kali; rather, she is more akin in her reformation to Shiva's wife, Parvati, a goddess linked to fertility, love, devotion and gentleness. Where Kali represents the destroyer, Parvati, by contrast, suggests nurturing functions. In this connection, the lyrics to the reciprocity song spring to mind, for Shiva and Parvati traditionally have need of each other; theirs is an ongoing relationship in which complementary forces are continually evolving. If *Nanjundi Kalyana* occupies a final position with respect to male-female relations, then a constantly developing, but also deeply co-dependent, union is the idea we are invited to contemplate.

Conclusions

M.K. Raghavendra writes that, in the Kannada-language film, there are 'two overlapping narratives, a local one pertaining to the immediate milieu and another pertaining to the nation.'[24] *Nanjundi Kalyana* is a film which answers to this dual imperative. At once, the film mobilises local registers in its representation of women, family and *dharma*, investing in a regionally based dialogue as part of its negotiation with the gendered questions thrown up by Shakespeare's play. As earlier parts of this essay have argued, there is, in the interstices of the film's engagement with gender, a backstory. In more ways than one, *Nanjundi Kalyana* is concerned with the situation of the 'modern woman', and, interestingly, in common with the Victorian satires on which it might be said to draw, the film finally answers its questions on this score by espousing, in Partha Chatterjee's words, notions of 'modesty, or decorum' which extend to 'orderliness, thrift, cleanliness, and a personal sense of responsibility.'[25] Or, to make a similar point for a later period, as does Tejaswini Niranjana, although, in the post-Independence period, there were 'spaces for women' and 'a new visibility', this was often illusory or short-lived, 'folded back into the very spectacularization that some feminists might challenge.'[26] As part of its discovery of this process, *The Taming of the Shrew* is updated not only via a reimagining of the Petruchio/Katharina relationship but also by a cultural and, specifically, Karnataka-based transposition that imbues the original play with new meanings and applications. In this sense, *Nanjundi Kalyana* accords with a definition elaborated by Julie Sanders: 'adaptation', she writes, can fruitfully be understood as a 'transposition' that takes 'a text from one genre and' delivers 'it to new audiences ... in cultural, geographical and temporal terms.'[27] More broadly, the figure of Devi/Katharina, it might be suggested, operates as a cipher for some of the hopes and aspirations of a regional film industry pitted against the 'Bollywood' cinema machine. As this essay has suggested, *Nanjundi Kalyana* is distinctive in the ways in which it takes 'Bollywood' conventions and plays with them, sounding subtle variations on a theme. In this connection, Shakespeare serves a key function, stressing the ways in which a classic English dramatist can be mortgaged to support the vitality and significance of southern Indian cinematic industries inside a larger national system. (It might be mentioned here that in Kannada there was for a period a move to ban Bollywood features so as to play up the value and contribution of a native *mentalité*). To judge from the previous productions of the director, M.S. Rajashekar (mainly adaptations of novels and remakes), there is no consciously enunciated political stance developed in *Nanjundi Kalyana* around these issues; rather, what may be deemed political is a by-product of the film's subscription to the local, an effect of its mode of representation. Shakespeare emerges from the work of adaptation as infinitely malleable, as a dramatist whose creations can find a 'home' in representational practices that compete with, even as they find inspiration in, the more mainstream forms of Indian cinema with which the Bard has most often been allied.[28]

Notes

1 Vijaya Guttal, 'Translation and Performance of Shakespeare in Kannada', in *India's Shakespeare: Translation, Interpretation, and Performance*, ed. Poonam Trivedi and Dennis Bartholomeusz (Newark: University of Delaware Press, 2005), 110, 116–18.
2 Guttal, 'Translation and Performance', in *India's Shakespeare*, ed. Trivedi and Bartholomeusz, 108.
3 M.K. Raghavendra, *Bipolar Identity: Region, Nation, and the Kannada Language Film* (Oxford: Oxford University Press, 2011), xi–xlvii.
4 Rajiva Verma, 'Shakespeare in Hindi Cinema', in *India's Shakespeare*, ed. Trivedi and Bartholomeusz, 752. Ruth Vanita notes that in modern India, a play such as *The Taming of the Shrew* possesses a particular force because 'members of the college-educated public routinely participate in the drama of family-arranged marriage and the exchanges of dowries, and often witness male violence against women' ('"When Men and Women are alone": Framing the Taming in India', *Shakespeare Survey*, 60 (2007), p. 86).
5 Quotations from *The Taming of the Shrew* are taken from *The Norton Shakespeare*, ed. Stephen Greenblatt et al. (New York: Norton, 1997).
6 For typical examples, see Rachel Dwyer, *100 Bollywood Films* (London: BFI Publishing, 2005), 18, 154.
7 Raghavendra, *Bipolar Identity*, 91.
8 See Dwyer, *100*, 94, 120.
9 Partha Chatterjee, 'Colonialism, Nationalism, and Colonized Women: The Contest in India', *American Ethnologist* 16, no. 4 (1989): 625.
10 *Hic Mulier* (1620), in Katherine Usher Henderson and Barbara F. McManus, eds, *Half Humankind: Contexts and Texts of the Controversy about Women in England, 1540–1640* (Urbana and Chicago: University of Illinois Press, 1985), 268.
11 The episode may refer to the fate in the *Ramayana* of Shurpanakhi (with whom Devi/Katharina is associated) who is reduced to covering her face after Lakshmana has cut off her nose.

Gendered Play and Regional Dialogue in Nanjundi Kalyana 237

12 The subtitles to the DVD targeted at an international market identify only some of the figures mentioned in the filmic dialogue, and the list continues by referencing such mythological types as Kannagi, noted for enacting revenge on the king who had murdered her husband.
13 Alain Daniélou, *The Myths and Gods of India: The Classic Work on Hindu Polytheism* (Rochester: Inner Traditions, 1991), 135, 286; Sisir Kumar Das, 'Shakespeare in Indian Languages', in *India's Shakespeare*, ed. Trivedi and Bartholomeusz, 54.
14 Nilima Chitgopekar, *The Book of Durga* (New Delhi: Penguin, 2009), 5, 15, 19.
15 Daniélou, *Myths*, 271.
16 See Daniélou, *Myths*, 271. It is also possible to see Devi/Katharina in this scene as a version of Durga (see note 13) or Chamundeshwari. There are several myths about this figure in Kannada-language and site-specific (Mysore) contexts. On Chamundeshwari, see 'Mysore District: Chamundi Hills', http://mysore.nic.in/tourism, accessed 30 April 2016.
17 Chitgopekar, *Book*, 39, 53. Durga is also a simultaneously destructive and nurturing mother; this aspect is kept alive in the figuration of Devi/Katharina in such a way as to bolster her ambiguity (particularly in the light of her eventual transformation).
18 See Chatterjee, 'Colonialism', 626, 627.
19 For typical theatrical manifestations in the West of the performed nature of Katharina's speech, see Elizabeth Klett, *Cross-Gender Shakespeare and English National Identity: Wearing the Codpiece* (New York: Palgrave, 2009), 160.
20 The film title is richly evocative. In Hindi, *kalyana* translates as welfare, prosperity and good fortune *and also* virtuous and auspicious action. By extension, in other linguistic and cultural contexts, the title invokes both Nanjundi's virtuous actions and his wedding/union.
21 By contrast, Kittu and Puttu, who marry Devi/Katharina's sisters, Lakshmi and Saraswati, and remain in Bangalore, discover to their discontent that they have, as in the play, joined not with demure women but 'shrews'. (The mythological associations – wealth/prosperity and knowledge/learning – embodied in the sisters' names, therefore, turn out to be fallacious.)
22 On the controversies surrounding consanguinity and marriage, see G. Kumaramanickavel, 'Problems with Consanguineous Marriages', *The Hindu*, 29 April 2004, http://www.thehindu.com.seta/2004. Accessed January 2016.
23 Danielou, *Myths*, 293, 297.
24 Raghavendra, *Bipolar*, xxi.
25 Chatterjee, 'Colonialism', 626, 629.
26 Tijaswini Niranjana, 'Nationalism Refigured: Contemporary South Indian Cinema and the Subject of Feminism', *Subaltern Studies* 11 (2000): 140, 151.
27 Julie Sanders, *Adaptation and Appropriation* (London and New York: Routledge, 2006), 20.
28 I would like to thank Poonam Trivedi and Paromita Chakravarti for their astute and enabling comments on an earlier version of this essay. I am also grateful to Sujata Iyengar and Mythili Iyengar for their generous and penetrating remarks concerning the local contexts for the film.

13 Not the Play but the Playing
Citation of Performing Shakespeare as a Trope in Tamil Cinema

A. Mangai

Even though postcolonial readings would like us to begin any study of canonical writers in English, especially Shakespeare, as 'masks of conquest', reality seems to have been more complex in India. Early post-independence studies on English in India argued that Shakespeare 'educated us for this new world'[1] and 'directed us back to our old world and Shakespeare himself came to us not so much as discovery but as a recovery.'[2] Chellappan quotes Krishna Chandra Lahiri (1966) as to how, in the Catalogue of Books in Fort St. George, Madras dated September 1719, copies of Shakespeare's plays were entered along with scriptural and theological works. In Calcutta and Madras, Shakespeare was made part of the curriculum from 1835 onwards. Textbooks based on Shakespeare's plays in the form of stories or extracts were introduced. The ripple effect seems to have been sustained until almost the last few decades of the twentieth century. My grandfather and first teacher, Subramaniam Iyer, who was a headmaster of a primary school in Nagappattinam, had not cleared his school leaving examinations. But he could quote Shakespeare by heart. When I joined the bachelor's course in English Literature, his dream was to hear me recite Shakespeare's soliloquies! I never fulfilled his dream, and he did not deem my degree valid until I could recite Shakespeare by rote. Such was the influence of Shakespeare in Tamil Nadu.

This essay will explore how Shakespeare, who entered the arena of literature and drama in Tamil from the late nineteenth century, returned to the popular realm through cinema. This passage was made possible by the playwrights and artists who were part of both Tamil drama and cinema. The essay hopes to document the overlapping space of these two genres in terms of form. Apart from translations and adaptations, Shakespeare appears as citations in school or college programmes, or even as performances staged by drama companies, as in the case of films like *Rajapart Rangadurai* (*Hero Role Rangadurai* 1973).[3] These scenes serve as subtexts of the main theme; sometimes they become parallel readings; at other times they serve as the primary force behind the plot, as in *Sorkkam* (*Heaven* 1970).[4] One can perceive the liberal attitudes towards bringing the bard into Tamil in recognisable formal aspects and palatable thematic ways, to the point of not even making the connections or drastically changing the focus of Shakespeare's play. This essay will deal in detail through its analysis of *Ratha Thilagam* (*Thilak of Blood* 1963)[5] with how the citation of *Othello* in the Tamil context shifts the theme of suspicion, not jealousy, from the personal, sexual realm to the political one of loyalty to the Indian nation. In the process 'Desdemona' becomes an assertive, decision-making and active woman, sacrificing her love for the service of India, which is her country of birth, while China is her country of migration. The two major preoccupations of this citation/adaptation seem to be those of nation and gender. Shakespeare fades into dim traces in this whole process, which is typical of popular forms.

Ka.Na. Subramanyam explains in his article 'Shakespeare in Tamil' (1964) how high schools and colleges had stagings of scenes or whole plays of Shakespeare as annual events. He relates how his grandfather, Rao Bahadur S. Appu Sastry, twenty-sixth graduate of the University of Madras, acted in Shakespeare plays at school. Subramanyam refers to *Manonmaniyam*, written by Sundaram Pillai in 1891, which is considered to be the first literary play in Tamil (never having been staged so far) and was a dramatic adaptation of a minor, mediocre poem of Lord Lytton called 'The Secret Way', very much structured in the usual Shakespearean pattern. The five-act play came into existence in Tamil, probably due to Shakespeare's influence. There had been no attempts to divide the play into acts and scenes before that. The scenes were called 'Kaatchi', which were numbered continuously, much in line with the divisions found in Shakespeare's plays. His influence seems to have ranged from awe and worship to easy or passing reference. Swami Vipulananda's translations/adaptations were motivated by a desire to illustrate Tolkappiyar's theory of *Meyppadu*.[6] He also saw the connection between *meyppadu* and *rasa*.[7] *Meyppadu* literally means bodily expressions and gestures. This was an effort to read Shakespeare from the perspective of indigenous grammars of performance. In *The Tempest* Vipulananda sees wonder as a dominant emotion and relates it to the wonder of Ariel and Miranda's vision of a new world. In *Macbeth*, he finds fear and awe. In *The Merchant of Venice*, he finds joy, and in *Timon*, he finds all the types of anger, as in Tolkappiyar. He divides Shakespeare's women into eight types, following Sanskrit dramaturgy. He also explores various prosodic possibilities that can parallel Shakespeare's verse and prose.[8]

Some of the early translations of Shakespeare have been motivated by moralistic concerns. Chellappan quotes T.S.D. Swamy's reason for translating *The Taming of the Shrew*:

> As I have already translated ('Isabella') *Measure for Measure* to explain that a wife should be deeply devoted to her husband and *Two Gentlemen of Verona* to exemplify that whatever fault she found

in him, the wife should not swerve from her loyalty, this *Taming of the Shrew*, I render to show that a wife's prime duty to obey her husband implicitly.[9]

Pammal Sambandha Mudaliar is a central figure in the history of bringing Shakespeare to the Tamil stage. He has also documented in detail his process of working with Shakespeare's texts in his *Nataka Medai Ninaivugal (Notes on My Stage Experiences)*. Written in six parts between 1932 and 1938, the volumes were compiled into a single edition in 1998 and published by the International Institute of Tamil Studies. Sambandha worked on *The Merchant of Venice, Antony and Cleopatra, Cymbeline, Hamlet* and *Macbeth*. Since he deployed these texts for stage adaptations, he Tamilised them without any reservations. Chief among his indigenisations were the names of characters and lands. Hamlet becomes Amalathiththan. Venice became Vanipuram. Instead of killing by demanding a pound of flesh, Shylock is hanged in *Kazhumaram*, a direct reference to Jains being punished by the Saivites in seventh-century Tamil history.[10] The casket scene, which in every sense is Portia's 'swayamvara' scene in which she chooses her life partner, is loaded with Hindu mythological references to Seetha and Damayanthi. Sambandha elaborates how a prolific writer like him took seven long years to write *Amalathiththan*, an adaptation of *Hamlet*. His most popular play, *Manohara*, later made into a box-office hit film by the same name, was a reversal of the theme of *Hamlet*. He takes up the plot line and does a broad adaptation by reversing the main issue at hand. In *Manohara* the father, who is the King, takes another woman as his second wife. Disapproving of the stepmother his father takes the hero remains patient until the end, only to have an outburst on his mother's orders to literally break the chains, both those binding him and those binding the nation.

The screen versions of Shakespeare's plays in Tamil have not yet been explored fully. Very often Shakespeare's name does not figure in the plot outline or story. Perhaps it did not come from Shakespeare at all. The story could have been gleaned from other Indian sources, as in the case of the Bengali film *Saptapadi*, discussed later in the essay. Therefore this essay is only a beginning. Ka.Naa. Sunramanyam has evasively commented that 'The Tamil screen has adapted one or two of Shakespeare themes as films with indifferent success changing them out of all recognition, as in the case of *Twelfth Night, The Comedy of Errors* and *The Taming of the Shrew*.'[11] Contrary to his view, use of Shakespeare plays in Tamil cinema has been ingenious, integral and of contemporary relevance.

Before I dwell on *Ratha Thilagam*, I would like to mention the films that use Shakespeare's plays as tropes in different degrees and at various levels. The adaptation of *King Lear* as *Gunasundari* in Tamil (1955) made *Lear* culturally part of the Dravidian milieu. The Telugu version of the same was produced earlier in 1949. *Arivaali (The Clever Man*

1963)[12] is a full-length adaptation of both *The Taming of the Shrew* and *Much Ado About Nothing*. The rich girl who detests marriage is convinced by the hero's ideas of 'companionate marriage'. She is therefore 'tamed' by her own will. The couple remains exemplary and solves problems that come their way, as in *Much Ado*. The film combines the plot of both the plays into a native romance story. There is no reference to Shakespeare either by the film-makers or by the reviewers at that time. *Anbu* (*Love* 1953),[13] on the other hand, has the protagonists perform the bed chamber scene from *Othello* in their college life. In real life, the hero becomes the object of suspicion – of having a sexual liaison with his recently widowed, young, pregnant stepmother. The film, however, tides over this theme in a light way. Once the hero clarifies his beloved's doubt, she trusts him, they lead a happily married life and everything ends well. This method of using the trope of Shakespeare's theme/scene/play as a central motif in the plot or deploying them as references to suggest the onset of modernity continues even today. Superstar Rajnikanth acted as Julius Caesar in *Priya* as late as 1978.[14] All that Shakespeare implied for the viewer of Tamil cinema was sophistication, knowledge of English texts, civilised taste and higher status. All these elements meant being 'modern' in a particularly popular way.

In *Rajapart Rangadurai*, Sivaji performs the role of a veteran stage actor. A male lead actor is commonly referred to as Rajapart. The film traces briefly how the 'Rajapart' actors usually take the other actors for a ride in drama companies. It documents the lifestyle of stage artistes in the pre-independent Tamil Nadu. It also suggests the commonly held view about the low moral standards of actors. In the film Sivaji replaces the existing Rajapart, who leaves the company after being criticised for his behaviour by the company owner. Sivaji represents all that is good and admirable in the ideal 'Rajapart'. However, when he marries the heroine, who is a fan of his acting, against the wishes of her father, troubles ensue. One such crisis is precipitated when the heroine's father's business partner sets up a rival film screening tent opposite their drama company's tent. This signals the contemporary transition of popular media from theatre to talkies. Sivaji is challenged by the dwindling audience to provide new entertainment and not the same old stories. He takes up the challenge. With the support of a workers' union in the neighbourhood, he strives for a second inning. He opens the new repertoire with *Hamlet*. The film shows Sivaji performing the soliloquy 'To be or not to be' and the scene in quiet and stillness. So restrained is the delivery that the rest of the lines are not even very audible. This style of rendering of the soliloquy is shown as the entry of a new aesthetics into Tamil stage acting. No song, no music, just stillness in the actor. It creates a commotion in the beginning, but this later turns into rapt attention as he begins to speak. The scene is one of the finest performances by Sivaji in the whole of his acting career in real life. This scene underscores the critique of melodramatic histrionics that was the hallmark of stage acting in those days. Sivaji himself was no exception to that. But voices against that style of performing had already begun in both theatre and film circles in a sporadic fashion by then. The film documents it without taking sides. The other new plays by the drama company in its new lease of life – like *Thiruppur Kumaran* (a local nationalist leader from Tiruppur who died in a police lathi charge during a satyagraha, holding the national flag in his hand) – are set in the old excessive, melodramatic style (Figure 13.1).

This film reads Shakespeare as a modern entity. It also places him within the history of Tamil stage. After all Shakespeare was introduced to the Tamil audience through the performances of Drama Companies. *Hamlet* is followed by plays based on nationalistic themes. The juxtaposition is interesting, since it does not bother the popular psyche that Shakespeare was English after all.

As Nandi Bhatia discusses in one of her early articles,

> The choice of Shakespeare indicates an easy familiarity with the bard. That this happens to be the case is reflected in traces of Shakespeare in India in both the popular and literary culture. Since the last century, Shakespeare has continued to be the subject matter of films, popular songs from Hindi cinema, and a dominant figure in the education curriculum.[15]

This mode of popularisation of Shakespeare gets reflected in *Rajapart Rangadurai* in the enactment of the single scene from *Hamlet*. It serves as a citation of the fact that Shakespeare was familiarised through

Figure 13.1 Sivaji Ganesan as Hamlet – a new lease of life on stage in *Rajapart Rangadurai*.

popular theatre in Tamil. In that sense, the film is only using this scene to draw attention to the history of popular theatre and not to the bard. Postcolonial theory harping on the colonial impact of Shakespeare at least in the early stages of British education system is questioned by this reference. This is a case of assimilating Shakespeare into Tamil cultural history. But the project is not to accept him as the universal, humanistic agent; he becomes an icon of the entry of modernity and a modernity that is legitimised.

Sorkkam (*Heaven*) features two friends. They perform *Julius Caesar* in their college days. The theme is about the hero trying to become rich – read: ambitious – and the friend supporting him in that mission. The climax of the film refers back to the Shakespearean scene that they had performed at college. When the story leads to a point where everyone is against the hero – again Sivaji – he reminds his friend about the line 'You too Brutus?'

The friend in a flash recovers from the frenzy of doubt and believes what the hero is saying. All ends well. The split between the actor and the character and the ways of working on characterisation have been played out here. Different theories of acting posit character-building in varied ways. The two most important schools of training are by Stanislavsky and Brecht: one working 'inside out' and the latter 'outside in'. The importance given to 'emotive memory' and physicalised emotions are common skills cultivated in acting. In this context, the friends recall the college play and that becomes the crucial turning point in 'recognition'. Even though the scene is negligible in terms of the story of the film, it is made the key focus. Shakespeare brings the friends back on track and acts as the deus ex machina. Shakespeare's play or just a few lines from the play, more particularly the experience of performing it, becomes integral to the plot structure. In this case just the thrust of friendship betrayed becomes the link to the plot. Brutus and his dilemmas do not figure. Julius Caesar is the poor victim surrounded by betrayers. His only 'flaw' is being ambitious. Still, reference to the play helps in resolving the conflict. And it actually makes the friend trust the hero, who is blamed by everyone else. What gets emphasised therefore is the fact of working together as a group in a play and not the theme of the play *per se*. In other words, the friend does not behave as Brutus; of course, there is no larger political context of a national crisis either.

I would like to argue then that the Shakespearean citation in the film is not so much in terms of the text or plot but the amateur performance of the play in college. The focus is on the bonding evolved between college friends while putting up the Shakespearean play and not the actual play. The film becomes a commentary on acting and characterisation. The friend is not like Brutus after all. He was only acting. The distance between the two had to be underscored for the problem to be solved. Friendship overpowers the historical references made through the play to Roman history. For me, as a theatre practitioner, this is extremely pertinent as it draws the echoes of the process of mounting a play. And this aspect is crucial in performance and media studies (Figure 13.2).

Ratha Thilagam (1963) is a film in which the last scene of *Othello* is staged in a college performance. Sivaji, as Kumar and Savithri, as Kamala are the protagonists in the film. Kumar is portrayed as a nationalist. Gandhi's portrait hangs on his wall. Savithri, on the other hand, is a Tamil girl from a family settled in China. They begin as usual fighting with each other. A famous basketball match scene introduces the hero and Nagesh, Savithri's brother, as being on rival teams. In auditioning for the College play, Savithri is cast as Desdemona, and she tries to convince Nagesh to take up Othello's role. The friends tease Nagesh, who is already diffident about this role. During Savithri and Nagesh's attempt to rehearse the lines in the room, they see Sivaji performing the part of Othello. On the day of the performance, Sivaji is pushed into taking Othello's role, and he does it masterfully. It resembles the rehearsal shown earlier. Sivaji and Savithri soon become admirers and lovers. They sing the farewell song together. Things, however, take a sudden turn. Savithri has to rush to China, as her father is on his death bed. Meanwhile, a war breaks out between India and China.[16] The love story takes a back seat.

Sivaji joins the Indian army and is posted at the border. Meanwhile, Savithri chooses to remain in China, despite her family leaving for India. She claims China to be the land of her birth and upbringing. She becomes the butt of suspicion in China at every step. In order to prove

Figure 13.2 Sivaji and Savitri as Othello and Desdemona in the college play in *Ratha Thilagam*.

her loyalty to China she marries a childhood neighbour-turned-Chinese army officer. Meanwhile the Indian army is able to sabotage the Chinese attacks successfully with the help of anonymous notes that are thrown on the Indian border. Doubts loom large on both borders about the espionage and counter-espionage. Sivaji kills a Tamil youth who is spying on the Indian army. But his family – mother and sister – protect Sivaji from the Chinese officers. Interestingly, the mother stops them from entering her daughter's room saying she is sleeping with her newly-wed husband and helps the Indian officer escape.

Savithri, on the other hand, postpones the sexual advances of her husband quoting the war as a reason. She, however, lovingly listens to all his exploits in warfare – much in the same way Desdemona is wooed by Othello, except it is reversed here and for another motive which is revealed later.

Finally it turns out that Savithri is the culprit giving away the Chinese military secrets to India. The army officer-husband catches her red-handed, and she is punished. She narrowly escapes when the Indian army enters the scene and wins over the Chinese assault. The husband is out to take his revenge on the wife. The ex-lover, having understood her intention, tries to save her. The husband discovers Sivaji and Savithri as they try to escape. The husband is in the guise of a Hindu sage in the Chinese-occupied Himalayan region. When Savithri seeks his blessing by falling at his feet, he shoots her. Sivaji then fights with him and, after finding out that he is the husband of Savithri, kills him. Sivaji holds the dying Savithri on his lap. They recall the song they sang during their farewell at College. After she dies, Sivaji gives her a military salute with 'Jai Hind' – Praise India – symbolising his patriotism. Later during a long scene of siege on both sides, Sivaji finds his battalion fighting a Chinese camp. He joins and leads them with an Indian flag. When he replaces the Chinese flag with that of India, a bullet hits him on his forehead, justifying the title of the film, the *thilak* of blood.

The film uses the framework of *Othello* in a dexterous fashion. Suspicion is the leitmotif of the film. However, it is the loyalty to the nation and not personal fidelity that becomes the focus of the film. The woman, like Desdemona, is innocent and chaste. Additionally, she is also clever and patriotic. The film is framed within the background of the Indo-Chinese war. References to the dates of the war and regions are made, and the effect of war on everyday lives of the people is also shown. In more than one way, *Othello* gets expanded into the public domain.

Othello is a text that has been interpreted in multiple ways. Studies on how *Othello* has been adapted to deal with racial tensions and gendered aspects of race are innumerable. Interestingly, a Bengali film *Saptapadi* (1961) uses *Othello* as 'a paradigm to validate this inter-racial marriage' between a Bengali boy and an 'English' girl.[17] The film is set in the 1940s against the background of World War II.

Ratha Thilagam shows an amazing similarity with *Saptapadi* in the early scenes. In both films the performance of the murder scene of *Othello* becomes the seed for romance between the protagonists. The difference is that in the Tamil film it is not a question of racial difference but national identities that comes to the fore since the heroine is a Tamil from China. Much in the same way as the Bengali film, the hero is not supposed to be performing the role of Othello in the College play. Unlike in the Bengali film, in which the tension is between a white man and a native, in Tamil, it is just a question of varying skills. Nagesh, who appears as the insignificant, comic brother of the heroine, was supposed to be performing Othello, but his nerves fail him at the last minute, and Sivaji is forced to step into the role. There has already been a tug of war between Sivaji and Savitri over the noise made by her during her birthday celebrations. As in the case of *Saptapadi*, the Western music played for the celebration of her birthday is drowned by the hero singing indigenous (Tamil) devotional music. The two enter into a tussle. He also irritates her by reading aloud Shakespeare's *Othello* in the Tamil film.

The famous enactment of *Othello* has been dubbed by Utpal Dutt in *Ratha Thilagam*, just as it is in *Saptapadi*. Sivaji Ganesan has performed this scene in two different films in *Anbu* (1953) and *Ratha Thilagam*. In *Anbu* the scene is performed in Tamil. In the other, it is staged in English. Sivaji mentions in his autobiography that Utpal Dutt gave voice to that scene:

> I did it in English. Since I was not conversant in English language, a Bengali actor called Utpal Dutt dubbed my role. The same play of Shakespeare done in two films evoked two different experiences. ... At times, this technique helped to suggest things that one did not want to state overtly.[18]

The scene done in English becomes a reference to English education and its accompanying social class and modernity. By assigning the female role to the heroine and playing with the actors performing the male roles it is already suggesting gender as performed. The female protagonists in both films are comfortable enough to perform Desdemona with ease. Their skills are not questioned at all. But the male actors, who should play Othello, cannot deliver at the last minute. In a way, it can be read as providing a mode by which to imagine a new masculinity through the context of the performance of the play. The hero, however, does not tremble but excels. It is possible that *Ratha Thilagam* has taken this sequence from the Bengali film *Saptapadi*. There is no reference to any direct influence anywhere. But in conversations film critics talk about a

'Bengali film' which had a war background and a scene from *Othello*. In the latter, however, the emphasis is on racial tension rather than on issues of national identity and patriotism.

Ratha Thilagam complicates the importance of loyalty in personal relationships by extending it to the public sphere – in this case the nation. The sexual loyalties are not highlighted at all. The hero has no time to lament the heroine's failure to return from China, because he is too busy fighting for the nation. Nehru's appeal spreads like fire, and all young men rally to defend India against the Chinese aggression. The heroine, on the other hand, uses marriage as a ploy to prove her 'loyalty' to China and also to stay on in the country to help India secretly. Even a minor character uses the ploy of the privacy of the bedroom to save the hero from being caught by the Chinese officers. The mother asks her unmarried daughter Sheela to stay with Sivaji in the room to save him from the Chinese military officers. Soon after, she realises that he was the one who shot her son dead for being the spy helping Chinese military. As a mother she is ashamed of her own son but valorises the son of the soil, Sivaji. Indian/Tamil nationalism is the main motif in her dialogues and action. The same is echoed in the character of the heroine, even though she chooses the most dangerous path. Her husband, finally, wants to take revenge from her – not for being disloyal to him but to China, his country. The 'private' sphere is not only subordinated but exploited to serve 'public' interest in the film version. In *Othello*, on the other hand, the anxieties of the public sphere, racial identities and the responsibilities of public office complicate private relationships. The way in which this film shifts personal, sexual loyalty to the realm of loyalty to the nation is almost aggressive. This allows the heroine to emerge as a strong, clever, decision-maker in a completely new fashion. Savithri performs this new role with dignity. One almost forgets the reference to *Othello* while watching the movie.

In fact, none of the early reviews or advertisements or even later studies of the film mention the way in which *Othello* is used in it. One of the earliest announcements of the film is found in *Pesum Padam*, a film journal, in the January 1963 issue, the announcement of this film is listed along with many others (11). The next three pages contain a marching song by Kothamangalam Subbu, a popular lyricist, choreographer and scriptwriter about joining the military to support India in the Indo-China war. The photographs of both Sivaji and Savithri appear in this section showing them as taking the pledge mentioned in the marching song. The song is very similar in sentiment to the one used in the film when Sivaji joins the army.

> Let us be born again to save India- even
> If we die in the war;
> Five year olds are reading the newspapers;

> Their marbles hit Chou en Lai head ...
> Those who have come to watch the show
> Join the fight;
> With Nehru's words in your mouth
> Sharpen your swords;

The Indo-China war and the urgency of the times called for this rhetoric of patriotism and loyalty to the country. And Shakespeare was used as a trope to discuss the question of loyalty and betrayal.

Richard Burt discusses how the question of the authenticity of Shakespeare has become close to obsolete. In his article 'Slamming Shakespeare', he refers to instances where 'Shakespeare's plays are performed live or re-cited aloud, and 'liveness' is generally equated with authenticity. Racial authenticity also becomes a matter of live performance: media sampling is represented only through voices imitating the sounds of boom boxes and deejays scratching records'[19] which might not be defined as authentic but real. The 'mediatization' Burt refers to, especially in popular culture, defies the existing categories of classifications. But the essence of popular culture lies in this very defiance of authenticity or literary canonical status. In the case of Shakespeare, his rightful place is in popular culture.

In Tamil Nadu, when films arrived, they generated ambivalent responses, especially from the elite. Pandian explains how the elite, Brahmanical, upper strata of Tamil society grudgingly accepted the power of entertainment, especially popular entertainment, and particularly the impact of cinema.

A small section of the Tamil elite clung on rather resolutely to this idea that cinema is incorrigibly a sign of low culture. C. Rajagopalachari is perhaps the most telling representative of this cinephobic minority, and even the invocation of nationalism could not convert this nationalist to cinema. In 1939, when the Indian Motion Picture Association sought a ban on anti-Indian foreign films, he, as the prime minister of Madras State, noted cynically,

> I have a notion that in most cases the objection comes from competing companies that want in the guise of patriotism to keep out as far as possible well executed films that carry away the money. There is so much objectionable matter in the films prepared in India that the 'anti-Indian' objection pales into insignificance.

His objection to cinema continued well into the post-1947 India.[20] This antipathy to popular culture among the elites is not exceptional, including the academia. Reality, however, was different. Shakespeare was referred, quoted, recalled, performed and mentioned in passing as a sign of modernity, and English education. All of these were done without a single mention of the bard. Therein lies the audacity and attraction of popular culture and Shakespeare fitted the bill perfectly. He has become part and parcel of Tamil culture, without any need for claiming knowledge, familiarity or minimum decorum of any kind. Vipulanandar, an early twentieth-century scholar in Tamil music, translated Shakespeare's name as 'Segappiriyar' ('Darling of the whole world'). By translating his name to suit the Tamil sound system, he has inadvertently captured the spirit behind the uses of Shakespeare performances in Tamil cinema.

This essay attempts to open ways of reading Shakespeare in the Tamil context as integral, rather than adaptive. Shakespeare is also nativised to such an extent that he does not seem non-Indian. I think it is to the credit of Tamil cinema to have delved into such explorations that have to be studied in depth as cultural markers of assimilation and indigenous interpretation in popular media and culture.

Acknowledgments

The author would like to acknowledge Dr K. Ganesh and Ms K. Latha, who helped make the connections in a continuum of sorts. Their enthusiasm for Shakespeare and Tamil cinema was infectious.

Notes

1. G. Muliyil, 'Why Shakespeare for us?' in *Shakespeare Came to India*, ed. C.D. Narasimhaiah, Bombay: Popular Prakasan, 1964, qtd in Valarmathi, M. ed. *On Translation* (Chennai: International Institute of Tamil Studies, 1999), 109.
2. Chellappan, K, 'Translating Shakespeare into Tamil' in Valarmathi, M. ed. *On Translation* (Chennai: International Institute of Tamil Studies, 1999), 110.
3. *Rajapart* and *Streepart* refer to the lead male and female roles, respectively, in Tamil Company/Special drama context. Usually the lead actors perform only the lead roles and not the secondary characters. The literal meaning of the term would be 'Rangadurai in King's attire'. In the film it acts as an ironic comment on his pitiable condition. The film was produced by V.C. Guhanathan and directed by P. Madhavan.
4. *Sorkam* was produced by T.R. Chakravarthi and directed by T.R. Ramanna.
5. The title refers to the adornment on one's forehead; in this case it is done with blood. It has the connotation of honour, clearly stating that the heroine is a woman of honourable virtues and her decisions cannot be questioned. It was produced by Panchu Arunachalam and P.V. Krishnan. It was directed by Dada Mirasi.
6. *Meyppadu* is a chapter in the ancient Tamil grammatical treatise *Tolkappiam* that describes the eight major expressions of human emotions. This is parallel to *Rasa* theory in Sanskrit.
7. *Rasa* is the major school of aesthetic theory attributed to Bharatha in Sanskrit.
8. See Valarmathi, *On Translation*.
9. Valarmathi, Ibid., 115.

10 Jainism was one of the dominant religions in Tamil Nadu until about the seventh century. With the advent of Vedic religion, attacks on Jains became rampant. Mayilai Seeni Venkatasami's *Samanamum Tamizhum* (1942) dealt with this phenomena in detail with poetic evidences from Saivite poetry.
11 Ka.Naa. Subramanyam, 'Shakespeare in Tamil', *Indian Literature* VII, no. 1 (1964): 124.
12 *Arivaali* was produced and directed by A.T. Krishnaswamy.
13 *Anbu* was produced and directed by M. Natesan.
14 *Priya* was produced by S.P. Tamilarasi and directed by S.P. Muthuraman.
15 Nandi Bhatia, 'Shakespeare and the Codes of Empire in India', *Alif: Journal of Comparative Poetics*, no. 18 (1998): 96.
16 Indo-China war of 1962 is the major upheaval faced by India during Nehru's rule. It remains a sore experience to date.
17 Paromita Chakravarti, 'Modernity, Postcoloniality and *Othello*: The Case of *Saptapadi*', in *Remaking Shakespeare: Performances Across Media, Genres and Cultures*, eds. Pascale Aebischer, Edward J. Esche and Nigel Wheale (New York: Palgrave Macmillan, 2003), 46.
18 Sivaji Ganesan, *Enathu Suyasarithai* (My Autobiography) ed. T.S. Narayanaswami, 2nd ed. (Chennai: Sivaji Prabhu Charities Trust, 2006) 110–11.
19 Richard Burt, 'Slammin' Shakespeare in Acc(id)ents Yet Unknown: Liveness, Cinem(edi)a, and Racial Dis-Integration', *Shakespeare Quarterly* 53: 2, Screen Shakespeare (Summer, 2002): 204.
20 M.S.S. Pandian, 'Tamil Cultural Elites and Cinema: Outline of an argument', *Economic and Political Weekly* 31, no. 15 (13, April 1996): 951–52.

14 Indianising *The Comedy of Errors*
Bhranti Bilash and Its Aftermaths

Amrita Sen

Shakespeare's influence on Bollywood and regional Indian cinema has been far-reaching and at times unexpected. This is more so when a single Shakespearean play inspires multiple adaptations in different Indian languages. The obvious question that comes to one's mind is the extent to which these films are indebted to Shakespeare and how much they owe their success to Indian cinematic traditions. One of the most popular adaptations of Shakespeare in Indian cinema in the last fifty years, cutting across regional borders, is that of his early comic drama *The Comedy of Errors*.[1] Shakespeare's play itself, of course, was an adaptation of Plautine comedy, which the bard embellished by adding a second pair of twins. Transplanted into the Indian context, this proliferation of identical twins offered more potential for comic confusion while continuing to attract audiences accustomed to the well-established subgenre of switched brothers and mixed identities in Indian cinema. Although stage adaptations of *The Comedy of Errors* were quite common in nineteenth- and early twentieth-century India, the first film version, *Bhranti Bilash*, made its appearance only in 1963. The Bengali film, however, was soon followed by Hindi productions *Do Dooni Char* (1968) and *Angoor* (1982). The regional adaptations continued with *Ulta Palta* (1997) in Kannada and most recently with *Double Di Trouble* (2014) in Punjabi. This list, of course, does not include films that reference or are indirectly inspired by the play, such as *Yeh to Kamal Ho Gaya* (1982) and *Bade Miyan Chhote Miyan* (1999).[2] What is noteworthy, however, is not only the sheer number of these Indian versions of *The Comedy of Errors*, far outstripping the adaptation of most other Shakespearean plays in Indian cinema, but also how each film appears to directly engage with its predecessor. The result is a unique clustering, wherein the films influence each other, informing the way each adaptation Indianises its retelling of Shakespeare.

The impact of Parsi theatre on Indian cinematic adaptations of Shakespeare has been well documented, richly enhancing our understanding of the diverse range of local influences.[3] What is equally important to consider, however, is the role of other Bollywood and regional films upon Indian Shakespeares. This cross-fertilisation perhaps helps explain the popularity of *The Comedy of Errors* in India. *Bhranti Bilash* and subsequent adaptations follow certain stock devices of Indian cinema – such as the opposition of urban and rural life, the fair or 'mela' and the convenient pairing up of lovers – to achieve its comic impact. Furthermore, as Rajiva Verma observes, it is in fact this cinematic medium, allowing for the possibility of showing 'twins who are actually identical', that also accounts for the 'fascination' that the play holds among audiences and film-makers.[4] Unlike the stage, the films offer up *more* of the favourite stars, whether this means the legendary Uttam Kumar in *Bhranti Bilash*, Sanjeev Kumar in *Angoor* or Dharmendra in *Double Di Trouble*.

Shakespeare himself was, of course, also aiming for more. While adapting Plautus's *Menaechmi* during the late sixteenth century, Shakespeare decided to add a second set of twins and an unmarried sister-in-law, Luciana. The result, as Richard Allen succinctly notes, is 'a *reductio ad absurdum* of the narrative of mistaken identity.'[5] The play opens with Aegeon, a merchant from Syracuse, who is brought before Duke Solinus of Ephesus on charges of violating a travel embargo. While trying to defend himself against an inevitable death sentence he reveals the rather strange story of his life. A father to twins, he had bought for his sons another pair of twins born to a poor couple at an inn in Epidamnum. Shortly afterwards the two sets of twins were separated. As the play unfolds Antipholus of Syracuse along with his slave Dromio of Syracuse famously arrive in Ephesus, unaware that their brothers are actually residents there. What ensues is comic confusion, with the ever-present threat of wife-swapping and incest since both Antipholus of Ephesus and his Dromio are married. While Shakespeare rather unusually adheres to the classical unities, the Indian cinematic adaptations mostly do not, utilising the night that is spent in confusion to exploit sexual undercurrents and romantic couplings between the visiting brothers and the women of Ephesus.

This chapter will thus adopt two strands of enquiry. The first will situate the Indian *Comedy of Errors* within the larger context of Indian cinema, exploring how these films exploit well-established devices, particularly relating to the depiction of twins on screen. The second strand will turn specifically to the clustering effect of the adaptations that I have mentioned. It will examine the borrowings and departures within this group of movies that are *outright* adaptations of the play. Hence, this chapter will primarily rely on *Bhranti Bilash*, *Angoor*, *Do Dooni Char*, *Ulta Palta* and *Double Di Trouble*, and not on the larger corpus of films that might briefly or tangentially reference the play. The purpose of this is to trace what one might describe as a 'genealogy' of the Indian *Comedy of Errors*. In the final section I will turn to the newest addition to this family to explore how *Double Di*

Trouble both belongs to and radicalises the comic traditions of the Indian Shakespeares.

Setting the Scene: *Bhranti Bilash*, Shakespeare and Indian Cinema

When it comes to Shakespearean adaptations on the Indian screen, *The Comedy of Errors* is actually a late arrival. Directed by Manu Sen, *Bhranti Bilash*, as mentioned before, was released only in 1963. The Bengali film does not come directly via Parsi theatre but through the 'non-rhetorical' nineteenth-century prose translation by the social reformer Ishwar Chandra Vidyasagar.[6] As has been frequently noted, the introduction of Shakespeare in India is tied to the colonial agenda, best articulated in Thomas Babington Macaulay's 'Minute' in 1835, which sought to create a new 'class of people Indian in blood and colour, but English in taste, in opinions, in morals and intellect.'[7] This is not to suggest that Shakespeare was unknown in India prior to this date; as Poonam Trivedi has shown the bard's plays have a long history of performance on the subcontinent from at least the late eighteenth century.[8] Macaulay's Minute, however, did broaden the scope of English education and by extension the influence of Shakespeare. Vidyasagar himself was a product of this education designed to create hybrid colonial subjects. Vidyasagar's contemporary Bankim Chandra Chattopadhyay, in his essay 'Shakuntala, Miranda and Desdemona', upheld the Shakespearean heroines as embodying higher domestic virtues than their Indian counterparts.[9] The classical Sanskrit poet and dramatist Kalidasa's Shakuntala was thus dismissed for not being a viable model for emulation among contemporary women. Chattopadhyay's preference is telling, and it is within this altered colonial aesthetics, one created by the introduction of English education, that Vidyasagar translates *The Comedy of Errors*. His *Bhranti Bilas* (1869) follows Shakespeare's plot quite closely, although the names of characters and places are Indianised. Instead of Ephesus and Syracuse, Vidyasagar locates the story in fictional old kingdoms named Hemkut and Jayasthal.[10] Antipholus thus becomes Chiranjeev, while Dromio becomes Kinkar. In 1888 Vidyasagar's translation was dramatised and staged successfully in Calcutta.[11] Still, with the advent of motion pictures in India, *The Comedy of Errors* was initially nowhere on the scene.

As Verma documents, Indian cinema turned to Shakespeare for its subject matter fairly quickly. Barely fourteen years after the first silent movie *Raja Harishchandra* (1913), Excelsior Film Company produced *Dil Farosh* (1927) based on *The Merchant of Venice*. Adaptations of *Hamlet*, *The Taming of the Shrew*, *Measure for Measure* and even *Antony and Cleopatra* soon followed.[12] In light of its subsequent popularity among film-makers, the absence of *The Comedy of Errors* from this list is noteworthy. We must therefore ask ourselves why did the play suddenly make its appearance on the Indian celluloid in the 1960s, and how may we begin to understand its continuing appeal? Allen locates the success of *Bhranti Bilash* in the move towards realism, and the Bengali film and each of the subsequent adaptations do indeed discard the fantastical setting of Vidyasagar's translation in favour of a more modern bourgeois context. In this, films seem to return to the bourgeois spirit that Shakespeare's play showcases, emphasising the mercantile lives of its principal characters.[13] There is, however, another aspect which also needs to be taken into consideration: namely the affinity of the Indian *Comedy of Errors* to the vastly popular subgenre of Bollywood and regional films dealing with twins.

Unlike the double pairing in Shakespeare, most of these twin movies (much like Plautus) concern themselves with just the single set. The Tamil classic *Apoorva Sagodharargal* (1949), closely inspired by Alexandre Dumas's *The Corsican Brothers*, was one of the first films to work in the plot of twins separated at birth and mistaken identities. Shortly after, Baldev Raj Chopra's *Afsana* (1951), starring Ashok Kumar, brought the story of separated twins and conflicting love interests to mainstream Hindi audiences. The Bengali film *Lookochuri* (1958), on the other hand, made it possible for each twin to have his separate love interest, conveniently providing, much like *The Comedy of Errors*, two sisters for the brothers. In subsequent years, this premise of separated twins became a stock device, proving extremely popular in the box office. D. Rama Naidu's blockbuster *Ramudu Bheemudu* (1964) triggered remakes in Tamil, Malayalam and Hindi. The Bollywood version *Ram aur Shyam* (1967), with heart-throb Dilip Kumar, proved equally successful, ensuring that more remakes would follow. While *Kishen Kanhaiya* (1990) and *Judwaa* (1997) had twin brothers, *Seeta aur Geeta* (1972) and *ChaalBaaz* (1989) turned things around with twin sisters. These films, of course, did not follow a Shakespearean plot, although some did resort to scenes inspired by the bard.[14] What these films did provide, however, was a ready market for plots with twins. Like *The Comedy of Errors*, they depended on delayed recognition, swapped sexual partners and new romantic liaisons for full comic effect. The coveted double roles also allowed the stars – Dilip Kumar, Ashok Kumar, N.T. Rama Rao and Uttam Kumar – to show off their acting prowess, taking pains to depict subtle differences in character. *Bhranti Bilash* and *Angoor* thus show one brother as more irascible than the other, one addicted to snuff while the other, more urbane twin is a smoker. Moreover, many of the actors who would go on to be part of one of *The Comedy of Errors* adaptations already had experience with productions revolving around twins. Thus Kishore Kumar, who played twins in the Bengali film *Lookochuri*, would also star in the Hindi *Do Dooni Char*; Sanjeev Kumar and Dharmendra, both appearing as love interests of Hema

Malini in *Seeta and Geeta*, would go on to play the part of Antipholus in *Angoor* and the Punjabi *Double Di Trouble*, respectively.

What this subgenre of twin movies also helps highlight is an integral feature of Indian cinema: chiefly the cross-fertilisation of Bollywood and the regional film industries. In what has become almost standard practice, successful films in Bengali, Tamil or Telugu found themselves remade in Hindi and vice versa. Given this inbuilt tradition of local adaptations, it is perhaps not so surprising that the Indian *Comedy of Errors* would continue the pattern, drawing upon previous versions of the bard's play as well as other films. *Bhranti Bilash*, the first of Indian *Comedy of Errors*, thus owes as much to Shakespeare as it does to the indigenous cinematic traditions. The same is true for the films that follow *Bhranti Bilash*, particularly *Do Dooni Char* and *Angoor*. For instance, in the original play, both Adriana and her sister Luciana spot the visiting twin Antipholus of Syracuse in a 'public place'. In *Bhranti Bilash*, it is only Bilash (Luciana) who publicly confronts the man she mistakenly believes to be her brother-in-law, thus setting in motion the eventual romantic pairing. This departure from both Shakespeare and Vidyasagar's translation is perhaps easier to understand when we compare it with other twin films, especially *Lookochuri*, which ensured that the unattached pair met alone, optimising the new romantic possibilities. While the title of *Bhranti Bilash* has unusually been translated as 'The Play of Errors,'[15] there is clearly a pun here, and the story is also about the error ('bhranti') of Bilash, the younger sister. Bilash, holding a purse and wearing her sari in the modern style, unlike her sister Chandra, who is demurely clad in an older 'sabeki' style, represents the New Woman.[16] In this Bilash shares affinities with the younger sister in *Lookochuri*, who works for an insurance company. What makes this new image of Bilash possible is the fact that the film completely modernises Vidyasagar's text (Figure 14.1).

Where Bilash meets Chiranjeet (Antipholus of Syracuse) is equally significant; for while the play text mentions a public space, the film interprets it as a fair. The fair or 'mela' is notable as yet another stock device in Indian cinema, as a space where characters, particularly siblings or lovers, meet or are separated. In *Afsana*, for instance, the twins Ratan and Chaman (played by Ashok Kumar) are torn apart in the chaos of a fair. In the groundbreaking *Acchut Kanya* (1936) it is again the fair that separates Kasturi, the untouchable heroine, from her companions, forcing her to ride home with her childhood sweetheart, Pratap. She is distracted while watching a dance drama similar to the Parsi theatrical style, not realising that her jealous friends from her village have slipped away. In *Bhranti Bilash* it is the fair that brings Chiranjeet and Bilash together. After completing his preliminary business affairs, the visiting Chiranjeet is told of a local fair that draws people from all around. We are taken to the fair scene, and the camera pans down so that we can catch a glimpse of the carousels and food stalls. Lamps flicker everywhere, and we realise that darkness has fallen. While the initial confused exchanges between Chiranjeet and the two Kinkars had taken place in daylight, closely following Shakespeare's banter, the new complications will arise in the cover of night. As Allen notes, the film incorporates 'the idiom of Indian folk theater' through 'song and dance or choreographed movement.'[17] Nowhere is this more evident than in the fair scene. We get to hear a wide range of music, from the flutes to the low beats of the animal performers and, finally, to the enticing songs of the puppet show. The fair is, nonetheless, a space that exacerbates the chaos and confusion. Similar to a Bakhtinian world things go topsy-turvy. The unmarried Chiranjeet is switched with his married brother Chiranjeev. This collapse of order is illustrated by the shock on Chiranjeet's face when a totally unknown woman grabs hold of his hand and smiles.[18] Bilash, of course, thinks that this is her brother-in-law, but Chiranjeet, like the audience, recognises the scandal of the gesture. He cries out *Sharbonash koreche! Apni ke?*' (Oh Destruction! Who are you?). To make matters worse Bilash pulls Chiranjeet out of the puppet tent and continues to coax him to return home, still holding his hand. Soon people gather, and Bilash accuses Chiranjeet of creating a scene in public by still refusing to accompany her home. As the bystanders quickly point out, there is something incongruous about a respectable woman, a '*bhadramahila*', holding the arm of a man.[19] A semblance of order is restored when Bilash clarifies that he is her brother-in-law, and Chiranjeet is bullied into going with her.

Apart from a chaos inducing, topsy-turvy realm, the fairground also comes across as one of the 'other spaces', a heterotopia that stands outside of everyday life but yet comes to define it. Its role thus becomes one

Figure 14.1 Bhranti Bilash: Chiranjeet and Chiranjeev finally meet, as do the two Kinkars.

of 'creat[ing] a space of illusion that exposes every real space, all the sites inside of which human life is partitioned.'[20] The fairground with its bright lights and disorienting crowds that jostle from one stall to another is a world far removed from the domesticity of Chiranjeet's house in Kolkata or even the marital life that his twin Chiranjeev (Antipholus of Ephesus) enjoys in the unnamed small town. And yet, the central attraction of the fair, a puppet show called 'Ahalya Upakhan' or the story of Ahalya, very closely mirrors what might possibly happen in the lives of the twins. Taken from the *Ramayana*, the puppet show reminds the audience of the fate of Ahalya, the wife of the sage Gautama. Smitten by her beauty, Indra, the king of the gods, comes disguised as her husband. In some versions of the *Ramayana* Ahalya sees through the deceit but still makes love to Indra on the floor of the house she shares with her husband, flattered that she has caught the eye of a god.[21] Her husband returns, catching them together in the act, and curses both his adulterous wife and Indra. As punishment Ahalya is turned to dust but not forever. Gautama promises that she will be released and returned to her human form when Rama, the seventh avatar of Vishnu, finally arrives. Indra's punishment is harsher; because of Gautama's curse, he sprouts 1,000 phalluses on his body.

The puppet show in *Bhranti Bilash* tells a slightly different story. Ahalya genuinely mistakes the disguised Indra for her husband, thus making her less culpable. The moral of the story therefore shifts from a cautionary tale against adultery to the necessity of the wife being able to distinguish between an imposter and her husband. At the beginning of the puppet show the male narrator explains why Ahalya has been turned to stone, and a female voice sings, '*O Meye, bhul koro na chine nite apon potike*' (O woman do not make a mistake in recognising your own husband). The puppet show thus clearly comments upon the main plot of the film but does so within (an)other space, tying it back to Indian mythological narratives about switched spouses. This effort to indigenise the Shakespearean play is evident elsewhere as well; for instance, nowhere does the film explicitly acknowledge its debt to Shakespeare, identifying instead Vidyasagar as its source. The opening credits juxtapose the nineteenth-century reformer with the Hindu mystic Ramakrishna while repeating a popular anecdote regarding their meeting.[22] Unlike *Angoor*, *Ulta Palta* or even *Double Di Trouble* which openly acknowledge Shakespeare, the first Indian adaptation of *The Comedy of Errors* is thus curiously silent about its roots in the English dramatic tradition. The puppet show about Ahalya further underscores this desire to firmly anchor the story to local traditions, and it does in fact bring together various strands of folk music, ending with the tunes celebrating the amorous union of Radha and Krishna. The irony is evident for it is through the love song that we learn that Ahalya has inadvertently committed adultery.

The puppet show therefore opens up an alternate space, staging what the film does not, the possibility of Chiranjeev's (Antipholus of Ephesus) wife sleeping with the wrong man. The Ahalya puppet wears a sari in the older *'sabeki'* form,[23] drawing a sharp visual parallel with hapless Chandra, especially since none of the other younger women dress like her. The fairground, with the puppet show as its highlight, encourages the audience to consider the other possibilities of the Shakespearean plot line. In Shakespeare's play itself there is a similar moment which hints at an illicit union that must not be explored because of the dangers it poses to a comic ending. Soon after the first confounding encounter between Antipholus of Syracuse and Dromio of Ephesus, the servant returns home to report to his mistress the full details of her husband's strange behaviour. He tells Adriana, 'Why, mistress, sure my master is horn-mad'. When she retorts angrily, Dromio hastily tries to recover the situation: 'I mean not cuckold-mad;/ But, sure, he is stark mad' (II.i.59–60).[24] Because the two brothers are finally in the same city, there is, however, a very real danger of Antipholus of Ephesus finding himself cuckolded. The threat is even more pronounced in *Bhranti Bilash*, and the subsequent Indian adaptations which without fail depict a night spent under mistaken assumptions. Making matters worse, in the Indian versions the Adriana figure starts off by fighting with her husband, only to repent as soon as he leaves the house in a huff. Thus, when the wrong brother is brought before her, she is full of love, and ready to make up. Much like the incongruity between the traditional love tune in the puppet song and its disastrous message, the threat remains that Adriana's renewed amorous intentions might result in unsavoury consequences.

In an attempt to counter this sexual danger, the Indian *Comedy of Errors* play up the love plot between Antipholus of Syracuse and Luciana. Again it is the magic of the fair that makes possible this coupling in both *Bhranti Bilash* and *Do Dooni Char*. For Chiranjeet and for Sandeep, his counterpart in the Hindi movie, the shock of being accosted by a beautiful stranger amidst the general backdrop of festivity and merry-making has long-lasting effects. When the bachelors are brought to their brothers' homes, they are already too distracted by the unwed sister to pay much attention to the married woman. *Bhranti Bilash* thus sets a trend that the later films take up, interpreting this moment within their individual context of music and revelry. *Do Dooni Char* being the closest adaptation of *Bhranti Bilash* is also truest to it in spirit. Much like Chiranjeet, Sandeep lands up at a fair. Instead of a puppet show he stops to watch a folk dance. The lyrics *'uparwaala neeche dekh neechewaala upar … chakkar chaliye, chakkar chakker'* (One above looks down, one below looks up … everything is a circle, circle) foreshadow the confusion that will soon ensue, while the dancers heighten the sense of ambiguity with their use of masks. In *Angoor*, the fairground becomes a music recital hall. Ashok (Antipholus of Syracuse) listens with rapt attention to the beautiful singer who turns out to be Tanu (Luciana). Much like her predecessors, she accosts Ashok right afterwards, grabbing his arm in an effort to bring him home. When he refuses, she too pleads with him not to cause a public scandal. *Double Di Trouble*, which as we shall see later, radicalises the comic structure of the Indian adaptations, also abides by this stock motif. Right before the switch, Ajit Singh (Antipholus of Syracuse) and Fateh Singh (Dromio of Syracuse) visit not a fair but a nightclub, hoping to absorb all the entertainment that the city has to offer. The Club Oyster transports them to darkness and psychedelic lights, although it is still daytime. The nightclub also becomes an alternate space, similar to the fairground, allowing the duo to flirt harmlessly and dance with the extremely sensuous crooner. The camera follows the gyrating women, and even the usually self-contained Ajit lets down his guard. Inebriated, the two stumble out of the club, only to run straight into the arms of Pammi (Adriana), her brother Gunni Mama and Pammi's daughter-in-law. Shakespeare's public space therefore comes to signify something completely different in the Indian *Comedy of Errors*, allowing the directors to comment upon the characters and to steer them in new directions, all to the accompaniment of the indispensable song and dance number. Shakespeare's play text specifies that the characters meet in the marketplace, a space that seems to be shaped primarily by the economic exchanges that take place – it is here that an unnamed merchant cautions Antipholus of Syracuse about his goods and money (I.ii.1–5). Not surprisingly, this economic subtext remains valid for the remainder of the play, even as the romantic plot takes hold. In contrast, the public spaces in the Indian movies are flamboyantly spectacular, in a way that the Shakespearean space is not, with the song and dance setting the mood for the romantic complications rather than the economic context.

Repetition and Difference in *Comed(ies) of Errors*

The Indian cinematic adaptations of *The Comedy of Errors*, as is becoming clear, form a cluster or even a family, incorporating or revising the previous incarnations. This self-reflexivity is not as extensive in any of the other Indian Shakespeare productions. For instance, Vishal Bhardwaj's *Haider* (2014) is very different in its choice of geographical and political setting from Sohrab Modi's *Khoon Ka Khoon* (1935). When it comes to *The Comedy of Errors*, each film modernises its setting and departs from Shakespeare in ways that are often similar. In the original play text Syracuse and Ephesus are both independent cities, their long-standing feud making commerce very difficult. When the play opens, Aegeon has been arrested and will be executed by the Duke until his bond is paid. The Indian adaptations without exception completely do away with the theme of political strife. Even when the father is shown (which is rare), he is not a prisoner, nor is he facing any immediate crisis that his sons need to rescue him from. Instead, the films focus on the theme of travel and (self) discovery.

In *Bhranti Bilash*, Chiranjeet's journey takes him away from the bustling city to the charms of a small town situated amidst rolling hills and forests. No longer is this a tale of two cities but one that explores and exoticises the difference between urban living and the open country. We accompany Chiranjeet as he surveys the terrain, and the dense forests that supply his city business with wood. Debu Sen's *Do Dooni Char* takes this further, and Sandeep (Antipholus of Syracuse) overwhelmed by the beauty of the Himalayan foothills bursts into song: '*Hawaon pein likh do hawaon ke naam*' (Write on the breeze the names of the breezes). Gulzar, the lyric writer for the film, would go on to write and direct *Angoor*. Not surprisingly, the small-town setting is present in Gulzar's version as well, as it is also in *Ulta Palta*. *Double Di Trouble*, on the other hand, in a rather tongue-in-cheek way reverses this convention, and begins with a village in Punjab and then moves to the capital city of Chandigarh. It is urban life that is now held up as a spectacle, with its nightclubs and swank mansions.

There are other parallels that run across the movies, both in terms of major interpretations of the play text as well as through the smaller devices utilised for heightening the cinematic effect. For instance, a commonplace strategy that is adopted to heighten the sense of doubling is the use of neutral attires. The preferred sartorial choice for the Antipholuses are nondescript white shirts or kurtas, while the Dromios wear the grey or striped uniform reserved for domestic staff. It thus makes it harder for the other characters as well as for the audience to differentiate between the twins, but it also results in a visual continuity between the films. But there are more obvious borrowings across the films, mostly centring on the sexual repercussions that the Indian adaptations throw up by defying Shakespeare's unity of time. In *Angoor*, for instance, Sudha (Luciana), eager to appease the man who she thinks is her husband, tries to ply him with alcohol. Soon after she coyly asks Ashok (Antipholus of Syracuse) to remove his dhoti. When he looks shocked, she reassures him by saying that she has seen him nude many times before. Horrified, Ashok says, '*Kya! Mujhe nanga dekha hai aapne!*' (What! You have seen me naked!). At the end, once the confusion is finally sorted out with the two sets of twins standing next to one another, we are reminded of this highly sexually charged encounter in Sudha's bedroom. In a comic reversal, it is now her turn to be mortified. Prompted by her agitation, when her husband asks whether anything happened the previous night, she responds by reassuring him that she was saved by the breadth of a hair. Just as the audience is lulled into dismissing the sexual possibilities of the night, the camera pans to Tanu (Luciana), who seems to have fainted, and blurts out that she was in fact kissed by Ashok. *Angoor* thus deftly shifts the visiting Ashok's sexual attraction away from the married Sudha to her sister. In this, of course, Gulzar follows Shakespeare who provides us with the figure of Luciana, and Antipholus of Syracuse's growing interest in her, precisely to avoid actual incest. But he is also guided here by both *Bhranti Bilash* and *Do Dooni Char*, which play up the more legitimate romantic pairing.[25] There is, however, no such safety net for the other set of twins.

Unsurprisingly, class plays a very important role in *The Comedy of Errors*, with the 'lower' characters being subject to a more vulgar comedy. Thus even though a night is not spent, the sexual implications of switched identities do get staged – not so much through the bourgeois characters but via the exploits of Dromio. When Antipholus and Dromio of Syracuse attempt to take stock of their bizarre encounter with the women of Ephesus, the servant cheekily tells his master about the 'kitchen wench' (Nell) whom he has just met. The two bandy jokes back and forth, itemising her body, comparing it to different countries:

ANTIPHOLUS OF SYRACUSE: In what part of her body stands Ireland?
DROMIO OF SYRACUSE: Marry, in her buttocks: I found it out by the bogs.
ANTIPHOLUS OF SYRACUSE: Where Scotland?
DROMIO OF SYRACUSE: I found it by the barrenness; hard in the palm of the hand.
....
ANTIPHOLUS OF SYRACUSE: Where Spain?
DROMIO OF SYRACUSE: Faith, I saw it not; but I felt it hot in her breath.
ANTIPHOLUS OF SYRACUSE: Where America, the Indies?
DROMIO OF SYRACUSE: Oh, sir, upon her nose all o'er embellished with rubies, carbuncles, sapphires, declining their rich aspect to the hot breath of Spain; who sent whole armadoes of caracks to be ballast at her nose.
ANTIPHOLUS OF SYRACUSE: Where stood Belgia, the Netherlands?
(III.II.110–28)

This, of course, is grotesque comedy but one that, even while it parodies, upholds the familiar conflation of land and the eroticised female body in the sixteenth century. Walter Raleigh, for instance, famously declared that 'Guiana is a country that hath yet her maidenhead', thereby casting it as a nubile woman, available for deflowering and possession by the English colonisers.[26] Commenting on this phenomenon, Michel de Certeau notes that

> what travel literature really fabricates is the primitive as a body of pleasure. [...] Such eroticizing of the other's body – of the primitive nudity and primitive voice – goes hand in hand with the formation of the ethics of production. At the same time it creates a profit, the voyage creates a lost paradise relative to a body-object, to an erotic body.[27]

Angoor, like its cinematic predecessors and Shakespeare's original play text, is also premised on travel, and Ashok and his servant Bahadur, much like the other incarnations of Antipholus and Dromio of Syracuse, experience a new geography through their encounters with the women. While Antipholus and Dromio's jokes about Nell take on increasingly sexualised tones, in *Angoor* the scenes containing the greatest physical proximity involve the visiting Bahadur and Prema. Alone in the kitchen with the man she believes to be her husband, high on fries laced with cannabis, her clothes and hair dishevelled, she rolls seductively on the floor, wrapping herself around him. The scene switches abruptly to the jewellery shop where her rightful husband is waiting with his master, and thus the outcome of Prema's amorous intentions are left open. When we return to the house, Bahadur is climbing the steps, evidently having succeeded in pacifying or satisfying Prema.

While the hint of sexual dalliances downstairs is no doubt titillating, *Angoor* still tries to contain the effects of any transgression. Before Bahadur starts drugging everyone, we find out from Sudha that Prema is pregnant. *Double Di Trouble* replicates this strategy. Ekom's young wife is also pregnant, minimising the reproductive dangers of spending the night with a stranger. This, of course, is a departure from Shakespeare's play text as well as from *Bhranti Bilash*. *Angoor*, however, repeatedly raises these prospects of sexual transgressions only to rein them in. For instance, in the opening scene where we find Ashok playing cards with his wife and sister-in-law, Sudha jokingly reminds him that when her father first got the two sets of twins, he mixed up the servant for the master until the error was rectified. She tells him that she might well have become Bahadur's wife, and Ashok retorts that she would then have married an ass. In the same scene while playing footsie, Ashok kicks his sister-in-law instead of his wife until he is eventually told off. These little errors foreshadow the bigger confusions of identities and sexual partners that will follow (Figure 14.2).

There are, however, also significant differences in how the Indian *Comedy of Errors* interpret other aspects of sexuality in Shakespeare's play text. The most notable instance of this is the portrayal of the character identified as the courtesan. As Allen points out, the films retain some version of the quintessential 'other woman.'[28] In *Bhranti Bilash*, *Do Dooni Char* and *Angoor*, the husbands refused entry into their own homes, spend the night at the house of this woman. In the first two movies, she is symbolic of 'a new woman of independence and agency', but contrary to what Allen suggests, they are not stripped of their sexuality.[29] In *Bhranti Bilash*, for instance, Chandra (Adriana) sees the studious Aparajita who lives by herself as a rival to her husband's love. When Chiranjeev (Antipholus of Ephesus) accompanied by Kinkar shows up at the dead of night she is all alone, and the following morning he tells her of his wife's jealousy. In *Angoor*, Alka is dressed in saffron robes,

Indianising The Comedy of Errors 263

Figure 14.2 Angoor: Ashok, Sudha and Tanu play cards.

symbolising her role as a renunciate, and although this should alleviate all sexual anxieties, this is not the case. After the night is spent the two seem to be on extremely familiar terms as she chats with Ashok while he is wearing a towel and shaving himself. These latent sexual moments find full expression in *Ulta Palta*. Returning to Plautine as well as Shakespearean roots, the Kannada movie gives Devaraja (Antipholus of Ephesus) a mistress, aptly named Mohini. Before the mix-up begins, Devaraja visits Mohini's house where she serves him tea wearing shorts and a white shirt. She strokes his head, and he begins to fantasise through an elaborate song and dance sequence – the first of such scenes in the movie. In the sequence Mohini dressed in black leather takes Devaraja for a ride on her motorcycle, drawing on well-known romantic stereotypes in Bollywood and regional cinema. Devaraja's wife has a similar fantasy in which she sails out in a coracle dressed all in white to meet her husband. The music sequences thus pitch the two women against one another, with the dominating mistress dressed in black and the submissive wife in white.

Double Di Trouble and the Apotheosis of *The Comedy of Errors*

Smeep Kang's *Double Di Trouble* begins, like *Angoor*, by acknowledging its debt to Shakespeare. However, this Punjabi film adds a new twist to the plot: the twins Ajit and Manjit separated from one another from their childhood are unaware of each other's existence. Childless, each brother adopts a son, not realising that the boys (Fateh and Ekom) are also twins. Thus while the film retains the structure of the two sets of twins, it alters the relationship between them. There is no master and servant pairing; instead we have fathers and adopted sons. In the opening credits Kang asks us to blame it all on Shakespeare, but it becomes clear that *Double Di Trouble* deliberately subverts the play's romantic possibilities as well as the social moorings that each of the previous adaptations relies upon.[30] For instance, in Kang's version there is no Luciana; Pammi (Adriana) has a brother instead who provides comic relief and is generally not interested in the antics of the married couples around him. Moreover, the figure of the courtesan is completely absent, although for the first time we find both the old parents (Aegeon and Aemelia) who are reunited at the end, following Shakespeare's script. However, in keeping with the cinematic tradition set in place by *Bhranti Bilash*, the parents are switched around, and it is Ajit (Antipholus of Syracuse) who gets the mother, while Manjit lives in the same city as his father (Figure 14.3).

The most significant departure, however, is in the way that the film treats Dromio. In transforming the master and slave/servant pairing into one of father and son, *Double Di Trouble* offers a resounding critique of the class hierarchies that Shakespeare's play stages and that the subsequent Indian adaptations leave intact. Fateh and Ekom (Dromios), much like their predecessors, are adopted, but their birth into poverty (as in Shakespeare) or early abandonment (as shown in *Angoor*) does not inevitably mean that they must be placed in positions of servitude. In Shakespeare's play the Dromio twins are born to 'a meaner woman' (I.i.55) of Epidamnum where Aegeon was stationed after his factor's death. The acquisition of the twins is thus tied with the emergent global

Figure 14.3 Double Di Trouble: Switched father and son.

Indianising The Comedy of Errors 265

commerce of the late sixteenth century, and Epidamnum, though famous from Plautus's *Menaechmi*, was also a city in Illyria. As scholars of the *Twelfth Night* have noted, Illyria, situated in the Balkans, stood at the crossroads of the East and the West, a site of both commerce and of conflict.[31] While the underlying racial implications of the *Twelfth Night* (which also features separated twins) have been frequently explored, it is perhaps worth reminding ourselves of this contested geography while considering the enslavement of the Dromio twins. These questions become even more pertinent given that during the early modern period the terms race and class were deeply interconnected.[32]

The Indian cinematic adaptations from the 1960s through the 1990s continue to restage not only this hierarchic relationship but also the accompanying violence associated with the power disparity. In Shakespeare's play the two Dromios are constantly being beaten up or facing threats of physical harm (I.ii.92–93; II.i.79), and the movies follow suit. Even in the absence of beatings, the verbal abuse remains, with the upper-class characters rebuking, taunting or mocking their Dromios. In contrast, *Double Di Trouble* avoids showing any domestic worker, although it takes us inside the homes of the Indian middle class. Fateh and Ekom far from bearing the brunt of abuse from their ill-tempered masters, stand in for the promises that the new generation brings. This sense of rejuvenation dependent on the Dromios is heightened by the fact that the Antipholuses of the film are older men. There is no doubt, however, that Fateh and Ekom are the Dromios, for we get the classic Shakespearean sequence of encounters between the two sets of twins starting with the early quibble about Antipholus's wife down to the confusion over money towards the end. However, it is Ajit (Antipholus of Syracuse), shown as an older widower, who is left without a romantic partner, while Fateh goes on to secure his sweetheart. The logic of the play is thus turned on its head, with the comic dénouement dependent on the future marriage of Dromio of Syracuse. This is not to suggest that Antipholus (played by Dharmendra) does not have a central role, but it is the needs of the two Dromios that for the first time become an important factor. This is set in place from the very beginning, for unlike the other movies the twins from Syracuse do not travel for the sake of Antipholus's business but to help out Dromio's love interest. The movie opens with a love song starring Fateh (Dromio of Syracuse) and Harleen, the village belle. When ruffians threaten to destroy the school that Harleen sets up, Fateh and his father, eager to sort out the matter, travel to the city, where unbeknownst to them their twins Manjit (Antipholus of Ephesus) and Ekom (Dromio of Ephesus) reside. Antipholus's trade is thus no longer the incentive for travel; instead it is the desire of the young Dromio of Syracuse (Fateh) that determines the action of the film. The final resolution again does not depend upon Ajit (Antipholus of Syracuse) finding a bride but on ensuring that Fateh (Dromio of Syracuse) secures his.

Double Di Trouble thus goes where no other Indian *Comedy of Errors* has gone before, and in shifting the attention away from Antipholus onto Dromio, it dramatically alters the very basis of a comic resolution predicated on finding new love.

Conclusion

The Indian *Comedy of Errors* stand apart from the adaptations of other Shakespearean plays not only in numerical terms but, more importantly, because they seem to form a family of films, bridging regional borders. As we have seen, the films draw upon one another, expanding or radicalising themes and scenes that come before. The Bollywood versions *Do Dooni Char* and *Angoor* interpret in their own way not only Shakespeare but also the older Bengali film, *Bhranti Bilash*, and, in turn, the Kannada and Punjabi adaptations follow from them. Through this Shakespeare gets thoroughly Indianised, his play, like any other blockbuster script, remade again and again in different spiced up combinations.

Notes

1. *The Comedy of Errors* was quite popular on Indian stage as well, being the second most performed play after *The Merchant of Venice*. See Poonam Trivedi, 'Introduction', in *India's Shakespeare: Translation, Interpretation, and Performance*, ed. Poonam Trivedi and Dennis Bartholomeusz (Newark: University of Delaware Press, 2005), 17.
2. For a detailed list of the cinematic off-shoots of *The Comedy of Errors*, see Rajiva Verma, 'Shakespeare in Hindi Cinema', in *India's Shakespeare: Translation, Interpretation, and Performance*, ed. Poonam Trivedi and Dennis Bartholomeusz (Newark: University of Delaware Press, 2005), 279.
3. See, for instance, see Richard Allen, 'Comedies of Errors: Shakespeare, Indian Cinema, and The Poetics of Mistaken Identity', in *Bollywood Shakespeares*, ed. Craig Dionne and Parmita Kapadia (New York: Palgrave Macmillan, 2014), 165–92.
4. Verma, 276.
5. Allen, 165.
6. Verma, 276. Vidyasagar has many claims to fame and is viewed as one of the most important figures of the Bengal Renaissance that saw widespread social and religious reform in the nineteenth century. Most importantly, Vidyasagar was responsible for pushing the colonial English government to pass the Widow Remarriage Act in 1856.
7. Paromita Chakravarti, 'Modernity, Postcoloniality and Othello: The Case of *Saptapadi*', in *Remaking Shakespeare: Performance Across Media, Genres and Cultures*, ed. Pascale Aebischer, Edward J. Esche and Nigel Wheale (New York: Palgrave Macmillan, 2003), 41.
8. For a comprehensive history of early Shakespearean performances in India, see Trivedi, 'Introduction', 13–17.
9. Chakravarti, 44.
10. Ishwar Chandra Vidysagar, *Bhranti Bilas* (1869), (Kolkata: Pathok Publishers, 2015), 4.
11. Verma, 276.

12. See Verma, 270–75.
13. Richard Strier, for instance, considers *The Comedy of Errors* 'Shakespeare's most wholehearted evocation and celebration of bourgeois life', outranking both *The Merry Wives of Windsor* and *The Taming of the Shrew*. See Strier, *The Unrepentant Renaissance: From Petrarch to Shakespeare to Milton* (Chicago: University of Chicago Press, 2011), 153.
14. See Verma, 279.
15. Verma, 276.
16. For more on the emergence of the New Woman in the nineteenth century as a new model of educated, independent womanhood and its effects on Indian literature and cinema, see Chakravarti, 43–44.
17. Allen, 169.
18. See Allen, 173–75.
19. The 'bhadramahila', literally translated as 'gentlewoman', is the counterpart to the 'bhadralok' or 'gentleman' and the result of the codification of behaviours centred on chastity that began in nineteenth-century Bengal.
20. Michel Foucault, 'Of Other Spaces', *Diacritics* 16, no. 1 (Spring, 1986), 27.
21. Ramesh Menon, *The Ramayana: A Modern Retelling of the Great Indian Epic* (New York: North Point Press, 2001), 43–45.
22. The anecdote concerns a pun on the sobriquet 'Vidyasagar' which literally means the ocean of knowledge.
23. The modern way of wearing the sari in Bengal was introduced by Jnanadanandini Tagore after her trip to Mumbai (then Bombay). The Parsi or Bombay style of draping the cloth was believed to be more aesthetically pleasing and functional for women who wanted to step out of the inner quarters and into public life. It was initially adopted by other women of the Brahmo Samaj, before becoming popular in the rest of urban Bengali society. The older form, with less pleats, became known as the 'sabeki' style. For more, see Chitra Deb, *Women of the Tagore Household*, trans. Smita Chowdhry and Sona Roy (New Delhi: Penguin Books India, 2010).
24. William Shakespeare, *The Comedy of Errors* (1594), *The Bedford Shakespeare*, ed. Russ McDonald and Lena Cowen Orlin (New York: Bedford St. Martin's, 2015).
25. For more see Allen, 178–82.
26. Walter Raleigh, *The Discovery of Guiana*, 1595 (New York: Createspace, 2015), 76.
27. Michael De Certeau, *The Writing of History* (New York: Columbia University Press, 1988), 227.
28. Allen, 179.
29. Allen, 180.
30. Rather tongue in cheek, the opening credits state, 'Blame it on Shakespeare that the ones they adopt turn out to be twins too'. *The Comedy of Errors*, of course, does not stage a multigenerational mix-up with fathers and sons being twins, and each pair not knowing the existence of the other.
31. See Patricia Parker, 'Twelfth Night: Editing Puzzles and Eunuchs of All Kinds', in *Twelfth Night: New Critical Essays*, ed. James Schiffer (London: Routledge, 2011), 45–64.
32. For more on the origins of the word 'race' and how it initially denoted hierarchies of class, see Ania Loomba, *Shakespeare, Race, and Colonialism* (Oxford: Oxford University Press, 2002), 81.

15 Regional Reflections
Shakespeare in Assamese Cinema

Parthajit Baruah

Shakespeare in Assamese Drama

The year 1826 is significant in Assamese history because through the Treaty of Yandaboo, signed in this year, Assam came under British rule, facilitating Assam's contact with the Western world, even as it initiated a period of colonial domination. During the second half of the nineteenth century a section of Assamese youth went to Calcutta for higher studies and got acquainted with the world of Shakespearean plays and their Bengali adaptations.

The group of four young Assamese men who studied in Calcutta colleges included Ratnadhar Borua (1864–1894), Gunjanan Borua (1860–1936), Ghanashyam Borua (1867–1923) and Ramakanta Borkakoti (1860–1935). Together they produced the first full-scale translation of Shakespeare: *Bhrama Ranga*, the Assamese *Comedy of Errors*. Namrata Pathak comments,

> *Bhrama Ranga* (1888) is regarded as a benchmark in the annals of Assamese literature. It is a translation of Shakespeare's *Comedy of Errors*, jointly undertaken by R.D. Barua, R.K. Barkakoti, G. Barua and G.S. Barua in Calcutta under the guidance of Lakshminath Bezbarua. This prose translation, while emulating Shakespearean technique, also deviated from it. The use of a local venue and local adaptation of the characters lend a native touch to this play.[1]

But it was Lakshminath Bezborua (1868–1938) and Padmanath Gohain Barua (1871–1946) who tried to bring Shakespeare closer to the people of Assam. Nanda Talukdar writes in 'Shakespeare and Assamese Literature' that Shakespearean characterisation and the form and technique of his plays influenced Bezborua and Gohain Barua. While Shakespeare's Falstaff has inspired the characters of Gajpuria and Priyaram in Bezborua's play *Chakradhwaj Sinha* (1923), Shakespearean cross-dressed heroines have influenced characters in Assamese drama, such as Padmanath Gohain Barua's *Lachit Borphukan* (1914), Sailadhar Rajkhowa's (1892–1964) *Pratap Sinha* (1926) and Prasannalal

Chowdhury's (1898–1985) *Nilamber* (1933). Gohain Barua and Bezborua represent Shakespeare's influence on the technical aspects of Assamese drama.[2]

Prasannalal Chowdhury's *Nilamber*, an adaptation of Shakespeare's *Othello*, is set in the sociopolitical context of Assam. Nilambar, the Assamese counterpart to Shakespeare's Othello, is a young king of Komotapur, in ancient Assam, who has a beautiful queen, Chandrawali. Nanda, the lieutenant of Komotapur and the bastard son of the last queen of the Pal dynasty, believes himself to be the rightful ruler of Komotapur. Nanda plots revenge against Nilambar by planting false suspicions in Nilambar's mind about his wife Chandrawali, insinuating that she is having an affair with Manuhor, another lieutenant of Komotapur. Nanda explains his malicious intentions in his speech, 'the cunningness of the fox, the greedy look of the tiger, venomous breath of the snake, the terror of foetus killing – all bundled together in me'[3] (1.4.67–68), which echoes Iago's psychology, 'I am not what I am' (1.1.66).[4] Nanda succeeds in destroying Nilambar's nobility. It is too late when Nilambar learns about Chandrawali and Manuhor's innocence.

Prasannalal Chowdhury's *Nilamber* laid the foundation for the new generation of playwrights to appropriate Shakespeare within Assamese sociocultural contexts. A contemporary young Assamese playwright, Hillol Kumar Pathak, who has adapted Christopher Marlowe's play *Dr. Faustus*, comments,

> I have just completed writing my script on Shakespeare's *King Lear*. In my *King Lear*, the setting is an interior village of Assam where simple village girls are his daughters. The conflict of a joint family in an Assamese society will be showcased in my *King Lear*. The Sutradhar will narrate the story to the audience and my Sutradhar will be Shakespeare himself. Shakespeare is a character in my *King Lear*. He will come to the audience off and on to narrate the story. At the end, my tragic hero will question the Sutradhar i.e Shakespeare how the playwright determines the destiny of a tragic hero.[5]

Shakespeare has been adapted, reconstructed and reinterpreted in Assamese drama; he has been assimilated within the sociocultural context of Assamese life from the nineteenth century onwards and continues to provide cultural resources to contemporary Assamese theatre practitioners and writers.

Assamese Cinema: History and Contexts

Historically, Assamese cinema has struggled to articulate a distinctively Assamese identity by focussing on social issues. The first Assamese film, *Joymoti*, released in 1935, was directed by Jyotiprasad Agarwala, the father of Assamese cinema, who was educated in Calcutta, Edinburgh and UFA (Universum Film AG) in Berlin. He was determined to make a film in Tezpur, a small town in Assam. He built an improvised film studio at Bholaguri, a remote place, almost 50 km away from the Tezpur town. Agarwala set the foundation for Assamese cinema, fighting against all odds. Sahitya Akademi Award-winning writer Apurba Sarma writes about the social condition of Assam during the 1930s:

> Assam in the thirties of the last century was just beginning to get the feel of modernism having already acquainted itself with the Macaulay-designed British colonial collegiate education, but in all other aspects of life it was extremely backward and undeveloped. The scientific and technological infrastructure for a modern society was non-existent, the outlook, the attitude, the ambience of modernism were still to take shape.[6]

Agarwala adapted the first Assamese film, *Joymoti*, from the renowned litterateur Lakshminath Bezborua's play, which narrates the seventeenth-century story of a valiant Ahom princess, Joymoti, who sacrifices her life to save her husband, Gadadhar Singha, and the Ahom kingdom. Writer-director Bobbeta Sharma comments on how Agarwala tried to make cinema a cultural medium:

> Jyotiprasad who believed in complete cultural emancipation, thus found a platform to express his thoughts through his poems, songs and plays, and it was but natural that it found expression in his film *Joymoti* (1935) as well. It also helped that the maker of *Joymoti* was a prodigy at a time when a culture was looking for self-identity. Language became the source that gave rise to, and sustained, the sense of a separate, unique, social entity, of having a distinct cultural identity, and of being Assamese.[7]

Although the film's subject was historical, the issue of a woman's sacrifice is foregrounded. Joymoti's silent protest against the cruelty of the puppet King made the film a strong statement on feminist politics. Film critic Manoj Barpujari writes in 'Assamese Cinema: dreams, reality and dichotomies',

> the film can be viewed as the very first attempt by any Indian director to depict the narratives in a true feminist light. The uncompromising resistance shown by Joymoti and other female characters seems to have overshadowed their men folk in the narration. In the 1930s women protagonists in Indian cinema were very passive, always sidelined, and hardly out from the veil. *Joymoti*, on the other hand, had a powerful, assertive, die-hard and self respecting woman as its central character who could ignore imminent death for her prestige.[8]

After *Joymoti*, some of the film-makers following in Agarwala's footsteps made films like Rohini Kumar Barua's *Monomati* (1941), Parbati Prasad Barua's *Rupahi* (1947), Kamal Narayan Choudhury's *Badan Barphukan* (1947) and Phani Sarma's *Siraj* (1948). These films were replete with history and patriotism. In the next decade, films like *Mak aru Maram* (Mother and Affection), dir. Nip Barua, 1958; *Ronga Police* (Police with Red Cap), dir. Nip Barua, 1958; and *Puberun*[9] (Sunshine), dir. Prabhat Mukharjee, 1959 addressed social values and themes in a sentimental, melodramatic mode.

Alternative Cinema: Challenging Stereotypes

With the arrival of Padum Barua, Bhabendra Nath Saikia and Jahnu Barua during the 1970s and 1980s, Assamese cinema entered the world of alternative cinema. Challenging the conventional narrative techniques these new film-makers started making serious artistic films, often experimental, choosing aesthetics over commerce. They had distinctive authorial styles; rejected dance and songs; focussed on serious contemporary themes like the crisis of the middle-class, political and women's issues; and used social realism. Their cinematic discourse and grammar was distinctive and new, using non-linear narratives, music as motif and slow camera movements.

Padum Barua depicted the social dynamics of an Assamese village through his film *Gonga Silonir Pakhi* (Wings of the Tern, 1976). Set in 1960s Assam, the film portrays the story of a young village girl, Basanti, who is forced to marry against her wishes, loses her husband in an accident and fails to build a new life with her former lover. Bhabendra Nath Saikia, in his film *Sandhya Raag* (Evening Song, 1977), based on the story *Banaprastha* (Third Spiritual Stage, 1969), shows the middle class' exploitation of the poor. Jahnu Barua's *Halodhia Choraye Baodhan Khai* (The Catastrophe, 1987), based on Homen Borgohain's novel of the same title, shows farmers' exploitation by landowners.

After this extremely productive phase there has been a slump in the Assamese film industry in recent years. The industry is celebrating its golden jubilee this year, but so far, it has produced only 350 films. From 2000 to 2006, it produced 86 films, and from 2007 to 2011, only 21 films were produced. The major reasons for the decline in productions are the insurgency, limited market for Assamese films and the poor condition of cinema halls. There are only about 100 mini cinema halls operating in all of Assam, and more than 60 cinema halls have been shut down.

Contemporary Assamese Cinema and Politics

Contemporary film-makers of Assam have continued making films on the themes of identity politics and political issues. In the multilingual demographic and culturally diverse structure of Assamese society, ethnic groups and the tea-tribes of Assam have been marginalised and alienated by mainstream Assamese society. The ethnic clash in Assam in 2012 was between indigenous tribal Bodos and Bengali-speaking Muslim migrants from Bangladesh.

Jadumoni Dutta's *Jetuka Pator Dore* (The Challenging Life, 2011), set in a remote village during the 1970s, narrates the story of Radha, a young woman of lower caste belonging to the fishing community. She fights for the rights of her community and against the exploitation of a rich villager. Timothy Das Hanse's film *Ronga Modar* (The Subdued Cry, 1990) depicts the Adivasis' quest for an identity and for liberation from exploitation through Raghav, the labour union leader. Monjul Baruah's *Antareen* (Quest for Sanctuary, 2015), not yet commercially released, bagged the Best Feature Film Award at the Third Indian Cine Film Festival – 2015 in Mumbai. The film narrates how Tarali discovers her Adivasi roots when she comes to know her real mother's identity.

Another section of film-makers have taken up political themes in their films, such as *Surya Tejor Anya Naam* (The Blood Red Sun, 1991), directed by Dinesh Gogoi; *Sesh Upohar* (Final Gift, 2001) by Gopal Borthakur; and *Sankalpa* (Vow, 1986) by Hem Bora. These films were based on the two major political upheavals in Assam: namely the Assam Movement (1979–1985) and the rise of the ULFA (United Liberation Front of Assam). The popular Assam Movement led by All Assam Students Union (AASU) and the 'All Assam Gana Sangram Parishad' (AAGSP) was a non-violent programme of protests demanding the identification and expulsion of illegal immigrants. However, the movement turned violent, with the Nellie massacre of 18 February 1983, which claimed the lives of 2,191 people, mostly Muslims. The ULFA was founded in 1979 with an aim to establish a sovereign Assam through armed struggle against deprivation and economic exploitation by mainland India.

Gogoi's *Surya Tejor Anya Naam* addresses the ULFA political insurgency. In the film, Bijoy, a cadre of People's Court (suggesting the ULFA), believes in the ideology of Che Guevara and targets corrupt engineers, businessmen, politicians and bureaucrats for ransom. Borthakur's *Sesh Upohar*, set in the 1990s, depicts the political questioning caused by the surrender of several noted ULFA revolutionaries to the government. In the film, Nanak Baruah, chief commander of militant group, desists from exploding a bomb in a train when he sees his wife and daughter boarding it, thus saving many lives. The film throws up questions on politics, ideology and human relationships.

Hem Bora's *Sankalpa* depicts the social life in the 1980s during the Assam Movement. Ramen Dutta, a student leader, organises anti-government agitations demanding the identification and deporting of illegal immigrants. But the government spreads a rumour among Muslim migrants that only they were being targeted, while the Hindu foreigners were not to be deported. Afzal, a student leader, reacts: 'The Assam Movement will go on until the last foreigner is left. A foreigner is a foreigner. There is no religious sentiment'. The last frame of the film freezes with the lines, 'Can the country be built by ignoring youth?/Is it possible to hold back time by bullets?/This is only the beginning of such questions'. These films, although politically audacious, did not experiment with technique and cannot really be categorised as alternative films, except for Monjul Baruah's *Antareen*. But these films have built up a rich legacy of political film-making in Assam. This is demonstrated in the 2014 film *Othello (We Too Have Our Othellos)*, directed by Hemanta Kumar Das, produced by Manabendra Adhikary and based on Shakespeare's *Othello*, in which a story of suspicion, jealousy and betrayal has been transformed into a narrative of a political identity quest.

Shakespeare in Assamese Cinema

In Assamese cinema, we get only indirect and oblique representations of Shakespearean themes except for Hemant Kumar Das's 2014 debut film *Othello (We Too Have Our Othellos)*. Hence this essay focusses on this film with a brief exploration of the allusive references to Shakespeare in Manju Borah's *Baibhab – A Scam in Verse* (1999) and Jahnu Barua's *Aparoopa* (1982). The voice of Shakespeare distinctly echoes in the first film, whereas in the others it appears only implicitly.

The producer of the Assamese *Othello*, Manabendra Adhikary, explained why he produced the film:

> I am a great fan of William Shakespeare, the master playwright whose plays have almost been reconstructed in India and in some other countries. One day, when I read the Assamese script of *Othello (We too have our Othellos …)*, I was overwhelmed. I read the script many times and found that Shakespeare's tragic hero Othello is represented in a different social context of Assam. Moreover, this was the first Assamese film that speaks of Shakespeare in a strong voice. So, I decided to produce the film.[10]

Commenting on the role Shakespeare plays in Assamese cinema, National Award-winning Assamese film-maker Manju Borah said,

> Shakespeare may not be present overtly in Assamese cinema, but Assamese filmmakers have dealt with the themes of cultural racism, woman's position, characters' alienation. In our films too, Hamlet's psychological position, Othello's question of identity, King Lear's love of flattery and Macbeth's ambition are presented through many characters in the Assamese context. Shakespeare is a larger than life

figure. As far as Shakespeare is concerned, I am planning to adapt Shakespeare because his themes are universal.[11]

Othello: A Modern Assamese Adaptation

Hemanta Kr Das's debut film *Othello*, a modern-day Assamese adaptation of Shakespeare's *Othello*, is the first film in Assamese cinema to address Shakespeare explicitly. It uses Shakespeare to construct a new discourse about the 1990s insurgency by ULFA and other groups and their violent clashes with the Indian army. Set in contemporary Assam, the film poses questions about social and political identities. An intense political and psychological drama, its narrative involves two generations of characters: Bankim, Pabitri and Mun, who represent the older order, and Arjun and Tina, who are the younger characters and who are connected through complex turns of events and relationships. All the characters in the film are united in their struggle to assimilate into a changing sociopolitical order. The film revolves around Bankim Bhattacharjee, a seventy-two-year-old ex-revolutionary, who suffers from Alzheimer's disorder and Mun an autorickshaw driver who has leukoderma (a 'whitened' man among brown people). In Shakespeare's *Othello*, Roderigo and Iago use racist epithets, like 'an old black ram' and 'a Barbary horse' to describe Othello who is a cultural and racial outsider in Venice. But here, in the sociopolitical context of Assam, both Bankim and Mun are outsiders. Ranjit Sarma, the screenplay writer of the film, describes how he brought Shakespeare's *Othello* into Assam's social framework:

> Shakespeare's *Othello*, the moor of Venice stood apart in a white dominated society of Venice. Othello was a dark skinned man in a white society who became a general by dint of his hard work, merit and intelligence. I have tried to give a new dimension to my *Othello*. Mun, the protagonist of my film *Othello*, is an auto rickshaw driver who has a skin disorder - leukoderma – a white man in a dark skinned society. I have made an attempt to showcase the predicament of Mun and Shakespeare's Othello. The colour of the two skins separates the two characters namely Mun and Othello from their respective societies in their respective eras-one representing 20th century cultural and racial prejudices of Assam, while the other, 16th century England.[12]

Bankim has come to believe that the armed struggle he followed during his youth was wrong, and he is seen, at the beginning of the film, walking up to the jail and asking to be imprisoned. Realising that he is an Alzheimer's patient, the jail sends him back in Mun's autorickshaw to the very police station where Tina, Bankim's tenant and a call girl, has gone to lodge a complaint about her missing landlord. It appears that this situation of Bankim wandering off to the police and demanding to be jailed is an oft-repeated one. Tina meets Mun at the police station. Later, a bomb blast at Mun's auto stand that kills many innocent people and destroys Mun's auto is discovered to have been engineered by Arjun, Bankim's illegitimate son and a young Turk in the Communist Movement. However, Arjun escapes unnoticed. The film ends with the suggestion that despite political turmoil, the lives of ordinary people like Tina, the call girl and Mun, the autorickshaw driver continue against all odds. Pranjal Borah writes in his article '*Othello: An Assamese Film*',

> Life is like a perennial river that has to keep on flowing. Life and river both appear to have a smooth run when seen from a distance but in fact they have a fierce current within that is full of intricacies.

This is the theme of Assamese '*Othello*.'[13] The apparently complacent lives of the characters contain hidden depths: all of them, Bankim, Mun, Arjun, Tina and Pabitri, hide within their ordinariness some revolutionary impulses. They all have at some time resisted or countered the conventional norms of the society.

Though commercially not released yet, the film was screened at the Brahmaputra Valley Film Festival in Guwahati (Assam, 2015) for the public and was well received. The film got critical appreciation for using Shakespeare as a frame to narrate the story of Assamese society and politics. Lyle Pearson, a curator, has written to the film's producer that his *Othello* film brings the 'inside story out' with all the values changed.[14] The film bagged the Rajat Kamal (Silver Lotus) at the Sixty-Second National Awards for the Best Assamese film in 2014, and Best Screenplay, Best Debut Director, Best Cinematography, Best Actor (male), Best Supporting Actor (male), Best Sound at Prag Cine Awards North-East Festival, 2015. It has also travelled to several international film festivals.

Three Othellos

The Assamese *Othello* speaks of three Othellos – Mun, Bankim and Arjun. While Shakespeare's Othello was a greatly respected and powerful Venetian General, the Assamese Othellos are ordinary human beings, although like Shakespeare's Othello, they are all outsiders in mainstream Assamese society. Bankim is an ageing and frustrated revolutionary and a Bengali, Mun is an autorickshaw driver who is a Muslim and Arjun is a political fugitive and a socially outcast son.

Mun is socially ostracised for his skin disorder. Despite paying for his sister's marriage he is asked to stay away on the wedding day because of his leukoderma. Mun's college friend Anju laughs at him and mocks him for being a fake Othello, a white-skinned man among brown people.

He almost identifies himself as an outsider and labels his autorickshaw 'Othello' (Figure 15.1).

The issue of Bangladeshi migrants has been regarded as a major political problem in Assam. Muslims are often suspected to be behind insurgent activities and become victims of the anti-Bangladeshi prejudice. Mun is arrested when a bomb explodes at the autorickshaw stand. As he is a Muslim, the investigating police officer harasses him by asking him questions like 'Are you a member of SIMI, IM, AL-QUIDA, ULFA?,'[15] though he is later released.

Mun's autorickshaw is destroyed in the bomb blast. When he buys a new one, he organises a party at Bankim's house to celebrate. At the party, Bankim says to Mun, 'The name of your auto is Othello. You are also an Othello, a white Othello in the land of black'. Bankim's ironical remark is a scathing attack on Assamese society.

Bankim too is another Othello, an expelled Communist and a lapsed revolutionary who bears an identifiably Bengali name in an Assamese society which has a history of anti-Bengali movements.[16] As Ranjit Sarma says, 'Bankim is a character who does not belong to Assamese society. It is usually a name common to the Bengali community. Bankim is from Karim Ganj. So, Bankim is, in a sense, an outcast, a deserter.'[17]

Bankim Bhattacharjee has been expelled by the communist party. His comrade Dharani died for him. He leads an isolated life. Mun says to Bankim at the party, 'You too are an Othello. You had joined the Movement and were jailed. Your party expelled you. Now, you spend your time

Figure 15.1 Mun with his autorickshaw named 'Othello'.

making masks. Does society accept you?' Bankim's act of making masks – of Karl Marx, Fidel Castro, Che Guevara, Lenin and other revolutionary figures – is deeply ironic revealing his hankering to continue to belong to causes which have failed him and the society. As Arjun, the active rebel, points out later, these are mere effigies, while he, Arjun, is the one carrying out their ideals of violent change. All these characters signify an otherness: Mun, as a leukoderma patient; Tina, as a sex worker; Bankim, as an expelled communist; and Pabitri, as a former member of the communist party, as they struggle to carve out a life within an otherwise hostile world.

The third Othello is Arjun, a terrorist on the run, who is discovered to be the illegitimate son of Bankim and his former comrade, Pabitri. Bankim says, 'Arjun was born because of my mistake'. He has chosen to lead an underground life of an outsider, as a revolutionary. He dreams of a new identity in his own world which he tries to forge through violent activities like the bomb blast which kills innocent people (Mun's only friend, a teenage boy who runs the tea shop next to the auto stand and who also lives with him is one of those killed) and changes nothing. If the early revolution 'failed' as the film says explicitly, the present generation is confused about its ends and means and is shown only causing havoc through their indiscriminate violence.

Subject to discrimination and deprivation, the three Othellos suffer from their own identity crises in specific ways. Bankim, a failed communist, is torn between dream and disenchantment. Mun suffers marginalisation because of his skin colour, while Arjun discovers that Dharani Rajbongshi, a former communist, Pabitri's husband, is not his father.

Ideological Conflicts in Das's *Othello*

Bankim and Pabitri in *Othello* are shown as communists who were involved in the failed CPI (ML) Movement in Assam during the 1970s. Their son Arjun represents the Maoist upsurge in different Indian states like Chhattisgarh and lately in Assam. The Left movement in Assam became dominant just after Independence. Assamese youth, inspired by Pannalal Dasgupta, joined the Revolutionary Communist Party of India. Dasgupta, however, was influenced by and became a follower of Gandhi's political methods causing resentment within the party. Eventually the Left movement led by Dasgupta failed. But almost simultaneously, another Left mobilisation started under the United Communist Party of India which supported participation in parliamentary politics. However, CPI (ML) Party in the 1960s and early 1970s, led by Charu Majumdar and Saroj Dutta, advocated armed revolution and denounced participation in the electoral process. Later, they decided to give up armed struggle saying that there were no objective conditions for the struggle to succeed. After almost twenty years, the ideology of violent Left revolution against the government was revived by the CPI (Maoist) led by Kishenji.

The different turns and phases of Left movement had a strong cultural impact on Assamese society. Revolutionary Left-wing figures like Kalaguru Bishnu Prasad Rabha (1909–1969), who gave the slogan *Haal Jaar Maati Taar* ('Those who cultivate should own the land'), became household names. Bhupen Hazarika's (1926–2011) songs full of the voices of farmers and poor fishermen inspired people to work for an egalitarian society (Figure 15.2).

The film seeks to capture this complex history through its Othello-like outcast figures who represent various stages and versions of Assamese politics. Bankim and Pabitri were active members of Communist Party of India (MarxistLeninist) who dreamt of changing the socio-economic condition of Assam. Bankim's ideological differences with the party after its decision to give up armed struggle led to his alienation. He is shown leading an isolated life sculpting faces of communist leaders like Fidel Castro, Che Guevara, Lenin and Mao Tse Tsung in his room. Suffering from Alzheimer's disease, Bankim has forgotten most things but not the communist leaders. He is also unable to forget that it was he who sent Dharani Rajbongshi, Pabitri's husband, on an action where he was shot dead by the police. He also remembers that it was because of his mistake that Arjun was born. Since then, Pabitri, Arjun's mother and Bankim's former comrade, looks after him and cooks for him. Frustrated with the Movement and his own ideological contradictions, Bankim says, 'The day I die, the world will not be lost/ Few will know my absence/ The flowers will continue to bloom, the breeze will move on, the stars will be in their orbit, orbit, orbit'.

Arjun is trapped between the old and new forms of communist struggle. In the film, Arjun is introduced through a guerrilla attack on the police. Then he is shown escaping in a boat captured through a fixed frame within which the boat moves slowly against the current, metaphorically signifying Arjun's movement against the system.

At Pabitri's behest Bankim offers shelter to the fugitive Arjun in his house, in the room where he makes earthen masks. Bankim believes that the new forms of communism espoused by Arjun's generation would fail just as their own movements had. Arjun relentlessly questions Bankim about his politics and expresses his own lack of faith in Chinese models of communism which characterised older Left movements. He says to Bankim, 'We have to shock the people into awareness to make them think of the revolution'. The film, however, does not suggest that his politics have any more chance of succeeding than Bankim's.

Tina: Desdemona of Our Times

In the Assamese *Othello*, Tina is Bankim's tenant. Her father is in hospital, and she resorts to prostitution to earn a living. She too is an outcast – her clients use her services but disown her. Her status as an isolated and unaffiliated individual in society is reflected by her refusal to use a surname. Tina is shown signing papers when she goes to the police station to report Bankim's disappearance. An extreme close-up shows her signature to be only her name.

At the party in Bankim's house to celebrate Mun's new autorickshaw, Arjun asks, 'Who is Desdemona here?' Tina says that she is Desdemona, to which Arjun replies sarcastically, 'Desdemona of our time is a call girl'. Defiant like Desdemona in rejecting social and patriarchal expectations, Tina befriends Mun, the social outcast, using his auto to visit her clients. When Mun's autorickshaw is destroyed in the bomb explosion Tina gives him money to buy a new one. In a particularly poignant scene, Tina kisses Mun to comfort him after he is beaten up, trying to protect Tina from goons. Humiliated by society, Mun finds a new meaning in his relationship with Tina.

In contrast to Shakespeare's Desdemona, Tina – the modern Desdemona – is not a passive character. Like the legendary Joymoti on whose valiant life one of the earliest Assamese films was made, she resists the traditional norms of femininity to live on her own terms. She hates the world, but towards Mun and Bankim, she is compassionate and caring.

Othello within *Othello*

At the party at Bankim's house Mun plays a DVD of an English movie version of *Othello* which everyone watches. This 'Othello within Othello' scene acts as a moment of revelation. During the viewing of *Othello*,

Figure 15.2 Bankim, the failed Communist, spends his time making busts of revolutionaries in *We Have Our Othellos Too*.

the discovery of Arjun's birth details exposes that Pabitri, mother of an illegitimate child also has a past which is not unlike Tina's, although it is only Tina who is reviled as a woman with questionable virtue. They are thus both revealed to be social outcasts. The watching of the film also transports the audience to another time and space – to Shakespeare's England. 'It is a question of preparing the audience to be transported to Shakespeare's times and comparing my *Othello* with that. In fact, this scene is a metaphoric representation of the whole film', says Sarma (Figure 15.3).[18]

It may seem incongruous for the characters like Bankim, Mun and Tina to watch a film like *Othello* in its English version, yet it is a significant part of the narrative of the film. It becomes an aesthetic and critical intervention which obliquely draws a parallel between the Shakespearean Othello as a victim of racism and the modern Assamese Othellos in a distant world – yet subject to almost similar experiences of marginalisation. This is the only scene where three Othellos and modern-day Assamese Desdemona are brought into one cinematic frame with the Shakespearean Othello.

Other Assamese Films with Shakespearean Resonances

While *Othello* is the only Assamese film with a direct engagement with Shakespeare, a couple of other films reveal some Shakespearean resonances. Manju Borah's *Baibhab – A Scam in Verse* focusses on the disturbed psychology of Samiran Choudhury, a thirty-seven-year-old man who is haunted by a childhood trauma of accidentally killing his younger brother. He suffers from a quasi-Hamletian alienation, and his

Figure 15.3 Arjun, Tina, Bankim, Pabitri and Mun in the '*Othello* within Othello' scene.

inner turmoil is reflected when he speaks out in a soliloquy, 'I have never been able to make myself understood to anyone'.

Jahnu Barua's *Aparoopa* presents a character named Jeevon who is reminiscent of Shakespeare's wise-fools. Barua admitted in an interview: 'While creating the character of Jeevon in my film, I was influenced by Shakespeare's fools, but it was created in the cultural context of Assam.'[19] A *bahua* or a buffoon in *khulia bhaona* (Assamese folk drama), based on the stories of *The Mahabharata* and *The Ramayana*, amuses the audience with satirical songs and comical comments and acts as the link between the stage and the audience. Unlike a stereotypical comedian Jeevon is not dressed in Shakespearean motley. He is a village drunk and a rustic philosopher who sagely says to his friend Rana: 'Do you remember Ganesh Gogoi's poem: *Who hasn't come here/ who hasn't gone away! Everyone has to come/Everyone has to go/You too have to come/ You too will go/ When we meet/It's always here and now!*' recalling the wise pronouncements by Shakespeare's fools on earthly transience and mortality. But while there are slight echoes and glimpses of Shakespeare in Assamese cinema, the only and first full-length, self-conscious deployment of a Shakespearean play occurs in Hemant Das's *Othello*.

From the very first film, serious Assamese cinema has shown a political slant, using the medium to comment on society. Hence it follows that the first Shakespeare film too is a serious critique of the political scenario of the state delving into the upheaval caused by the insurgency movement. The Assamese *Othello* does not represent a conventional story of a betrayal of love; rather its narrative indicates a more complex story of political betrayals – of ideologies, comrades and parties. It is not a domestic drama of collapsing faith and crumbling relationships but one in which the very credibility of communist ideology which once promised to deliver a more equitable society is under question. The Assamese *Othello* tells a story of the failure of the Left movement in Assam. The film's ironical representation of the characters' failure to achieve their revolutionary ends clearly signifies a quiet but firm rejection of the political ideologies that have haunted the state for the last fifty years and more.

The adaptation of Shakespeare's *Othello* into Assamese, with a new focus on identity construction reiterates how Shakespeare has come to represent the cultural, aesthetic and theoretical ground, on which new narratives can be created.

Notes

1 Namrata Pathak, *Trends in Contemporary Assamese Theatre: Theatre in Assam, Tradition and Transition* (Partridge India, 2015), 48.
2 Nanda Talukdar, 'Shakespeare and Assamese Literature', *The Indian Review*, https://indianreview.in/shakespeare-and-assamese-literature. Accessed January 2016.

3 Prasannalal Choudhury, *Neelambar* (Guwahati: Banalata Publication, 2002), 19.
4 Peter Alexander, *William Shakespeare: The Complete Works* (London and Glasgow: Collins, 1964), 1115.
5 Personal interview with the author, 20 June 2015.
6 Apurba Sarma, *Jyotiprasad as a Filmmaker and the Forsaken Frontier* (Gauhati Cine Club: ADI Publication, 2005), 7–8.
7 Bobbeta Sharma, *The Moving Image and Assamese Culture, Joymoti, Jyotiprasad Agarwala, and Assamese Cinema* (New Delhi: Oxford University Press, 2014), 46.
8 K. Moti Gokulsing and Wimal Dissanayake, *Routledge Handbook of Indian Cinemas* (New York: Routledge, 2013), 52.
9 The title of the films like *Monomati, Badan Barphukan, Siraj, Piyoli Phukan* are the names of the central characters in the films. I have tried to give the literal meaning of the films' titles where necessary.
10 Personal interview with the author, 8 June 2015.
11 Personal interview with the author, 8 July 2015.
12 Personal interview with the author, 28 June 2015.
13 Pranjal Borah, '*Othello*: An Assamese Film Portraying Life as a Perennial River', 28 November 2014, www.kothasobi.com/news/othello-assamese-film-portraying-life-perennialriver/. Accessed January 2016.
14 Lyle Pearson personal note to the producer, 28 June 2015.
15 *The Students Islamic Movement of India* (SIMI), *Indian Mujahideen* (IM) and *Al-Qaeda* founded by Osama bin Laden are Islamic fundamentalist organisations, who want to convert everyone to Islam by force. They have carried out several attacks against the civilians in India. While *United Liberation Front of Assam* (ULFA) is a separatist group in Assam, the government of India denounced this organisation in 1990 as a terrorist organisation and thus banned it. ULFA also carried out several attacks on civilians in Assam. They choose Bangladesh as their hideout for operating their activities.
16 A significant political phenomenon centred around identity in Assam, known as *Bhasha Andolon* (The Bengali Language Movement in Barak Valley, Assam), emerged in 1960s. It was a protest against the decision to make Assamese the only official language of the state by the Assam Government. The then popular Chief Minister of Assam Bimala Prasad Chaliha presented a bill in the Legislative Assembly on 10 October 1960 and wanted to legalise Assamese as the official language of Assam, and the bill was passed on 24 October in the Assam Legislative Assembly, thus making Assamese the one and only official language of the state. In the Barak Valley, the Bengali-speaking people constituted the majority of the population. Ranendra Mohan Das, the legislator from Karimganj (North) assembly constituency, raised his strong voice against the bill. When the Bengali Hindu settlers in Assam opposed the bill appealing to the Government of Assam that would suppress the Bengali language by derecognising it, the Assamese attacked them and destroyed their houses. They were forced to flee from the Brahmaputra Valley and take shelter in the Barak Valley. People of Silchar, Karimganj and Hailakandi protested vehemently against the injustice of the Assamese Government. Many lost their lives, and eventually, the Assam Government withdrew the bill, and Bengali was given official status in the Barak Valley.
17 Personal interview with the author, 28 June 2015.
18 Personal interview with the author, 8 July 2015.
19 Personal interview with the author, 18 July 2015.

Part V
Interviews

Interview with Pankaj Butalia by Paromita Chakravarti and Poonam Trivedi, 20 September 2015

Pankaj Butalia is a documentary film-maker who happened to start his film career with *When Hamlet Went to Mizoram* (1990) about the unsuspected popularity of *Hamlet* in the 1980s in Mizoram, a north-eastern state of India. As he tells us, he stumbled upon this fortuitously and found Hamlet's soliloquies being played on audio cassettes in the market place. Subsequently, he has made a number of films, one of which, *Moksha* (Salvation), won several national and international awards. Recently he has done a trilogy of documentaries on Manipur, Kashmir and Assam, border areas with endemic violence.

POONAM: Tell us about your journey as a film maker and before that as a film enthusiast?

PANKAJ: In the late 1960s and 70s film societies were mushrooming everywhere. While I was in University I became very interested in films. In 1974 I helped to found Celluloid, the Delhi Film Society and between 1975 and 85 I was actively involved with the Society ... There were a group of enthusiastic people who were associated with the Society – Harish Trivedi, Vina Das, Radhika Chopra, Ravi Vasudevan, Sumit Chowdhary and other friends from St. Stephens, also from the Sociology department, Delhi University. We started getting films for screening and organizing discussions around them. Lots of foreign embassies in Delhi helped us to get international films.

POONAM: So when and how did you take the step into film making?

PANKAJ: From the involvement in Celluloid I slowly got interested in film making. I bought a Super 8 camera but getting stock was a huge problem. In those days you could not buy film – you needed a license for it. I often asked friends abroad to bring stock for me and I would store it in the fridge till it rotted! Initially I only wanted to make fiction films – we had a sense of arrogance about the Indian feature films that were being made and I wanted to do something better. Then in 1986 I had the opportunity to organize the documentary section of the International Film Festival. From then on, I got interested in documentary films. I went on to organize three documentary film festivals for IIFI in Delhi, Hyderabad and Trivandrum. I used all my contacts to get good international films. Around this time, in 1986 a group of people had come to India to do a film on Partition. My sister Urvashi was helping them to gather stories for the film. One day their sound recordist left suddenly and I was roped in to do the sound. The cinematographer Peter Chapel taught me how to record sound. On the next day I recorded sound for a very complex shoot. That is how it all began.

PAROMITA: How did the idea of making the film *When Hamlet went to Mizoram*, the first such Indian film of this kind, come about?

PANKAJ: I had been going to the North East most of my adult life as a table tennis coach. I had coached the Assam team in 1973. I had also coached the Meghalaya team for several years. I used to go to the Jaintia Hills regularly for this work and I would put up at the Pinewood Hotel. When I was there I had been thrilled by a post-harvest festival called *Bein Dia Khlem* which was celebrated with huge totem poles. There would be flute and drums and fanfare as the totem poles would be carried into an amphitheatre like space and then immersed in water. There would be an audience of women carrying umbrellas since it rains there most of the time – it was quite close to Cherrapunji. I was interested in filming this festival and got in touch with some film maker friends – Deepa Dhanraj and her husband, a cinematographer. However, before they could arrive, there was a big student strike and they got held up. While I waited I got talking to a student from Mizoram who told me about the fascination with Shakespeare in Mizoram, particularly with *Hamlet*. Eventually we could not make the film we had planned on the harvest festival since the Church tried to shut it down. Around this time the RSS had become very active and the Shah Bano case had started a few years earlier. At this time to oppose the Church action seemed too much like playing into the hands of the RSS [Shah Bano case 1985, 1986 Ram Janmabhoomi agitation begins, Rath Yatra 1990, demolition of Babri Masjid 1992].

So we returned without being able to make our documentary but the germ of the idea about the popularity of *Hamlet* in Mizoram stayed in my head. Soon after I went to Prague as part of my work for the Federation of Film Societies and from there I took a Eurorail trip to the UK. I stayed with friends there. This was the time when the UK was promoting its multicultural policy and the Bandung File had been commissioned on Channel 4 by its commissioning editor for multicultural programmes, Farrukh Dhondy. I knew Tariq Ali who was the series editor of the Bandung File. He had a free one hour slot and I told him about the *Hamlet* in Mizoram idea. This is how I was commissioned a 26 minute film on *Hamlet* in Mizoram in 1987. But when I went to him with the complete film it was 52 minutes long. But I did not get double the money for it. So in effect Tariq Ali got a film double the length for half the money. I did feel a little cheated. But the important thing is that he trusted me to make the film. For my next film, *Moksh*, I went directly to Channel 4 and not through intermediaries. It was 84 minute film which won me awards and gave me money.

PAROMITA: Is your film, *When Hamlet went to Mizoram* a documentary?

PANKAJ: Yes, it is – it is also a bit of an essay. In this film I am really trying to challenge the anthropological lens which is often used in documentary films. I am trying to use my own perspective here. The first shot of the film has this local chap sitting on a slope looking contemplatively at a panoramic view of the city of Aizawl. But in the very next shot he gets into his jeep and starts blaring out popular rock music. This helps to immediately shatter the myth about the North Eastern tribals, of a people cocooned in a traditional culture. The film has many such moments of surprise where it deliberately challenges audience expectations.

POONAM: What difficulties did you encounter in making the film? Tell us about your experiences in shooting the film. Also tell us about how the film was restored?

PANKAJ: I encountered many technical problems while making the film. On the seventh or eighth day of the shoot, the camera was on a tripod and we were shooting in the marketplace. Suddenly the camera was knocked down. The cinematographer Ranjan Palit's assistant K.U. Mohanan was sent to Bombay to check the damaged camera and the footage. When we checked, we found a light leak because of the camera damage. This was the pre-digital age when the laboratory's technical work was hugely expensive and the film industry was not really geared towards the 16mm films – since feature films were all 35mm. So a lot of footage was lost. Later I went back for another shoot with Mohanan to fill in the gaps. There is still a lot of footage lying in the laboratory in negative, but most of this would be junk. Even the final negative of the film is gone now. I did not have the time to make copies. When I revisited the film several years later I did a cut and paste job taking sections from the original footage and a video version. So much of the film was destroyed. I have managed to salvage most of it now. I have done the work myself because now I have the technology.

PAROMITA: Why was *Hamlet* so popular in Mizoram? And why in the mid 80's?

PANKAJ: We shot the film in 1988–89. But the phenomenon of the popularity of *Hamlet* started much earlier from 1984. But this huge popularity of the play waned after the actors got married and got busy with their professions. Redemption Theatricals was the group, and they did several plays, *Romeo and Juliet* and *Salome* and others,

288 *Interview with Pankaj Butalia*

but *Hamlet* worked better than others. Hence in the mid 80's there were several performances of the play both in indoor and outdoor theatres. There would be about three performances a year. They also made audio cassettes of the play which circulated widely and helped to popularize it further.

POONAM: What is the history of Mizo translations of Shakespeare? Which translation did you use?

PANKAJ: In the performances we filmed, they used the Laldailova translation. J.L. Laldailova was an interpreter in the British Indian Army and created a Mizo-English Dictionary. He also translated five Shakespearean plays including *Hamlet* into Mizo. He translated other English plays like *Salome* too. Interestingly, the Mizo *Hamlet* does not have the play within the play, they are broad translations. The group didn't perform the entire play either. It was the emotional drama which interested them, the father mother relation, the romance, the brother sister and the father son angles.

POONAM: Were these translations printed?

PANKAJ: They were available mostly in cyclostyled form. At that time, Aizawl had no printed newspapers. People made cut and paste versions of local handwritten and printed news which were cyclostyled and sold. Maybe the translations are in printed versions now.

PAROMITA: What about the sub-titles used in the film? Some of them seem to be English translations from the Mizo version of the play – but some of them use the exact Shakespearean lines. Why this discrepancy?

PANKAJ: I had the play's lines translated back into English from the Mizo language by my Mizo friends in Delhi. But the translations are not always very reliable. So I substituted lines from Shakespeare's *Hamlet* where there seemed to be close correspondence with the Mizo translation.

POONAM: Where was the film screened? What was the reaction?

PANKAJ: The film was screened extensively five or six years after it was made. In 1991 it was shown in the Museum of Modern Art, New York. I then took the film to the universities of Cornell, Columbia, New York University, William's College – mostly in the East Coast. I got a very good response. I have also shown it at the Toronto Film Festival and also in the Cinémathéque Française in Paris (in 1991). At all these screenings I have had good discussions on the film.

PAROMITA: Do you see your film as political? What is the politics of the film? Do you see *Hamlet* as being connected in any way with the politics of insurgency in Mizoram?

PANKAJ: When I made the film in 1988 Laldenga was already out of power. Insurgency in Mizoram was no longer an issue. Ania Loomba in her essay on the film asks the question why the film is not political. For me, the essence of the film must arise from the protagonists of the film, not from my own point of view. If I had to put across my own perspective, I would make fiction and not documentaries. There is a basic ethics of making a documentary – you have to be true to its characters ... I did not want to manipulate my subjects. People open up to you and trust you – if you do not respect that then you are going against the ethics of documentary film making. Ania Loomba wanted a political Shakespeare and she wanted politics in the film. But I need to be true to the sentiment and feelings of my characters. So I needed to work with why the people playing the main characters relate to them. The woman playing Ophelia does talk about how she can identify with Ophelia's grief for her father and her brother. She says that Laertes' departure makes her think of the many young men who leave home in Mizoram for livelihood reasons and never return. Here there is a veiled reference to the young men who used to go underground to join the insurgency movement and never return. Also bringing in the local lamentation songs for the dead into the *Hamlet* performance helps to connect it to the political situation in Mizoram, to its oral tradition and transference of memory, of old songs, from generation to generation. You have to be able to read politics into the images – the deeper meanings are for the audience to find. For instance, even an insignificant image like eating *paan* and buying a cigarette can convey a politics of indigenous and western cultures. My politics is not to give you an overt statement, a crass political reading – not just 'slogan *baazi*'. But there is a definite and explicit politics in every film I make. I would call myself a political film maker – but I must be loyal to the form. So, my politics will be knitted into the film. It will not be an overt statement which will put people off.

POONAM: The role of Christianity in the film – seemed celebratory, with shots of the Christian rituals of sermonizing, psalm singing, Sunday school etc. Is that what you wanted to convey? Or is there an implicit contrast being suggested between the indigenous festivals and Christian celebrations?

PANKAJ: I would not say that. The film seems to implicitly say to Christians: 'Do not do here what you have done to rest of the world – do not destroy the local culture'. The 'steep and thorny way to heaven' quote suggests that. Ophelia says to her brother Laertes' advice to guard her virginity: 'But good my brother,/Do not as some ungracious pastors do,/Show me the steep and thorny way to heaven,/whiles like puff'd and reckless libertine/Himself the primrose path of dalliance treads,/And recks not his own rede' (1.3.46–51). The lines urge the Christian pastor to heed his own counsel rather than forcing it on others. The image of the Cross and the 'Christian' quotes from *Hamlet* are used ironically in the film. The film begins with the sound of traditional Mizo drums and then cuts to a shot of a Cross on the hill – this shows a transition from traditional tribal culture to the dominance of the Church. The moral regimen of the Church has dislocated the local culture. The Mizo Church is a combination of various denominations and it is also relatively mild. But it is still authoritarian and moralistic – the Sunday School and psalm singing shots towards the end of the film shows this aspect of Christianity.

Yet it is true that Shakespeare is a consequence of the Church, he arrives in Mizoram with the British and the Evangelists. And equally the Church provides a shelter to the Mizos against the cultural domination of mainland India. But the Mizos have successfully effected an indigenization both of Christianity and of *Hamlet*, infusing them with their own traditions.

PAROMITA: There are many shots of Mizo everyday life in the film – did you wish to indicate how both Christianity and Shakespeare are embedded in Mizo quotidian lives?

PANKAJ: Yes – those shots convey the surprise and comfort of the everydayness in Mizoram. Some shots like that of the boy on a bicycle riding through Aizawl streets also conveys a sense of freedom of spirit which allows the Mizos to adapt Shakespeare so freely. They are not encumbered by any sense of the iconic Shakespeare. This is communicated by the audio cassettes of *Hamlet* playing in the middle of the vegetable market and ordinary women buying them. As a matter of fact, I missed out an important clinching shot because the camera man was taking a break, when in the market place I saw a woman stop by the stall blaring out the *Hamlet* cassette. She asked for it to be rewound and then had it played fast forward and then actually dug into her purse and bought it. I did not want to 'restage' it for the camera because that would go against the ethics of documentary film making.

The two children who lie in bed and recite dialogues from *Hamlet* randomly are like Indians who know dialogues of the popular film *Sholay* by heart. And it was the audio cassette which made it a part of popular culture. Hamlet's soliloquies in the Mizo language have a certain rhythm and musicality – there appears to be something in the Mizo language which lends itself to the rhythm of Hamlet's soliloquies. And this language is common street language. Is there a certain incipient orality in Shakespeare's language which matches the predominance of oral cultures in Mizoram? People don't know that this is a British play. The advent of script in Mizoram happened in 1890 with the coming of the Roman script.

POONAM: Does Mizoram have indigenous theatre traditions? How does *Hamlet* fit into it? There seems to be no use of indigenous theatre conventions or costumes in the *Hamlet* performances?

PANKAJ: Mizoram does not have any indigenous theatre tradition – there are traditions of music and dance. The quasi-Western costumes are part of their desire to be modernized.

POONAM: Tell us about your relationship with Shakespeare and Shakespeare films. Which is your favourite *Hamlet* film?

PANKAJ: I am not a literary person – I like some five or six Shakespeare plays. I am fascinated by *Hamlet* – it is a very understated play. So there is so much scope for interpretation. I like the other tragedies too. There is so much meaning in Shakespeare's plays – you can spend a lifetime on two lines. My favourite *Hamlet* film is Grigori Kozintsev's 1964 *Hamlet*. I am not a great fan of Shakespeare on film – Kurosawa's *Throne of Blood* is probably the best cinematic adaptation of Shakespeare. I liked *Shakespeare in Love* too – it was fun.

PAROMITA: What about Vishal Bhardwaj's Shakespeare films? Particularly his recent film *Haider* based on *Hamlet*?

PANKAJ: I think there is too much overt machismo and theatricality in his films. I have seen *Haider* – I feel he chickens out on the incest angle after having opened it up. He flirts with it and then backs out. I liked the scene when Haider returns and sees his mother and uncle engaged in singing. But the second half of the film seems to be merely resolving the issues broached in the first half – it does not add anything new.

PAROMITA: Thank you. This has been very informative.

Interview with Roysten Abel by Poonam Trivedi, 26 February 2016

Roysten Abel, theatre director and playwright, is credited with being the first to devise and direct a widely successful contemporised version of *Othello* in India; this won the Fringe First award at Edinburgh in 1999. He then turned the play into an art film, *In Othello* (2003), directed by himself. He has subsequently turned to devised theatre with folk musicians.

P: Let's start at the very beginning. Tell us about your love for Shakespeare because, as I told you, this interview is for a book, *Shakespeare and Indian Cinemas: 'local habitations'* and you were one of the earliest young directors to perform a kind of contemporary Shakespeare, in an adapted and localised fashion. You were not afraid to mess around with it and you did it very successfully, *Othello in Black and White* (1999). And before that for your graduate performance you did a Shakespeare, *Merchant of Venice* (1993), which I had viewed. So tell me, why this special interest in Shakespeare?

R: The answer is very simple. You see, this is the only playwright I knew. For the simple reason, he was the only playwright who was taught in school. And I took a liking to Shakespeare at a very early age, around ten or eleven, and the one I took the very first liking to was the play within the play of *Hamlet*.

P: Really? This was in school?

R: I was in sixth standard or so.

P: What part were you doing?

R: No, no I directed it.

P: That's really starting early.

R: We did not have a clue at that time and at school every week you had to do something as a part of your extra-curricular activity and when I was in sixth standard we were taught abridged versions of many Shakespearean stories and that was when I first came across *Hamlet*. Then *Merchant of Venice* was taught to us in ICSE (Indian Certificate of Secondary Education). I also had a great teacher who orated Shakespeare very well and I just took a liking to him. Once at NSD (National School of Drama) I was lucky to have Raghunandan (theatre director and critic) in my first year, and in the second and the third year you would have to do a Shakespeare scene work. It was a two-part exercise: one was, we had to pick up a text and a scene from Shakespeare, and I think I chose *Macbeth*.

R: And Raghunandan and Anamika Haksar (director/teacher) were doing scene work with the whole class on *Othello* and it was interesting to see how, especially Raghunandan, was approaching the text. Of course, as students, we had to do our own stuff, but observing him working as an actor was a turning point because he was one person who was physicalizing a lot of the Shakespearean imagery and thereby making the text fully available for the actor. This is what was interesting for me and that's what I tried with the *Merchant of Venice*. Then you can go deeper into the text, and then you kind of start to like it and … it's like your favourite drink. … Then you want to try the other plays.

P: Great! That's a quotable quote that 'Shakespeare is like a favourite drink'.

P: You also went to the Royal Shakespeare Company.

R: Very very short period. I was there for a very little while. But RSC was almost like the National Repertoire Company, it was so boring. I left there and went then into other theatres, watching and rehearsing.

P: When you came back from England you did a production of *Macbeth* for the Shakespeare Society at St. Stephen's College in which you cast the witches as a rock band in punk gear. Was this RSC influence?

R: No, no it wasn't. We were looking for how to interpret the three witches for the modern day and we were also trying to have the play in a college, so.

P: It was quite electrifying, I saw that production.

R: Shakespeare to me is a lot of fun, and for me, theatre is fun and I need to have my share of fun when I do these things. And my pent-up angst of not becoming a rock star.

P: Ha ha, I see, that is the other dream, is it? Can you say something about the *Merchant* you did? It was a graduate course production, right?

R: Strictly, it wasn't because it was done by all the first year, second year and third year students in their free time which was not a part of their coursework. So it was my own and then it became so big, that it kind of started to become my diploma production.

P: It was very striking. Again, I saw it. It was one of the first Indian productions that admitted something of Antonio's sadness, it clearly hinted at a subterranean level of homosocial attachment, let's say. So therefore, I thought that it was bold and brought in new resonances. Then you added a very colourful masque sequence.

R: Yes, Jessica's elopement. And I used Handel's *Hallelujah*, I remember, as the music score, which was basically because the Christian was eloping with the Jew and the whole masquerade of it. It was an act of sacrilege within the religion ... and it had that feel of opera. I certainly enjoyed creating that scene, it was one of my favourite scenes ... trying to create a baroque-ish experience because the music is very baroque. And, I was a final year student, so it was all the more exciting.

P: Coming to the *Measure for Measure* that you did with Arjun Raina in 1995. That was interesting because *Measure* is a play that is not much read in India, nor has been performed often.

R: I think nobody has ever done it after that!

P: That is such a pity because it's such a great play!

R: It's an extremely dramatic play.

P: Full of contemporary relevance, the exploitation and personal gratification by public figures.

R: And today, you know that kind of literature is very relevant with all your Pachauris and others. But, for me then, the take was on the Duke and you remember there was this *hawala* scam and all this crime going on.

P: Did you pick *Measure for Measure* or was it Arjun Raina (actor) or the group?

R: No, no. It was me and I went to Arjun and asked him if he could do it with me.

P: And he was happy to do that.

R: Yes, he obliged, he was my teacher.

P: Then you did a *Romeo and Juliet in Technicolour* (2000) and *Much Ado About Nautanki* (2001)?

R: The *Much Ado About Nautanki* had nothing to do with Shakespeare (laughs).

P: Okay, other than the title.

R: But *Romeo and Juliet* was technicolour, did you see it?

P: Yes, I did and found it also quite interesting. You brought some Bollywood dimension into it.

R: Yes.

P: And it was how this story circulates, because it's a perennial story and how Bollywood treats it and how you treat it in theatre, something like that.

R: I really enjoyed doing that production. Because then I was trying to experiment with Shakespeare and new writing; it was me and Shakespeare collaborating and binding within the Indian context and just exploring the layering within the text, within the context and thereby elevating it. Likewise, with *Goodbye Desdemona* and the post *Othello*. Now that I am talking to you I am revisiting those days and I must say I quite like that! But then I was trying to re-contextualize Shakespeare. And for me that was a great joy and great fun.

P: Why did you feel that Shakespeare needed to be re-contextualised?

R: His plays/lines are so multidimensional that they can work in so many contexts and not just the one he had written it in. Just the greatness of the lines and the words and the drama. For example, the love scene between *Romeo and Juliet*, in *Goodbye Desdemona* it was put in a completely different context: they had to breakup because you know they could not complete the play and the political pressure that they were going through – these were two gay men who were in love with each other. And then when they see that one was a Muslim and one was an Englishman and then when you speak the lines, 'O Romeo wherefore art thou', 'deny thy name' the whole thing gets a wholly different dimension and becomes more poignant. Shakespeare is the only playwright who can go into so many places.

P: And your *Othello*, it became so popular, because I think it was the first theatre production of Shakespeare in India that was contemporised in an acute and vivid manner. What do you think?

R: You know, that's a mystery. Maybe, two, three things because none of us thought it was going to be so successful. One was the way Shakespeare was juxtaposed with new writing and how the story was told within a contemporary milieu of a theatre company which was interesting for people. Then it had a multicultural cast. And it had two great performances of Adil (Husain) and Barry (John). They were both very good.

P: And this duo worked very well. To have an older man do the other, the villain, that kind of reverses the dynamics in a very interesting and poignant manner.

R: The reason for me to have cast Barry as an older Iago ... I was a young director surrounded by these older men acting and being on the stage, so the villains available to me were all older men, so Barry as old Iago. And then, by providence, I got to explore a purely traditional form like Kathakali, the usage of Kathakali which was happening here, and we tried our version of the experiments and lot of these elements came together which I think made the play work and made it very electrifying. And the supporting cast was all very good and they all kind of fitted into place and all these things worked. We ran that play for ten years! And each time we changed it a little, we reworked it each time.

P: In what manner?

R: In the sense that, maybe I said that we should change one scene or we should not act it like this but in another way, in a different way.

One of the conversations that I would go in again and again while rehearsing was that, 'let's not try and repeat actions, just repeat the lines like we know them, since the last time we've played it. Let's just keep to the Shakespearean part of it but be open and respond to what is actually happening just here'. So, then it started becoming more fresh.

P: So, it was the stage business and the performance that you were improvising. The script remained more or less the same.

R: And we did a lot of performances after the film.

P: Okay. So how did the film happen? Tell us more about it. You changed the title right? The play was *Othello in Black and White* and the film is called *In Othello*.

R: The film happened because of my late producer Amit Bhatia. He asked me if I wanted to make a film and at that time I said if you want to do a film then let's do a thriller. But he had already done this kind of film, though at that time I actually had a film script ready. Then a few other people came in and they were ready to do something and Amit was game and everybody else was there and the film just happened. We had three performers I think.

P: The film was very tightly done and artistically composed. I was just wondering whether the DVD version, which I was watching yesterday, had been edited a little bit?

R: I have no clue.

P: There were some scenes in my memory from the first viewing which I could not find here. Some scenes of Desdemona in the dressing room and Othello lying on the bed with the red counterpane and there's an image of you in a red dress like a Venetian noble.

R: But I don't think there could be a different version unless my producer went ahead and edited it. Not that I know, I haven't seen the film for a very very long time.

P: What was the reception of the film like?

R: Very mixed.

P: Why was that?

R: I mean, for the reason that it only got through to a very niche audience, it did not get a wider release. But all the people who saw it kind of liked it.

P: So why not a commercial release?

R: At that point, I was wishing for a release at a larger level, reaching a lot more people and now I feel I was completely wrong. But people loved the film, they write to me, they talk about it. Now, when I see the film I feel like that I could do this in a much much better way.

P: Well, what would you have changed?

R: I would have changed the whole thing.

P: The striking thing about the film is that it's all of one piece and all the issues of the play have been transposed within your film which is also in a distinctive cinematic style, isn't it? This kind of darkness and green room mirrors and sharpness of the stage light …

R: Too much of it I think.

P: You think it's too much and you want it to be more 'opening up to the outdoors' although there is only one scene I think, a dream sequence, with the elephant, in the open?

R: Which I kind of like.

P: It is beautiful, very poetic and … sexy. And it was inevitable, I suppose, the comparison between the play and the film.

R: You know some like the play better while some like the film.

P: So why do you think some people like the play better than the film?

R: I think there are two or three things here. For many people, the play was their first experience of the text and in a play, it's not just what you see that you experience, there is also the *you* in it, the audience who contributes in it, who contribute to your experience and that's what completes the whole experience of theatre. You know when your imagination and your life experiences contribute to that theatrical happening you have a different picture altogether. When you are watching a film you do not see that happening. Because in a film things are way more concrete, so the element of identification, the ephemeral contributory experiences are lesser in cinema. So mostly it does not reach your expectations. You know, you read a book and you watch a film and you say that the experience of reading the book is much better than watching the movie of the same. But the thing is you got to deal with a lot of what is happening in your head as well.

P: What do you think the film gained?

R: The film is more poetic, I guess.

P: Especially towards the latter half I feel.

R: Yes, yes, the way in which everything worked, especially the camera, each and every shot was planned that way, too much I think, but everything had so many layers. In cinema, you know there is much more layering and hence it was more poetic. But I could not get through the cinema techniques, and I did not understand lenses, magnification etc. so I feel that it could have been more focused and a lot more dramatic.

P: You also used a lot of symbolism: the colour red, Desdemona in red or black rather than in white through which she is always symbolised, the mirror images, the spiral staircase and then the song, the song was very important, '*Ram kare naina na uljhe*' [Lord, let the eyes not get entangled]. It is there as voice over in the beginning and then is repeated at the end.

R: Yes, because a film is also about the gaze, isn't it? So it's also the way in which he sees Desdemona and the way he sees himself and it also has to do with being oneself, dealing with the other person, looking at one self and looking at the other and the mirror, so much of it was the mirror.

P: So, the mirror was a means of viewing the inner reality you think you know, because they were facing the mirror.

R: And also, seeing, looking at yourself and seeing the other person. And it has to do with fear and insecurity, so much of it, and also what is real and what is an illusion.

P: In the film, you have a striking statement very early on, 'what is acting, it is lying and an actor has to lie to bring out the convincing truth.' I felt that was what the film was doing, which is intermeshing fiction and reality. Because others get confused, the chief actor confuses his real emotions with his actor-ly emotions and he suffers because of that.

R: I would not have that line in the play, in the film, if I would do that now though.

P: Really?

R: Too much of a statement. I did it at that point because, I suppose, it was me at that time trying to understand what acting is like, and compassionately, the film kind of records it.

P: For always! What is the experience of directing a film *vis a vis* directing the play? You will not make another film, right?

R: There are two or three things to it I guess. Anyway, directing a play is anyday much more fun than directing a film because the constant adrenaline rush that you have over those forty, forty-five days that you are directing is unmatchable. In making a film the experience is of a much longer time. There's too much of technique and science involved in it and too much importance is given to that, and people who try to make films are people who actually enjoy that process. But for me it was getting a bit tedious. Also, a film is a much lonelier process because after you shoot, it is only you left. You are in the lab and you are in colour correction going through it, it is such a lonely experience and you are accountable for everything unlike the theatre where you share all the experience. So that was number one, and number two is that I just got busy with all the other stuff that I was doing. I did want to make another film after *Othello*, I did have everything needed but I found another love, of theatre with music and musicians and it took up a lot of time.

P: You've changed direction quite substantially and since then, 2003, it's been ten years, and you have neither made a film and nor have you gone back to Shakespeare.

R: But it looks like I am going to make another Shakespeare now.

P: What kind? A play?

R: I am going to be doing *The Tempest*. *The Tempest* is one play in Shakespeare where there is a lot of music, it probably has the most amount of music and it's his last play and all this magic business is

the magic of theatre and the music is a big part of this magic. So, I want to work with actors and creators of music to come together and work towards it.
P: So, when are you targeting this for?
R: In 2016 or 2017.
R: The British Council will be part of this anyway since it is the Shakespeare anniversary year. They have been after me but I never had an idea. I can't just go and do something because it is the anniversary you know. You need to have a real reason and real inspiration to do something. And so, when the music composer also asked me if I would be interested in doing something, he had just composed the music for the songs in *Tempest*, so I said let's wait. ... I am literally looking at using these musicians as Prospero's cloak, you know, the cloak of magic.
P: That's fascinating.
R: And Prospero is like a theatre director who is creating all these scenes.
P: And Prospero is also many times seen as Shakespeare himself.
R: It is actually that vulnerable Shakespeare at the fag end of his career. It is the time when he is moving to Stratford-upon-Avon and there are other playwrights who have come into the scene. It's an insecure Shakespeare who says give me your hand, who wants applause, he says 'come' and we are asked to applaud, he really needs applause now. It's a Shakespeare who wants help, a Shakespeare who wants to forgive and is not bitter in his last act. He also wants to create a different reality for himself because doing theatre in London at that time would not have been the easiest of things, it must have been a lot of dirty cloak and dagger stuff. And so, for me that's very interesting, it's one play that I could not figure out for a long time. For me it was the most difficult play and suddenly it looked interesting to me. And I am now living by the sea, at the end of a village; I am covered on three sides by the sea, I feel like Prospero marooned on an island.
P: To come back to the film, how did you think this kind of play-within-the film genre worked? There are several other films which use this motif, and there are also Shakespeare films where there are scenes of rehearsing and acting like *Kiss me Kate*. Do you see your film in line with these?
R: No! Because, no, what I am trying to do is also a play within a play within a film.
P: And what would you say were the cinematic influences on you as you conceived this film?
R: In this film? All the films that I saw till then, and especially whether it was Masami Taura or Bergman, or whether it was Wong Kar-Wai. I had a lot of these influences but not just one. I was trying to do scenes like those between Sheba and Adil and me and the way the

300 *Interview with Roysten Abel by Poonam Trivedi*

camera starts with one person and by the time it comes on to the other side it will be on another person, and it comes back geared at the third person, which can only be done in cinema. Thereby using the magic of cinema to create those scenes, it was just not about doing a play within a play, but doing that extra thing. I don't think I have answered your question but for me it's like, I am just going back to the film so I am trying to see what happened. I have not watched the film for a long time.

P: When you used Adil, there were a lot of comments about him which had to do with his Assamese background and whether he was comfortable in his own language speaking Shakespeare and being called an outsider. All this politics of the northeast had an electrifying effect because it made the play contemporary with an immediacy for us. What did you think?

R: I did not know that things would get so much worse now, things were bad then. Now, I think so bad that it is crazy. At that time, it was happening. ... My wife you know is Assamese and she was not cast in a play, even though, you know, she was in the NSD repertory company, because she looked Assamese and the play dealt with Indian royalty and the big question arose how can an Assamese qualify as an Indian?! And this was a very senior director, very well qualified, and this just came out of his mouth while telling me. Very very leftist, a director who was ideologically left. I was so shocked at that point that I could not respond. And it was also at that point the first stage of the 'chinky chinky' business was happening in the universities in Delhi with the north-east people.

P: So did you put in Adil consciously or did it just happen because he was from Assam?

R: No no no, it was very conscious, that was the reason I picked this play. I made *Othello* for this reason.

P: To foreground the outsider.

R: Yeah. Unlike most other *Othello* plays, the thing for Othello is the complex that he is only feeling within himself and Iago is instigating it. But no one is actually looking at why Othello has this complex. So, for me it was a very strong thing. Look at what happened last year with all the north-easterners getting beaten up, unbelievable.

P: Prejudice seems to be growing.

R: Yes, and now you have to prove that you are a nationalist, you can't just be a nationalist but you have to prove you are one, unbelievable.

P: You must have heard about or seen the film *Hamlet in Mizoram*?

R: No, I have not seen it but I may have heard of it. Whose is it?

P: It has been made by Pankaj Butalia.

R: Ok. Pankaj did it?

P: Of course, it is a little different because it is really a documentary and speaks about *Hamlet* being performed by several groups and in Mizo language. But he has the same cinematographer as yours, Ranjan Palit. So, I wondered if there was some connection.

R: Did that happen before me or after *Othello*?

P: It was before yours, 1990 in fact.

R: No no no no, I have not seen it. I took Ranjan because I liked the film he had done on the *Bauls*, there's a documentary.

P: Have you seen Jayaraj's *Othello*, in Malayali? What did you think of it?

R: Yes, I have seen that and I feel it was a great film.

R: Actually, we just finished shooting with Jayaraj who is also a friend. He is shooting *Macbeth*, he has just gone back into the shoot, he told me day before yesterday.

P: There is a new *King Lear* film, again in Malayali, where the daughters become the sons.

R: Who did that? Even though I live in Kerala, I'm pretty cut off and I live on the sea, I am not on an island but my house is at the very end of the village; after my house, there is just the sea.

P: Just have one or two more questions about the film: In your play there is this Italian director who wants to come and do a production of *Othello* and then wants it in Kathakali to take it abroad so isn't that kind of orientalising and exoticising India and Indian tradition? Did you see it like that?

R: You are asking about orientalising and exoticism as being in the play? You are saying that it is not there in the film but in the play?

P: Yes, it is not there in the film but it is there in the play. The use of Kathakali, especially ten years ago or so, was so often used to represent the exotic India. So what's your take on that?

R: Why it was not in the film?

P: Yeah, why it was not in the film. But also, traditional dance and song and craft, why attention to it is so often misplaced, used only for its surface and veneer and colourfulness and not really in depth about its philosophy, how did it come about and what does it mean?

R: Precisely why it was in the play. I think it has to do with two things: the western eye trying to look at it, at the peripherals. But on the other hand, if you went in deeper there was something in there as well, because it has much to go deep into. And that was the reason why people make fun of it in the play. And later when Adil does the last scene he does it with Kathakali being a strong influence. So, it wasn't all black and white in that way. In the film, we thought that it wasn't one of the strong points that we wanted to talk about.

P: And, could you comment on the role of the *Behroopiya* (folk impersonator)? Because again he seems to be a kind of a symbolic figure and the film ends with the figure of the *Behroopiya*.

R: The film is ultimately speaking about the multiple meanings of being an actor. You know, whether it's actor on stage or the actor in life and all the colour that you put on yourself, all the make-up you put up in life and on stage, and you have to remove all the make-up, the whole purpose of life at some point is to remove all the makeup and hence the *Behroopiya*.

P: The language of Shakespeare, there was a great focus on the language of Shakespeare and to get the lines right and actors having to speak in that language. Do you think that Shakespeare's language poses a problem for actors today?

R: No. I think it's a problem for people who understand Shakespeare like that.

P: Like what?

R: Like he is just the language or just the words. Of course, there is no one who has played with words so well, he is a master with his play of words and there are no two ways about it. But it is not just the words, of course they have a lot of layering, but sometimes the words have come out so masterfully by Shakespeare but not because he wanted to create the words like that. The words are an outcome of something much more intrinsic to what he was experiencing or what he wanted people to experience.

P: And do you think Shakespeare translated into Indian languages can work as well? In Malayali for example?

R: I will be honest to you, I am still yet to see a good translation. Because it's a very difficult act to match. With all being said and done, who are you trying to translate? I mean it's Shakespeare and you will never be able to reach that level. Not just the words, you might find meaning, there may be measuring, but there is just so much more to it. It's so good that you can't blame the translator but it's just the hard act of translating.

P: So, which is your favourite Shakespeare film?

R: One is Kozintsev's *The Lear* and Kurosawa's *Ran* and I love *Shakespeare in Love*. But apart from these two I have not seen any recent ones. I kind of liked Bhardwaj's remake of *Hamlet*. I did not like the *Macbeth* and *Othello*, but I liked and loved the way he interpreted the ghost.

P: It's a very clever film in that sense and very well made. But it is more about Kashmir than Hamlet. Somewhere you have to keep the balance.

R: At the end of the day you can't take away the words, there is so much to it, Shakespeare's greatness. Shakespeare took his plots from all over, so it's not just taking a plot and doing a turn. There is so much there if you can get actors. One of the joys of playing Shakespeare is that there is also the language, the words, and when you take away that then you take away a substantial amount from the total *rasa* experience and that is why I did not like Vishal's film. It's there for an actor to be a joy, it's one of the things, there's nobody who writes

like that for an actor. After so many years it's so relevant even today and people are still doing it.
P: So, you will do *The Tempest* in Hindi?
R: Yes, I think so.
P: Okay, thank you so much. This has been enormously enriching and informative.

Interview with Aparna Sen by Paromita Chakravarti, 3 January 2016

Daughter of film critic and director Chidananda Dasgupta, Aparna Sen is a leading Bengali film actor (who has acted in the films of Satyajit Ray, Mrinal Sen and Rituparno Ghosh), an editor of a popular women's journal and an award-winning film director. She won a National Award for *36 Chowringhee Lane* (1981), her debut directorial venture. Her most recent film, *Arshinagar* (The Mirror City), based on *Romeo and Juliet*, was released in 2015 December.

P: Tell us about your involvement with Shakespeare, in school or college, on stage?

A: It was not a great involvement. In school we read a little bit and started with, I think, Lamb's Tales from Shakespeare. Not the best beginning. But Baba[father] used to read to me ... from *Antony and Cleopatra* and so on. Baba read Shakespeare to me just as he would read [Kalidasa's] *Meghaduta* to me. Then the involvement increased in college because we had *Macbeth* as our text. By then I had read some more plays like *As You Like It, Twelfth Night, Hamlet* and *Othello*. *Othello* was earlier because in *Othello* I played Desdemona while I was still in school. I always found Desdemona a little silly and found it very difficult to play Desdemona. ... unless one assumes that she was very naïve – why didn't she tell him? – I found that difficult to grasp till I saw, much later, an *Othello*, played very badly by Lawrence Olivier who was much more the Moor with a rose in his hand and with this panther walk. But in that, if I remember correctly, Maggie Smith played Desdemona [very interestingly] and she was an older Desdemona – she did it as if she found it very humiliating to explain – which I found very interesting since it felt more credible. Then when I did *36 Chowringhee Lane* ... I delved into *Lear* and got to know *Lear* quite well. We also watched 'Shakespeareana' doing plays, and *Richard III* played by Lawrence Olivier, on film. Then, I saw Zeffereli's *Romeo and Juliet* and various versions of *Romeo and Juliet* and, then down the years, *Westside story* which had a profound influence. But when I saw it later I found it very dated. At that time, that clicking of the fingers, that really captured our imagination. When I decided to do *Romeo and Juliet*–I had already seen Zeffirelli's *Romeo and Juliet* and then I saw Baz Luhrmann's.

P: What did you think of Lurhmann's film?

A: Luhrmann's did not speak to me, emotionally. He used the television as the chorus – the newscaster. One can use any number of things – I have used Reshma Bai, the puppeteer. So many Hindi films have been made on this play – none of which are really *Romeo and Juliet* at all. I made it a point to see these films. In *Ishaqzaade* you have Romeo almost raping Juliet in order to take revenge which I found [to be] against the idea of pure love in the middle of strife which is what I think Shakespeare's main idea was – that there is a certain purity, ... a poignancy in love – which is very close to my idea in *Mr and Mrs Iyer* – love in the middle of violence, and that is what *Romeo Juliet* is and that is why it appealed to me. I saw *Ram Leela* which started off okay except that it was too colourful for me.

P: *Ram Leela* was Lurhmannesque you thought?

A: Except that Baz Lurhman is more stylish, *Ram Leela* was not. *Ram Leela* was just lots of colours. Anyway, it started out okay – the balcony scene was there which was not bad, but then afterwards these two people [Romeo and Juliet] went and sided with their own kinsmen which is not at all *Romeo and Juliet* and then they started fighting each other ... and joined the strife. For me they stand for love as opposed to strife which is why in my film when I used a colour palette I gave Romeo and Juliet whites and pastel shades, all colours of purity and I gave the other two gangs red and black

P: I thought that was very Stendhalesque.

A: Oh – because of the red and black? It wasn't taken from Stendhal. I have always thought of having them in two different colours so that people who see this film will immediately know that these are the Khans and these are the Mitters; these are the Capulets and these are the Montagues. I found out later that actually in Verona, a long time back – oh no, this was in Florence, you had the Guelphs and the Ghibbelines –the Guelphs wore white and the Ghibbelines wore black. ... apparently Dante was a part of it all. It's very interesting and you get the first reference in Dante. In canto six you get that reference and [they] call them the Capelletti and the Montecchior – something like that. Anyway, when I started out all this was very far from my mind – all this was a later exercise. I started out because I was always attracted to the idea of love winning over violence and that has been a continuing theme ... and will remain that way. I did an interview on NDTV which some of you may have seen where I have said all this ....

P: At this juncture, I think, to be able to make a film like this is important.

A: I think so too, and I have transposed the gangs and all the civil strife that used to go on in Verona and Europe of that time to our present times where it still fits ... extremely well.

P: ... [In] *36 Chowringhee Lane* the use of both *Twelfth Night* and *Lear* are so important and the cat is called Sir Toby and she (Violet Stoneham) teaches Shakespeare.

A: She teaches *Twelfth Night* and teaches it very badly, unfortunately, and nobody is interested and the children read love comics. ... somebody brought me that model of Globe theatre ... which we used on [her] desk.

P: One of the very poignant points of the film is where she is sitting in front of the Victoria Memorial reciting Shakespeare. I am very interested in how you have shown Shakespeare as a fading presence in Bengali life. So how do you look at the continuing relevance of Shakespeare for the Bengali? The fact that he is seen as an imperial icon but at the same time indigenised in different ways?

A: I think he is seen as more than an imperial icon. I think he has grown above that. See, there are two or rather three classes of people. One, who have just heard about *Romeo and Juliet* and maybe read about it or (have) seen films about it and think that *Ishaqzaade* or *Ram Leela* is *Romeo and Juliet*. There is a class that does not know anything about *Romeo and Juliet* and hasn't even heard the name – or they have heard the name as lovers like Laila-Majnu, Romeo-Juliet like that – and then there are people who have actually read the play and who know about *Romeo and Juliet* and who love Shakespeare. Shakespeare lives on among the people who are fond of literature. I don't think even in England all people know Shakespeare. But I think Shakespeare lives on. There is a relevance [even] if you take it away from the Shakespearean language which people can't understand anymore. It is like Bankim Chandra, he is simple if you understand the Bengali. If you understand Shakespeare's English then I don't think there is a problem because it is a simple enough story. But what one can do is keep reinventing him and I think his greatness lies in the fact that his texts allow themselves to be reinterpreted in so many times and in so many ways. I mean 400 years after his death he is still ... Now two more Shakespeares are being done. Anjan Dutt is doing *Hemanta* as *Hamlet* and Srijit is doing *Zulfikar* which is *Julius Caesar* and *Antony and Cleopatra*.

P: Does it have a historical context?

A: No no – it is set here, in the docks in Khidderpore ... these are all mafia. I think Vishal Bharadwaj started the trend of the mafias. But mine is not quite mafia, but yes, land mafia, you can say ... the families in Verona had armed gangs and so how do you transpose it here? – it has got to be oil mafia or land mafia, something like that.

P: You mentioned Vishal Bharadwaj who has now become synonymous with the category of 'Bollywood Shakespeares'. What do you think about his films?

A: I liked *Maqbool* very very much but I must say that I didn't like *Omkara* or *Haider*.

P: Why not?

A: Because for Othello ... he has to have the qualities of a tragic hero which I felt that Ajay Devgan did not. Somehow being mafia ... he did not reach those noble qualities that the tragic hero must have along with the tragic flaw. He has to be noble otherwise why do you care for him? There was no nobility there.

P: And the nobility does not need to be lineage ... it can just be the character?

A: The character – the conceptualization of the character where you have noble qualities – otherwise you cannot be the tragic hero. *Haider* I didn't care for. I just liked the idea of Rooh as the Father's ghost. You know, Ophelia, why did she wind a lot of twine around her and die is something I could never figure out. ... in Shakespeare ... Ophelia, is very young, very vulnerable, very fragile, which is why she could not take it all. But here[in *Haider*] she had a mind of her own ... she rebelled, she was a journalist, so why would she do that? It just did not work for me. What did work for me was the fact that he placed it in Kashmir and the politics of Kashmir. The other thing that worked for me was ... the play within the play ... [with] those fantastic dances. ... . But in the end, you know that it has to appeal to your emotions which it didn't.

P: And it was too full of stories ... the Kashmir strand and the *Hamlet* strand ... were not meshing very well?

A: Anjan Dutt apparently did not like *Haider* and then decided to make his own *Hamlet*.

P: [Is this film] something that you have been thinking about because of the quatercentenary of Shakespeare's death?

A: Oh no, no. We started the film late. We were supposed to start it in Feb. 23, 2014 and ended up making it in 2014 December and then it took very long for the film to get a release slot. I hadn't thought of it but I guess it is very fortuitous that it has turned out like this.

P: And the spate of Shakespeare films coming out from the Bangla film industry?

A: I think it is fortuitous but it was not all planned in that way. It was the same with *Mr. and Mrs. Iyer*. The day we ended the shoot, on the 20th of February ... Godhra happened and we ... felt, what have we unleashed? Because it was almost clairvoyant ....

P: Art anticipates life?
A: Well you can say that. But you know lot of riots had been happening already ... the Bombay riots ... I had been very disturbed about communal enmity ever since the demolishing of the Babri Masjid which my father and I discussed many times and we never thought it would happen in secular India. And then when I was an editor [of *Sananda*, a Bengali women's magazine], I think about fifty or sixty percent of my editorials were about communal harmony. Then it found its way into *Mr and Mrs Iyer*, which I never intended to be a film about Hindus and Muslims. It was just supposed to be a love story during a journey because I felt that a physical journey was a great metaphor for an internal one. But as I wrote, it found its way – and this [*Arshinagar*] I had always thought [about]. I have thought of different kinds of *Romeo and Juliet* ... one ... I thought of was the sister of a rebel in Manipur and a Jawan ... from different camps. But then another film like that had been made but set in Kashmir ... called *Yahan* which has the sister of a rebel and an army officer. So I scrapped that idea and in any case Manipur is almost impossible to shoot in. Then I thought of this.
P: To what would you attribute the popularity of the *Romeo Juliet* films in our film industry?
A: Everyone loves a lover. Love stories are popular.
P: Not love stories with tragic endings?
A: Well – even with a tragic ending. One of the grouses against my film was that there wasn't enough of the lovers – they want more love scenes. But for me this was enough since my intention ... was to show the strife. There were many political elements that came into the film. Land grab is something I have been very interested in ever since Singur and Nandigram [sites of people's movements against the State's land acquisition]. Then also the way in which the Gujarat riots were fanned by distributing petrol to the rioters. The way the fire brigade and the police were not allowed to be called until some hours had passed. And this was largely the work of politicians to further their own ends.
P: I think the most brilliant thing about the film is the naming because it lays out the context which is picked up by the music.
A: Yes because it's a Sufi name.
P: Yes, and this whole thing about '*porshi*' [neighbour] as being someone you don't know.
A: I believe in this song [alluded to in the title, *Arshinagar* or 'mirror city'], the '*porshi*' refers to ...
P: An aspect of yourself?
A: No, no. In Lalon's songs it actually refers to Shiraj ... '*Shiraj Lalon eksaathe roy lokkho jojon dure*' [Shiraj and Lalon remain together although a million miles apart]. So the *murshid* and the *chela* [mentor

and mentee], exist in the same space but far away. But it can also be interpreted as *'porshi'*, whom you have never seen – as somebody you perceive as the other but who is not actually the other. You just haven't seen him properly and it could be a mirror image of yourself. This harks back to *Advaityavaada* where nobody is the other. You remember the Shaivite poems of the tenth century, which both my husband and I love – one of them I remember – maybe the words are not exactly right – I used it in *Mr and Mrs Iyer* and this is translated by A.K. Ramanujan. It says: 'into what shall I plunge a dagger my lord, and what shall I take it out of when you are all the world?' Even when you are plunging a dagger into somebody you are really plunging it into yourself or into the lord. 'When you are all the world' – that means that I am part of you, he is part of you and that means we are one. So, what is the point of this futile violence?

P: When you were planning the film, was music dictating the way in which you were writing it?

A: I wanted to make it a musical. I was very charged with the idea of a musical ever since I made *Goynar Baksho* [Ornament Box] and we had that Bangla rap – *Zigaayo ore* [Ask her] – ever since then both Debojyoti Mishra, my music director and I have been thinking of making a musical. And then I thought that *Romeo and Juliet* lends itself very well to the idea of a musical.

P: And you thought of *Westside Story*?

A: *Westside Story* was also a musical – yes. I reviewed it. I felt that I had to see it again and was it still as exciting as I thought it was when I first saw it. It wasn't. But there were lots of good things in it – they were migrants in New York – here it was completely different. But I wanted to use dance. I wanted to depict violence – this violence that takes place between the gangs is an everyday affair and there is no point in showing actual violence. I thought let me show it symbolically through choreography. I wanted to stylize the violence. You can stylize violence in many ways – you can make it slow motion ... But here I wanted to make it as part of a dance. There was another dance which we had to take out because it was getting too long – this dance borrowed from the Manipuri martial arts. Only at the end when he slashes the neck of the other boy that you realize that, this was real violence. This was partly inspired by *Chicago* which is a great favourite, where you had real scenes interspersed with songs which were take-offs. Then it's also there in Brecht. So these were some of the inspirations. It is stylized, stylized, stylized and suddenly it is real – that's the form. And this a lot of people found difficult to accept largely because they have not had enough exposure. I think, the point is that this film needed an audience that had some exposure to world cinema, world theatre.

P: How do you locate the film? Because it has Dev [a popular male star who plays Romeo] in it, he has a fan following ... an audience.

A: That was the problem in fact. See Dev was taken because we could not find a young newcomer ... we wanted two new people. The girl was unseen enough.
P: I thought that Juli[Juliet] worked very well.
A: Yes, someone said, it was the Juliet of their imagination. Juliet works very, very well. She had this innocence and I didn't allow her to wear any makeup. The first thing that I would do in the morning was to really come and check whether she had secretly worn it! She was not allowed to back comb her hair and she was very obedient. Her role was also fairly simple – naïve, young girl. Now Dev we took finally, when we could not find a new comer, because he carries with him ... a romantic association of a romantic hero and also because there is a certain innocence about his face. I did ask him to lose about ten kilos which he never managed to do, sadly. But he was very cooperative. Another thing is that when you have a film which has a large budget you have to fall back on some box office stars ... that is a reality. As I am fond of saying, 'cinema is the art of the possible', because it involves so much money.
P: The other thing which worked really well for me was the use of Parvati Baul [a female folk singer] and that she is in the foreground while the riots are happening.
A: I am so glad that you like that. I think for some people it went on too long.
P: What was it like, working with Parvati Baul?
A: Wonderful. I had seen Parvati Baul on stage ... Later when we went backstage ... I asked her – 'if I ever want you to work in a film of mine, will you?' And she said 'why not?' But both she and I were noncommittal. I had initially wanted to use the Pakistani qawali singer Abida Parveen. But I found out that Abida Parveen had apparently not been singing much recently. She was having some lung problem .... She was not being able to reach the high notes – I have seen her live and she is absolutely wonderful but we could not get her. Then I saw Parvati Baul and her dreadlocks forming a sort of halo around her. I was struck by her energy. And so we photographed her like that, the locks going in front of the camera. Always right from the time that I wrote it, even when it was not supposed to be a musical, it was supposed to be Abida Parveen singing in the middle of a riot.
P: So that was the central image?
A: That was the central image, the counterpoint of the whole thing – like a musical counterpoint – you have the fire, people running and killing each other and you have this Sufi singer singing in the middle of it all, unaware almost. So it's the two opposite sides of human nature, one that is able to love and the other that only hates. Basically using love as a counterpoint to hate.

P: I was also struck by the fact that on the one hand it is a political film – there is a gritty edginess about the politics but there is this stylization, choreography and singing [too].

A: Even in the middle of the politics we have singing. [But] we [also] have a very sarcastic song called *'Percentage er khela dada'* [it is all a game of percentages] and the light changes.

P: I think the audience found it difficult to switch between the modes?

A: Perhaps. But this is what I wanted to do. I wanted to have realism and then just switch … this is very Brechtian actually.

P: And Shakespearian. I think there is a lot of realism in Shakespeare

A: But do we have this stylization?

P: I think so.

A: Because of the poetry?

P: Yeah. This is something that interests me about the play – the tone. The fact that you use rhyme and also humour – because it is a tragedy with a lot of humor and that is very Shakespearean to have humor in the midst of tragedy.

A: Did you find the humour? I mean a lot of people did not.

P: I thought there was a lot of humour in the give and take between Romeo and Juliet, also in scenes. Partha Chatterjee [reviewer of *Arshinagar* in *The Telegraph*] writes about that scene in the bathroom.

A: I think Partha Chatterjee got it right – he really understood the film.

P: So there is a certain lightness to it?

A: I did not want to make an earnest film. Sometimes subjects are such that you have to be – but I like a lightness of touch.

P: So when you were writing, were you thinking about the tone of the film?

A: You know the process of writing is a very instinctive one. Sometimes I think 'is this becoming too heavy?' But usually I am not thinking 'is this the tone I want to set?' When I work initially it's just instinctual – a lot of the stuff comes from the subconscious and that's the magic of writing or creating. You don't always know the source. Which is very different from you academics – you are always looking for intertextual [references].

P: The credits mentioned as screenplay writers, your name, Kunal Basu's [writer] and Srijato's [Bengali poet] names – how did that collaboration work?

A: I had said that I wanted to do a *Romeo and Juliet* where Juliet was Muslim and Romeo a Hindu and Kunal wrote the basic story line. I wanted to make it contemporary. But … I veered away from it quite a lot. I introduced, again my husband's idea, the relationship between Romeo's mother and Juliet's father to indicate that nothing had actually changed in thirty years … and I like the way it was photographed.

P: And Srijato?

A: Srijato came in when I decided to make it a rhymed musical. I had seen Koushik Sen's production of *Korkotkranti Desh* [Land of the Tropic of Cancer] which was written by Srijato in verse and that was brilliant and I thought Srijato was just the right person to do this.

P: In Bhardwaj's film ... if he didn't mention that it was taken from Shakespeare it wouldn't matter, but it would matter for your film, would it not?

A: Well, I think both for Vishal's film and for my film ... (I will just take *Maqbool* since it was very close to Shakespeare) certainly a knowledge of Shakespeare would make for a more enhanced viewing. Even without knowing it, the story is simple enough – lovers killed etc. But certainly if you know your Shakespeare then it's a much more enriched viewing. While you are watching *Maqbool*, you are getting all the, 'Oh, so these are the witches' – you get that extra little, it's a bonus.

P: You mentioned the framing of the puppeteer telling the story. What's the significance of that? Because she is also a gypsy figure, she moves around.

A: She does not move around a lot as the puppeteer but you do see her again in the graveyard. You can call her the chorus, the narrator – it is like the voice at the beginning ... 'Where civil strife makes civil life unclean'.

P: Is she like a prologue?

A: Yeah – she's like a *Sutradhar*, a narrator. The fact that she is a puppeteer makes it poignant that these kids are really puppets in the hands of society, no matter how adventurous they might try to be.

P: I wanted to ask you about the female characters – the Waheeda Rehman [Juliet's grandmother] character – it is as if the nurse character got split between the puppeteer, nurse and the [grandmother]?

A: This is another Brechtian element that I brought in – the puppeteer is also the nurse – she admits that when she winks at the audience and says, '*thakbo na ar ei para te, theke ki ar phal, dure kothao chole gie khulbo putul nacher dal*' [I will leave this neighbourhood and open a puppet show somewhere else]. She is taking the audience into confidence in a very Brechtian way. And Dadijan, I wanted as a kind of remnant of the old order. Her ancestors probably came along with Bahadur Shah as his entourage. They all came away from Awadh and she is the descendent of one of these. Tayeb says: "'*Bahadur Shahr Ujir amar dadur dadur dadu*' [Bahadur Shah's minister is my grandfather's grandfather's grandfather]. That could have been an exaggeration. But it is also something that I drew upon – she brings into the film that *tehzeeb* [courtesy] of the inside of the old Muslim household which is very interesting and you don't normally see. She still speaks with a smattering of Urdu and Hindustani whereas the others have become more Bengali with time.

P: And there's a certain graciousness about her.

Interview with Aparna Sen by Paromita Chakravarti 313

A: I wanted to show that Juliet's household was much more sophisticated than Romeo's who were very crass.

P: I wanted to ask about the Tybalt figure – Jishu [a popular Bengali film actor] playing Tybalt and we always associate Jishu with positive roles. Tybalt becomes a kind of a hero?

A: Tybalt is a character that I absolutely love. Tybalt is really my favourite character in *Romeo and Juliet*. What makes him interesting is his flamboyance and that smouldering anger that he has. I was wondering why he has that anger against Romeo? It's not there in the Shakespeare text but I decided to put it in anyway because it wouldn't hurt the film or the text – that he had a romantic weakness for Juliet and even though cousins do marry among Muslims, he would not ever be considered as Juliet's suitor because he was *asrito* – he had taken shelter, his mother was poor and his father had been poor and he just was one of the gang. I don't think Juliet's father or mother wanted Juliet to marry a gangster .... There was a song called, '*Shatash peti maal re, shatash peti maal/aaj loote ne, kal ki hobe, dyakha jabe kal*' [Twenty-seven containers of the stuff, loot today and think tomorrow] in which this has come out very well, but unfortunately it had to be taken out – where you show that these people deal in drugs nefariously which Reshma Bai mentions in the beginning. We cut in between [the song] with the two fathers relaxing with their whiskeys ... The words were something like: '*Construction site? Shob booked! Ekhon shudhu delay delay, bank e barche shud*' [Construction site? All booked! Now there will be delays while the interest multiplies in the bank]. This is what they [builders] do – they take the money, payments are complete now just delay it, delay it so that the interest grows. And they harbour these boys and give them instructions quietly and they do all their fighting for them whereas they themselves lead a sophisticated, refined life. And they want Juliet to have that refined life. It is okay to plot and plan – like Pervez/Paris and Sabir Khan, Juliet's father, they say: '*Ekhon aagun jwalte daao, chhai e dhelo jal/Arshinagar bosti bhenge, uthbeArshi Mall*' [Let the fire burn now, pour water on the ashes/The new Arshi Mall will rise on the ruins of the Arshinagar slum]. They are all part of the plot – they have this thing of how much percentage you will pay me and then the song '*Percentageer khelaa*' comes. So both the Khans and the Mitters pay this politician and the politician takes from both and his job is to clear out the slum. ... How does he clear the slum? Because he is supposed to be taking care of the place, he is the minister for urban development and the party has an image, as his assistants point out. So he engineers a riot so that the slum is cleared. ... Tayeb being a gangster would not be the right choice for Juliet. They fixed up somebody who lives in Dubai – they have got all their daughters married elsewhere. The older daughter is in

America, the younger daughter is going to be sent off to Dubai, they don't have to be a part of this murkiness.

P: But in my reading of *Romeo and Juliet* Mercutio appears to be the stronger character and Tybalt is somebody who just accidentally gets killed?

A: But if you see Baz Luhrmann ... that's the part I really like, and if you see the text – I read the text over and over. Actually, Tybalt lunges out at Romeo and Mercutio comes between them and gets killed. So that's exactly what I did.

P: So that's the Montey figure?

A: That's the Montey figure, Mercutio ... he shoves Romeo aside and he gets killed. Then later on he [Romeo] gets into some sort of daze – because his best friend has died and that's exactly there in the text. And then he kills Tybalt. He shoots Tybalt with Mercutio's gun and then Lady Capulet comes and she says that Romeo must die. Then all these people come, the police and all. But I did not have it like that. I had Tybalt's mother rather than Lady Capulet coming and that *hahakaar* [howling] like crying which became a metaphor for the grief of all mothers whose sons had died – that is why I enhanced it so much.

P: Any more Shakespeare adaptations in the offing?

A: I don't think so. I would love it – but let me see how these two come out, *Zulfikar* and this other one. And I don't know if I will get funding for it either, because this film is not doing that well. The form is too new for the general audience and Dev's fans.

P: Dev really gets beaten up in this film and I don't think his fans like it.

A: I don't think his fans like it. And I think they expected a blockbuster and this is not a blockbuster. This is basically a film against violence. Dev gets beaten up – that's another thing.

P: That I thought was excellent.

P: Romeo was not involved [in the violence]. But do you think it is excellent because you don't like Dev?

A: That too! But I think the anti-violence statement really comes across because he is the hero and he does not do it.

A: But I think in that scene he acted rather well actually. He is not reacting violently at all – and even when he shoots his face is a blank as if he is in a kind of daze. I think there he was quite good ... Romeo was trying to be not violent. He appealed to Tybalt, almost as a brother, a kinsman because he is Juliet's kinsman. So I had '*Tayeb, Tayeb bhai*' [Brother Tayeb] but we did not keep it because we had shot it in slow motion and we couldn't fit the dialogue to the lips ... But that is what we had – and Tayeb says: '*Bhaai bole tui daakish Jodi aar!*' [If you dare to call me brother ever!].

P: Would you consider making a Shakespeare film in English? I ask you because I am very intrigued by Rituporno Ghosh's *Last Lear*.

A: It's not really Shakespeare you know.
P: It's a take off.
A: I did not care for it but then that's me, that's subjective.
P: I think he said something which is interesting – he said that when *Saptapadi* [classic popular 1960s Bengali film] was made it still had an audience which was a purely popular, commercial Bengali film audience who would come and sit through fifteen minutes of Shakespeare in English.
A: I think people were less impatient ... I don't understand their brand of impatience though – because they will sit through a song like *Khokababu* or something [popular Bengali film song] ... but they will not sit through some Shakespeare ... their impatience is very selective.
P: Some people have said that the audience has objected to the use of rhyme. But on what grounds? Shakespeare also used blank verse! Is this because audiences have become divided?
A: Audiences have become divided and impatient and everything has to have a great pace. I think *Arshinagar* has a lot of pace – I don't think the pace is the problem. The thing is they will not accept something that is new. As Partha Chatterjee said in his article, they are very ensconced in the familiar, they don't want to get out of that comfort zone.
P: I think the objection to rhyme is part of that.
A: Yeah. Even Shirshendu Mukherjee said that in his review – every time you do something new, this is the risk you run. But then can you stop doing something new because of that? Not for me.
P: What new projects are you thinking of?
A: Nothing at the moment. Let me recover. And you know ideas take their time ... you can't just sit down and say, okay, now I am going to hatch an idea .... As you are walking or reading or watching a play or have gone to a music concert and suddenly the idea will come. It is very important to have continuous touch with the sister arts.
A: And you are very interested in theatre?
P: I am very interested in theatre and I have borrowed everything from theatre in this [film] and I think that's a great thing. I thought one of the USPs of the film is that I have borrowed from theatre. But instead of delighting in it people will say, 'what is this? I don't understand.' In *15 Park Avenue* too, in the end where I make a surreal leap – 'I don't understand, what is this?' 'Okay, leave it then, you don't have to understand it' – is all I can say. I can't explain everything, underlining everything. I have said to some people – 'do you understand poetry completely?' I don't always understand poetry completely – I mean unless it is explained by a professor or something – I don't. But that doesn't stop me from enjoying the poem. In fact ... often it is the little understood or not understood nuances that make it very interesting – make it so multidimensional and rich.

P: And I think that's the thing about Sufi music or Baul music as well – it's a language you see through a veil, a coded language. And if you don't know the codes, you are getting half of it and you are not getting the other half. But that is the fun.

A: Exactly. Somebody asked me – they liked the film ..., but it's always very iffy – they asked 'what were you trying to say when you had a Hindu kill a Hindu and a Muslim kill a Muslim?' I said, 'that's known as irony.' Shirshendu Mukherjee has pointed it out – he calls it *slesh* – it is irony. If you don't understand this transcendental leap into surrealism, if you don't understand a bit of irony – well, am I supposed to bring my language down and make it simpler until I am down to the lowest denomination? I don't think so.

P: Do you think people are uncomfortable with political satire? Have we lost the tradition of political satire?

A: There was a wonderful film called *Kangaal Maalshaat*. [A satirical Bengali novel by Nabarun Bhattacharya, made into a film by Suman Mukhopadhyay] My husband said it reminded him of Dario Fo. But I think it hardly played a week. So you put all this money into a film and it is not really fair on the producer ... Luckily this one isn't that bad. There are lots of people still going to see it and enjoying it. Audience opinion is divided very sharply – either they love it or they hate it.

P: How is it doing outside India?

A: Not yet. People are asking – but not yet.

P: Thank you.

Part VI

Shakespeare Films in Indian Cinemas
An Annotated Filmography

Antony and Cleopatra

1936, *Zan Mureed* (also listed as *Kafir-E-Ishq* in Urdu and *Nastik Prem* in Hindi), dir. A.H. Essa, Urdu/Hindi – possibly based on the stage adaptation by Anwaruddin Makhlis titled *Kali Nagan*, which had a moralistic happy ending.

1950, *Cleopatra*, dir. Raja Nawathe, Hindi – based on Cecil B. De Mille's *Cleopatra* (1934), with a moralistic view of the love affair.

2001, *Kannaki*, dir. Jayaraj, Malayalam – based loosely on Shakespeare's *Antony and Cleopatra*.

As You Like It

1959, *Sollu Thambi Sollu*, dir. T.V. Sundaram, Tamil – loosely based on Shakespeare's *As You Like It*.

Cymbeline

1923, *Champraj Hado,* dir. Nanubhai Desai, Silent, story by Vinod Kant – the earliest Indian Shakespeare film traced so far. Based on a play by Vaghji Asharam Oza and first performed in 1884, it adapted a Rajput story and Mughal setting with Shakespeare. A 1932 talkie version, *Sati Sone* aka *Champraj Hado* aka *Sone Rani*, dir. Madanrai Vakil was adapted by Joseph David.

1928, *Kusum Kumari*, dir. Saki, Silent – probably based on Chandrakali Ghose's popular adaptation in Bengali, *Kusum Kumari*, first performed in 1874. The film had Elizer and the director as lead players. A shorter version released again in 1929.

1930, *Mitha Zahar*, dir. A.P. Kapur, Silent – story by M.R. Kapoor, based on Narayan Prasad Betab's adaptation of *Cymbeline*, first performed in 1900 as *Mitha Zahr*.

1947, *Katakam*, dir. T.G. Raghavachari, Tamil – based on Sankaradas Swamigal's adaptation of *Cymbeline*, the film is primarily remembered as the only Tamil film featuring Suryakumari as heroine and its twelve songs, most of which were sung by Suryakumari.

Hamlet

1928, *Khoon-E-Nahak*, dir. Dada Athawale, Silent – based on the popular stage adaptation by Mehdi Hassan Ahsan.

1935, *Khoon Ka Khoon*, dir. Sohrab Modi, Hindi/Urdu – credited as the world's first full-length talkie of the play.

1936, *Manohara*, dir. unknown, Tamil – based on Pammal Sambandha Mudaliar's adaptation of *Hamlet* entitled *Amaladhithan* with Mudaliar playing a minor role.

1954, *Hamlet*, dir. Kishore Sahu, Hindi – a free adaptation heavily influenced by Lawrence Olivier's *Hamlet* (1948) with Sahu playing the title character.

1954, *Manohara*, dir. L.V. Prasad, Tamil (dubbed in Telugu and Hindi as well) – a remake of the 1936 *Manohara* based on Mudaliar's adaptation of *Hamlet* and inspired by the legend of Samson and Delilah.

1957, *Aasha*, dir., M.V. Raman, Hindi – a comedy/crime film which uses the Mousetrap device and claims inspiration from *Hamlet*.

1959, *Raja Makutam*, dir. B.N. Reddy, Telugu and Tamil – close to the plot of *Hamlet*.

2009, *Hamlet: Prince of Denmark*, dir. S. Nathan, English – feature film with Kabir Ahamed as *Hamlet*.

2009, *8 × 10 Tasveer*, dir. Nagesh Kukunoor, Hindi – a reworking of *Hamlet* as a murder mystery set in modern day Canada.

2012, *Karmayogi*, dir. V. K. Prakash, Malayalam – advertised as an adaptation of *Hamlet*, the film tells the story of Rudran Gurukkal, the lone male descendant of the Chathothu family of the Yogi community, in which Lord Shiva is believed to have been born.

2014, *Haider*, dir. Vishal Bhardwaj, Hindi – a contemporary adaptation of *Hamlet* and of *Curfewed Night* by Basharat Peer set in the insurgency-hit Kashmir conflicts of 1995.

2016, *Hemanta*, dir. Anjan Dutt, Bengali – adapts Hamlet as a thriller which deals with the intrigues of the Bengali movie industry.

Julius Caesar

2016, *Zulfiqar*, dir. Srijit Mukherjee, Bengali – adapts *Julius Caesar* and *Antony and Cleopatra* as a mafia thriller set in the Calcutta docks involving gang lords, a corrupt police force and politicians.

King John

1936, *Said-E-Havas*, dir. Sohrab Modi, Hindi/Urdu – based on Agha Hashr Kashmiri's adaptation of *Richard III* and *King John*.

King Lear

1949, *Gunasundari Katha*, dir. Kadiri Venkata Reddy, Telugu – based loosely on Shakespeare's *King Lear*, the film has supernatural and religious elements and a happy ending.

1997, *Rui Ka Bojh*, dir. Subhash Agarwal, Hindi – based on Chandra Kishore Jaiswal's novel *Gawah Ghair Hazir* and *King Lear*.

2003, *Baghbaan*, dir. Ravi Chopra, Hindi – thematically based on *King Lear* and marketed as an adaptation, it is also inspired by films like *Make Way for Tomorrow* (1937) the Marathi *Oon Paoos* (1954) and the Kannada *School Master* (1958).

2016, *Natsamrat*, dir. Mahesh Manjrekar, Marathi – based on a well-known play by V.V. Shirwadkar about an aging theatre actor abandoned by his children.

Macbeth

1930, *Khooni Taj* aka *All for the Crown*, dir., screenplay and camera by Pandurang Taligeri. Silent. Marathi title *Raktacha Rajmukut*.

1938, *Jwala*, dir. Vinayak, Hindi – loosely based on *Macbeth*, the film ends with Lady Macbeth and Banquo joining forces with the people against Macbeth.

1951, *Marmayogi*, dir. K. Ramnoth, Tamil – based on the novel *Vengeance* by Marie Corelli and *Macbeth*, this fantasy film was shot simultaneously in Hindi as *Ek Tha Raja*.

2001, *Yellamma*, dir. Mohan Koda, Telugu – set in 1850s India during the Sepoy Mutiny.

2003, *Maqbool*, dir. Vishal Bhardwaj, Urdu/Hindi – a crime drama set in the Mumbai underworld with the witches recast as corrupt police officers.

2016, *Veeram*, dir. Jayaraj, Malayalam/Hindi/English – epic historical film based on a ballad of North Malabar, it is about the fatal ambition of Chandu, a Kalarippayattu warrior, to wrest leadership of the clan.

Measure for Measure

1940, *Pak Daman* (aka *Shaheed-e-Naaz*), dir. Rustom Modi, Urdu/Hindi – based on Agha Hashr Kashmiri's stage adaptation of *Measure for Measure*.

Midsummer Night's Dream

2010, *10 ml Love*, dir. Sharat Katariya, Hinglish (Hindi + English) – set in contemporary India concerning three couples and with the mechanicals reimagined as a group of amateur *Ramlila* actors.

Othello

1961, *Saptapadi*, dir. Ajoy Kar, Bengali – a romantic drama set in wartime colonial Bengal based on a novel by Tarasankar Bandyopadhyay, the film is loosely based on *Othello* and features a performance of the murder scene as a play within the film.

1963, *Ratha Thilagam*, dir. Dada Mirasi, Tamil – a romantic war film based loosely on *Othello*, featuring Othello as an Indian army officer during the Sino-Indian war and Desdemona as a spy. Also has a performance of the murder scene as part of college theatricals.

1997, *Kaliyattam* (aka *The Play of God*), dir. Jayaraj, Malayalam – an adaptation of *Othello* set in the context of the *Theyyam* performance tradition and the caste politics of Kerala.

2006, *Omkara*, dir. Vishal Bhardwaj, Hindi – a crime drama set in the rural underworld of contemporary India.

2014, *Hrid Majharey*, dir. Ranjan Ghosh, Bengali – based on *Othello*, the film also incorporates elements from *Macbeth* and *Julius Caesar*.

2014, *Othello* (*We Too Have Our Othellos*), dir. Hemanta Kumar Das, Assamese – adapting the play to comment on the political unrest in the state of Assam.

Pericles

1935, *Khudadad*, dir. Fram Sethna, Hindi/Urdu – possibly based on Jehangir Pestonjee Khambatta's play, *Khudadad*, first performed in 1898.

Richard III

1936, *Said-E-Havas*, dir. Sohrab Modi, Hindi/Urdu – based on Agha Hashr Kashmiri's adaptation of *Richard III* and *King John*.

Romeo and Juliet

1937, *Ambikapathy*, dir. Ellis R. Dungan, Tamil – the film is about the poet Ambikapathy and his love for Amaravathi, daughter of the Chola king in AD 1083. The director, who did not know Tamil, used *Romeo and Juliet* for his inspiration and incorporated several scenes from the play in the script.

1948, *Romeo and Juliet*, dir. Akhtar Hussain, Hindi – based on the 1936 MGM *Romeo and Juliet* and influenced by the Parsi theatre tradition.

1957, *Ambikapathy*, dir. P. Neelakantan, Tamil – a remake of the popular 1937 film.

1970, *Heer Raanji* (aka *Rhanjha and Juliet*), dir. Chetan Anand, Hindi – based on the legend of Ranjha and Heer of Punjab and Shakespeare's *Romeo and Juliet*.

1973, *Bobby*, dir. Raj Kapoor, Hindi – Bollywood teen film based on *Romeo and Juliet* exploring caste, class and religious divides but with a happy ending.

1978, *Maro Charitra*, dir. K. Balachander, Telugu – with verbal quotations from *Romeo and Juliet*, the film features a cross-cultural romance between a Tamil boy and a Telugu girl.

1981, *Ek Duuje Ke Liye*, dir. K. Balachander, Hindi – a remake of *Maro Charitra*, now with a cross-cultural romance between a Tamil boy and a Marathi girl, with the lead actor of *Maro Charitra*, Kamal Hasan, reprising his role as Romeo.

1982, *Sanam Teri Kasam*, dir. Narendra Bedi, Hindi – referred to as a *Romeo and Juliet* appropriation starring Kamal Hasan, the film also has references to *Hamlet*.

1988, *Qayamat Se Qayamat Tak*, dir. Mansoor Khan, Hindi – a Bollywood cult film based on *Romeo and Juliet* and *West Side Story* (1961).

1991, *Saudagar*, dir. Subhash Ghai, Hindi – based on *Romeo and Juliet* the only Indian film on *Romeo and Juliet* which has a character parallel to Friar Laurence.

2000, *Josh*, dir. Mansoor Khan, Hindi – an adaptation of *West Side Story* (1961) and *Romeo and Juliet* with a happy ending against the backdrop of gang wars in Goa, and the only example of a director adapting *Romeo and Juliet* twice.

2012, *Ishaqzaade*, dir. Habib Faisal, Hindi – box-office hit based on *Romeo and Juliet* and the first film featuring a murder-suicide when the lovers agree to kill each other at the end.

2013, *Issaq*, dir. Manish Tiwari, Hindi – set in Banaras against the backdrop of the feuding sand mafia.

2013, *Goliyon Ki Raasleela Ram-Leela*, dir. Sanjay Leela Bhansali, Hindi – set in the fictional village of Ranjaar, infamous for its manufacture and sale of arms and the feud between two clans, Rajadi and Sanera.

2013, *Annayum Rasoolum* – dir. Rajeev Ravi, Malayalam – loosely inspired by *Romeo and Juliet*, the film is about a Muslim boy falling in love with a Christian girl whose family disapproves of their relationship.

2015, *Arshinagar*, dir. Aparna Sen, Bengali – a tragic musical adaptation in verse based in contemporary Kolkata against a backdrop of real estate gang wars between a Hindu and a Muslim clan.

2016, *Sairat*, dir. Nagraj Manjule, Marathi – featuring an inter-caste romance, the film's success has led to remakes being planned in Kannada, Telugu, Punjabi, Malayalam and Tamil.

The Comedy of Errors

1963, *Bhranti Bilas*, dir. Manu Sen, Bengali – based on Ishwar Chandra Vidyasagar's adaptation of *The Comedy of Errors* set in postcolonial Calcutta, this was the first full-length adaptation on film in the world.

324 *Shakespeare Films in Indian Cinemas*

1968, *Do Dooni Chaar*, dir. Debu Sen, Hindi – a loose remake of *Bhrantibilas* set in postcolonial Bombay.

1982, *Angoor*, dir. Sampooran Singh Gulzar, Hindi – a remake of *Bhrantibilas* and *Do Dooni Chaar*.

1997, *Ulta Palta*, dir. N.S. Shankar, Kannada – close to the original.

1998, *Ulta Palta*, dir. Relangi Narasimha Rao, Telugu – a remake of the Kannada *Ulta Palta*.

1999, *Heeralal Pannalal*, dir. Kawal Sharma, Hindi – with two sets of twins unaware of each other.

2012, *Aamait Asal Eemait Kusal*, dir. Ranjan Raghu Shetty, Tulu – a modern Indian adaptation of *The Comedy of Errors* in a language spoken mainly in south-west Karnataka and in the Kasaragod district of Kerala.

2014, *Double Di Trouble*, dir. Smeep Kang, Punjabi – an adaptation of the play based loosely on *Angoor* where the master-servant pairing is replaced with a father-son pairing.

The Merchant of Venice

1927, *Dil Farosh* (aka *Merchant of Hearts*), dir. M. Udwadia, Silent – based on Mehdi Hasan Ahsan's popular stage adaptation, this film was considered, until very recently, to be the first Indian adaptation of Shakespeare on film.

1940, *Shylock*, dir. S. Sarma, Tamil – based on *The Merchant of Venice*, the film was unsuccessful despite its authentic costumes and locale.

1941, *Zalim Saudagar*, dir. J.J. Madan, Hindi – the film is said to have enjoyed critical and commercial success in its time.

The Taming of the Shrew

1932, *Hathili Dulhan*, dir. J.J. Madan, Hindi – based on the popular Parsi theatre stage adaptation of the play, writer unknown.

1953, *Aan* (aka *The Savage Princess*), dir. Mehboob Khan, Hindi – based loosely on *Taming of the Shrew*, this was India's first technicolour film and one of the first Indian films to have had a worldwide release.

1958, *Mane Thumbida Hennu*, dir. B. Vittalacharya, Kannada – partially inspired by *Taming of the Shrew*.

1959, *Abba! A Hudgi*, dir. H.L.N. Simha, Kannada – a feminist president of the Anti-Marriage League is tamed by her lover with the help of a theatre group.

1962, *Gundamma Katha*, dir. Kamalakara Kameswara Rao, Telugu – a critically and commercially successful remake of *Mane Thumbida Hennu*, starring N.T. Rama Rao. Remade in Tamil as *Manithan Maravillai*.

1963, *Periya Idathu Penn*, dir. T.R. Ramanna, Tamil – one of the earliest of the 'taming' genre in Tamil. It starred M.G. Ramachandran and B. Saroja Devi.

1963, *Arivaali*, dir. A.T. Krishnaswami, Tamil – one of the most popular Shakespeare adaptations, starring Sivaji Ganesan.
1966, *Kumari Penn*, dir. Ramanna, Tamil – with Jayalalithaa. A loose adaptation of the clever woman tamed.
1971, *Savale Samali*, dir. Mallaiyam Rajagopal, Tamil – a variant on the 'taming' genre, it starred Sivaji Ganesan and was remade into Telugu, Malayalam, Kannada and Hindi.
1972, *Pattikkada Pattanama*, dir. P. Madhavan, Tamil – one of the most successful films of the year earning commercial and critical acclaim.
1973, *Manchali*, dir. Raja Nawathe, Hindi – based loosely on *Taming of the Shrew*, the film is an adaptation of Satyendra Sharat's novel *Swayamber*.
1976, *Bahaddur Gandu*, dir. A.V. Sheshgiri Rao, Kannada – close to the original, an upright soldier kidnaps egotistical princess and tames her.
1989, *Nanjundi Kalyana*, dir. M.S. Rajashekar, Kannada – a commercially successful romantic comedy drawing upon the Hindu mythology of Durga, the goddess of power and strength.
1990, *Mahajananiki Maradalu Pilla*, dir. Vallabhaneni Janardhan and Vijaya Bapineedu, Telugu – a remake of *Nanjundi Kalyana*.
2001, *Srimati Bhayankari*, dir. Anjan Banerjee, Bengali – based on the successful 1970s Bengali stage adaptation of *The Taming of the Shrew* of the same name.
2010, *Isi Life Mein*, dir. Vidhi Kasliwal, Hindi – the film was marketed as *The Taming of the Shrew – Reborn*, with 'Reborn' added to underscore that the original play had been modified to remove the alleged misogyny.

Twelfth Night
1929, *Bhul Bhulaiya*, dir. Vithaldas Panchotia, Silent, with Panchotia in the lead role.
1933, *Bhool Bhulaiyan*, dir. Jayant Desai, Hindi – adaptation from a play by Mehdi Hasan Ahsan, with elements of *The Comedy of Errors*.
1949, *Kanniyin Kaadhali*, dir. K. Ramnoth and A.K. Sekhar, Tamil – an adaptation, the film stars Madhuri Devi as the twins Adithan and Chandrika.
2009, *Dil Bole Hadippa*, dir. Anurag Singh, Hindi – a loose adaptation of *Twelfth Night*, the film tells the story of a young woman who disguises as a man to join an all-male cricket team.

Films with Shakespearean Scenes, Characters and References
1925, *Savkari Pash*, dir. Baburao Painter, Silent – adapted from Hari Narayan Apte's novel *Savkari Haak* (Call of the Moneylender), the film is also called *The Indian Shylock* where 'Shylock' represents the extortionist moneylender.

1953, *Anbu*, dir. M. Natesan, Tamil – enacts the bedchamber scene from *Othello* as part of college play.

1965, *Shakespeare Wallah*, dir. James Ivory, English – based on actor-manager Geoffrey Kendal's family and his travelling theatre company Shakespeareana, which earned him the sobriquet Shakespearewallah.

1968, *Izzat*, dir. T. Prakash Rao, Hindi – the film features Dharmendra playing a double role of the fair son of a zamindar and his black-faced illegitimate tribal son and references *Othello*.

1970, *Aranyer Din Ratri*, dir. Satyajit Ray, Bengali – references and quotes from *Romeo and Juliet*, balcony scene.

1970, *Sorkkam*, dir. T.R. Ramanna, Tamil – references the senate scene from *Julius Caesar* at a crucial point in the plot.

1973, *Rajapart Rangadurai*, dir. P. Madhavan, Tamil – cites and visually quotes *Hamlet* as a new type of play.

1974, *Eradu Kanasu*, dir. Dorai and S.K. Bhagavan, Kannada – references *Romeo and Juliet*. It's about a teacher of English who carries a copy of the *Complete Works* in several scenes and during a lecture on *Romeo and Juliet*, mistakenly calls Juliet, 'Lalitha', the girl he loves.

1980, *Karz*, dir. Subhash Ghai, Hindi – a revenge drama, the film makes sensational use of the Mousetrap device from *Hamlet*.

1981, *36 Chowringhee Lane*, dir. Aparna Sen, Bengali – the film tells the story of an Anglo-Indian English teacher, Violet Stoneham, who struggles to teach Shakespeare to uninterested schoolgirls in postcolonial India. Quotes *Twelfth Night* and *Lear*.

1990, *When Hamlet Went to Mizoram*, dir. Pankaj Butalia, English and Mizo – a documentary about the popularity of *Hamlet* in Mizoram.

1994, *1942: A Love Story*, dir. Vidhu Vinod Chopra, Hindi – set during the decline of the British Raj in India, the film visually quotes *Romeo and Juliet* through the forbidden love of Naren and Rajeshwari and references the iconic balcony scene.

1998, *Kuch Kuch Hota Hai*, dir. Karan Johar, Hindi – a coming-of-age romantic comedy which visually quotes Baz Luhrmann's *Romeo + Juliet* (1996).

2001, *Dil Chahta Hain*, dir. Farhan Akhtar, Hindi – the film references *Much Ado about Nothing* through the relationship between Akash and Shalini and visually cites *Troilus and Cressida*.

2002, *Such a Long Journey*, dir. Sturla Gunnarsson, English/Hindi – adaptation of the novel by Rohinton Mistry with strong echoes of *King Lear*.

2003, *In Othello*, dir. Roysten Abel, English – the film is about an Indian theatre group attempting to stage *Othello*.

2003, *Second Generation*, dir. Jon Sen, English/Bengali – Ch.4 UK two-part TV film on the lives of Bengali immigrants with overtones of *King Lear*.

2007, *The Last Lear*, dir. Rituparno Ghosh, English – based on Utpal Dutt's semi-autobiographical play *Aajker Shahjahan* and *King Lear*.
2007, *Om Shanti Om*, dir. Farah Khan, Hindi – a tribute to and spoof of 1970s Bollywood, the film is a revenge drama/comedy that uses the Mousetrap device from *Hamlet* in imitation of *Karz*.
2007, *Eklavya: The Royal Guard*, dir. Vidhu Vinod Chopra, Hindi – set in princely Devigarh, the film is about revenge and *dharma* with quotations from the sonnets, strong allusions to *Hamlet* and echoes of *Lear* and *Macbeth*.
2008, *Shakespeare M. A. Malayalam*, dir. Shyju and Shaji, Malayalam – the film is about a stage play writer Pavithran who is also known as Shakespeare.
2009, *Life Goes On*, dir. Sangeeta Datta, English – the film is about a Hindu family with three daughters in Britain coping with the death of the wife and mother, Manju with references to *King Lear*.
2013, *Matru ki Bijli ka Mandola*, dir. Vishal Bhardwaj, Hindi – a black comedy about land scams with a spoof inset of the Macbeths' conspiracy scene.
2013, *Fandry*, dir. Nagraj Manjule, Marathi – the film locates the sentiments of the wronged Shylock through the story of a low-caste boy, Jabya, who dares to fall in love with an upper-caste schoolgirl in a Maharashtrian village.
2014, *Jyobinte Pusthakam*, dir. Amal Neerad, Malayalam – a period thriller set in mid-twentieth-century Munnar about Jyob and the sibling rivalry of his three sons, the film has echoes of *King Lear*.

Complied with inputs from Koel Chatterji and Thea Buckley.

Filmography Chronological

Year	Name	Original Play	Director	Language
1923	*Champraj Hado*	Cymbeline	Nanubhai Desai	Silent
1925	*Savkari Pash*	Referencing Shakespeare	Baburao Painter	Silent
1927	*Dil Farosh (aka Merchant of Hearts)*	The Merchant of Venice	M. Udwadia	Silent
1928	*Kusum Kumari*	Cymbeline	Saki	Silent
1928	*Khoon-E-Nahak*	Hamlet	Dada Athawale	Silent
1929	*Bhul Bhulaiya*	Twelfth Night	Vithaldas Panchotia	Silent
1930	*Mitha Zahar*	Cymbeline	A.P. Kapur	Silent
1930	*Khooni Taj aka All for the Crown*	Macbeth	Pandurang Taligeri	Silent
1932	*Hathili Dulhan*	The Taming of the Shrew	J.J. Madan	Hindi
1933	*Bhool Bhulaiyan*	Twelfth Night	Jayant Desai	Hindi
1935	*Khoon Ka Khoon*	Hamlet	Sohrab Modi	Urdu/Hindi
1935	*Khudadad*	Pericles	Fram Sethna	Urdu/Hindi
1936	*Zan Mureed*	Antony and Cleopatra	A.H. Essa	Urdu/Hindi
1936	*Manohara*	Hamlet	Unknown	Tamil
1936	*Said-E-Havas*	King John and Richard III	Sohrab Modi	Urdu/Hindi
1937	*Ambikapathy*	Romeo and Juliet	Ellis R. Dungan	Tamil
1938	*Jwala*	Macbeth	Vinayak	Hindi
1940	*Pak Daman (aka Shaheed-e-Naaz)*	Measure for Measure	Rustom Modi	Urdu/Hindi
1940	*Shylock*	The Merchant of Venice	S. Sarma	Tamil
1941	*Zalim Saudagar*	The Merchant of Venice	J.J. Madan	Hindi
1947	*Katakam*	Cymbeline	T.G. Raghavachari	Tamil
1948	*Romeo and Juliet*	Romeo and Juliet	Akhtar Hussain	Hindi
1949	*Gunasundari Katha*	King Lear	Kadiri Venkata Reddy	Telugu

Year	Name	Original Play	Director	Language
1949	Kanniyin Kaadhali	Twelfth Night	K. Ramnoth and A.K. Sekhar	Tamil
1950	Cleopatra	Antony and Cleopatra	Raja Nawathe	Hindi
1951	Marmayogi	Macbeth	K. Ramnoth	Tamil
1953	Aan (aka The Savage Princess)	The Taming of the Shrew	Mehboob Khan	Hindi
1953	Anbu	Referencing Shakespeare	M. Natesan	Tamil
1954	Hamlet	Hamlet	Kishore Sahu	Hindi
1954	Manohara	Hamlet	L.V. Prasad	Tamil
1957	Aasha	Hamlet	M.V. Raman	Hindi
1957	Ambikapathy	Romeo and Juliet	P. Neelakantan	Tamil
1958	Mane Thumbida Hennu	The Taming of the Shrew	B. Vittalacharya	Kannada
1959	Sollu Thambi Sollu	As You Like It	T.V. Sundaram	Tamil
1959	Raja Makutam	Hamlet	B.N. Reddy	Telugu and Tamil
1959	Abba! A Hudgi	The Taming of the Shrew	H.L.N. Simha	Kannada
1961	Saptapadi	Othello	Ajoy Kar	Bengali
1962	Gundamma Katha	The Taming of the Shrew	Kamalakara Kameswara Rao	Telugu
1963	Ratha Thilagam	Othello	Dada Mirasi	Tamil
1963	Bhranti Bilas	The Comedy of Errors	Manu Sen	Bengali
1963	Periya Idathu Penn	The Taming of the Shrew	T.R. Ramanna	Tamil
1963	Arivaali	The Taming of the Shrew	A.T. Krishnaswami	Tamil
1965	Shakespeare Wallah	Referencing Shakespeare	James Ivory	English
1966	Kumari Penn	The Taming of the Shrew	Ramanna	Tamil
1968	Do Dooni Chaar	The Comedy of Errors	Debu Sen	Hindi
1968	Izzat	Referencing Shakespeare	T. Prakash Rao	Hindi
1970	Heer Raanji (aka Rhanjha and Juliet)	Romeo and Juliet	Chetan Anand	Hindi
1970	Aranyer Din Ratri	Referencing Shakespeare	Satyajit Ray	Bengali

(*Continued*)

Filmography Chronological

Year	Name	Original Play	Director	Language
1970	Sorkkam	Referencing Shakespeare	T.R. Ramanna	Tamil
1971	Savale Samali	The Taming of the Shrew	Mallaiyam Rajagopal	Tamil
1972	Pattikkada Pattanama	The Taming of the Shrew	P. Madhavan	Tamil
1973	Bobby	Romeo and Juliet	Raj Kapoor	Hindi
1973	Manchali	The Taming of the Shrew	Raja Nawathe	Hindi
1973	Rajapart Rangadurai	Referencing Shakespeare	P. Madhavan	Tamil
1974	Eradu Kanasu	Referencing Shakespeare	Dorai and S.K. Bhagavan	Kannada
1976	Bahaddur Gandu	The Taming of the Shrew	A.V. Sheshgiri Rao	Kannada
1978	Maro Charitra	Romeo and Juliet	K. Balachander	Telugu
1980	Karz	Referencing Shakespeare	Subhash Ghai	Hindi
1981	Ek Duuje Ke Liye	Romeo and Juliet	K. Balachander	Hindi
1981	36 Chowringhee Lane	Referencing Shakespeare	Aparna Sen	Bengali
1982	Sanam Teri Kasam	Romeo and Juliet	Narendra Bedi	Hindi
1982	Angoor	The Comedy of Errors	Sampooran Singh Gulzar	Hindi
1988	Qayamat Se Qayamat Tak	Romeo and Juliet	Mansoor Khan	Hindi
1989	Nanjundi Kalyana	The Taming of the Shrew	M.S. Rajashekar	Kannada
1990	Mahajananiki Maradalu Pilla	The Taming of the Shrew	Vallabhaneni Janardhan and Vijaya Bapineedu	Telugu
1990	When Hamlet Went to Mizoram	Referencing Shakespeare	Pankaj Butalia	English and Mizo
1991	Saudagar	Romeo and Juliet	Subhash Ghai	Hindi
1994	1942: A Love Story	Referencing Shakespeare	Vidhu Vinod Chopra	Hindi
1997	Rui Ka Bojh	King Lear	Subhash Agarwal	Hindi
1997	Kaliyattam	Othello	Jayaraj	Malayalam
1997	Ulta Palta	The Comedy of Errors	N.S. Shankar	Kannada

Filmography Chronological

Year	Name	Original Play	Director	Language
1998	Ulta Palta	The Comedy of Errors	Relangi Narasimha Rao	Telugu
1998	Kuch Kuch Hota Hai	Referencing Shakespeare	Karan Johar	Hindi
1999	Heeralal Pannalal	The Comedy of Errors	Kawal Sharma	Hindi
2000	Josh	Romeo and Juliet	Mansoor Khan	Hindi
2001	Kannaki	Antony and Cleopatra	Jayaraj	Malayalam
2001	Yellamma	Macbeth	Mohan Koda	Telugu
2001	Srimati Bhayankari	The Taming of the Shrew	Anjan Banerjee	Bengali
2001	Dil Chahta Hain	Referencing Shakespeare	Farhan Akhtar	Hindi
2002	Such a Long Journey	Referencing Shakespeare	Sturla Gunnarsson	English and Hindi
2003	Baghbaan	King Lear	Ravi Chopra	Hindi
2003	Maqbool	Macbeth	Vishal Bhardwaj	Hindi
2003	Second Generation	Referencing Shakespeare	Jon Sen	English and Bengali
2003	In Othello	Referencing Shakespeare	Roysten Abel	English
2006	Omkara	Othello	Vishal Bhardwaj	Hindi
2007	The Last Lear	Referencing Shakespeare	Rituparno Ghosh	English
2007	Om Shanti Om	Referencing Shakespeare	Farah Khan	Hindi
2007	Eklavya: The Royal Guard	Referencing Shakespeare	Vidhu Vinod Chopra	Hindi
2008	Shakespeare M. A. Malayalam	Referencing Shakespeare	Shyju and Shaji	Malayalam
2009	Hamlet: Prince of Denmark	Hamlet	S. Nathan	English
2009	8 × 10 Tasveer	Hamlet	Nagesh Kukunoor	Hindi
2009	Dil Bole Hadippa	Twelfth Night	Anurag Singh	Hindi
2009	Life Goes On	Referencing Shakespeare	Sangeeta Datta	English
2010	10 ml Love	Midsummer Night's Dream	Sharat Katariya	Hinglish
2010	Isi Life Mein	The Taming of the Shrew	Vidhi Kasliwal	Hindi
2012	Karmayogi	Hamlet	V.K. Prakash	Malayalam
2012	Ishaqzaade	Romeo and Juliet	Habib Faisal	Hindi

(Continued)

332 Filmography Chronological

Year	Name	Original Play	Director	Language
2012	Aamait Asal Eemait Kusal	The Comedy of Errors	Ranjan Raghu Shetty	Tulu
2013	Issaq	Romeo and Juliet	Manish Tiwari	Hindi
2013	Goliyon Ki Raasleela Ram-Leela	Romeo and Juliet	Sanjay Leela Bhansali	Hindi
2013	Annayum Rasoolum	Romeo and Juliet	Rajeev Ravi	Malayalam
2013	Matru ki Bijli ka Mandola	Referencing Shakespeare	Vishal Bhardwaj	Hindi
2013	Fandry	Referencing Shakespeare	Nagraj Manjule	Marathi
2014	Haider	Hamlet	Vishal Bhardwaj	Hindi
2014	Hrid Majharey	Othello	Ranjan Ghosh	Bengali
2014	Othello (We Too Have Our Othellos)	Othello	Hemanta Kumar Das	Assamese
2014	Double Di Trouble	The Comedy of Errors	Smeep Kang	Punjabi
2014	Jyobinte Pusthakam	Referencing Shakespeare	Amal Neerad	Malayalam
2015	Arshinagar	Romeo and Juliet	Aparna Sen	Bengali
2016	Hemanta	Hamlet	Anjan Dutt	Bengali
2016	Veeram	Macbeth	Jayaraj	Malayalam
2016	Natsamrat	King Lear	Mahesh Manjrekar	Marathi
2016	Sairat	Romeo and Juliet	Nagraj Manjule	Marathi
2016	Zulfikar	Referencing Shakespeare	Srijit Mukherjee	Bengali

Index

Aajker Shahjahan 163, 167, 327
Abel, Royston 17, 326, 331, interview 292–303
Abhinavabharati 128
Abhinavagupta 128–129
Abraham, John 77
Adhikary, Manabendra 273
Aebischer, Pascale 195, 199n44
Agarwala, Jyotiprasad 269–270, 282n6, 282n7
'Ahsan', Mendhi Hasan 118, 121–123, 320, 324–325
Al Bassam, Sulayman 37
Allen, Richard 108n20, 252, 254, 256, 262, 266n3
Al Hamlet Summit 37
Ali, Tariq 286–287
Anandan 209
Anand, Mulk Raj 117–118, 125n18
Annals and Antiquities of Rajasthan 120
Apte, Narayan Hari 122
Aravindan 77
Assamese: identity 270, 300; drama 268; insurgency 271– 272, 274, 282n15, 281; impact Left movement 277– 278, 281; language politics 270, 282n16; outsiders in 275–276; plays influenced by Shakespeare: *Chakradhwaj Sinha* 268; *Lachit Borphukan* 268; *Nilamber* 269; *Pratap Sinha* 268
Ashcroft, Bill 9, 19n22
Art film 1, 3–4, 17, 45–46, 157, 292
Athawale, K. B. (Dada) 118, 121, 320, 328

Bahri, Deepika 158, 159n 12, 160n 43
Balachander, K. 104, 109n28, 323, 330
Banerjee, Dibakar 181

Barpujari, Manoj 270
Barua, Jahnu 271, 273, 281
Barua, Nip 271
Barua, Padmanath Gohain 268, 269
Barua, Padum 271
Barua, Parbati Prasad 271
Barua, Rohini Kumar 271
Baruah, Monjul 272–273
Baruah, Parthajit 16
Baskaran, Theodore. S 204, 206, 213n9, n16, 214n27, 215n45, n51, n54, n57, n58, n60, n62, n72, 216n88, n89, 217n110
Basu, Kunal 310
Beeman, William O. 206, 215n59
Bengaliness 13–14, 161–178, anti-Bengali 276; identity 14, 163–164, 166–170, 173, 175–177, 276, 312; language 108, 118, 162, 170, 255
Berges, Paul Mayeda 144–145
Bergman 299
Betab, Narayan Prasad 121, 319
Bezborua, Lakshminath 268
bhadralok 171, 176, 178n23, 267n19
Bharathan 77
Bhardwaj, Vishal 11, 23–44, 103, 133, 302, 312, 320–322, 327, 331–332; global 23; *rasa* in 13, 135, 139; Shakespeare tragic trilogy 2, 5–6, 10–11, 19n12, 23–44, 45, 94, 106, 118, 180; women 24–25, 28–30, 32, 37–38, 41, 43n20; transnationalism 196, violence 11, 23, 26, 24, 30, 31–33, 35–42, 139; *see also* Hindi cinema
Bharucha, Nilofer 173
Bhattacharya, Nabarun 316
Bhatia, Nandi 242
Bhushan, Pandit 122

Bollywood *see* Indian cinema
Bombay 7, 13, 54, 65–66, 115, 324; riots 308
Bora, Hem 272
Borah, Manju 273, 280
Borah, Pranjal 275, 282n13
Borgohain, Homen 271
Borkakoti, Ramakanta 268
Borthakur, Gopal 272
Borua, Ghanshyam 268
Borua, Gunjanan 268
Borua, Ratnadhar 268
Bose, Mihir 202, 214n30
Bose, Shonali 181
Bradshaw, P 32
Brians, Paul 143, 158n5
Brecht, Bertolt 243, 309, 311, 312
Buchanan, Judith 113, 124n2
Buckley, Thea 14–15, 327
Burnett, Mark Thornton 8, 15, 34, 45, 94
Burt, Richard 8–9, 19n16, n17, n18, n19, 61n9, 248, 250n19
Butalia, Pankaj 17, 300, 326, 330, interview 285–291

Caird, John 186
Calbi, Maurizio 48, 61n10
Callahan, Dympna 185
Cartelli, Thomas 68, 74n17, 196, 197n11
Carroll, W. C. 43n11, n15
caste 46, 83, 94, 98, 172, 202, 322; *chekavan* 88; divisions 82; inter-caste 323; lower caste 79, 82, 92n3, 272, 323, 327; Kerala 322; Tamil 202–212; unseeing caste 82; untouchability 49–55, 58; warrior caste 78, 89
de Certeau, Michel 261
Chadha, Gurinder 144, 170
Chakravarti, Paromita 13–14, 237n28, 250n17, 267n16
Chakravorty, Swapan 162, 169, 177n6
Champraj Hado and Sona Rani (Gujarati play) 119
Chapel, Peter 286
Charulata 166
Chatterjee, Koel 12, 327
Chatterjee, Partha 162, 177n5, 227, 235, 311, 315
Chattopadhyay, Bankim Chandra 15, 253, 306

Chaudhuri, Sukanta 187, 197n26
Chellappan, K. 217n97, 238, 239, 249n2
Chitgopekar, Nilima 229, 230, 237n14, n17
Chekov, Anton 76
Chicago 309
Chowdhury, Anjan 176
Chowdhury, Prasannalal 268, 269
cinematic realism 64
Chopra, Vidhu Vinod 11, 45, 56, 61n7, 198n34, 326–327, 330–331
Chowdhary, Sumit 285
Cohen, Ruby 30
colonial: education 14, 66, 91, 168, 270; Minute 159n20, 177n1, 253; modernity 163, 173, 177
The Complete Works of Shakespeare 148–149, 326
Coppola, Francis Ford 135
The Corsican Brothers 254
Cukor, George 14, 201–205, 207, 209, 214n18
culture: acculturation 9, 24, 26, 48, 65; Anglo-Indian 164; Bengali 163, 166, 168, 171, 175, 178n20; difference 172; English/British 47, 147, 169–170; Folk 68, 78; high 97, 144, 167, 169; Intercultural 13–14, 65, 73, 159n18, 200–202, 208, 213; Kerala 91; Kannada 222–224; Muslim 97, 108n20, 108n21; *nawabi* 97, 108n21; oral 290; parallel culture 202; Parsi 150, 153, 157; popular 77, 96, 104, 225, 248, 290; of resistance 200; Tamil 201, 204, 249; Telugu 65; Western 162–164, 174, 200, 289; multiculturalism 157, 171

Dabke, D. D. 121
Daniel, J. C. 77
Daniélou, Alain 229
Das, Hemanta Kumar 16, 273–280, 322, 332
Das, Sisir Kumar 117, 121, 122
Dasgupta, Chidananda 7, 11n19, 304
David, Joseph 120
death 11, 12, 16, 25, 26, 28, 31, 33–34, 36–37, 40, 41, 43, 50, 52, 55, 57–60, 80–82, 84, 86, 88–89, 94–95, 100–101, 104–106, 117, 134, 136–137, 167, 182–186, 207, 217n103, 244, 252, 270
Delwadakar, Gopalji 121
Desai, Jayant 122, 325, 328

Desai, Jigna 168, 172, 178n15, 196n9
Desai, Nanubhai 119, 319, 328
Dhanraj, Deepa 286
Dharma: as duty 11, 46, 49–50, 53–60, 223, 232–235, 327; as religion 15
Dharamsey, Virchand 114, 118, 120, 123, 124, 125n6, n20, n23, n26, 126n32
Dhondy, Farrukh 286
diaspora 172; Bengali 166, 170, 171; British films 172 (*My Beautiful Laundrette, East is East, Bend It Like Beckham*); 'Diaspora pudding' 157–158; film 144–145, 147–148; Indian 23, 143, 170; Parsi 143–144, 146; queer 172
Dickey, Sara 213n1, n4, n15, 214n32, 215n50, n70, 216n85, 92, 217n109
Dickson, Andrew 2, 18n2, 197n24, 198n28, 198n31, 215n75
Dionne, Craig 8, 19n14, 196n4, 210, 217n102
Divakaruni, Chitra Banerjee 144
Dr. Faustus 268
Dumas, Alexandre 254
Dungan, Ellis. Roderick 14, 67, 201, 203–205, 209, 213n7, 215n69, 216n83, 322, 328
Dutt, Utpal 96, 163, 167, 246, 327
Dutt, Anjan 176–177, 306, 307, 320, 332
Dutta, Sangeeta 14, 144, 161, 166, 327, 331
Dutta, Jadumoni 272
Dwyer, Rachel 7, 180, 195n4

Earth 145
Eisenstein, Sergei 127, 130
Eliot, T. S. 157
erotic 39, 41, 81–82, 88, 90–91, 261, 209

Faiz, Ahmed Faiz 39
Fassbender, Michael 31
feminist criticism 27–28, 36, 38, 42n9, 42n10, 44n25, 235
feminist politics 270
Fire 145
Freleman, William C. 43n18
Fo, Dario 316
folk traditions 62, 64, 67, 72; *baul* 301, (Lalon) 308, (Parvati) 310, 316; *Bein Dia Khlem* 286;

buffoon 79, 281; dance 258; *harikatha* 64; impersonator 301; *janapadam* 11, 64–65, 68–71; *jatra* 96, 164; *kalari* 12, 78, 85, 89–90, 321; *kaliyattam* 79, 81; *kathaprasangam* 76, 92n2; *komalikolam* 80; *komali theyyam* 79; lore 11, 27, 34, 64–65, 68–69, 71–72, 78, 89, 91, 94; music 5, 62, 89, 257, 292; 'Northern Ballads' 78, 89–90; performance 68, 79; *poorakkali* 85–86, 92n6; singer 310; theatre 64, 164, 256; *theyyam* 12, 79–82, 85, 92n3, 92n4, 322; *thira* 79, 92n3; *theechamundi* 79, 80, 92n4; *tholu bommalata* 64, 68
fool figure 55, 72, 79, 113, 151–155, 169, 281
Frémaux, Thierry 194, 199n43
Freud, Sigmund 186

Galsworthy 76
Ganesan, Sivaji 211, 213n5, 217n99, n112, 242, 246, 259n18; *Enathu Suyasarithai*(My Autobiography) 325
Gangar, Amrit 12
Garga, B. D. 123, 125n12, 126n34, 213n15
gender 15, 158, 172–174, 196n9, 201, 221, 239; and genre 41; dynamics 201, 210; flouting norms of 226–235; inversion of roles 32, 109n30; and power 28; as performed 246; and race 245; reformulating genre 11; re-gendering 25; segregation 108; stereotypes 103, 106; Tamil cinema 210; violence 26, 42n9, 43n10
George, K. G. 77
Gesta Danorum 113
Ghatak, Ritwik 167, 176, 178n14
Ghosh, Chandrakali 121, 319
Ghosh, Rituparno 14, 161, 163, 176, 178n11, 304, 327, 331
Gitanjali 157
globalisation 8, 9, 98, 170
The Godfather 135
Gogoi, Dinesh 272
Gopalakrishnan, Adoor 77
Gopalan, Lalitha 27, 42n9, 107n4
Gopinath, Gayatri 172, 178n28
de Grazia, Margreta 185–186, 197n20
Grease 144

336   Index

Greene, Graham 204n40
Gulzar 260, 261, 324, 330
Gunnarsson, Sturla 13, 143–145, 147–152, 157–158, 159n9, 159n17, 326, 331
Gunratane, Antony 29
Gupt, Somnath 117, 122–123, 125n16
Gustad, Kaizad 180, 181, 196n6
Guttal, Vijaya 221, 236n1
Guy, Randor 205, 211, 215n48, n52, n61, 216n89

Habba Khatoon 40
Haksar, Anamika 293
Halle, Randall 157
Hanse, Timothy Das 272
Hariharan, K. 208
Hariharan, T. 90
Hashr, Agha 118, 320–322
Heidenberg, Mike 34
Henderson, Diane E. 42n23
Hepworth 118
Hic Mulier 227, 228, 231, 236n10
Hogan, Lalitha Pandit 34
Hollywood 2–3, 9, 13–15, 18, 47, 201, 206, 210; anti-Hollywood 196n11; *Broken Horses* 47; cinematic norm 146; collaboration with Kollywood 200–206; conventions 146, 208, 212; cultural translatability 209; early films popular in India: *Exploits of Elaine* 116; *Perils of Pauline* 116; *The Black Pirate* 116; *The Iron Claw* 116; *The Mark of Zorro* 116; *The Thief of Baghdad* 116; *The Three Musketeers* 116; intermeshing with Bollywood 18, 19n16, 46; Shakespeare 14, 200, 212; early teleseries popular in India: *Lucille Love* 116; *The Black Box* 116; *The Broken Coin* 116; *The Purple Mask* 116
Howard, Anthony 24, 42n5
hubris 28
Hunter, Lynnette 97
Hussein, Nasir 95
Hutcheon, Linda 201, 204, 206, 214n23
hybrid 47, 170–175; colonial subjects 253; as generic of Hindi cinema 45; heritage in Tamil cinema 14–15, 200, 73; Parsi theatre 6

Ibsen 76
In A Grove 134
Indian cinema 1–18, 23, 25–27, 38–39, 42n8, 47, 63, 73n10, 77, 93, 107n4, 114, 120, 125n11, 164, 178n12, 178n14, 181, 194, 196n9, 200, 203, 210, 212, 213, 222, 225, 236, 251–253, 255, 259, 265, 270, 319
  Assamese 4, 16, 268–282; *Antareen* 272, 273; *Aparoopa* 273, 281; *Badan Barphukan* 271, 282n9; *Baibhab-A Scam in verse* 273, 280; *Gonga Silonir Pakhi* 271; *Halodhia Choraye Baodhan Khai* 271; *Jetuka Pator Dore* 272; *Joymoti* 269–271, 279; *Makaru Maram* 271; *Monomoti* 271, 282n9; *Piyoli Phukan* 282; *Puberun* 271; *Ranga Police* 271; *Ronga Modar* 272; *Rupahi* 271; *Sandhya Raag* 271; *Sankalpa* 272; *Sesh Upohar* 272; *Siraj* 271, 282n9; *Surya Tejor Anya Naam* 272; Films (Shakespeare): *Aparoopa* 273, 281; *Baibhab-A Scam in verse* 273, 280; *We Too Have Our Othellos* 5, 16, 274–280
  Bengali 3, 4, 13, 16, 161–177, 178n12, 178n14, 240, 245–247, 251, 253–254, 266, 272, 315; *Apur Sansar* 167; *Balaka* 169; *Charulata* 166; *Goynar Baksho* 309; *Kangaal Maalshat* 316; *Korkotkranti Desh* 312; *Lookochuri* 254, 255; Films (Shakespeare): *Arshinagar* 17, 108n22, 177, 304, 308, 311, 313, 315, 323, 332; *Bhranti Bilash* 3, 16, 251–266, 323, 329; *Hemanta* 177, 320, 332; *Saptapadi* 16, 177, 240, 245–246, 266n7, 315, 321, 329; *Zulfikar* 306, 314, 332
  Bollywood 2, 18n4, 19, 106; adaptation 9, 12; affinity for twins 254; aversion to tragic ending 101; *filmi* style 3, 107n5; global reach/critical esteem 4–5, 9, 26; Hindi film industry 3; item number 181; typical (romantic musical sequence) 47, 94, 96, 108n18; (representative of) 93; (thematic trope) 95, 100, 204;

(vocabulary) 101; (astrologic belief) 102; regional vs local 4–5, 10; remakes in 4–5, 9; transformative power 9–10; women in 109n27; *see also* Hindi cinema

diaspora 144–145, 147, 157, 170; *Bend It Like Beckham* 172, 174; *Bollywood Hollywood* 46; *Bombay Talkie* 147; *Brick Lane* 170; *Bride and Prejudice* 144; *East is East* 172, 174; *Heat and Dust* 147; *Monsoon Wedding* 144, 198n37; *My Son The Fanatic* 174; *Salaam Bombay* 144; *The Householder* 147; *The Mistress of Spices* 144, 145; *The Namesake* 170; *Trishna* 144; Films (Shakespeare): *Life Goes On* 5, 14, 144, 161, 166–176, 179n29, 327, 331; *Such a Long Journey* 13, 159n11, 326, 331, 143–158, 326, 331; *Second Generation* 5, 14, 161, 173–176, 326, 331

English *Mr and Mrs Iyer* 305, 307–309; *15 Park Avenue* 314; Films (Shakespeare): *In Othello* 17, 292, 296, 326, 331; *36 Chowringhee Lane* 14, 17, 161, 163–165, 167, 176, 304, 306, 326, 330; *Last Lear* 14, 161, 163–169, 176, 314, 327, 331; *Shakespeare Wallah* 47, 147–148, 159n18, 167, 178n13, 326, 329

Hindi 5, 7–10, 15, 23, 25–26, 34, 37, 42n8, 45, 47, 93, 95, 98, 100–106, 109n25, 135, 139, 161, 170, 176, 196n4, 198n27, 224, 242, 251, 254, 305, 319–332; *Acchut Kanya* 255; *Afsana* 254–255; *Alam Ara* 6, 114, 120, 122, 124; *Bade Miyan Chhote Miyan* 251; *Baharon ke Sapne* 95; *Bandit Queen* 27; *Beta* 100; *Betaab* 222; *Chaal Baaz* 254; *Chori* 222; *Damul* 33; *Dil Se* 38; *Dilwale Dulhaniya Le Jayenge* 100; *Gulaal* 187; *Hum Dil de Chuke Sanam* 100; *Judwaa* 254; *Kabhi Khushi Kabhi Gham* 174; *Kagaz Ke Phool* 98; *Kaminey* 24; *Kishen Kanhaiya* 254; *Maine Pyaar Kiya* 102; *Madhumati* 98; *Mother India* 38; *My Brother Nikhil* 188; *Parinda* 47; *Ponga Pandit* 222; *Raja Hindusthani* 100; *Ram aur Shyam* 254; *Seeta Aur Geeta* 254–255; *Tezaab* 101; *The Terrorist* 38; *Yahan* 307; *Yeh to Kamal ho Gaya* 251; Films (Shakespeare): *1942: A Love Story* 47–48, 198n34, 326, 330; *Angoor* 7, 251–252, 254–255, 257–258, 260, 262–264, 266, 324, 330; *Do Dooni Char* 251–252, 254–255, 258, 260–262, 266; *Ek Duuje Ke Liye* 2, 95–96, 100–101, 103–105, 108n22, 323, 330; *Eklavya: The Royal Guard* 11, 45–60, 61n22, 327, 331; *Haider* 5, 7, 11, 13, 23–25, 35–42, 44n27, 45, 60, 87, 118, 133, 138–139, 180, 186, 195n4, 259, 291, 307, 320, 321, 332; *Issaq* (Hindi)12, 161, 323, 332; *Ishaqzaade* 12, 105, 161, 305, 306, 323, 331; *Josh* 105, 109n32, 323, 331; *Kuch Kuch Hota Hai* 198n34, 326, 331; *Maqbool* 5, 11, 42n8, 43n13, 43n16, 45, 52, 60, 94, 130–131, 134–135, 161, 180, 195n4, 198n34, 307, 312, 321, 331; *Matru ki Bijli ka Mandola* 24, 327, 332; *Omkara* 5, 11, 13, 19n12, 23–24, 32–36, 38, 42n8, 43n23, 45, 94, 161, 180, 195n4, 214n31, 307, 322, 331; *Om Shanti Om* 109n31, 327, 331; *Qayamat Se Qayamat Tak* 12, 93–96, 98–106, 106n1, 109n25, 323, 330; *Ramleela* 12, 105, 305–306, 323, 332; *Zalim Saudagar* 122, 324, 328

Indie 13–14, 180–188, 193–195, 195n4, 196n9, 196n11; *Bombay Boys* 180–181, 196n9; *Hyderabad Blues* 180; *Ugly* 181; Films (Shakespeare): *10ml Love* 14, 180, 186–187, 190–192, 194–195, 195n2, 195n4, 321, 331; *8×10 Tasveer* 14, 180–186, 195, 195n3, 195n4, 197n14, 197n17, 320, 331

Kannada 4–5, 15–16, 25, 63, 170, 200, 221, 225, 235–236, 251, 263, 266, 321, 323–326,

329–330; *School Master* 321; *Priya* 241; Films (Shakespeare): *Ulta Palta* 5, 251–252, 257, 260, 263, 324, 330; *Nanjundi Kalyana* 15, 221–236, 325, 330

Malayalam 4–5, 11, 62–63, 75–92, 301, 302, 331–332; *Adbhutam* 78; *Bibhatsa* 78; *Karunam* 78; *Kattathe Kilikkoodu* 77; *Oru Vadakkan Veeraghadha* 90; *Santham* 78; *Vigathakumaran* 77; Films (Shakespeare): *Kaliyattam* 11, 77–79, 81–82, 91–92, 322, 330; *kaliyattam* 81, 92n5; *Kannaki* 11, 78, 83–84, 89, 92, 319, 331; *Karmayogi* 5, 11–12, 78, 84–87, 89, 91–92, 118, 320, 331; *kelipatra* 5, 84–89; *Veeram* 5, 7, 11, 78, 89–92, 321, 332; lack of Shakespeare 76–77

Marathi 123, 180, 206, 209, 321, 323, 327, 332; *Poona Raided* 123; *Prabhavati* 123; Films (Shakespeare): *Fandry* 327, 332; *Natsamrat* 18n7, 321, 332; *Oon Paoos* 321; *Sairat* 5, 323, 332, 18n7; *Savkari Pash-Indian Shylock* 122, 325, 328

Mizo Films (Shakespeare): *When Hamlet Went to Mizoram* 17, 285–287, 300, 326, 330

Punjabi *Khamosh Pani* 34; Film (Shakespeare): *Double de Trouble* 251–252, 255, 257, 259–260, 262–266, 324, 332

Silent cinema 114, 118–119, 121, 125n20; *Raja Harishchandra* 114; *Shakuntala* 115; Films (Shakespeare): *Bhul Bhulaiya* 122–123, 325, 328; *Champraj Hado* 7, 12, 114, 119–120, 124, 319, 328; *Dil Farosh* 114, 121, 125n28, 253, 324, 328; *Khoon-E-Nahak* 114, 117–118, 120–121, 320; *Khooni Taj* 26, 123, 321, 328; *Kusum Kumari* 114, 120, 121, 319, 328; *Meetha Zahar* 114, 121, 319, 328; *Raktacha Rajmukut* 123, 321

Tamil 201, 202, 204–206, 209–210, 212–213, 213n10, 213n16, 215n52, 215n54, 216n89; cinema audience 204–205, 208–209; film music 200, 204, 206–207; singing Shakespeare 213, 213n3, 214n44; heroine 216n94, 217n101; Kollywood 213n8; love stories 200–201, 203; motherland/nation 202, 208, 210; stage 206; talkies 63, 205, 213n15, 214n43; womanhood 210, 216n95; *Apoorva Sagodharargal* 253; *Kalidasa* 63; *Priya* 241; *Srinivasakalyanam* 204; Films (Shakespeare): *Aalayamani* 200, 212, 213n5; *Ambikapathy* 14, 64, 200–217, 322, 329; *Anbu* 240, 246, 250n12, 326, 329; *Arivaali* 241, 250n12, 325, 329; *Kanniyin Kaadhali* 67, 325, 329; *Katakam* 67, 319, 328; *Manohara* 240, 320, 328–329; *Marmayogi* 5, 67, 321, 329; *Rajapart Rangadurai* 5, 15, 212, 238, 241–242, 326, 330; *Ratha Thilagam* 15–16, 212, 239–240, 244, 246–247, 322, 329; *Shylock* 67, 324, 328; *Sorkkam* 238, 243, 326, 330

Telugu 4, 11–12, 18n6, 62–74; *Baahubali / Baahubali 2: The Conclusion* 4, 18n6, 62, 73n1; *Balanagamma* 64; *Bhakta Potana* 68; *Bhakta Prahlada* 63; *Devatha* 68; *Patala Bhairavi* 64; *Ramudu Bheemudu* 254; *Ratnamala* 64; *Sumangali* 68; *Swarga Seema* 68; *Vandemataram* 68; *Yogi Vemana* 68; *bhakti chitralu* 64; *pauranikam* 63; Films on Telegu plays: *Pandava Udyoga Vijayalu* 63; *Satya Harishchandra* 63; *Sati Savitri* 63; *Sri Krishna Tulabharam* 63; *Prahlada* 63; Films (Shakespeare): *Gunasundari Katha* 5, 11, 62–73, 321, 328; *Marmayogi* 5, 67, 321, 329; *Maro Charitra* 104, 323, 330; *Ulta Palta* 5, 324, 331

Urdu Film (Shakespeare); *Khoon ka Khoon* 3, 7, 26, 118, 259, 320, 328

film festival: international 194, 196n10, 285, 288; national 4, 77–78, 272, 275, 286; first feature film 114; first talkie 120; National Film Archive 114

Indian: epics 48–49, 63–65, 202–216, 226–229, 267n21, 321; identities 14, 104, 16, 166; India-China war

15, 247–248, 250n16; middle/upper-middle class 167, 170, 176–177, 187, 190, 196n4, 265, 271; mythology 34, 41, 48, 65, 228, 325; regional identities 13–15, 170 *see also* local habitations; South 65, 67, 73n5
insurgency in: Assam 271–272, 274, 281; Kashmir 5, 24, 35, 161, 320; Mizoram 288, 289; intertextual/intertextuality 13, 16–17, 27, 37, 46–47, 73, 96, 103–104, 106, 109n32, 143, 166, 179n29, 201, 204, 208, 210–211, 311
Ivory, James 147, 326, 329

Jackson, Russell 2, 18n3, 214n28, 214n40
Jayaraj 11–12, 77–78, 82–84, 89–92, 214n35, 301, 319, 321–322, 330–332, *see also* Malayalam cinema
Jhabvala, Ruth Prawer 147
Jhala, Angma Dey 45
Jha, Prakash 33
Joshi, Manilal 121
Joshi, V. B. 120
Journey of the Magi 157

Kagalwala, Fatema 133, 139n2
Kakar, Sudhir 7, 19n11
Kali 28, 31, 33, 35, 229, 230, 235
Kalidasa 67, 115, 253, 304
Kambar 14, 201–202, 208, 214n33
Kamath, Sudhish 38
Kant, Vinod 119
Kapadia, Parmita 8, 19n14, 210, 217n102
Kapoor, M. R. 121, 319
Kapoor, Prithviraj 118
Kapoor, Raj 198n34, 322, 330
Kapoor, Shekhar 27
Kapur, A. P. 121, 319, 328
Karnad, Girish 170, 182
Kar-Wai, Wong 299
Kashyap, Anurag 181, 188, 196n10, 198n29
Kashmir 5, 40, 302–308, 320, 321; documentary 285; dystopia 133, 139; insurgency 24, 35–42, 161, 186; as Hamlet 38; as paradise 39; *see also* Hindi cinema, *Haider*
Katariya, Sharat 14, 180–181, 186–193, 195n2, 195n4, 197n24, 197n27, 198n37, 321, 331
Kent, Charles 122

Khadilkar, K. P. 123
Khan, Farah 109n31, 327, 331
Khan, Iqbal 31
Khan, Mansoor 12, 94, 95, 104–105, 106n1, 108n19, 109n32, 323, 330, 331, *see also* Hindi cinema
Khan, Mehboob 38, 324, 329
Kiss Me Kate 298
Kitchen, Lawrence 19n9
K. Lalitha 208
Koda, Mohan 67, 321, 331
Kollywood 200, 213n8
Kozintsev, Grigori 291, 301
Kramer, Lucia 9, 19n21
Krishnamma, C. S. R. 67
Krishnamurthy, Kalki 211
Krishnaswami, A. T. 67, 217n113, 250n12, 325, 329
Kukunoor, Nagesh 14, 180–186, 189, 195n3, 195n4, 196n7, 197n12, 197n15, 320, 331
Kurosawa, Akira 13, 130, 132–134, 136–139, 139n3, 291, 302
Kurzel, Justin 31
Kyd, Thomas 113

Lahiri, Krishna Chandra 238
Laldailova, J. L. 288
Lanier, Douglas 48, 61n12
Lehmann, Courtney 94
Levin, Harry 96–97, 108n23
Lichtenfels, Peter 97, 108n24
Life of Christ 115
Litvin, Margaret 44n27
Liz, Mariana 157, 160n40
local habitations 1, 4, 10, *see also* culture
Lokadharma 129
Loomba, Ania 288, 289
Lothspeich, Pamela 49, 61n14, 61n23
Luhrmann, Baz 197n11, 305, 314, 326
Lutgendorf, Philip 42n7

Macaulay, Thomas Babington 148, 177, 253, 270
Madan, J. J. 122, 324, 328
Madan Theatres 116, 118, 120, 124
Madras 62–63, 67, 200–201, 204, 206–207, 213n12, 215n55, 215n71, 238–239, 248
magic 43n23, 132, 223, 258, 298–300; as a film's formula 72; of the film-maker 64; forest 189; as resolution 71–72, 194; as show 194; as simple moral resolution

340 Index

72; and women 90, 132; of writing 311
Mahabharata 11, 27, 47–52, 54, 56, 60, 60n6, 61n14, 75; influence on regional theatre 64, 202, 216n77; parallels with Shakespeare 202, 208, 229; in Shakespeare film 45–61, 281
Mangai, A. 15–16, 217n113
Manonmaniyam 239
Marlow, Christopher 268
materialist: critique 193–194; reading of Shakespeare 181, 185–186
Mathavan, P. 15
Maurice 118
McKellen, Ian 23
Meghaduta 302
Mehta, Deepa 46, 145, 170
Méliès's, Georges 114, 118
Menaechmi 252, 265
Mirasi, Dada 15, 249n5, 322, 329
mise-en-scène 13, 25–26, 76, 98, 127, 129–130, 133–134, 136, 225, 229, 231–232
Misra, Vijay 7, 19n11
Mistry, Rohinton 13, 143–145, 147–153, 155–158, 158n1, 158n2, 159n21, 159n23, 160n34, 326
Mizoram: cinema 4, 17, 285–291, 326, 330; insurgency 288–289; politics of behaviour 289; Shakespeare in Mizo (translation) 288, (onset) 290; traditions of learning 289, (oral tradition) 290
modernity 7, 15, 19n22, 43n14, 16, 161, 171, 225; Bengali 14, 162–163, 165–166, 171, 173–174, 176, 178n23; colonial 162–163, 171, 173, 177; and English education 241, 246, 248; Indian 162; literary 162; Muslim 172; national 16; Shakespeare as symbol of 162, 241, 243; Tamil 15, 243; templates of 15; and tradition 7, 13–14, 161, 172; Western 162–163
Modi, Sohrab 3, 6, 26, 118, 259, 320, 322, 328
Modenessi, Michel Alfredo 42n4
Moksha 285, 287
Moliere 76
Morey, Peter 149, 159n21
Mudaliar, Pammal Sambandha 240, 320
Mukharjee, Prabhat 271
Mukherjee, Shirshendu 315–316

Mukherjee, Srijit 177, 320, 332
Mukhopadhyay, Suman 316
Muliyil, G. 250n1

Nair, M. T. Vasudevan 90
Nami, Abdul Alim 122
Nandy, Ashish 7, 19n11
native 13, 107n4, 147, 159n12, 162, 173, 221, 236, 241, 246, 268
Natyadharma 129
Natyashastra 11, 25, 127–130, 133, 135
Nayakan 135
Neely, Carol Thomas 193, 199n41
Niranjana, Tejaswini 235, 237n26

O'Flynn, Siobhan 201, 204, 206, 214n23
Onir 181, 188, 198n30
Orfall, Blair 31, 43n16
Orwell, George 113–114, 124n1
Oza, Vaghji Asharam 114, 119, 120, 319

Painter, Baburao 122, 325, 328
Palit, Ranjan 287, 301
Panchotia, Vithaldas 122, 325, 328
Pandian, M. S. S. 250n20
Panjwani, Varsha 14
Parsi 143–168, 159n13; Bombay 145; community 13, 143, 151; culture 150, 153, 157; history 146, 157; identity 13, 148; population 145; post-colonial subject 143; relationship to the Raj 148, 152; sari style 267n23; Shakespeare 125n17; women 152–157, 158, 160n29
drama groups 66–67; adaptations of Shakespeare 13, 117–118, 121, 322, 324; tradition 118, 148; circulation of Shakespeare 6, 116; impact of 251, 253, 322; style 255
Parsi theatre 6, 77, 125n16, 148, 126n33
Parthiban Kanavu 211
Partition 169, 173, 175, 180, 286; of Bengal 119, 178n14; violence 147, 169, 171; history 147; narratives 38; film *Khamosh Paani* 34–35; territorisation of female body 38
Paterson, Ronan 106
Pathak, Hillol Kumar 269
Pathak, Namrata 268
Pawar, Ambadas 118

Index   341

Pawar, A. D. 121
Pearson, Lyle 275
Phalke, Dadasaheb 64, 73n9, 114–115
phallicity 30, 33, 37
phallic authority 228
Philippose, Ummen 75
Pillai, Kainikkara Kumara 76
Pillai, N. Krishna 75–77, 92n1
Pillai, Sundaram 239
Pitard, Derrick 93, 107n6
Plautus 252, 254, 265
Polanski, Roman 138–139
postcolonial 7–9, 13–14, 19n22, 68, 74n17, 113, 143, 146, 157, 159n12, 160n27; Bengal 165–166, 178n9, 197n27, 238, 326; Bombay 324; Calcutta 323, critique 148, identity 210, injunction 149, 155; via Shakespeare 161, 163, 210, 250n17, 266n7; theory 243; transnationality 168
Prakash, V. K. 11, 78, 84, 92, 118, 320, 331
Prasad, Madhava M. 7, 64, 73n5, 216n83, 18n4, 19n11
Premchand, Munshi 7, 19n10
Pullaiah, C. 64
Pulp Fiction 29
Pulugurtha, Nishi 11
puranas 64–65, 76
Pursell, Michael 103

Rabha, Kalaguru Bishnu Prasad 278
Raghavachari, T. G. 67, 319, 328
Raghavendra, M. K. 18n4, 224, 235, 236n3, 236n7, 237n24
Raghunandan 293
Rajadhakshya, Ashish 18n4, 64, 124, 126n31
Rajagopalachari, C 248
Rajamouli, S. 62
Rajashekar, M. S. 15, 221, 236, 325, 330
Rajkhowa, Sailadhar 268
Raleigh, Walter 261
Ramayana 64, 92, 191–192, 202, 211, 214, 216, 228, 236, 257, 281
Ramanujan, A. K. 308
Ramnoth, K. 67, 321, 325, 329
Ran 133, 302
Rangan, Baradwaj 45, 60n1, 60n2, 61n22
Rangoonwalla, Firoze 7, 125n24
Rajadhyaksha, Ashish 18n4, 64, 73n8, 124

Rao, Kamalakara Kameswara 69, 72, 324, 329
Rao, P. S. Ramakrishna 64
Rasa 12–13, 17, 60, 111, 127–130, 139n1; *Adbhuta* 74, 78, 128, 131–137; *Bhayanaka* 128, 134–138; *Bibhatsa* 78, 128, 131–138; *Hasya* 128, 135, 137; *Karuna* 78, 128, 134–139; *Raudra* 128, 131–138; *Shantam* 11, 60, 128, 135–139; *Shringara* 128, 135–139; *Veera* 128, 131–137; *nava-rasas* 78, 91; films on see Jayaraj; process of: *Charvana* 127, *Rasika* 129, *Sahrudaya* 129; *Rasa siddhanta* 127–128
Rashomon 133–134
Ray, Satyajit 1, 166, 167, 169–170, 176, 178n12, 304, 326, 329
Ratnam, Mani 38, 135
realism 7, 64, 189, 196n4, 254, 311; aesthetic 77; cinematic 64; in films 100; in Parsi theatre 116; social 271
Reddy, B. N. 320, 329
Reddy, H. M. 63
Reddy, Kadiri Venkata 11, 64, 65, 69, 321, 328
Reddy, H. M. 63
revenge 27, 42n9, 43n10, 54, 326–327; as duty 49–50, 54, 58–60; freedom and 40–41; ineffectual 46, 60, 88, 184, 305; poetic 212; politics of male revenge 11, 35–38, 85, 183, 245, 247, 269; and rape 27–28; treachery and 32; and violence 38, 93; by women 84, 89, 212, 230, 237n12
Richie, Donald 134, 139n3
Rodolfiby 118
Rodgers, Amy 42n1
Rothwell, Kenneth. S. 1, 26, 114, 124n5
Rushdie, Salman 68, 74n16

Sahu, Kishore 118, 320, 329
Saikia, Bhabendra Nath 271
Saki 120, 319, 328
Salome 287, 288
Saltz, Rachel 36
Samanta, Shakti 176
Sambasivan, V. 76
Sanders, Julie 92n8, 203, 214n36, 235, 237n27
Sarkar, Kobita 205, 215n49
Sarma, Apurba 270, 282n6
Sarma, Phani 271
Sarma, Ranjit 274, 276, 280
Sarma, Serukalathur 67, 324, 328

342 Index

Savkari Hak 122, 325
Scorsese, Martin 194
Semenza, Greg Colon 120
Sen, Amrita 15, 16
Sen, Aparna 14, 17, 108n22, 161, 164, 167, 176–177, 304–316, 323, 326, 330, 332
Sen, Debu 260, 324, 329
Sen, Jon 14, 161, 173, 175, 179n33, 326, 331
Sen, Koushik 312
Sen, Manu 3, 253, 323, 329
Sen, Mrinal 176
sexuality 19n11, 29–32, 38, 43n10, 43n23, 262; female 144, 152, 154, 262; gender and 172–174
Shah Nama 157
Shakespeare in Love 291, 302
Shakespeare, William 1, 67, 77, 124, 134; *Segappiriyar* Tamil name of 249; 'Shakespeare commons' 76; Shakespeare tragedy in India 10–12, 25–26, 41–42, 42n6, 42n10, 50, 83–84, 88–89, 132, 143, 191, 200, 203, 206, 217n102, 311; sonnet 50, 52;
  Antony and Cleopatra 11, 73n14, 78, 83–84, 177, 214n35, 240, 253, 304, 306, 319, 320, 328–331; Films: *Kannaki* (Malayalam); *Zulfikar* (Bengali); stage adaptation 240; translation(Telugu) 73n14
  As You Like It 304, 319, 329
  Cymbeline 7, 12, 60, 319, 328; Films: *Champraj Hado* (silent); *Katakam* (Tamil); *Kusum Kumari* (silent); *Meetha Zahar* (silent); see also silent Indian cinema 119–121; stage adaptation (*Sati Sone aka Champraj Hado aka Sone Rani*) 120, (*Meetha Zahar*) 121, 240; talkie *Kusum Kumari* 121
  Hamlet 2–3, 5–7, 11–12, 14–15, 17, 23, 25–26, 35–44, 45–47, 49–55, 57–59, 73, 75, 77–78, 84–89, 113–114, 117–119, 121, 123, 133, 138–139, 180–186, 197, 240–242, 253, 273, 285–292, 300, 302, 304, 306–307, 320, 323, 326–329, 331–332; Films: *Hamlet Segment* (silent)114; *Haider* (Hindi); *Hamlet* (Hindi); *Hemanta* (Bengali); *Karmayogi* (Malayalam); *Khoon-e-Nahak* (silent); *Khoon ka Khoon* (Urdu); *When Hamlet went to Mizoram* (Mizo and English); *Rajapart Rangadurai* (Tamil); *8×10 Tasveer* (Hindi); stage adaptations: *Amalathiththan* (Tamil) 240; *Manohara* (Tamil) 240; in colonial India 119; translation (Telugu) 73n14, (Malayalam) 75;
  Julius Cesar 67, 77, 177, 243, 306, 320–326; Films: *Sorkkam* (Tamil); *Zulfiqar* (Bengali); translation 73n14
  King John 2, 117, 121, 320, 322, 328; Film: *Said-e Havas* (Urdu/Hindi); Stage adaptation (Malayalam) 116
  King Lear 11, 13, 47, 55–56, 58, 62, 65, 68–74, 113, 133, 143–144, 149–151, 157, 159n23, 161, 163–168, 173, 179n30, 240, 269, 273, 301, 328, 330–332; Films: *Baghbaan* (Hindi); *Gunasundari Katha* (Telegu); *Life Goes On* (English); *Natsamrat* (Marathi); *Rui ka Bojh* (Hindi); *Second Generation* (English/ Bengali); *Such a Long Journey* (English); *The Last Lear* (English); Assamese 269, 273; Bengali 161, 163, 166–168, 173; Malayalam adaptation 116; translation (Telugu)73n14
  Macbeth 5, 7, 11, 23–32, 45, 47, 52, 61n22, 67, 78, 74n14, 91, 114, 123, 130, 133–136, 138–139, 180, 239–240, 293, 301, 304, 321, 322, 327–328, 331–332, 329; Films: *Khooni Taj* (Silent); *Hrid Majharey* (Bengali); *Maqbool* (Hindi); *Marmayogi* (Telegu); *Matru ki Bijli ka Mandola* (Hindi); *Veeram* (Malayalam); *Yellamma* (Telugu); performance Globe London 31; St. Stephen's College (English) 293; stage adaptation *Maranannayakana Drishthanta* (Kannada) 43n17; translations (Telugu) 73n14; Tamil 239, 240; witches in 32, 67, 130–131, 135–136, 138, 293, 321
  Measure for Measure 239, 253, 294, 321, 323, 328; performance

(English) 294; translation (Tamil) 239
Midsummer Night's Dream, A 14, 180–181, 187, 197n26, 197n27, 321, 331; Film: *10ml Love* (Hindi); translation (Malayalam) 75
Othello 5, 11, 15–16, 23, 32, 35, 45, 79, 82, 148–149, 163, 177, 239, 241, 244–247, 269, 274, 279, 280, 293, 320–322, 326, 329–332; Films: *Anbu* (Tamil); *Hrid Majharey* (Bengali); *In Othello* (English); *Kaliyattam* (Malayalam); *Omkara* (Hindi); *Ratha Thilangam* (Tamil); *Saptapadi* (Bengali); *We Too Have Our Othellos* (Assamese); performance *Othello: A Play in Black and White* (English) 17, 292–303; *Goodbye Desdemona* (English) 294–295; stage adaptation *Nilamber* (Assamese) 269; translations (Malayalam) 76, (Telugu) 74n14; bed chamber scene 241; as civilizing tool by British 148–149; racism in 273, 280; women in 227, 304
Richard III 117, 123, 304, 320, 322, 328; Film: *Said e Havas* (Urdu/Hindi)
Romeo and Juliet 2, 4, 12, 47, 76, 93–110, 200–217, 287, 295, 305, 308–309, 313–314, 322–323, 326, 328–332; Films: *Ambikapathy* (Tamil); *Arshinagar* (Bengali); *Bobby* (Hindi); *Ek Duuje Ke Liye* (Hindi); *Isaaq* (Hindi); *Ishaqzaade* (Hindi); *Josh* (Hindi); *Maro Charitra* (Telugu); *Qayamat Se Qayamat Tak* (Hindi); *Ram-Leela* (Hindi); *Romeo and Juliet* (Hindi); *Sairat* (Marathi); *Sanam Teri Kasam* (Hindi); *Romeo and Juliet* (Mizo) 287; and Bollywood formulae 102–106; Hollywood 14, 201, 208, 210; on-screen kiss 15, 103, 201, 208–209; in Tamil cinema 200–217; stage performance *Bhuli Nai Priya* (Bengali); *Romeo and Juliet in Technicolour* (Hindi/English) 294, (Kannada) 24; translation (Marathi, Tamil) 206
The Comedy of Errors 3, 5, 7, 16, 75, 122–123, 251–267, 325, 329–332; Films: *Angoor* (Hindi); *Bhool Bhulaiya* (Hindi); *Bhranti Bilash* (Bengali); *Do Dooni Char* (Hindi); *Double Di Trouble* (Punjabi); *Heeralal Pannalal* (Hindi); *Ulta Palta* (Kannada); *Ulta Palta* (Telugu); stage adaptation *Bhrama Ranga* (Assamese) 268; talkie *Bhool Bhulaiyan/ Hanste Rehna* (Hindi) 122
The Merchant of Venice 6, 67, 74n14, 75, 114, 121–122, 239, 253, 266n1, 292–293, 324, 328; Films: *Dil Farosh* (Silent); *Savkari Pash* (Marathi); *Shylock* (Tamil); *Zalim Saudagar* (Hindi); stage adaptation (Urdu/Hindi) 121; production (Hindi) 292–293; silent film 114; translations (Bengali) 6, (Tamil) 240, (Telugu) 67, 73n14
The Taming of the Shrew 2, 6, 15, 67, 121, 217n113, 221–223, 225, 227, 230, 233–235, 236n4, 239–241, 324–331; Films: *Arivaali* (Tamil); *Nanjundi Kalyana* (Kannada); *Srimati Bhayankari* (Bengali); stage performance (Gujarati) 6; translations (Tamil) 240; *The Tempest* 124, 214, 239, 298, 303; theatre performance (Hindi) 298–299, 303
Timon of Athens 239
Twelfth Night 67, 122–123, 214n38, 265, 306, 325–326, 328–329, 331; Films: *Bhool Bhulaiya* (Hindi); *Bhul Bhulaiya* (Silent); *Kanniyin Kaadhali* (Tamil); racial implications 265
Two Gentlemen of Verona 239

Shakespeare *Writing Julius Casear* 114
Shakuntala 115
Shankar, K. 212, 213n5
Shankar, N. S. 324, 330
Sharma, Bobbeta 270
Showalter, Elaine 28
Shyamala, C. G. 91, 92n9
Silappatikaram 27, 84, 203, 210
Singh, Suchet 115
Sivan, Santosh 38
Srijato 311, 312
Srinivasiar, S.V. 206, 208, 209, 215n65, 216n81
Sriramamurti, Gurazada 67

Index

Stendhal 305
Sumar, Sabiha 34
Swamy, T. S. D. 239

Tagore, Rabindranath 15, 157, 162, 166–167, 169, 171–173, 267n23
Taligeri, Pandurang 123, 321, 328
Talukdar, Nanda 268
Taneja, Preti 13
Tanselle, G. Thomas 102, 109n33
Taraporevala 13, 143–145, 147–148, 151–152, 157–158, 159n9, 159n14
Tate, Nahum 73, 172, 179n30
Tatspaugh Patricia 202, 214n29
Taura, Masami 299
Taylor, Neil 197n13, 197n23
Taylor, Sam 2
Thampuran, Kodungallur Kunjukuttan 75
Thanigachalam (pen name Elangovan) 204, 207, 212
The Thief of Baghdad 115, 116
The Throne of Blood 13, 31, 43n16, 130, 132–134, 136, 291
Tilak, Bal Gangadhar (Lokmanya) 115
Tod, James 120
translation 6, 9–10, 13, 16, 43n13, 44n26, 60n6, 66, 67, 70, 73n14, 74n15, 75–77, 92n9, 104, 110n38, 117, 124, 125n14, 125n21, 126n29, 163, 169, 197n26, 206–207, 209, 211, 214n35, 216n84, 217n103, 221–223, 227, 236n1, 238–239, 249n2, 253–255, 266n1, 268, 288, 302
transnational/transnationalism 8–9, 14, 19n12, 144, 157, 168, 170–171, 180, 195n4, 196n9
Tree, Beerbohm 2
Trivedi, Poonam 10, 11, 19n13, 19n20, 42n6, 50, 61n17, 74n15, 76, 92n2, 93, 107n5, 110n38, 125n14, 125n17, 125n21, 178n8, 197n26, 197n27, 236n1, 236n4, 237n28, 253, 266n1, 266n2, 266n8

Udwadia, M. 121, 324, 328
Urdu 3, 6, 38, 96–97, 108n22, 119, 177, 178n25, 206, 252, 312, 319, 320–322, 328

Vakil, Madanrai 120
Valicha, Kishore 7, 19n11

Valarmathi 249n1, n8, n9
vamp 28, 98, 109n26
Vasudevan, Ravi 7, 19n11, 285
Veeresalingam, Kandukuri 67
Venkiteswaran, C. S 11–12
Venning, Dan 147, 159n18
Verma, Rajiva 93, 106, 118, 198n27, 222, 236n4, 252–253, 266n6
Vidyasagar, Ishwar Chandra 16, 253–257, 266n6, 267n22
Vijayakar, R. M. 107n12, 108n14, n19, 110n37
violence 11, 23, 24, 26, 32–33, 35–38, 41, 55, 158; *see also* Kashmir; *see also* Vishal Bhardwaj

Wadia J. B. H. 115
Warerkar, Mama 123
Warrier, Anuradha 82, 92n5
Water 145
Weird Sisters 32, 137
Welles, Orson 33
Wells, Stanley 61n16, 197n25, 213n6
West Side Story 12, 96, 104–106, 109n32, 323
Westwood, Bruce 156
White, Robert S. 11, 61n21
Winterbottom, Michael 144
Witch/witches 67, 89, 90, 130–131, 135–138, 151, 160n27, 198n34, 293, 312, 321
women: assertive 270–271; avenging 10–11, 23, 23–44, 26–27, 33–34, 38, 42n9; Bengali woman 167, 172, 227, 308; *devadasis* 67; 'women's' films 25, 27; 'good woman' 98; Hamlet as woman 113; *Hic Mulier* 227, 231; and identity 17; Parsi 144, 152–158; *pativrata* 65; and modernity 15, 163, 172, 226, 235, 253; moral agency of 11; sexuality 144, 153; stunt heroine 28; suicide 34; shaming of 231; tragic 11, 24, 27, 28, 41–42; vigilante 27–28, 231; violence 11, 24, 26, 30–35, 236n4; *virangana* /warrior 27–28

Yajnik, R. K. 206, 215n64, 215n67, 215n68

Zankar, Anil. 12–13, 127, 215n66
Zeffirelli 304, 305